ANANT RAJE ARCHITECT

SELECTED WORKS 1971–2009

 Tulika Books

in association with

Anant Raje Foundation

ANANT RAJE ARCHITECT

SELECTED WORKS 1971–2009

Edited by **Shubhra Raje and Amita Raje**

Foreword by **William J.R. Curtis**

Introduction by **Gautam Bhatia**

First published in India in 2012 by

Tulika Books
35 A/1 Shahpur Jat, New Delhi 110 049, India
www.tulikabooks.wordpress.com

in association with

Anant Raje Foundation
302 Shaligram Apartments, off Dr Vikram Sarabhai Road,
Ahmedabad 380 015, India

ISBN: 978-93-82381-02-0

Designed by Shubhra Raje

Typeset in Frutiger at Tulika Print Communication Services, New Delhi
Images processed at Reproscan, Mumbai
Printed at Aegean Press, Greater Noida, Uttar Pradesh

Contents

7   Preface

8   Foreword I William J.R. Curtis

10   Introduction I Gautam Bhatia

15   Sources and Interpretations I Anant Raje

Projects at The Indian Institute of Management, Ahmedabad, 1971–1999
19   Continuation of a Language
21   Students' Dining Halls and Kitchens
31   Management Development Centre
43   Ravi Mathai Centre

Private Residences
61   Residence for Naushir Contractor, Ahmedabad
67   Studies in House Compositions, 1971–74
69   Residence for J.C. Parikh, Ahmedabad
81   Staff Housing for ATIRA, Ahmedabad
89   Residence for Kanubhai Patel, Ahmedabad
99   Wedding Wall, Ahmedabad
105 Residence for Nandan Mehta, Ahmedabad

Public Institutions
117 Indian Statistical Institute, New Delhi
127 Agricultural Produce Wholesale Market Complex, New Bombay
143 MAFCO Dairy, Bombay
148 Dairy Projects, 1971–79
153 Galbabhai Farmers' Training Institute, Banaskantha
167 Lintel Development
169 Testing Board Offices and Science Museum, Bhopal
175 Commissioner's Office and Walmi Subcentre, Morena

189 Indian Institute of Forest Management, Bhopal
220 Gas Tragedy Victims Memorial, Bhopal
225 Headquarters for the Bhopal Development Authority, Bhopal
239 Commercial Complex at MOG Lines, Indore
247 Mudra Institute of Communications, Ahmedabad
273 INTEC Polymer Factory and Laboratories, Silvassa
283 Museum of Minerals and Mines, Nagpur

Competitions
293 The Naval Academy, Ezhimala, Kerala
303 Ministry of External Affairs, New Delhi

Writings
308 Architecture, Building, Practice
310 Model Making
314 Sketching
317 What I Learnt from Kahn

320 **Epilogue**

Appendix
325 List of Works
328 Published References to Works
329 Biography
330 Awards, Exhibitions
331 Lectures–Seminars
332 Teaching, Consultations
333 Colleagues
334 Credits

335 Acknowledgments

336 Contributors

Preface

In the last few years before his death, Anant Raje had begun to put together a collection of his works, published and unpublished. This book is inspired by the intent and layout of that draft, unfinished at the time of his death. It is the first comprehensive presentation of the architect's oeuvre, an unbiased offering, which did not happen in Raje's lifetime; and it features over thirty projects that he had assembled into a draft – of built, unbuilt and competition work.

Each of these projects is extensively illustrated with photographs, models, drawings, sketches and reflections by the architect himself, meticulously collected from his office archives, diaries, interviews, publications, as well as lecture transcriptions. We have tried to respect the authenticity of the material by not reformating anything and by using much of the material directly from the archives – photographs of models, from the construction sites and of completed works, and plates made after completion of projects. Just as sketches and models were tools used by Raje during the design process, photographs were a means to record and assess his own work for himself. As a whole, the material in this book presents both the architect at work and in reflection of it.

The text accompanying the projects has been similarly selected from previously generated project descriptions. Raje not having been much of a man of words, these are inconsistent, with many of the projects lacking extensive written material. However he lectured extensively, and spoke about his work, his motivations and methods. A large part of the text in this book, especially that which accompanies the illustrations, is transcribed from these lectures.

This is material of such honesty compared to architectural publications these days, where so much is orchestrated and so much value is placed on the image. There is a timelessness in Raje's work and an agelessness in his personality that we hope, by maintaining a singular voice through the monograph, speaks for itself and positions the work for the pursuit of further scholarship.

Foreword

This book is long overdue. Anant Raje has deserved a monograph for many years. His contributions to the world of architecture far transcend passing fads and add something durable to the discipline. He belongs to a generation in India which came of age after Independence and which experienced the rapid modernization of the country. Architects faced the daunting task of constructing the institutions of a new society. They looked forward but they also looked back to the vast pre-colonial traditions of architecture in India. It was impossible to avoid the influence of both Le Corbusier and Louis I. Kahn, and in Raje's case it was a question of distilling lessons from these modern mentors while seeking longer-range touchstones in the past. Kahn was of course the major influence, especially since Raje worked in his office in Philadelphia and then oversaw the completion and extension of Kahn's Indian Institute of Management in Ahmedabad. But on this firm basis Raje established principles of his own.

These principles are fully demonstrated in works such as the Indian Institute of Forest Management in Bhopal designed in the mid-1980s, a particularly fruitful period in modern Indian architecture, especially in the public and educational sectors. The Institute occupies a hillside site, and is formed from platforms, a theatre, water basins, interstitial spaces, courts and sequences of indoor and outdoor rooms. The arches and structural expression clearly owe much to Kahn, but the underlying organization reveals Raje's fascination with ancient ruins including Hadrian's Villa at Tivoli (second century AD) and Indian palace/fortress complexes in the Deccan, such as Mandu (fifteenth century) with its courts, ramps, waterways and pavilions. These absorptions occurred at a deep level which had nothing to do with surface stylistic imitation. With each project Raje sought out an appropriate solution to the task at hand, whether an individual house or an entire institution like a small city as in the case of the ensemble of buildings for the Institute of Forest Management. But at the same time he researched the elements and combinations of an architectural language.

Raje responded to each site and programme in a unique way but there were recurrent patterns of organization. He often resorted to bold primary volumes and powerful voids. Combined together, these produced layers of structure and spatial complexity. He returned time and again to the theme of the shaded court surrounded by transitional spaces, rather like the streets and squares of a traditional city. The contrast between public courts and private rooms had something of the monastery about it. Orientation was crucial in catching prevailing winds, and he often had recourse to channels of water for both climatic and aesthetic effect. In plan and section, Raje organized buildings into legible hierarchies, using axes and symmetry when necessary. But he was wary of formalist recipes, and generated forms through continual study of each architectural problem in drawings and models. Structure was a central preoccupation but was not an end in itself: it embodied the character and aura of a work. As for materials, he used brick, concrete, stone and wood in a robust and direct manner, making the most of the craft available in India. Behind the bold arches, concrete tie-beams and insistent geometry, there was a striving for the expression of ideas, not in a theoretical sense of the word but at the level of poetic order. The best of Raje's buildings evoke primary qualities to do with the relation of ground to sky, light and shade, and an elemental sense of shelter.

This book has been assembled, organized and written by former collaborators of Raje, some of them family members, and it traces the emergence and crystallization of his characteristic spaces and forms in both realized works and unbuilt projects. It enables us to trace the development of his architectural language step by step. It is like a primer in bold black and white and shades of grey, and it reveals Raje's ways of architectural thinking. Drawing was one of his main tools for conceiving architecture, but also for perceiving it, capturing it and transforming it. He sought out the general lines and essential ideas of the buildings which he sketched. This book contains several of his sharp delineations of ancient buildings, but as we look at these we sense that he was creating anew even as he examined the old. Raje detested vainglorious, self-promotional theorizing and was a man of few words, but these words were carefully pondered and they reflected years of experience. He wrote relatively little, but some of his articles, such as the one on Kahn reproduced here, are gems. Like the man himself and his architecture, the writings are succinct, concrete and direct.

I first got to know Raje thirty years ago when, after several hard weeks trekking through central India studying Buddhist caves and early Hindu temples, my wife and I stumbled into the dusty Gujarati city of Ahmedabad with its Sultanate mosques and its industrial textile mills. But Le Corbusier and Kahn were also on the agenda. We were invited by Balkrishna Doshi to stay in his studio 'Sangath' and to meet members of the architectural community including of course Raje, who was at the time director of the CEPT School of Architecture. This first time in Ahmedabad was an introduction to a rich heritage running from stepped wells to Le Corbusier's Sarabhai House, from the tank and tombs of Sarkej (fifteenth century) to the shaded courts and bold brick volumes of Kahn's IIM. One could sense the deep continuities with the trabeated stone and wooden architectures of various periods of the past running back to the Solanki dynasties (tenth to thirteenth centuries) and beyond: the substructures of a tradition combining universal qualities with local accents. One evening, I gave a talk on the grassy steps of Sangath on the subject of two of my favourite buildings, the Assembly Building in Chandigarh by Le Corbusier and the Parliament building in Dhaka by Kahn, stressing the metamorphosis of archetypes in a modern form. This talk hit all the right notes and I quickly realized that Ahmedabad had generated a special culture of modern architecture of its own, combining new and old, modern technology and craft, local and general. I later expanded these thoughts to deal with matters such as post-colonial identity in Indian modern architecture.

During the 1980s I was often back in India and in Ahmedabad in particular. It became a sort of spiritual home. There were the articles and books of course on various Indian matters, but there were also the friendships and personal exchanges. At times we stayed in the Management Development Centre at IIM designed by Raje with its shaded undercrofts excluding heat and glare, a deliberate extension of Kahn's vocabulary. I recall the conversations with Raje on everything from cricket to geometrical patterns in Islamic architecture, to the brick cylinders of Albi Cathedral. I can still remember Raje's intense yet merry expression: 'You see Curtis, what many people do not realize ...', and then he would continue with a thought about brick construction or about the parallels between Kahn's IIM and Mandu. Pleasant get-togethers with Raje and his family were sometimes followed by strolls to Patel's icecream shop near the cricket ground. On one occasion Raje helped me to negotiate with tribals from the Rann of Kutch in a night street market near Law Gardens for a beautiful fabric which still hangs on the wall of our daughter's room. But one of the strongest memories of all was not in India at all but in the southwest United States when we overlapped briefly in the late 1980s at the architecture school of the University of New Mexico in Albuquerque. Driven by an obliging student, we set off on an expedition together to visit the ancient remains of Pueblo Bonito (AD 1000) with their amazing subterranean kivas in circular forms. Raje was quick to sense analogies between these stone and earth ruins of a lost civilization, and the stepped wells in western India. He was captivated by the silence of the canyons which seemed haunted by spirits from an archaic past. 'You see Curtis, architecture has its cosmic dimension, and that is what it is all about.'

William J.R. Curtis
July 2012

© William J.R. Curtis

Introduction

In order to live we 'have to be free of the authority of our immediate predecessors', wrote D.H. Lawrence. Anant Raje was a free man. His long association with Louis Kahn, from 1964 to 1974, and later, the twenty-six years as project architect for the Indian Institute of Management at Ahmedabad, were his first call to freedom. The rigorous link to Kahn, paradoxically, provided Raje with a significant platform for thinking freely – and enacting architecture in a larger frame of understanding that came from life itself. Such a view emancipated Raje from the narrow, cloistered, problem-solving bent of conventional practice, and laid before him a fertile plain of immense and limitless prospects. In eventually working out ideas, each project began as an equation between infinite possibility and architectural containment, within which lay all the pertinent questions about modernity and tradition, the role of history, the need to extend the masonry tradition, and to search for an inherent order beyond the merely visible, the literal and the prescriptive. Indeed, the move away from a pictorial outlook was realized in the conventions of elevations, facades, and all the lies and evasions by which ordinary architecture nourished itself. In an examination of a lifetime of work, it is hard now to pinpoint precise inspirations and influences. Doubtless there were many.

In a large part, the serious problem of the architect in India has been the unresolved conflict between private attitude, professional conduct and public expectation. At a personal level there remains the perpetual need to evaluate and assert your self-worth by being formally creative; professional demands necessitate mediocrity and conventions as primary value givers of acceptable architecture; the public meanwhile forms its opinions through visibility and experience. Acting together, the three forces have produced some serious misgivings in the profession and an unfortunate dreariness in the surroundings.

Within such an environment, Raje was an independent interpreter, an introvert – partly because of his reluctance to adapt to the methods of conventional practice. While his peers played within the ordinary vocabulary of the tested architectural alphabet, Raje refused to be enslaved by the visible, comprehensible language of buildings around him. He built only for himself, urging others around him to respect the privacy of his thoughts. In so doing, he created a counter-reality of his own, something suited to his own artistic rather than professional temperament. The growing detachment was palpable in a world which derived continual sustenance from public recognition. In that world he was a happy misfit, even distancing his work from the mundane vocabulary of daily inducements and regular back-pats. Over the years, in the fifty years of thinking, drawing and constructing, once he was comfortable with his own methods and explorations, he had even ceased to try and make peace with his profession.

Instead, Raje engrossed himself in his own expression – an engagement with the spirit of a personal architectural life. As a practitioner he was forever aware of the principles of time and place, but used them ahistorically, as the eternal 'now'. The 'nowness' of phenomena was essential to the passionate enthralment of all experience. To live was to be constantly and joyously aware, without the stifling apprehension of morality and convention. Raje opened up to all sources of cultural and intellectual nourishment – music, film, building, art, writing, dance, theatre, science, astronomy, even cricket. Indeed, to life itself. Listening to a piece of music once, he remained absorbed in its notes and, only when it was over, remarked, 'it seems to be coming from a great distance'. The casual statement had nothing to do with the composition itself, but it demonstrated an immediate and deeper comprehension of the piece, as something being performed in great space; at once, the construction of the music acquired a different, architectural strain. Aware always of the changing phenomena that suffused and surrounded all action, it was neither an analytical nor a static or logical interpretation, but merely the expression of a moment – Raje's private moment of connection and clarity.

In the life of most architects, the city of their residence often fuels the embers of architecture. For Kahn it was Philadelphia, for Vitruvius, Rome. Raje's fifty-year-long association with Ahmedabad remained an unfulfilled, clinical detachment. The place provided him the source of practice and teaching. However the city's suburban makeshift character, its thoughtless plotted development, left Raje to continue his sustaining links with

Bombay (now Mumbai), where he had studied and worked in his early years. He knew the fabric of south Bombay intimately, walking about its *gali*s, conducting workshops and student exercises within the urban congestion seething with humanity.

It was there, amidst the tumult of a changing cityscape, that he learnt the larger lessons of Indian urbanism, observing how streets were made, how edges between landscape and architecture were reconciled, indeed how buildings linked to each other, how in fact proximities and overlaps of structures made geometric relationships in space possible. Against the backdrop of such a beginning, it is not unusual to test the many geometric manipulations and collisions that took place in the development of building plans. At the Indian Institute of Forest Management (IIFM) and in later additions to the Indian Institute of Management (IIM), Ahmedabad, the angular fusions of walls are reminiscent of the accretions of a Roman plan – a Pirenesian assembly built in the restructuring of a ruin. The multiple layers attributed to circumstantial conditions in the Bombay streetscape here create private spatial dimensions. An urban street logic was applied to suggest the multiple layers of building functions. Because building context was absent on an empty site, the architect made his own, within the given constraints of the requirements. But by no means was it superfluous geometry for its own sake. The joining suffused with sudden moments of captive space and episodic possibility that went far beyond the stated building requirement, as in the IIFM library.

Unlike architects who use geometry as an organizing feature of the plan, Raje willed disturbances and distortions into the mix that challenged or restated geometry. Sometimes, so desperate was the urge to redefine the urban character of space, even remote individual projects formulated new attitudes to their surroundings. In places where campus buildings were conventionally viewed as autonomous objects floating freely in space, he used a skilled urbanism to create their position in space, before anchoring them. Such an idea of a plan made up of a variety of cellular accretions was part of an intuitive grasp of connections and exposures that came directly from the inner recesses of the architect. At the Mudra campus the conference building turns upon its axis, as does the assembly hall of the Mathai Centre at the IIM. The Romanesque joinings and subtle inflections announce the clear importance of one function above another. Moreover, the acci-

dental overlaps and collisions were part of the 'mysterious' inclination of the architect to forever extend space beyond established requirements.

So too it was with landscape. At the IIFM complex the remote hill site required monumental links and heroic axial geometries to make far-off connections, across terrain and landscape, to the surrounding lake. Whole hills and waterways were first brought into play in an architecturally inconceivable expanse. Only after the effort at such an epic anchoring could the more intimate, internal architecture of the Institute begin. Unable to find landscape variants in the competition for the Indian Administrative Service Academy, Raje similarly proposed a range of high plinths to situate buildings. In the bleached, featureless flatness of Haryana without outcrop or treeline, architecture was ordered out of a self-made terrain.

Connection to space as abstract and symbolic also extended to the architect's understanding of history. An integration of historic themes, though never consciously sought, was the natural outcome of a mind immersed in many classical traditions, including the Islamic geometric ideals of Persia, Turkey and, of course, India. Raje's use of these in his own work belies any direct visual links to monuments and ruins. It could be said that he derived a great deal of structural sustenance from the ruins of Mandu and Rome; so understated is the connection that equally it could be stated that the architects of Mandu foresaw their buildings' links to the future ruins of Morena and the Institute of Forest Management. The abstract nature of the inspiration does not leave the viewer gasping in supercilious delight but merely invested with a sensory evocation across the centuries, a slight disturbance in the mind's eye. If, as Kahn noted, 'in a blade of grass was the history of the universe', the architecture of masonry with studied openings, ruthless in its rhythms, could itself suggest a whole continuum of cultural development – a range within which the primitive and the civilized can exist together. The importance of relieving the building of the burden of expressing the time within which it was built was the only way to suggest the very essential 'eternal' of architecture. For Raje, the eternal was a nameless condition to which all his architecture adhered faithfully. Everything need not be stated. As in music, the absences in a building, like extended silences between musical notes, were the missing links to memory and association. The mind contemplated what the eye

11

saw, in much the same way that a ruin allows you to complete the missing parts in your own image.

As much as possible, Raje stayed away from the illusory architectural practice of comfort and security and painlessness. Never self-consciously belonging to the profession, he was freed of the fear of failure. He readily relinquished its built-in professional supports and possessions, and battled away headlong in a daily personal quest. With or without commissions, his pencil rarely fluctuated, the mind never wavered; projects were rarely the singular sources of sustenance, only the mystical dimension of some personal discovery was. And from that there was no escape, no compromise; the daily quest was much too fulfilling, charged with intimate experience, with more tests, more experiments and continual acts of faith. Every day he moved towards a new unknown, into a territory he created for himself. There was almost a stern engagement with destiny being played out each day – a sudden but partial revelation of an idea discovered in a model or held captive in a sketch. The goal was however always elusive. Raje moved tirelessly towards it, animated by his own drive and the multitude of draughtsmen and model makers that promoted every minuscule inclination towards an idea, towards coherence.

By adopting a private method for a public practice, Raje made a studio world which he dominated. In the large, airy room of multiple drawing boards he was the sole arbiter of power and authority, tolerating only the dictates of his own methods. The students he employed merely acted as the artist's extra hands. There the cumulative effort of architecture was assessed in a private collective of thoughts, ideas, sketches and model assemblies. The eventual measure of success was not the final product of construction, completed – but in the successful conclusion of the journey itself. Built or unbuilt, the project was merely the testing ground, a vigorous imaginative world he created for himself out of real situations. The drama lay as much in the testing of those ideas in the studio as on the real construction site. The tireless chipping away, testing, redrawing and correcting were part of a temperament that refused to settle with partial resolutions; that he built much more in his mind was but expected. Raje's consequent significance in the culture of thought and idea more than made up for his relative insignificance in conventional practice.

Again and again, the dimensions and material aspects of design called for exploration. Precise elements of structure would appear – attachments of porches, integration of landscape – requiring constant testing and refinement. The process was as deliberate and practical as it was personal and intuitive. It appeared everywhere: at the government headquarters at Morena, at the Museum of Mines and Minerals, even in the rarefied atmosphere of the Gas Tragedy Memorial. Elements were distilled and refined to a point of jewel-like iridescence, as if – as in the concrete lintel at Galbabhai Institute and again at the Mudra Institute of Communication – their singular presence was the defining moment of the architecture. As long as the precision was clearly enacted in form and material, it could be expressed in a myriad of changing circumstances. The lintel, the membrane arch, the independent light well, the screen wall, all became instruments in different projects. The personal struggle lay in discovering the physical form of each element before giving it application. Yet, despite the long process of model-making, sketching and note-taking, the elemental quality was all included in the search, the eventual outcome merely a lesson in rigour and patience.

Hard as it is to draw parallels in a work so independent, the nearest is perhaps Claude Batley, an architect whose reading of Indian traditional architecture Raje admired. Batley's struggle to reconcile the wide arc of Indian architectural history with the emerging international style found due sympathy and resonated with his own compulsions. Again, being both a teacher and a practitioner, Raje directed both towards similar ends. In the classroom the serious train of inquiry was made into a situation of play, alluding, as he did with his students, to specific moments in architecture from day-to-day situations: the curve of a stair, the afternoon light catching a wall, reflections in water, the fleeting piercing sound in a tunnel. The easily recognizable moments shared, pondered and dwelt upon as precursors to architectural ideas dissolved the difficult borders of prescriptive lessons, and evoked in class personal and indeed inspirational visual memories – both of his favoured city and his own days as a student.

Though he was forced to organize his thoughts and communicate them in a logical sequence, Raje used the classroom to vent his intuitions through young, supposedly experimental minds. Of his students, he said, 'I have forty minds to give me ideas.' Each class was a form of improvisation more akin to classical music than architecture. Always aware of the applied structure of notes, the music was open to many interpretations. It struck the chord of a thoughtful, fluent storyteller, rather than a grave and dogmatic professor. This is not to suggest an inability to academically engage; on the contrary, because of the personal fluent beginning developed with a striking spirit, the themes threw up unexpected and lyrical resolutions. Neither nostalgic nor sentimental, the process was always logical, much like the discovery initiated in his own workplace. 'Because I never discuss the outcome with the students, I am always surprised by the result.'

In a career that spanned sixty years, never was there space for the merely logical, the static or the analytical, and all the minor forces and conventions of architecture. Till the very end of his life Raje remained an astute and always enquiring student of architecture. In his late seventies, when he was asked to be the judge of a national architectural competition, his prompt reply was: 'What! Do you think I am too old to compete?'

The great penumbra of Raje's life exists outside a profession that eluded him, that left him to his own devices. And yet the prime difficulty such a life poses to chronological record is partly due to the acute obscurity necessary for creative work, and the secretive artistic urge within which Raje lodged himself. 'All artists have their secrets', he used to say. 'Their process is very precious to them.' The contradictory nature of such an existence makes the record of a life both impossible and wholly worthy of enumeration. For a man whose diligence of record – diaries, sketches, notebooks – was personal, and as much an attempt to explain life for himself as himself to life, a book on his work for public consumption was anathema.

Raje's obsessive record of the process of his sketches and thoughts that gave eventual direction to design, the meticulous development of construction details, and the eventual record of the building, is in itself a distressingly elaborate archive to place before the public. The collection of photographs, drawings and notes may be inadequate in clarifying his ideas, but together they do provide clues to the many fundamental problems and situations he constantly wrestled with. To monitor, sift and make selective pickings from such an archive is perhaps the only method of providing the first point of public contact with a very private, very varied and fulfilled life.

The need to perennially redefine architecture was a personal score for someone who treated the profession as a private discovery. It is hard enough to introduce the book of an enigmatic artist; it is harder still to do so, so close to his passing. Raje died in 2009. For the many who knew him, the book is a eulogy; for the others, a record of a working life.

Gautam Bhatia
with contributions from Rahul Mehrotra,
Amita Raje and Shubhra Raje
April 2012

KAILASH ELLORA

Sources and Interpretations

The history of architecture has for long responded to the making of places. Places have inspired the acts of architecture. It took centuries to build traditions, the forms of which were not intended by anyone but were worked on without knowing. These forms were closely connected with a way of life, crystallizing its inner structure in the process of what became a tradition.

What order was brought in the material realm and what order was brought into harmonious expressions of the spiritual realm are evident from the way the buildings were made. The way of life and the order in the material realm brought about the significant architecture of a given era.

The choice of material that encloses space is distinct from that which is unenclosed. A building is an enclosure, but without reaching its real fulfilment its technology remains only on the surface – that is, far from transcending into Architecture.

The lessons of past architectures show us an integrated solution to problems in their time. The complexity of those problems are not yet fully understood. Apparently, simple solutions have misled the present into false rationale and its academic acceptance.

A building programme can become innovative when worked with the climate of the place. The places realized within and outside the building become more meaningful. The culture of a place is very closely connected with its climate, lending further to its architectural expressions. The spaces in plan which seem to be outside any rationale are often intimately connected with ways of living and need to be discovered. These spaces are truly the life-force, generating in its wake the freedom to express and acknowledge its needs and values.

Long ago, magnificent buildings and complexes were made. Some of them are still standing, some in parts and some suggesting the place where they stood. All of them passed on to the present the inspiring moments of the time, raising continuous questions in the process and making it clear that no matter which direction architecture may take, the future will contain the ruins of the present.

July/September 1983

Projects at
The Indian Institute of Management, Ahmedabad
1971–1999

Original campus by Louis Kahn, until 1974

Campus extensions by Anant Raje, 1969–99

Selected projects, 1969–99

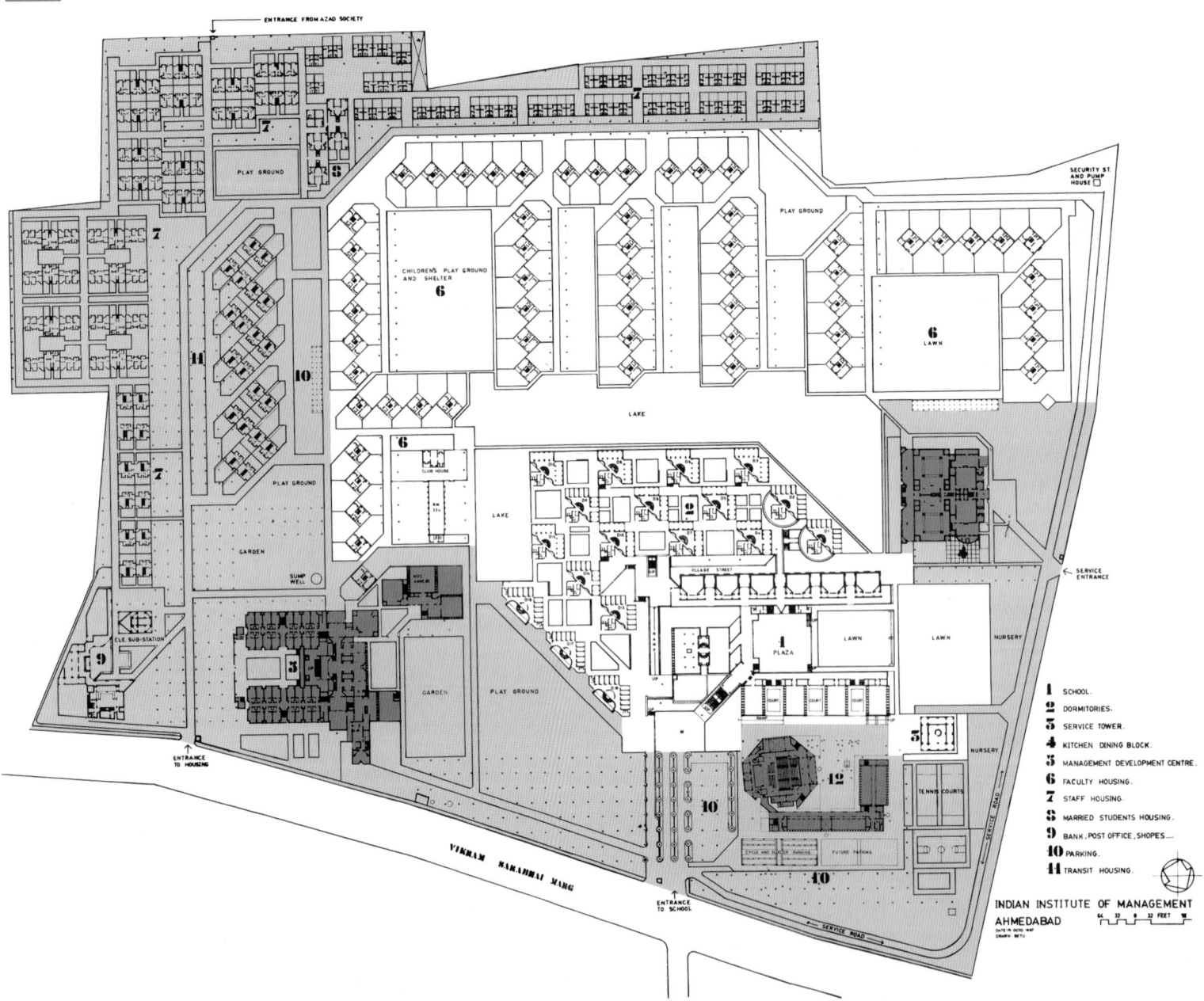

INDIAN INSTITUTE OF MANAGEMENT
AHMEDABAD

1 SCHOOL.
2 DORMITORIES.
3 SERVICE TOWER.
4 KITCHEN DINING BLOCK.
5 MANAGEMENT DEVELOPMENT CENTRE.
6 FACULTY HOUSING.
7 STAFF HOUSING.
8 MARRIED STUDENTS HOUSING.
9 BANK, POST OFFICE, SHOPES....
10 PARKING.
11 TRANSIT HOUSING.

Continuation of a Language

The Indian Institute of Management is sited on a plot of land of roughly 32 hectares, situated 6 kilometres west of the River Sabarmati. It is flat agricultural land without any features except for some mango trees. The plan constitutes three layers, starting with the core which is the assembly, a place of congregation, for student convocations. The first layer is composed of classrooms, library, administrative and faculty offices, followed by the students' living quarters – the dormitories. A large body of water, planned to separate the students' residences from the houses of the faculty and support staff, serves as a physical and psychological buffer. The three layers of the plan are tightly bound together by a geometry that orients the residences toward the prevailing wind direction. Kahn called the school a 'citadel of institution'.

The dormitories are an extension of the classrooms with open-to-sky courts between them to let the air cross-ventilate the rooms. Kahn loved the masonry walls of the Pompeiians who shaped their buildings with wall enclosures that made closed and open rooms. What he added to the openings made in the walls were reinforced ties to contain the horizontal thrust generated by the arches. These, in his words, were the composite order where both brick and concrete coexist. Material to Kahn was a choice in light. Light 'is the giver of all presences'. For him the room does not exist in nature. The room is so marvellous that its size, dimensions, walls, windows, light have an effect on what you say and what you do. If there is just one other person present besides yourself, what you say would be generative. The room is so sensitive that a third person entering it would change the event into a performance. A plan is a society of rooms.

To Kahn, the beginning of design is a question that invariably occupies the centre of a given space. The mark made for the question grows larger and larger until 'what to do meets the means of doing it'. This question and its mark, in the case of the Indian Institute of Management, started with the school building, with the open-to-sky building within. The periphery of the court grew larger until it broke up into several spaces, making class-rooms, library, offices, and further, in their wake, formed the layers of students' residences – which further broke up to accommodate the courts of light. In terms of 'poche' made by charcoal, the entire composition jelled into a plan where the first layers are apparent.

In Kahn's mind, the intuitive sense takes the uppermost position: 'The intuitive is the most accurate sense we have. Science can never reach it. Knowledge can never reach it. The beautiful thing that the intuitive gives is a sense of commonality, a sense of human agreement which is agreement without example. Something can be produced for the first time, and somehow it has a quality of having always been there.' Simply stated, Kahn raised the level of the intellect to a spiritual level, invoking humanistic and spiritual ideals in pursuit of timeless architectural solutions. His instinct for new technology, combined with abstract visual language and learning from the lessons of history, gave a new direction to the meaning and purpose of architecture.

Brick is the basic building material for all the buildings on the campus. The openings in the brick walls are spanned by arches, both segmental and flat. The plans, therefore, whether of school buildings or residences, reflect the order in brick construction. The mass is important in carrying the loads. The mass that makes the structure makes the light. The library stacks have the reinforced concrete frame within the enclosure of bricks where the book-loads on the floor slabs are carried on the concrete frame, leaving the peripheral brick walls to respond to the weather, create shade and bring in the light while keeping the glare out. The nature of the material that governed the brick construction generated arches, pilasters, buttresses. Walls brought about a composite order with concrete for frames and restraining members used for ties. Unplastered, both brick and concrete left their mark on all surfaces, and created a new architectural language that recognized craftsmanship and care in its making. This language instantly made connection with historical places like Mandu, Golconda, Bidar and Bijapur on the Deccan plateau in central India where the Sultanates built some of the most magnificent buildings in the fifteenth–sixteenth century.

The major works on the campus of the Indian Institute of Management after Kahn are the Management Development Centre, the Student and Faculty Mess Halls, Housing for various categories of supporting staff designed and built between 1974 and 1979, and the Ravi Mathai Centre.

Ahmedabad, 8 September 1997

Students' Dining Halls and Kitchens
Ahmedabad, 1970–79
(1970–74 as associate to Louis Kahn)

The two dining halls and the two separate kitchens were an outcome of the demand that the cooking done for non-vegetarian meals should be separated from that for vegetarian meals, with separate cooking equipment.

The roof over the dining halls supported by four brick masonry pilasters carried hollow beams to accommodate air-cooling supply air ducts and clerestorey ventilation system. The long covered porch connecting the two dining halls serve as entrances, as also places to meet before and after meals. Right above the porch are located the faculty dining spaces served by their own kitchens. The positions of these halls are at the end of the classroom corridor and at the end of the street that serves the dormitories. The building was completed for use in 1978.

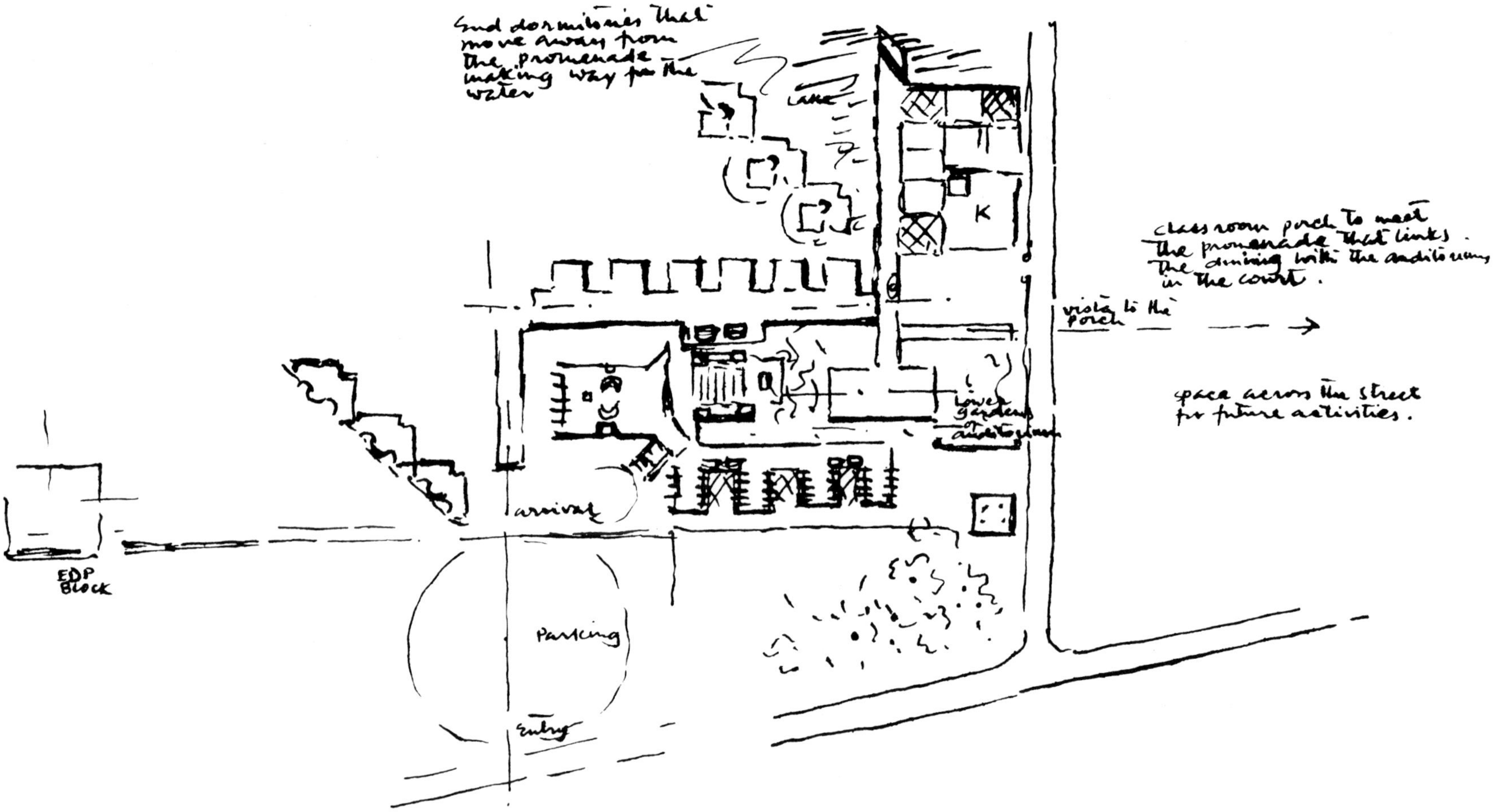
EDP
BLOCK
arrival
Parking
Entry
K
Lake

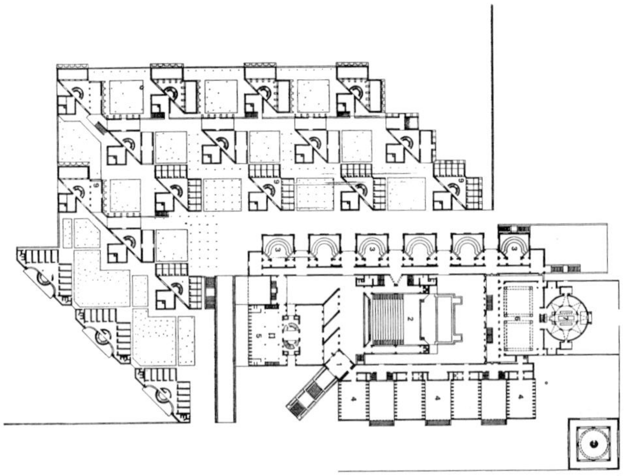

^ Development sketch showing revised location of the kitchen–dining complex, IIM, 1975. The kitchen–dining complex has been moved out of the school complex, leaving the plaza open at the northwest end. The notes, from the top, on the sketch read:
'End dormitories that move away from the promenade making way for the water'
'Classroom porch to meet the promenade that links the dining with the auditoriums in the court'
'Vista to the porch'
'Lower gardens of auditorium'
'Space across the street for future activities'

< The 1972 version of the kitchen–dining complex at IIM, by Louis Kahn, located at the northwest end of the plaza (now the Louis Kahn Plaza).
'The axial arrangement of the kitchen–dining area consists of a separate circular kitchen and twin square dining halls, one for the staff and the other for the students.' (Ronner and Jhaveri, 1987, p. 228)

> Wood model views of the IIM campus, locating the revised kitchen–dining complex, 1975.

23

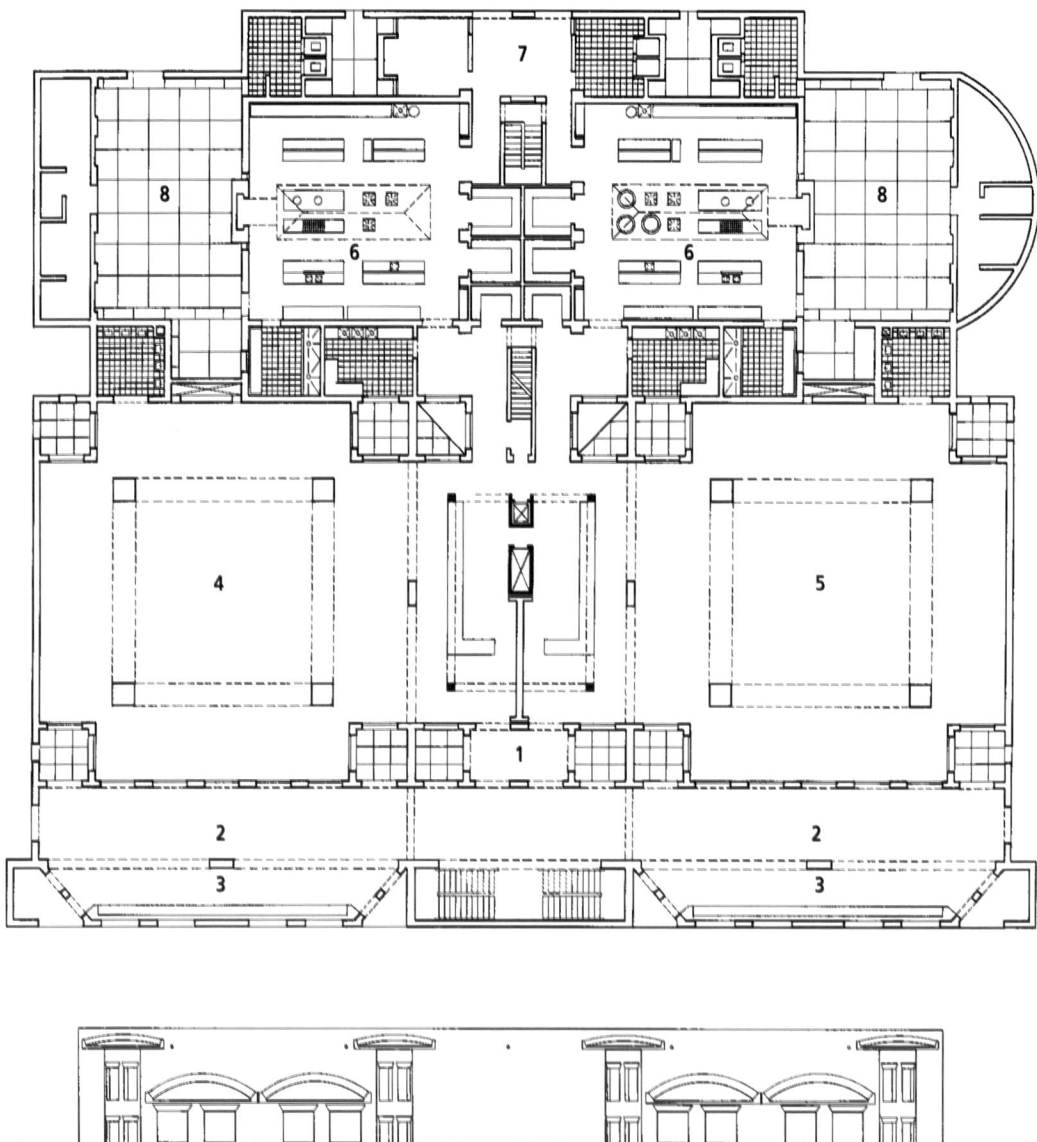

^ Ground floor plan.
1 Entrance lobby
2 Gallery
3 Alcove
4 Dining – students
5 Dining – staff
6 Kitchen
7 Service
8 Yard

> First floor plan.
1 Upper part of lower dining halls
2 Dining – faculty
3 Kitchen
4 Office
5 Light wells

> Section through dining halls.

> Section through kitchen.

^ Exterior elevation of loggia, looking towards the dormitories.

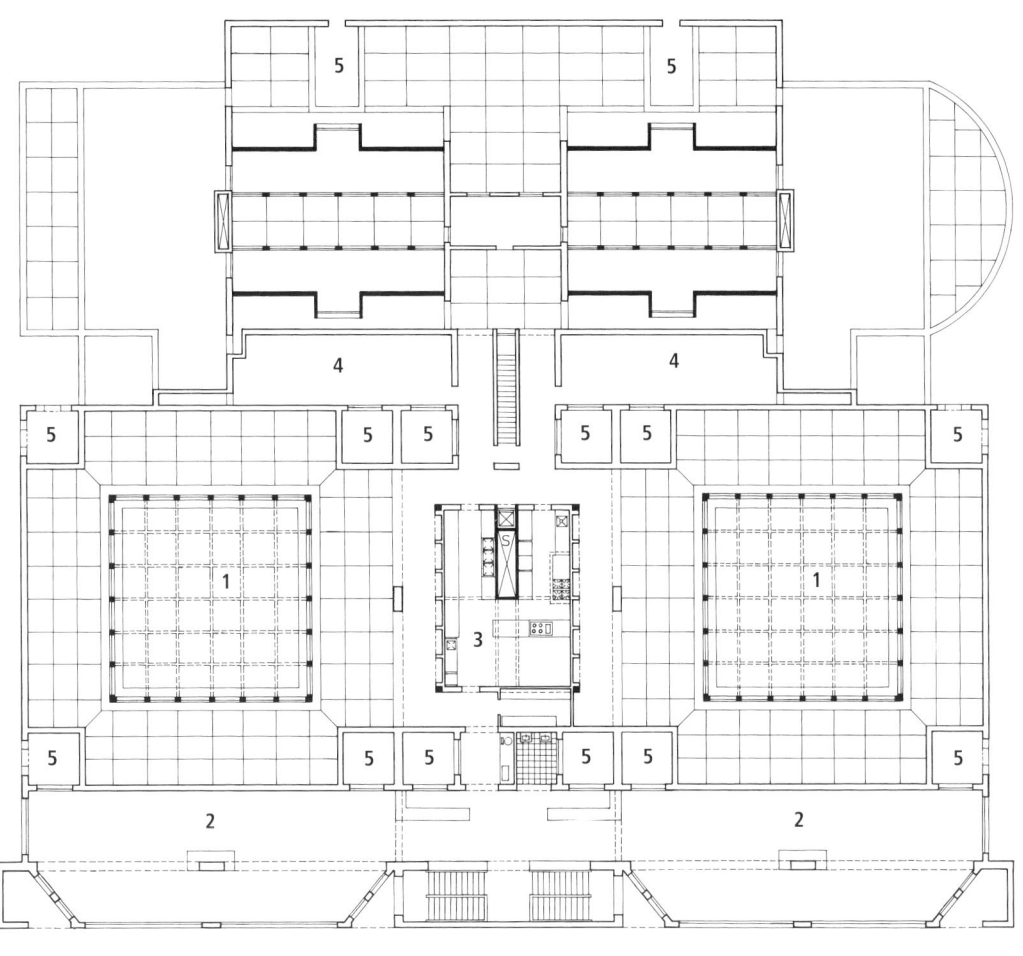

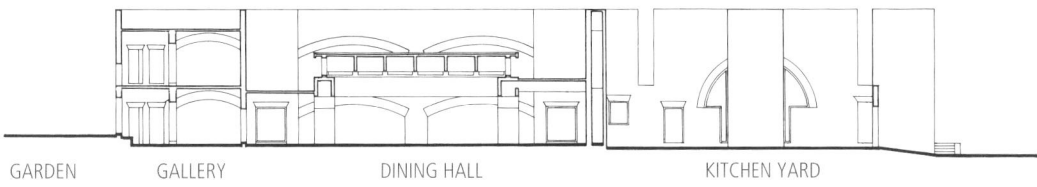

GARDEN   GALLERY   DINING HALL   KITCHEN YARD

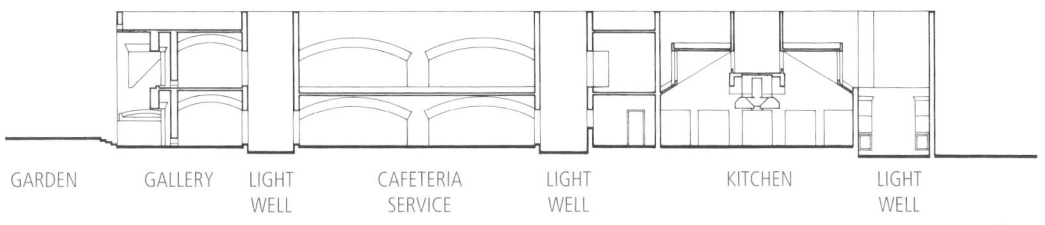

GARDEN   GALLERY   LIGHT   CAFETERIA   LIGHT   KITCHEN   LIGHT
                       WELL   SERVICE   WELL   WELL

25

> The loggia with two layers of exterior light to diffuse light
and reduce glare.

∨ Clerestorey lighting inside the dining halls.

Management Development Centre
Ahmedabad, 1974–89
(MDC Annexe 1987–89)

The Management Development Centre is considered a school within a school, to train managerial personnel of public and private enterprises. The early concepts were discussed with Kahn, but the later design and development were done by me. There were certain constraints in terms of scale that came about because it is right next to the faculty housing.

The building is basically an enlarged house, like a *haveli* or a *mahal*. A central court, flanked by two rows of rooms with a corridor that serves the rooms, connects on the front side with the classrooms, dining halls and lounge. The plans clearly indicate centrality (focus) in the form of an open-to-sky court, with rooms and lounges and concourses around it.

The making of openings in brick masonry follows the previous order in Kahn buildings. The exposed brick masonry-bearing wall is the predominant architectural decision. Brick arches span the openings with reinforced concrete ties as restraining members making a composite order. Concrete aprons with clerestorey light bring the light down to the basement, as interior light reflects better off concrete than brick. Strict geometry regulates the elements of architecture and helps make tighter composition of spaces in such a way as to make one building shade the other in the hot sun.

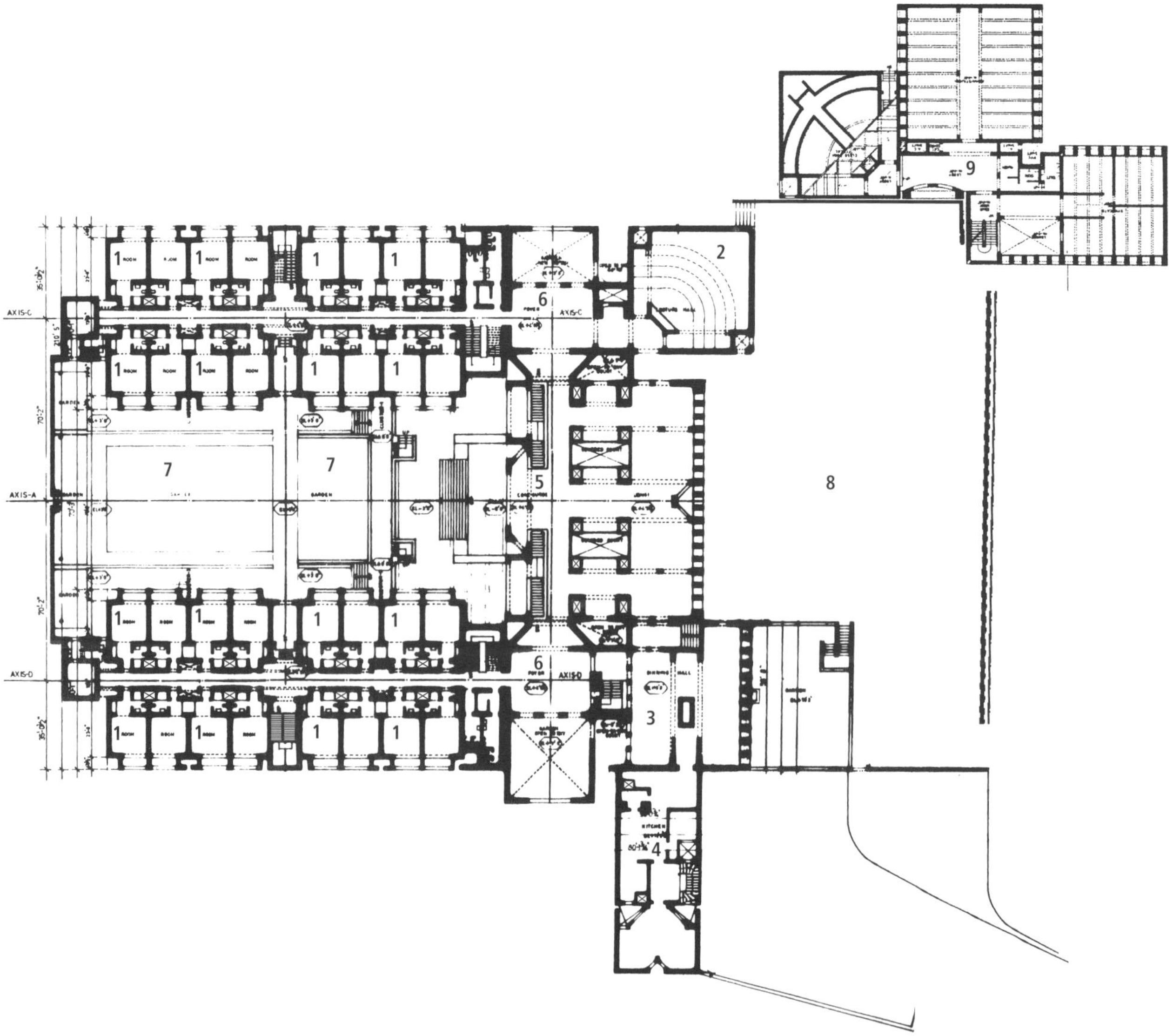

< Main floor plan.
  1 Room
  2 Lecture hall
  3 Dining hall
  4 Kitchen
  5 Concourse
  6 Foyer
  7 Garden
  8 Plaza
  9 Annexe

> Model view.

> Sections.

∨ Model view.

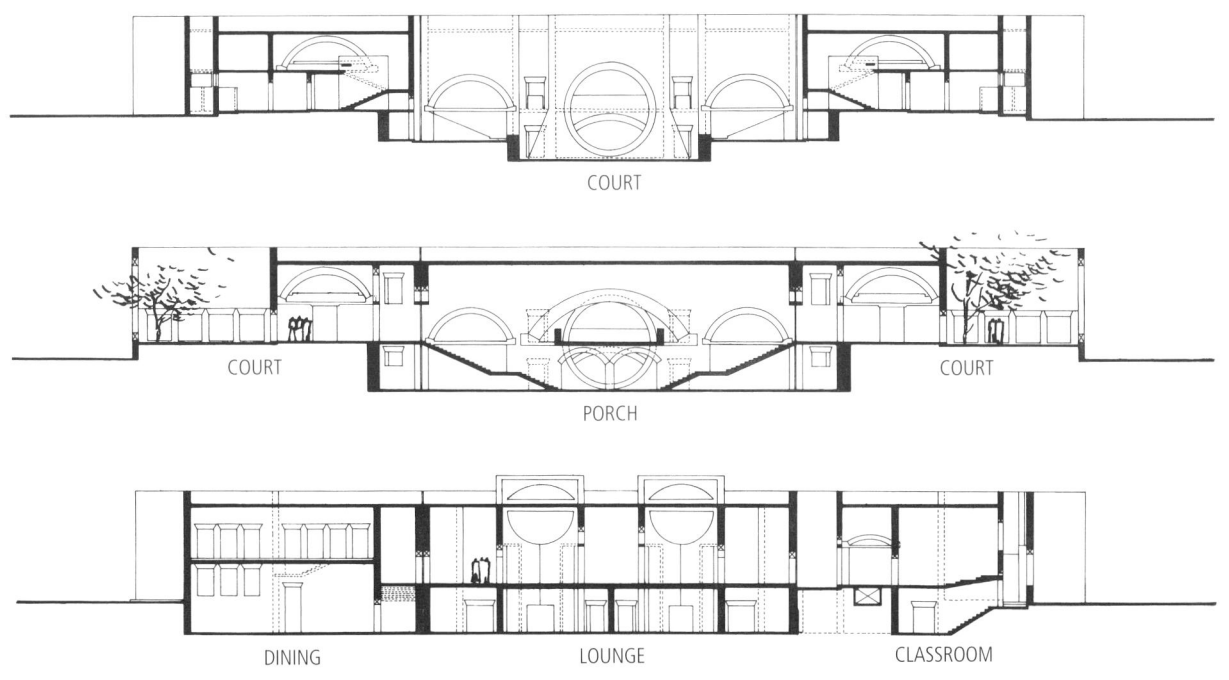

COURT

COURT   COURT

PORCH

DINING   LOUNGE   CLASSROOM

33

> A part of the building is brought down to get the outside scale to the scale of the adjacent faculty houses.

v Connections on axis from the lounges to the court, across the clerestorey, providing the completion of a circle.

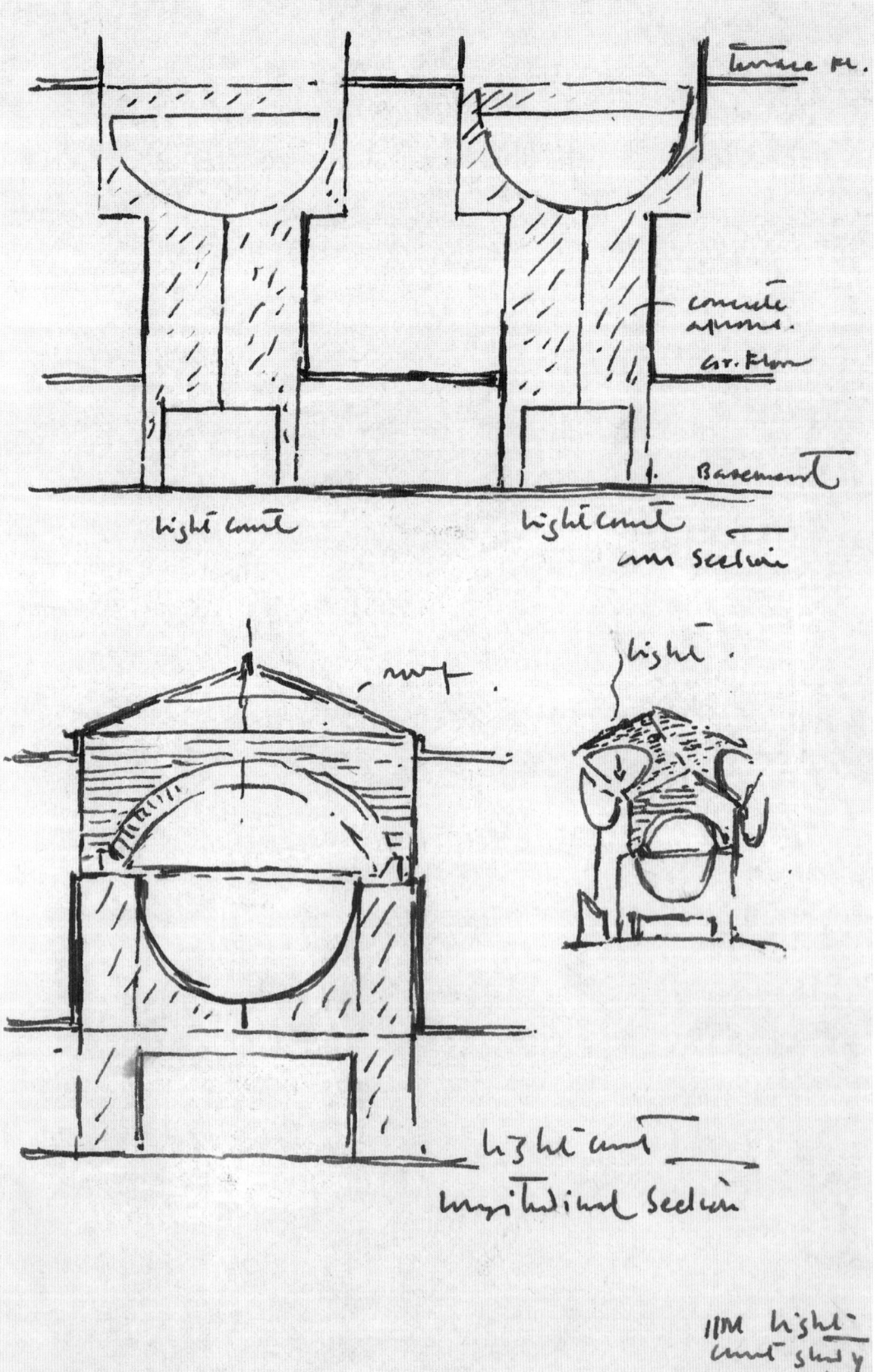

Terrace fl.

concrete
aprons.

Gr. Floor

Basement

light court

light court
cross section

roof.

light.

light court
longitudinal section

IIM light
court study
Aril 10/76

< IIM light court study: sketch, 1976.

> Aspect of the concrete clerestorey light
from inside the light element.

∧ Aspects of the central courtyard.

< Two layers of the exterior wall diffuse light and reduce glare.

^ Plastered wall in the interior of the participants' rooms is in the sense
  of an inlay; the room and common area furniture are designed to integrate
  with the architecture.

> Clerestorey light lifts parts of the corridor, removes the hot air and gives access
  to the rooms, in the upper floor corridor.

Annexe to
Family offices
HMA
Nov 88

Ravi Mathai Centre
Ahmedabad, 1987–89

The extensions to the school building by Louis Kahn were discussed several times at various stages of the construction. Kahn proposed an extension in the form of a mirror image to the faculty offices so that the courts between the offices extended, with the corridors facing each other across the extended courts. This proposal was schematically drawn on the board but was later dropped when priorities changed and the focus fell on other parts of the campus, as well as on new programmes. The requirements were broken down to three major spaces: computer laboratories for the students, accounts and other supporting offices, and an auditorium with a capacity of 500 seats.

When the new programme was introduced as a centre for innovative education, the new expansion needed an entirely independent concept. Yet it had to be a part of the 'Kahn campus' in its architectural language, and also meet the prevailing order of forming elements of composition, both in plan and elevation.

A visit to Italy in 1986 gave me an opportunity to study Renaissance architectural concepts in organizing public spaces. The twin plazas in the town of Padua are a striking example of bringing together administrative and commercial buildings, with residences on the upper floors. Each of the two public spaces has a separate identity, yet they form a unified whole.

Kahn's school building with its three major components, namely, classrooms, the library and faculty offices, encloses a large court. Its public nature lends it to the holding of student gatherings and assemblies, and, above all, yearly convocations on graduation day. It is therefore aptly called 'the court of free expression' and is named after Louis Kahn. This space is active and ceremonial in nature. It has a strong presence, and is Homeric in its scale and proportions.

The Ravi Mathai Centre was designed as a 'C'-shaped structure, where the supporting administrative offices form a linear building connected to the auditorium by a circular corridor on the inner side of the structure. The entire composition encloses a court facing the end elevations of the part of the building that Kahn designed, and leaving a linear space, around 10 metres wide, at its narrowest point. The broken edges of the end elevations form the courts between the faculty offices connecting the Mathai Centre Plaza with the Louis Kahn Plaza.

The Kahn Plaza has the library overlooking the convocation court. The main axis of the court is on the axis of the library, with classrooms and faculty offices on either side. The faculty office blocks enclose the courts and are served by a corridor facing the main court. The Mathai Plaza has no dominant axis like the Kahn Plaza. The suggestive axis is the axis of the auditorium, but it is independent of the plaza. The auditorium's position and the tilt of ten degrees towards the water tower swings the space of this court towards the courts of the faculty offices and onwards to the Kahn Plaza.

The twin plazas at Padua.

43

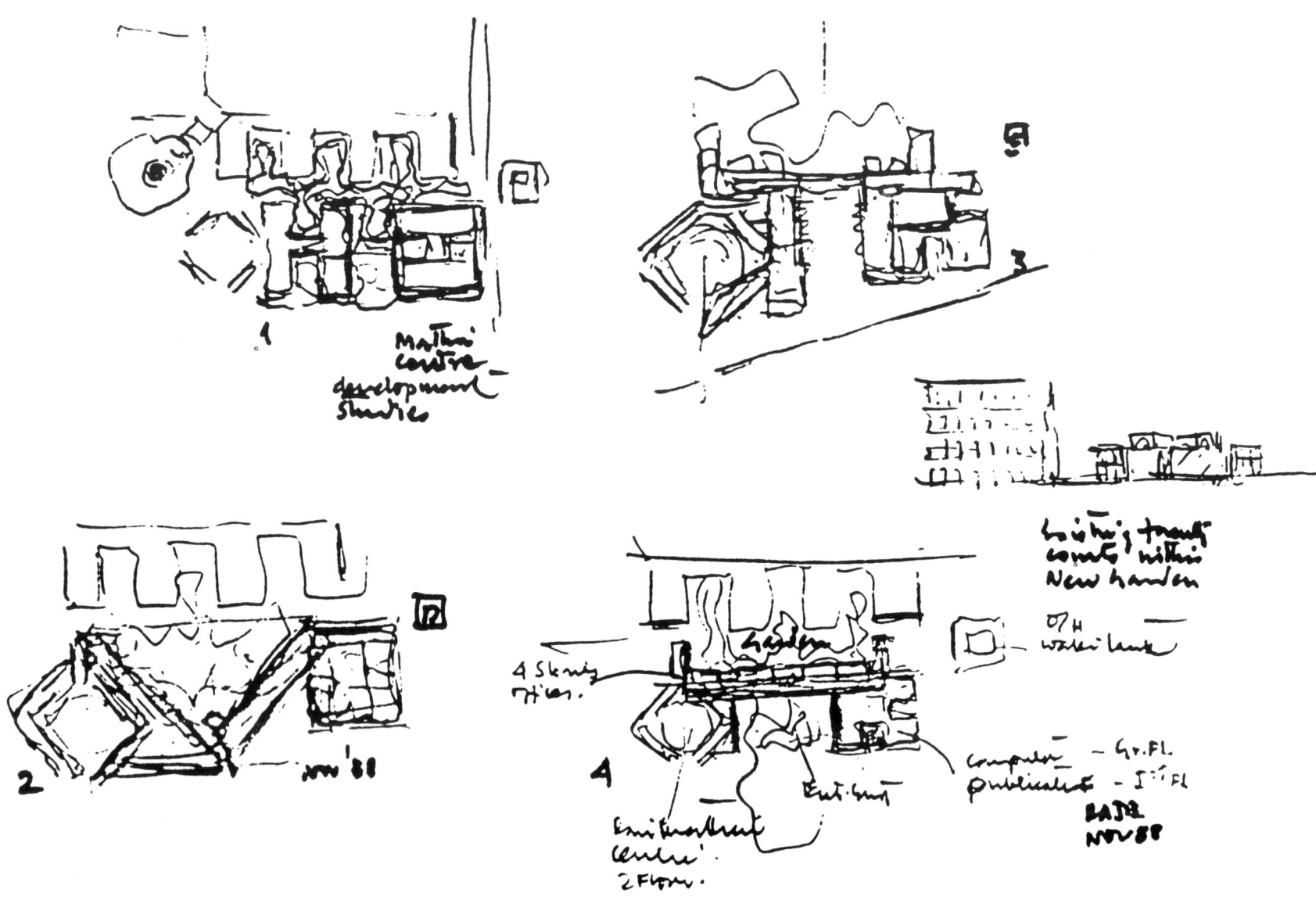

^ Development studies of Mathai Plaza as an extension of Louis Kahn Plaza, November 1988.

> Block model of Louis Kahn Plaza, faculty offices and Mathai Plaza, making an outdoor room.

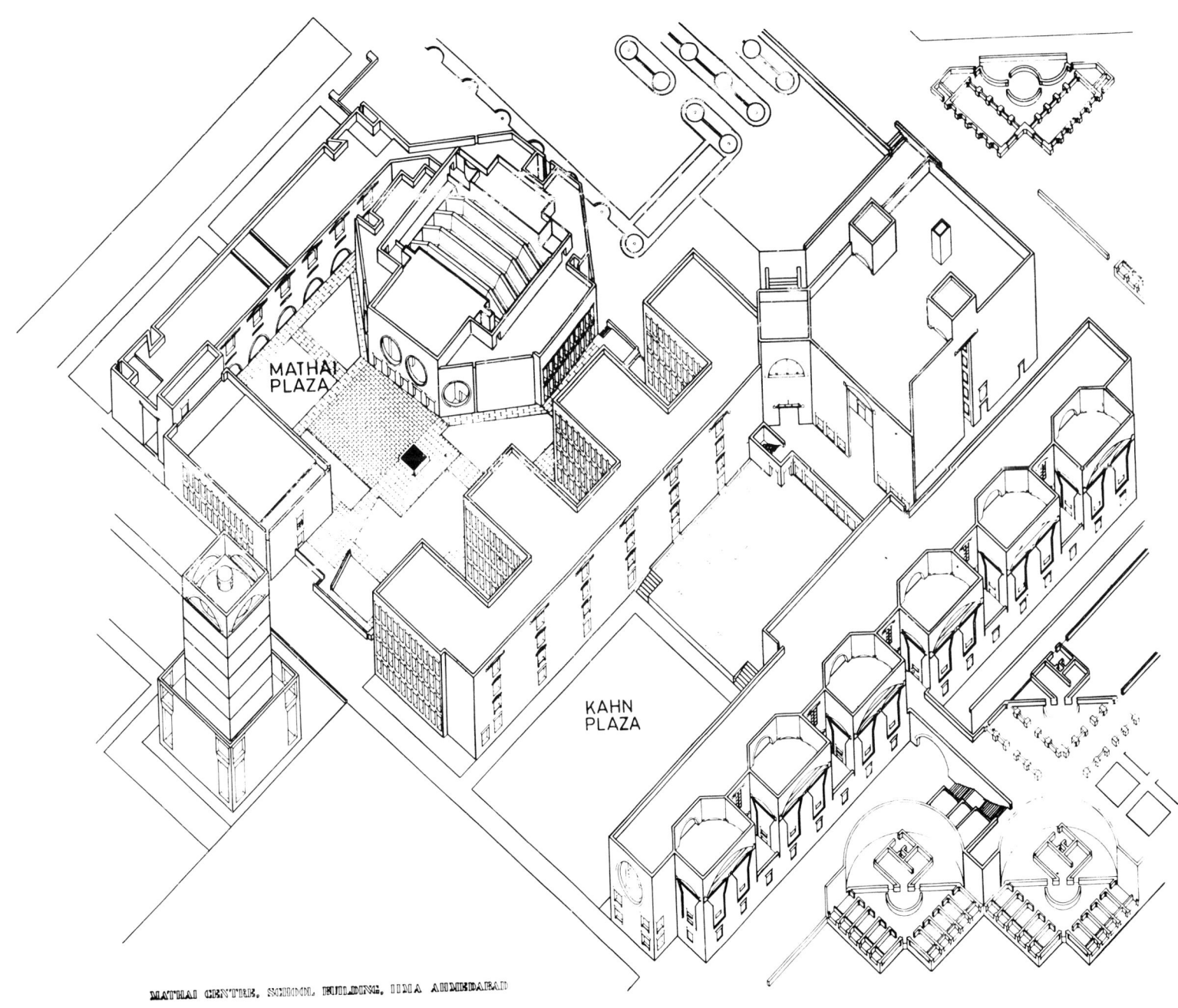

MATHAI
PLAZA

KAHN
PLAZA

MATHAI CENTRE, SCHOOL BUILDING, IIMA AHMEDABAD

^ Axonometric with the twin Kahn and Mathai Plazas.

< Definitive model with the convocation path between the faculty offices
and Mathai Plaza. The water tank termination suggests a turning into
Kahn Plaza to the left.

> Section through Mathai and Kahn Plazas.

> Layout plan.
  1 Parking
  2 Auditorium
  3 Computer wing
  4 Offices
  5 Corridor
  6 Faculty court
  7 Water/service tower
  8 Sport court
  9 Garden

∨ Auditorium core enclosed by brick walls with spaces within walls.
  Development studies of Mathai Centre auditorium, December 1988.

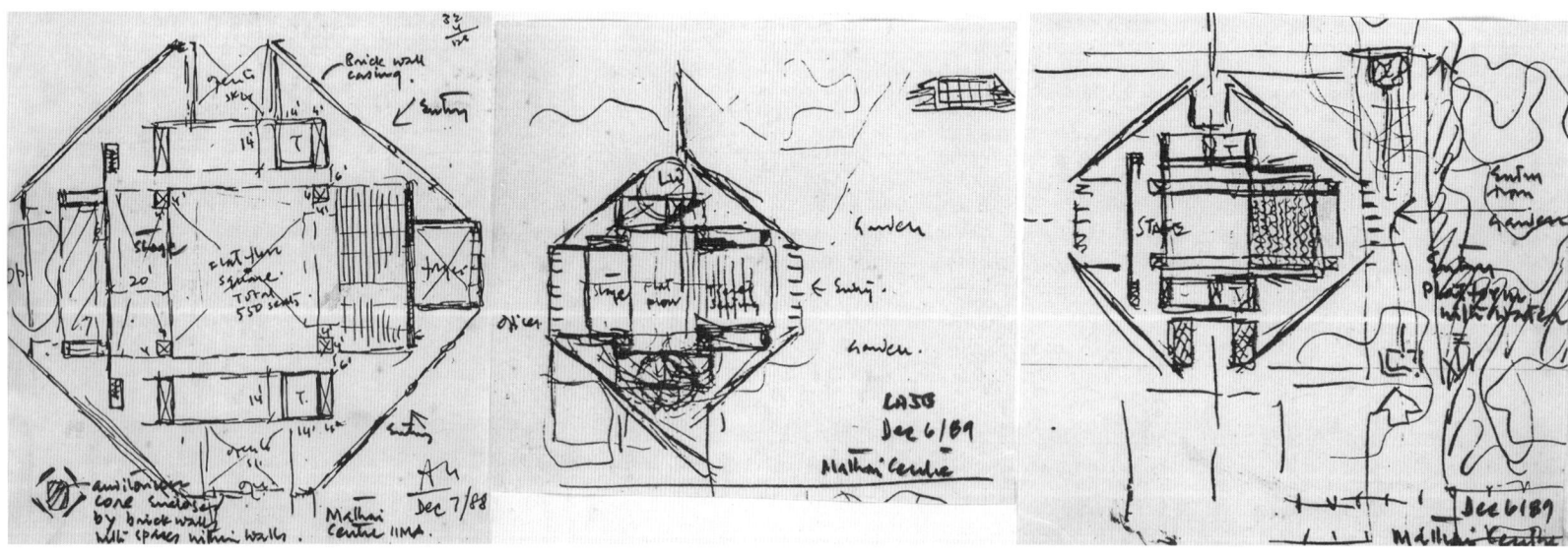

48

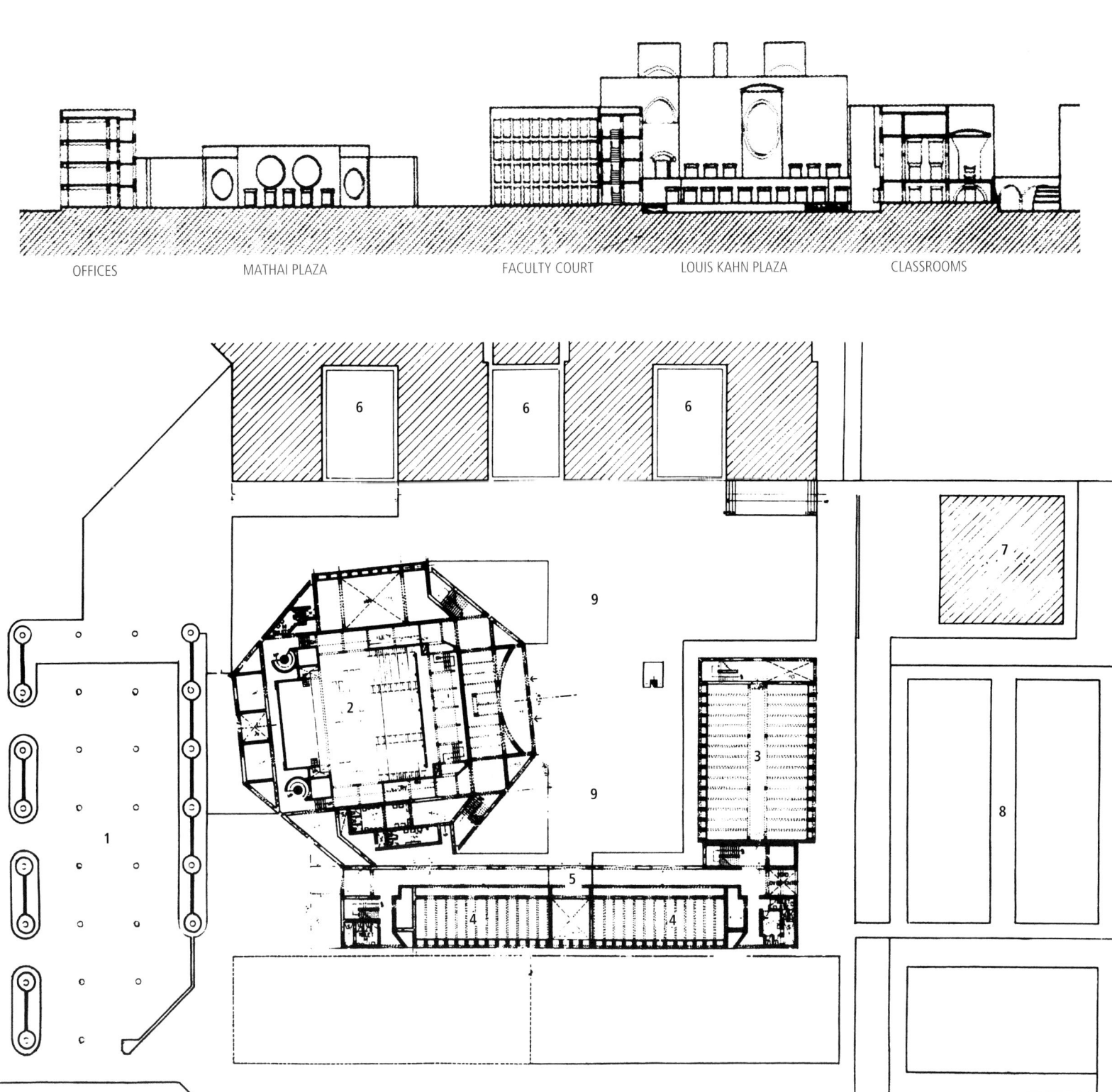

OFFICES   MATHAI PLAZA   FACULTY COURT   LOUIS KAHN PLAZA   CLASSROOMS

49

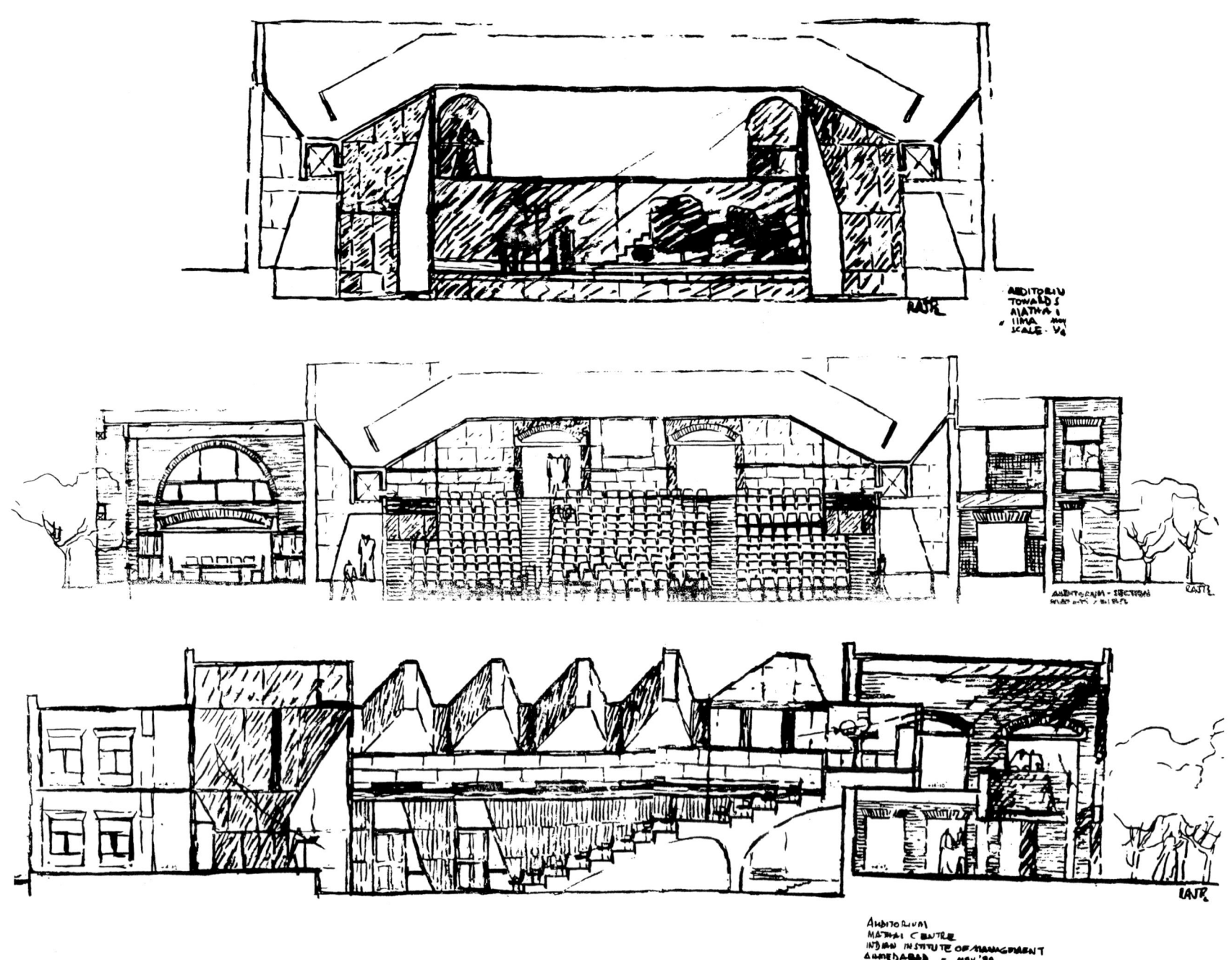

The auditorium serves the entire institute community besides being used for lectures, performances and syndicated simulation exercises. The extended stage area is a flattened floor, enlarging the space along the long axis of the hall beyond the proscenium up to the rear wall of the stage. The entire outside envelope, made of exposed brick masonry walls, contains management offices, toilets, seminar rooms, foyers and backstage facilities. This insulates the auditorium from external noise and temperature.

∧ Charcoal sketches showing the interior of the auditorium and foyer spaces, November 1989.

> Ground floor plan | first floor plan of Ravi Mathai Centre.

> Wood model: view from the Mathai Plaza with roof | view from parking without roof.

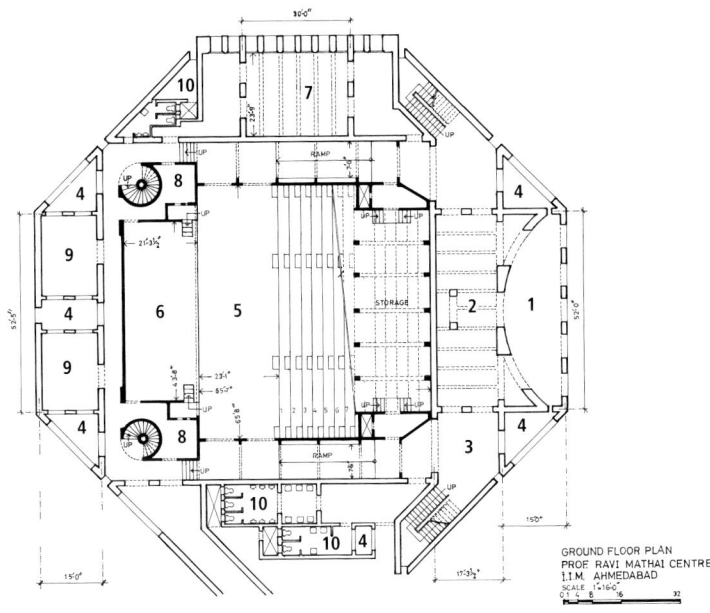

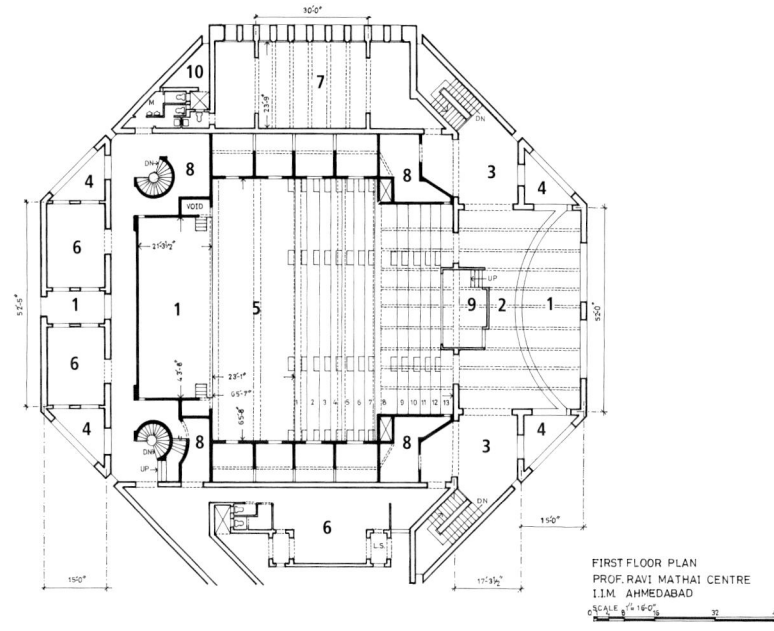

GROUND FLOOR PLAN
PROF. RAVI MATHAI CENTRE
I.I.M. AHMEDABAD
SCALE 1"=16'-0"

FIRST FLOOR PLAN
PROF. RAVI MATHAI CENTRE
I.I.M. AHMEDABAD
SCALE 1"=16'-0"

Ground floor plan.
1 Entrance lobby
2 Foyer
3 Lobby
4 Light shaft / court
5 Auditorium (550 seats)
6 Stage
7 Seminar hall
8 Utility
9 Anteroom
10 Toilets

First floor plan.
1 Open to below
2 Foyer
3 Lobby
4 Light shaft
5 Auditorium (550 seats)
6 Office
7 Seminar hall
8 Mechanical
9 Projector room
10 Toilets

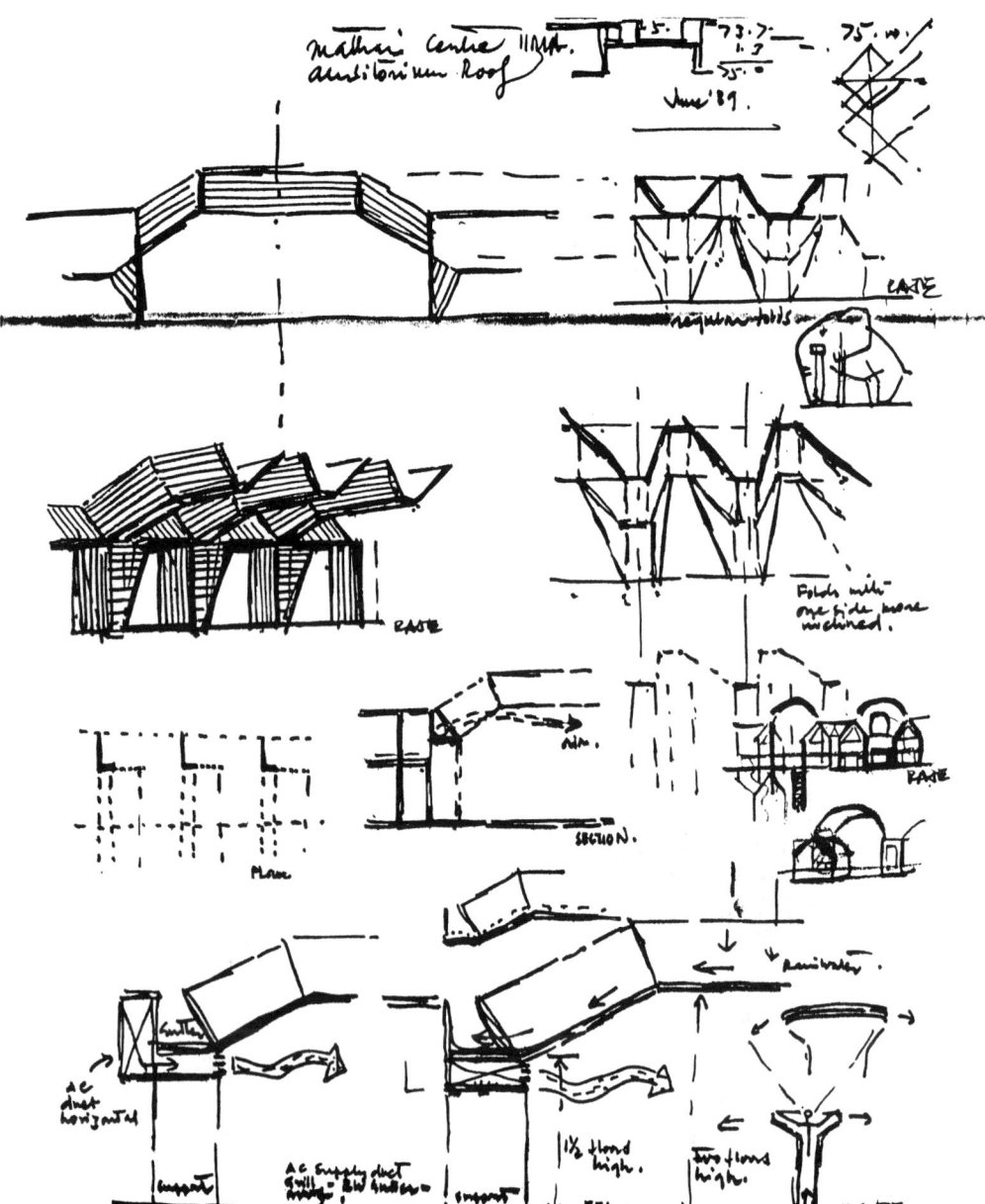

∧ Study model of auditorium roof.

< Mathai Centre auditorium roof studies, June 1989.

The structural form of the auditorium comes from the realization that acoustics are an inseparable part of the inner envelope of the roof, walls, seats and the floor.

The structure of the roof is an asymmetrical reinforced cement concrete folded plate, bending down at the two ends of the folds, 21 metres across the hall, and is supported on a three-dimensional reinforced concrete diaphragm, subsequently carrying the loads on eschewed reinforced concrete walls. The air-conditioning ducts, electric cables and rain-water gutters are integrated within the three-dimensional structure of the diaphragm, over the two ambulatory access ways on either side of the auditorium.

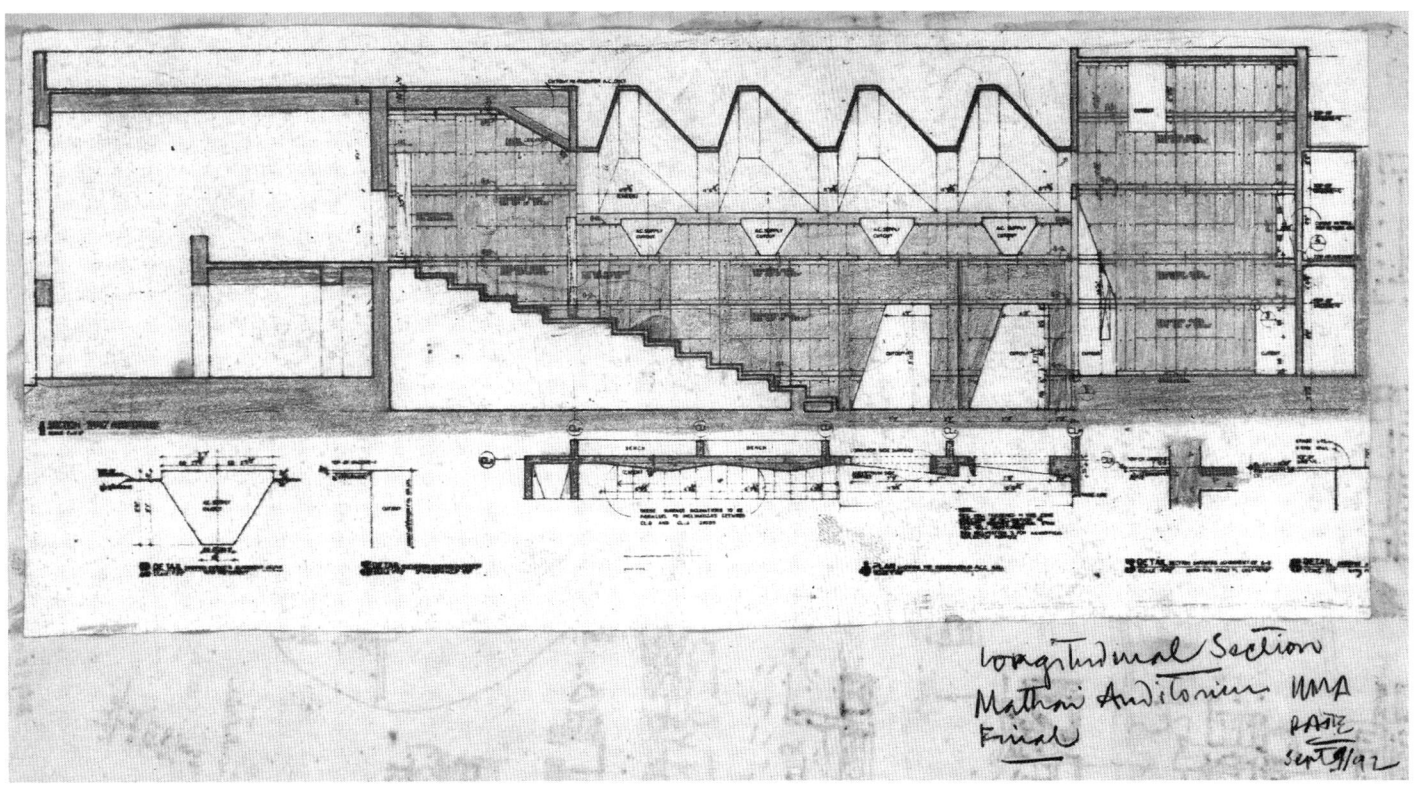

Longitudinal Section
Mathai Auditorium NMA
Final
RATZ
Sept 9/92

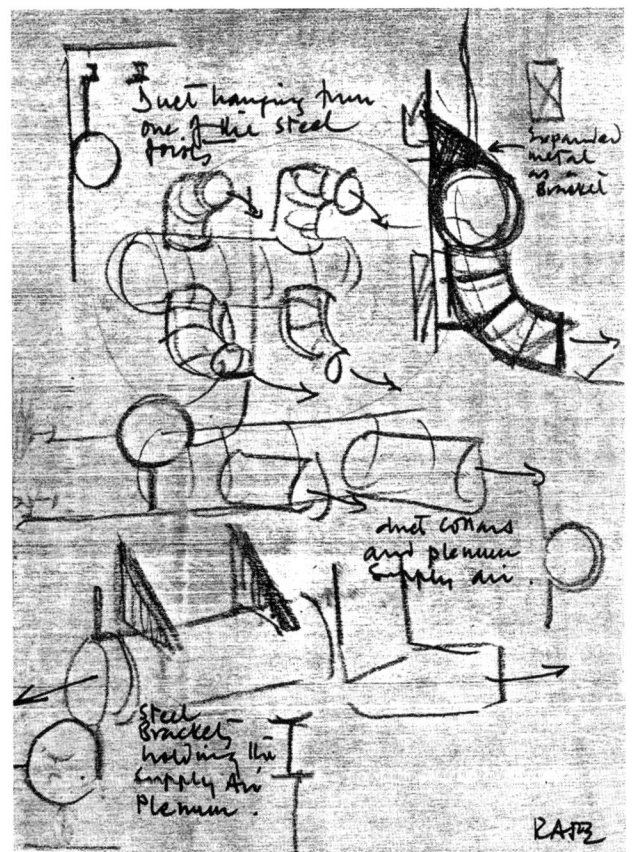

Duct hanging from one of the steel joists

expanded metal as bracket

duct collars and plenum supply air

steel brackets holding the supply air plenum.

RATZ

Mathai Auditorium Air condition Stage Side Ducting Studies

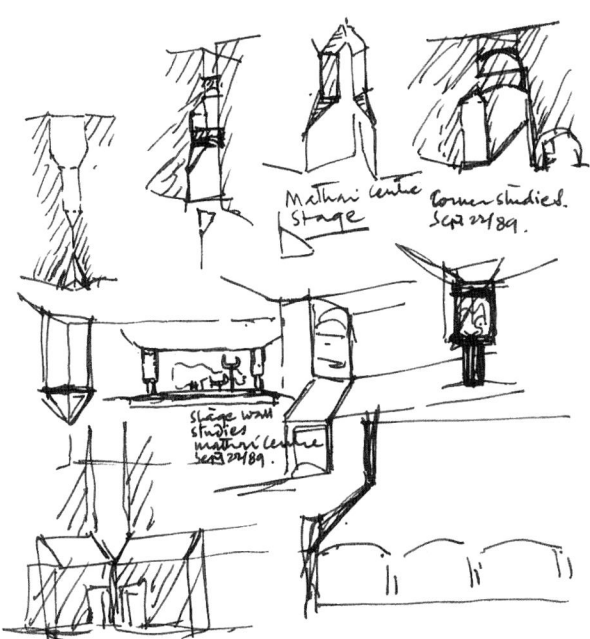

Mathai centre stage

corner studies. Sept 22/89.

stage wall studies mathai centre Sept 22/89

∧ Longitudinal section, final, September 1992.

∧ Auditorium stage wall and corner studies, September 1989.

< Auditorium stage side airconditioning ducting studies, undated.

53

Auditorium, interior views.

Exterior foyer in the sense of a mask. The idea of the entry to the auditorium from the court, and not the parking, makes greater sense. When people come out from a function, they must linger somewhere and not get straight back into their cars.

Private Residences

Study of light element, garden elevation, Contractor house, May 1976.

Residence for Naushir Contractor
Ahmedabad, 1983

A single family house with two bedrooms and a guest room that tries to find the centre of things. The house, in the process of reaching for light, forms alcoves and wall spaces to receive and diffuse the harsh glare from outside. The brick exterior folds on itself to create voids for shadows and the concrete aprons cut off the light glare. The walls are a semblance of parallel walls, but when they come to a termination, I wanted to have them not in a free flow that extends into the environment, but instead make a suggestion of a threshold between the inside and out. I was trying to see the two sides of the same coin – inside and outside – whether the inner realm, the interior of a space, has its own strength to be able to support itself, whatever may be the condition outside.

The two major volumes in cross-section create a third space which is the alcove of the living room and contains a wide seat. The end walls that meet the windows inside are articulated to extend the interior scales of the space to the exterior. The concrete aprons are oriented towards the west and south, and the living room alcove has a deep setback from the southern exterior wall.

The construction is of 35-centimetre-thick load-bearing walls kept exposed with flush pointing both inside and out. Some of the inside walls are plastered and painted. All concrete work is unplastered. Verandahs are paved with brick.

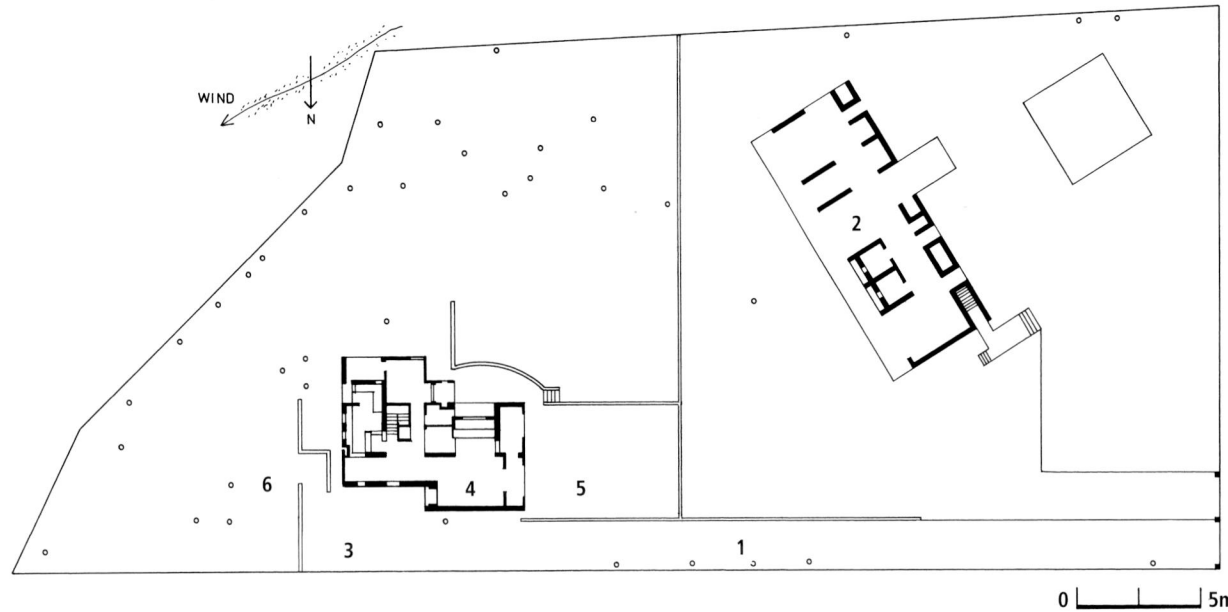

< Site plan.
1 Approach
2 Existing house
3 Parking
4 New house
5 Garden
6 Yard

> Section | West elevation.

> Floor plans.
1 Driveway
2 Car park
3 Entry
4 Living
5 Entry
6 Dining
7 Kitchen
8 Bedroom
9 Verandah
10 Terrace
11 Garden

> Detail at concrete light element.

WIND

N

0 ⌞___ ___⌟ 5m

On the right of the site is a house designed by me in 1957–58. A kind of linear space. The whole house was like a veranda, inspired to a certain extent by Manorama Sarabhai's house designed by Le Corbusier, though the language and materials were different. To the left is the house designed for the son of the family.

The focus of the house is at the centre, which is a window seat. On the ground floor, the cross-connections by way of the staircase, by way of the window seat, give a direction to the space – so that there are, constantly, relationships between one movement and the other, whether they are physical movements or visual interpretations of that movement.

The flow of air from the southwest escapes under the roof and also integrates the parapet. I am very much interested in integrating various kinds of elements to make one entity, or what one may call 'the integrity of an entity', so that it finally takes one particular position.

I like to work on elements of design, which I don't leave to chance. I work them out and apply them to a particular situation, and then try to recompose the entire space – either spaces that fall behind the element or those which are across.

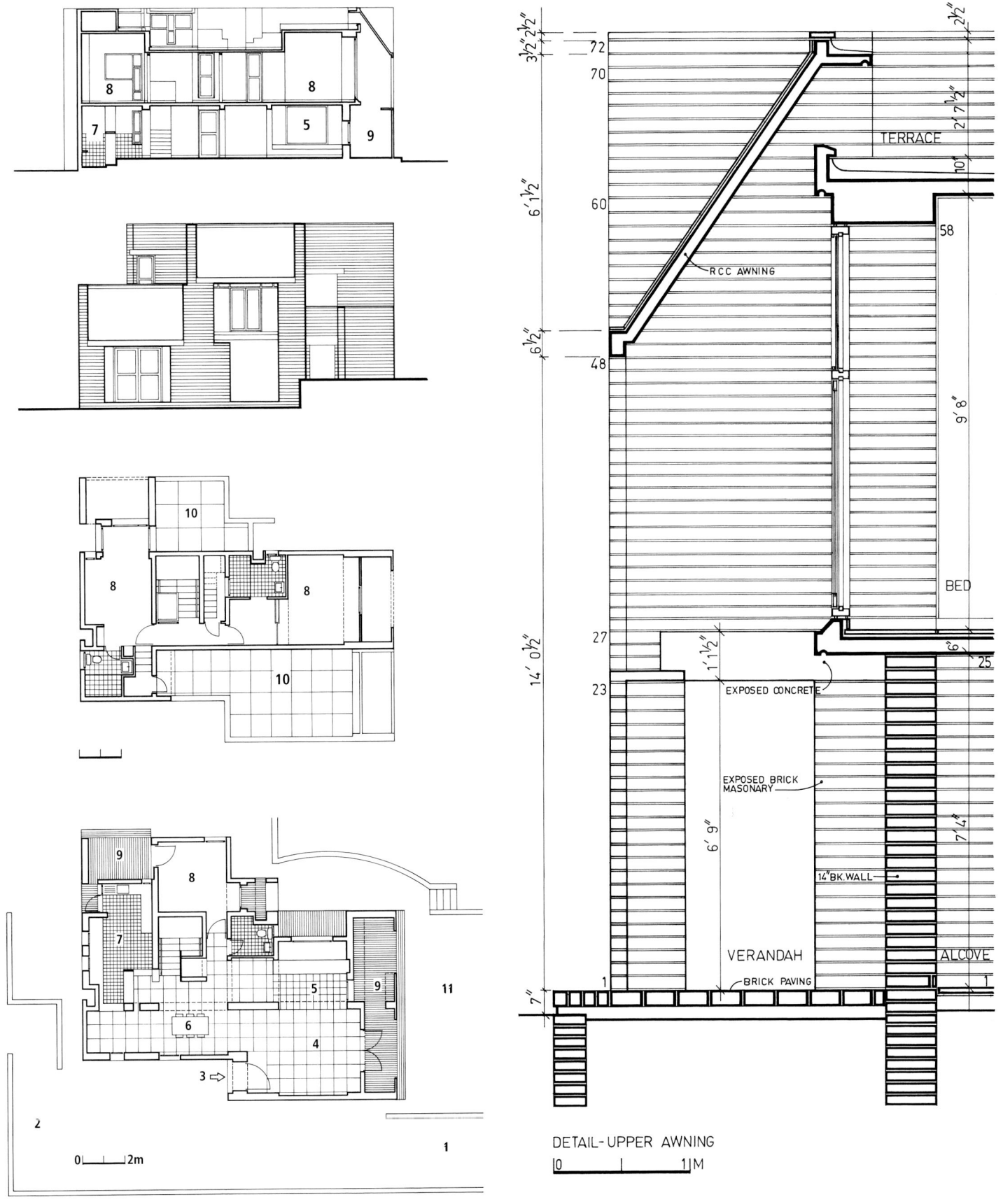

8

8

7

5

9

10

8

8

10

9

8

7

5

9

11

6

4

3 ⇨

2

1

0 ⌷⌷ 2m

TERRACE

RCC AWNING

72

70

60

48

27

23

1

3½ 2½

2½ 2½

2 7½

10½

58

9′ 8″

25

6″

BED

EXPOSED CONCRETE

1 1½

EXPOSED BRICK MASONARY

6′ 9″

14″ BK. WALL

7′ 4″

VERANDAH

ALCOVE

BRICK PAVING

7″

1

6′ ½″

6½″

14′ 0½″

DETAIL- UPPER AWNING

0 1 M

The window seat is one of the nicest things to have in a house – whereby the entire space comes to a point, or comes to peace within itself.

The focus is to develop 'pockets of shadows' – a good thing to handle in this country which has its lessons in so many historical buildings, from the Mughal architecture or the Deccan Sultanates, to the Portuguese and British architecture during colonial rule. They learnt something about the sun – keep the sun out and have the peace within.

> View of light element at living room verandah from the garden.

∨ Development sketches of the window seat.

∨ Living room window seat overlooking garden.

∨ Living room, view from dining.

64

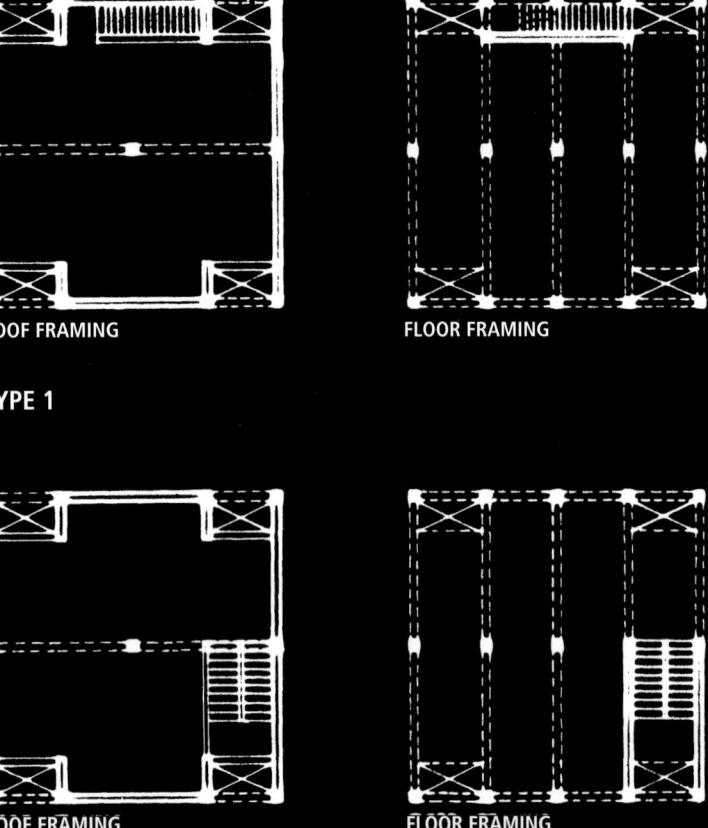

ROOF FRAMING

TYPE 1

FLOOR FRAMING

FLOOR FRAMING

ROOF FRAMING

TYPE 2

FLOOR FRAMING

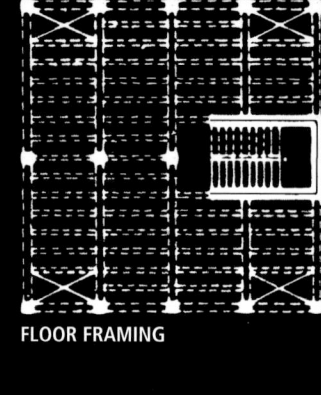

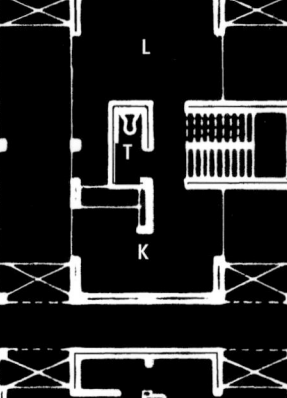

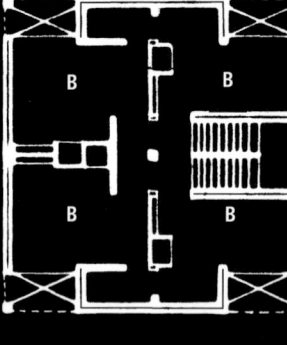

Top: Ground floor
Bottom: First floor
L   Living
K   Kitchen
T   Toilet
B   Bedroom

PROTOTYPE: STAFF HOUSING

Structural principles and staircase locations

PROTOTYPE: BACHELOR FACULTY HOUSING

Area: 1700 sq. ft (4 faculty per unit)

RCC frame structure, precast purlins and precast concrete blocks spanning 7'-6"

Ceramic fuse vaults spanning 15'-0" on roof

Studies in House Compositions, 1971–74
Attitudes within a Square: Light, Corners, Structure and Movement

Free form is like a forest fire. It is difficult to control unless you know the relationships in terms of their visual terminations.

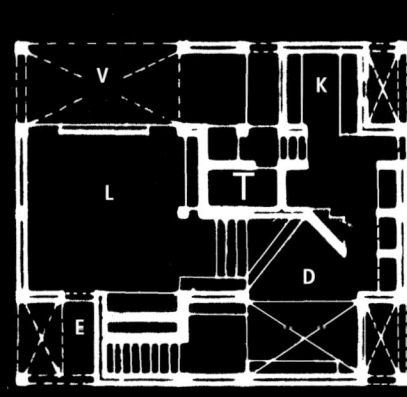

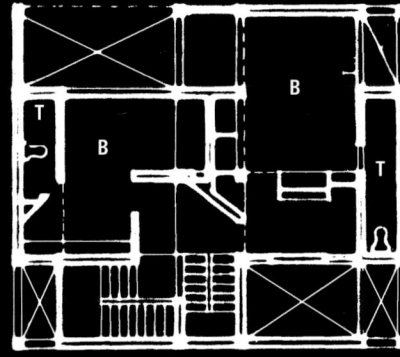

Top: Ground floor
Bottom: First floor
E Entry
L Living
D Dining
K Kitchen
V Verandah
T Toilet
B Bedroom

I took a box, and started to wonder about its composition: that if the inner spaces were that important, where would I put the staircase? What are the possible positions for the staircase in order to free the inner space of elements of that kind (a staircase, or a toilet)?

I carved out the four corners and started to recompose this whole space by way of the light that comes in, by way of the lower floor structure. As the floor goes up above, there is only one column there because there are vaults on top of it, and you don't need to repeat the columns because the system of flooring is different from the (vaulted) roof. There are two attitudes to this: the stairs between the two corners of light, and the circulation in the centre, which gives two sides within the same format of the square, and then introduction of more subsidiary spaces by way of toilets, alcoves, regrouping of smaller spaces around light and regrouping of larger spaces to the veranda. On the upper floor, with one column, and the axis of the staircase with four rooms around it.

As the house studies developed further, I wanted to find the conclusions to this story. Fortunately, a cousin of ours asked us to do a house. I was interested in testing a certain form and an idea to the particular requirements of the house.

PRIVATE RESIDENCE, AHMEDABAD
Area: 1600 sq. ft, 2 bedroom house
Application of principles based on the prototype

Residence for J.C. Parikh
Ahmedabad, 1976–82

The principal considerations for the plan organization of this house revolve around geometry and a roofing system which is the dominant feature of the house. With the roof demanding parallel walls, the modulation of space between the parallel walls is geometric.

Within the format of a square and the disposition of the elements (light and movement) as the four light corners, one corner becomes a verandah. The two rooms on the floor above overlook the verandah void. The upper floor and the subsidiary spaces, along with the elements of light, have a different dimension from the dimensions of the main spaces – the vault dimension for the latter and the dimensions of the light pockets for the former.

The cross-section illustrates a horizontal system of spanning (ribbed slab system) and the vaulted roofs. The vaults are paraboloids, not semicircular. The space between the vaults is a flattened terrace acting as a large gutter, separating the two vaults. The slight slope of the land results in a richness in volumes.

Ceramic fuses are used for the roofing system. When these are arranged to fit into one another, a parabola is the resultant curve. Structurally very sound, the final form is the direct expression of the material – the ceramic fuse. The walls are in exposed brick and the roof is finished in china mosaic. RCC pillars in the central bay allow for internal flexibility.

I put an emphasis on the entry; the rest of the elevation was the expression of the two vaulted volumes projected on flat surfaces.

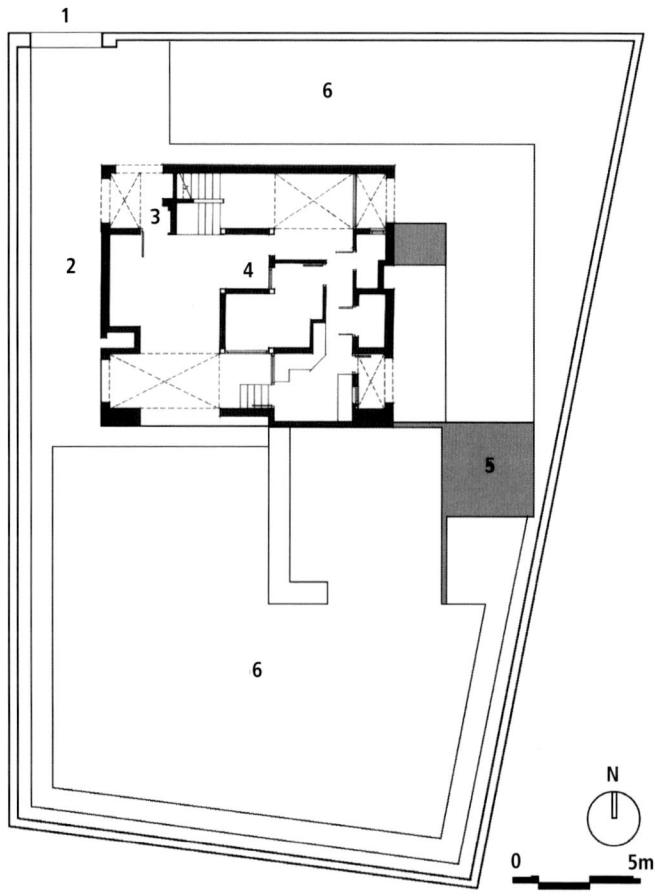

∧ Site plan.
   1 Site entrance
   2 Car port
   3 House entrance
   4 House
   5 Staff
   6 Garden

> Street side elevation.

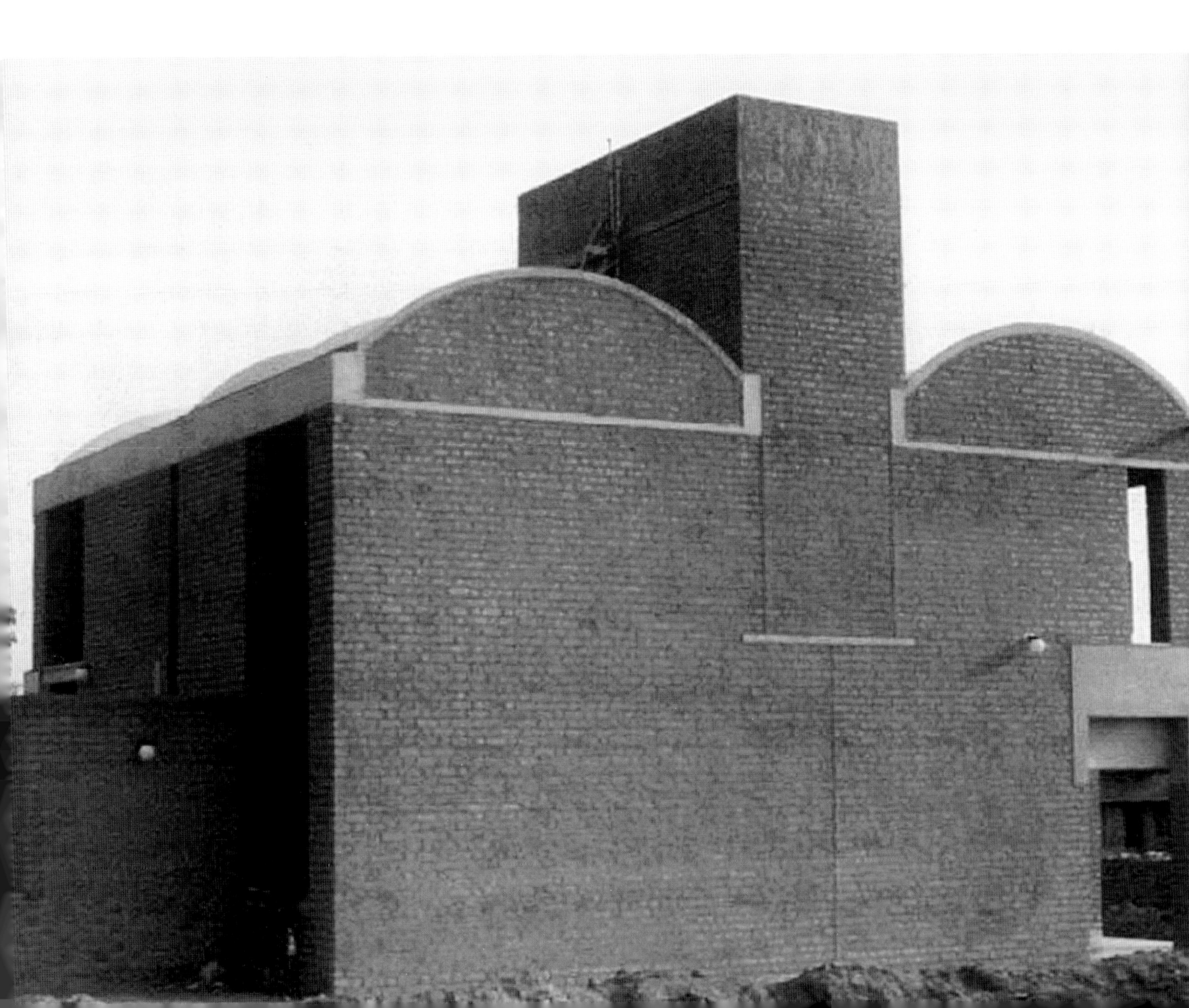

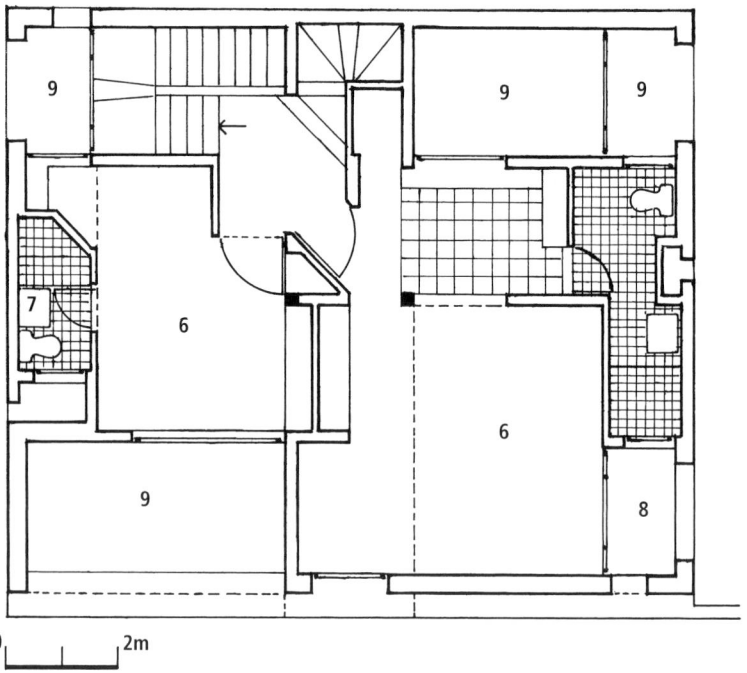

FIRST FLOOR PLAN

0 |___|___| 2m

Floor plans.
1 Entry
2 Living room
3 Dining room
4 Kitchen
5 Store
6 Bedroom
7 Bathroom
8 Verandah
9 Open to space below

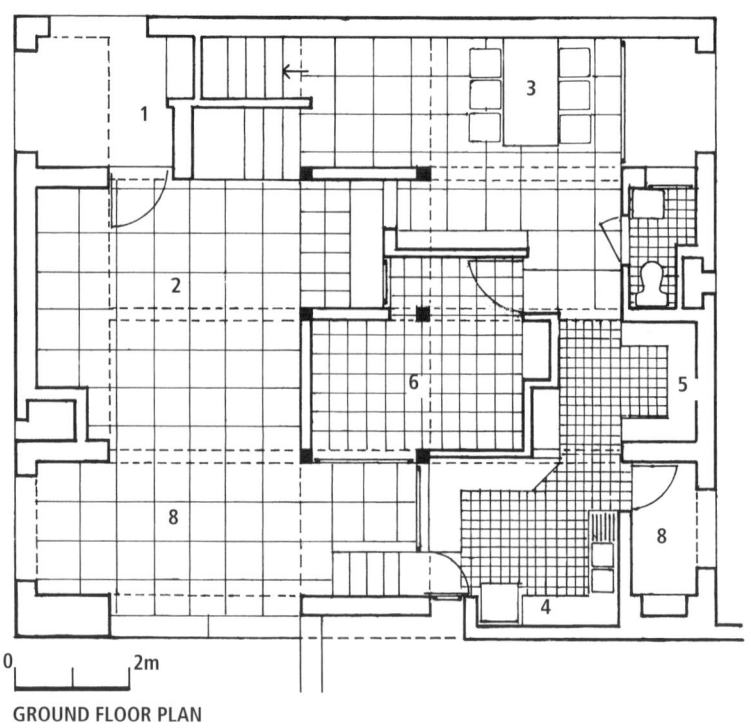

0 |___|___| 2m

GROUND FLOOR PLAN

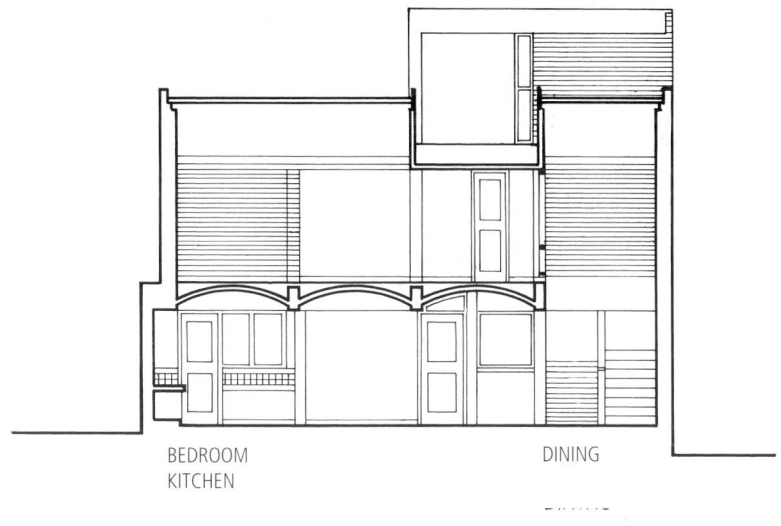

BEDROOM
KITCHEN   DINING

SECTION

LIVING VERANDAH   BEDROOM   KITCHEN VERANDAH
                             KITCHEN

SECTION

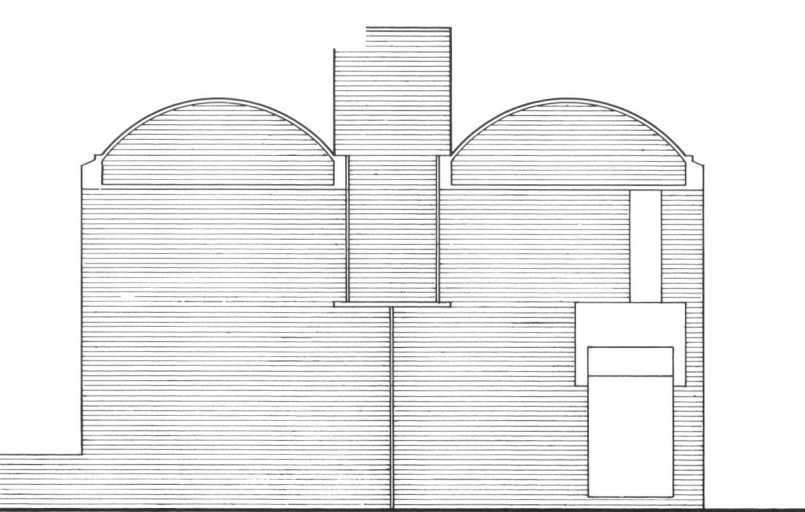

STREET SIDE ELEVATION

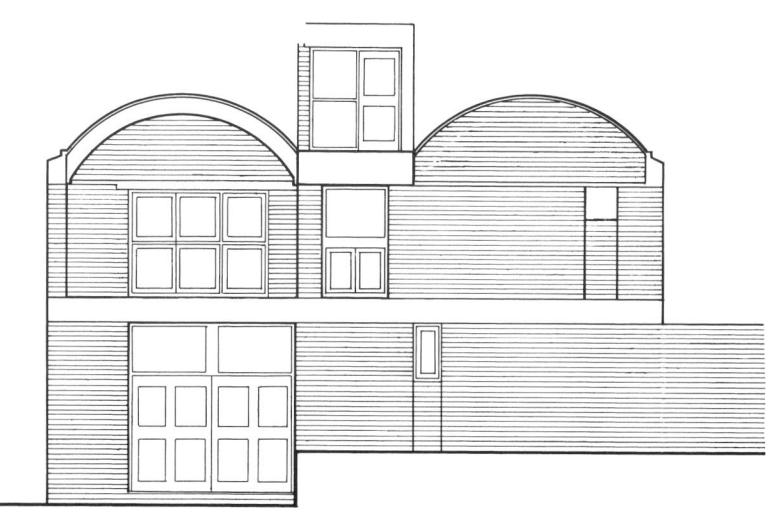

GARDEN SIDE ELEVATION

|0 | 2|m

73

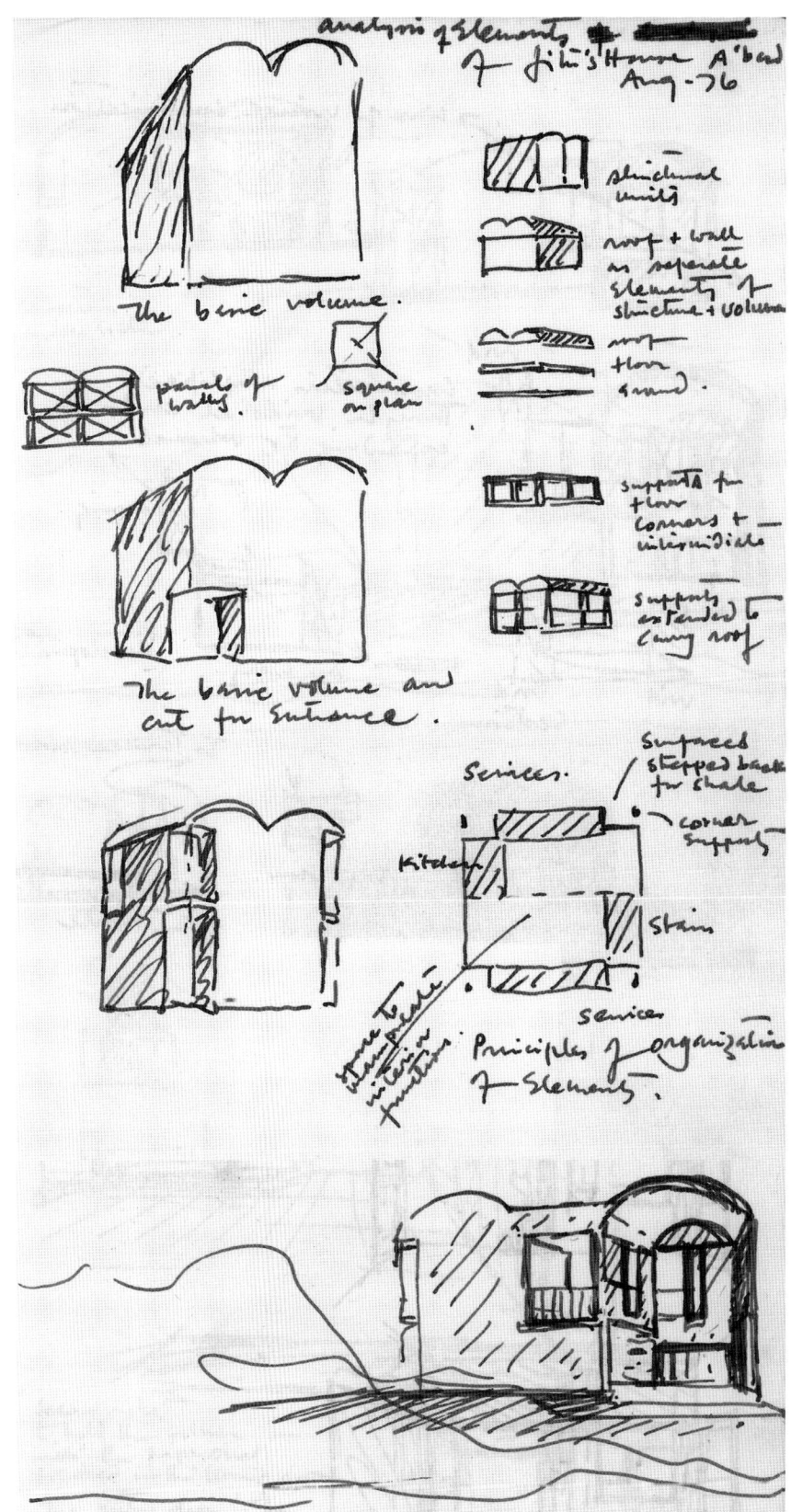

< Entrance corner developed into an entity.

> Analysis of elements, August 1976.
  Notes on the sketch:
  Left column:
  'The basic volume'
  'Panels of walls'
  'Square in plan'
  'The basic volume and cut for entrance'
  Right column:
  'Structural units'
  'Roof + wall as separate elements of structure + volume'
  'Roof – floor – ground'
  'Supports for floor corners + intermediate'
  'Supports extended to carry roof'
  'Principles of organization of elements: spaces stepped
  back for shade – corner supports stairs services space
  to manipulate interior functions – kitchen'

I work on a root-2 proportioning system. I find a tremendous satisfaction in the root-2 system (more than the Golden Section) as its properties ensure the tightness of composition. I find this true by my experience and observations, not theoretically.

> Garden side elevation.

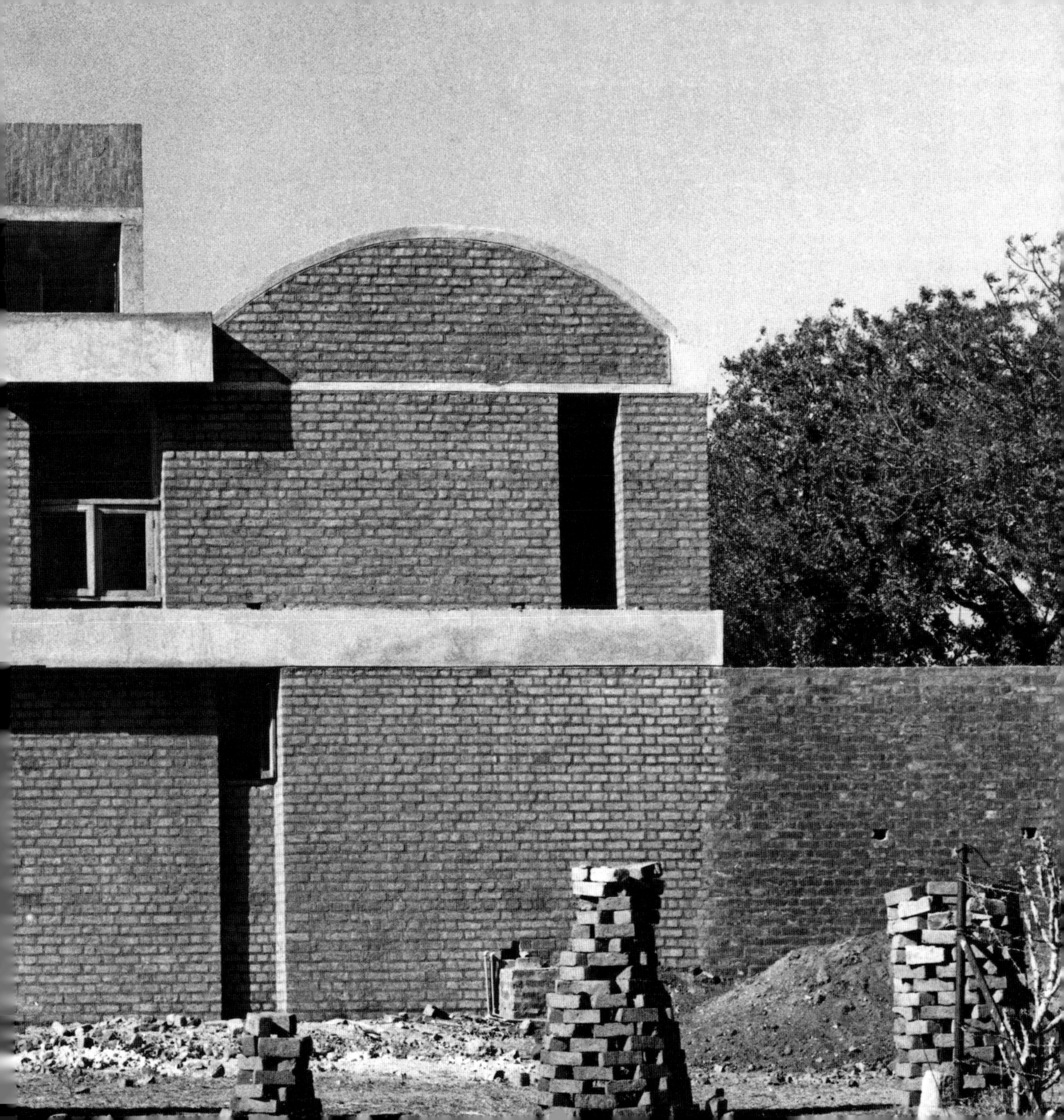

I have always felt that the strength of Buddhist caves and rock-cut temples lies in their being monoliths. They are not fragments of the whole, but are harmoniously related. This concept of the part and the whole in terms of its totality in our ancient rock-cut architecture has always intrigued me. That is why I use the word 'monolithic sense'. I refer to the 'deductive way' of doing things. That is, I get a mass which is finite in some way and I start taking material off from it to the point where the material on top will not crumble over the material below. So I introduce these vaulted forms by taking out unwanted material until there is a sizeable space that is acceptable.

'Space' in the language of a painter is a very abstract phenomenon, while in the language of a sculptor there is a three-dimensional aspect to it. When it comes to architectural space, it just cannot remain an abstract concept. I don't mean that space has to be looked at only in terms of its uses, because it also has an abstract aspect which concerns its evolution and formative stages. That is, in the making of a structure, at what point does this space get locked and frozen? As regards light and shadow, there are many architects, painters and sculptors who are extremely sensitive to the fact that light modulates and creates a kind of indescribable situation. Le Corbusier refers to this particular kind of space as 'ineffable space' which you cannot measure or touch, but through which you transcend the mundane aspects into the realm of architecture.

^ Fuses forming the paraboloids. Construction photo.

> Aspects of the interior.

ATIRA housing, the building corner, April 1982.

Staff Housing for ATIRA
Ahmedabad, 1984

Housing units for the research institute's staff – ground floor walk-up units built within the constraints of existing landscape. The plan is based on a square with open corners oriented towards the prevailing breeze direction.

Uncluttered usable space demands peripheral structure forming an enclosure; spaces that harbour the staircase; and toilets are outside this enclosure, ensuring efficient utilization of habitable space. The freedom of arrangement of the layout of rooms is guided by strict structural enclosure constraints, and openings for light and air in the most appropriate places. The open terraces in every unit reflect the response to the local climate. Each unit has three-and-a-half sides open for both light and cross-ventilation. Together, the layout brings a sense of connected clusters.

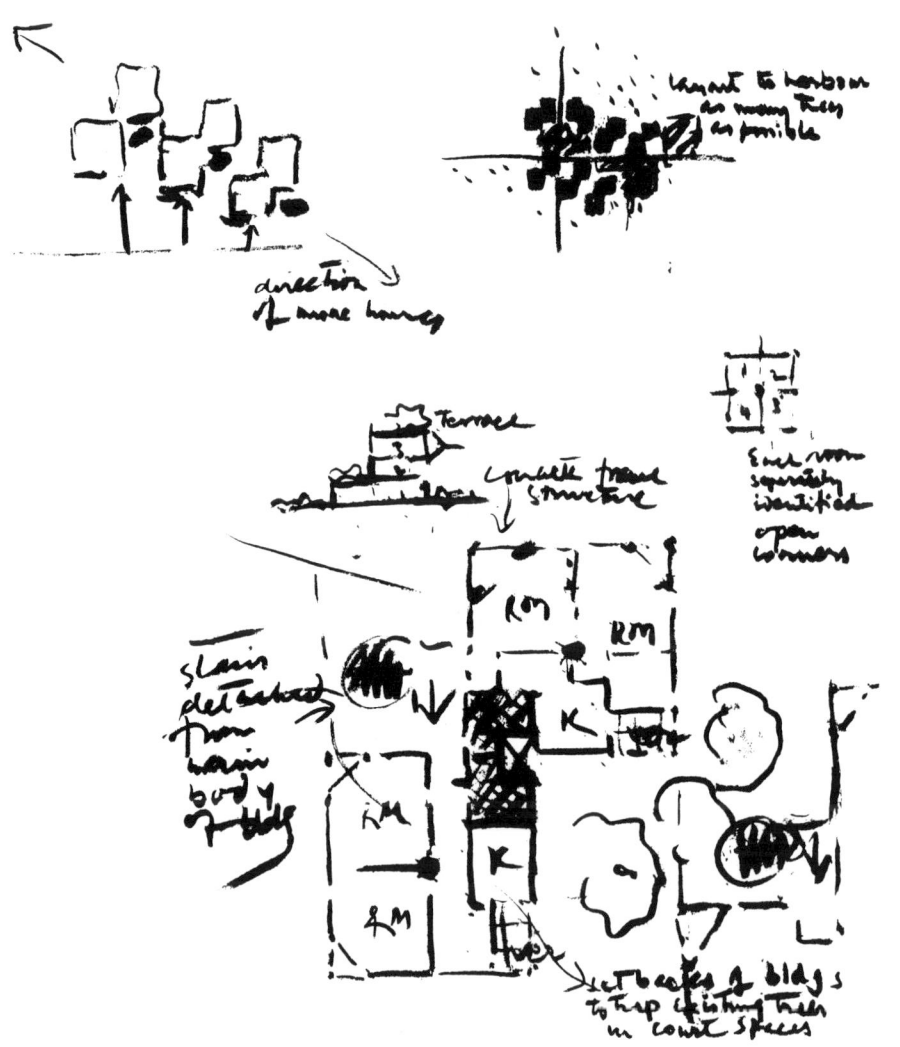

∧ Form study model in wood.

> Form study model in wood.

< Plan studies, undated.
  Notes on the sketch, from top:
  'Direction of more houses'
  'Layout to harbour as many trees as possible'
  'Terrace – concrete frame structure'
  'Each room separately identified. Open corners'
  'Stair detached from main body of building'
  'Setbacks of buildings to trap existing trees in court spaces'

Every pocket brings a sense of shelter with it. With the notches in the plan,
the existing landscape was kept as it was, creating an inner courtyard.

∧ Grey paint directly applied on the brick to express the textures of the wall, while
  sealing the porous brick.

> Floor plans. Four one-bedroom houses, two on the ground, two above.
  1   Entry
  2   Living Room
  3   Kitchen
  4   Bedroom
  5   Court
  6   Terrace

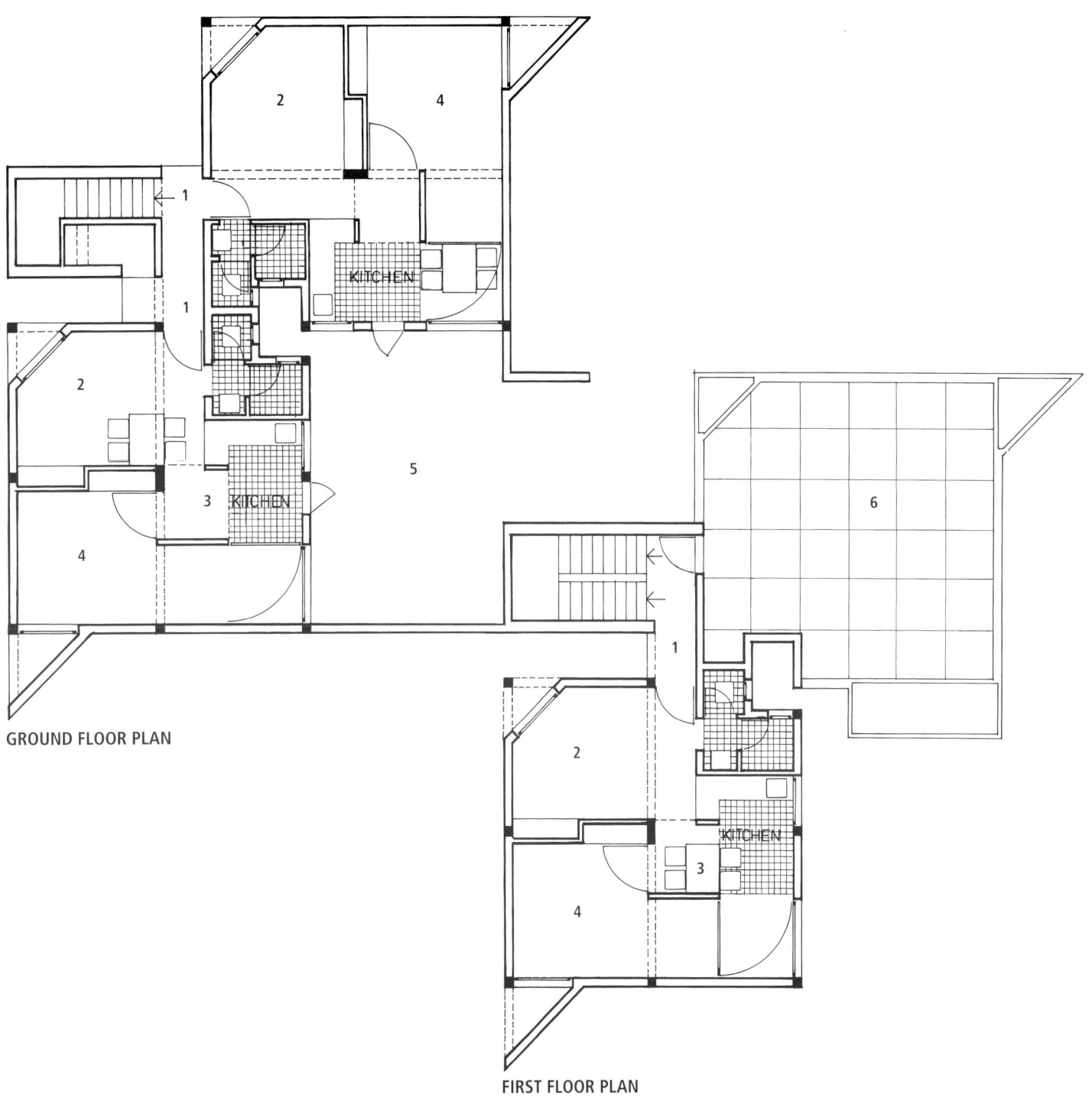

GROUND FLOOR PLAN

FIRST FLOOR PLAN

KITCHEN

KITCHEN

KITCHEN

KITCHEN

Residence for Kanubhai Patel
Ahmedabad, 1988

A house designed out of my experience with the Indian Institute of Forest Management (IIFM). Most of the language comes from the IIFM, with slate and washed grit as surfacing materials brought together in the composition by having horizontal strips and the elements of verandas as the spanning elements.

This is a single family house, where the garden side is a single-storey structure and the roadside is two storeys. I like the particular treatment of the roadside – Ahmedabad roads are rowdy – no environment, no footpaths. So I didn't want the house to sit there and enjoy the roadside hassles. The entry through the plinth of the house (or an expression of a plinth) is like a solid blow to the plinth wall, and sets up the arrival to the lower part of the house.

Above the plinth has a sense of freedom, to break out of the periphery of the house (via balconies) and get air.

> Floor plans.
  Ground floor plan | First floor plan
  1   Entrance
  1a Entrance lobby
  2   Living room
  3   Dining room
  4   Kitchen
  5   Verandah
  6   Light court
  7   Bedroom
  8   Bathroom
  9   Balcony
  10 Terrace
  11 Staff/servant room

> Definitive model in wood delineating concrete elements.

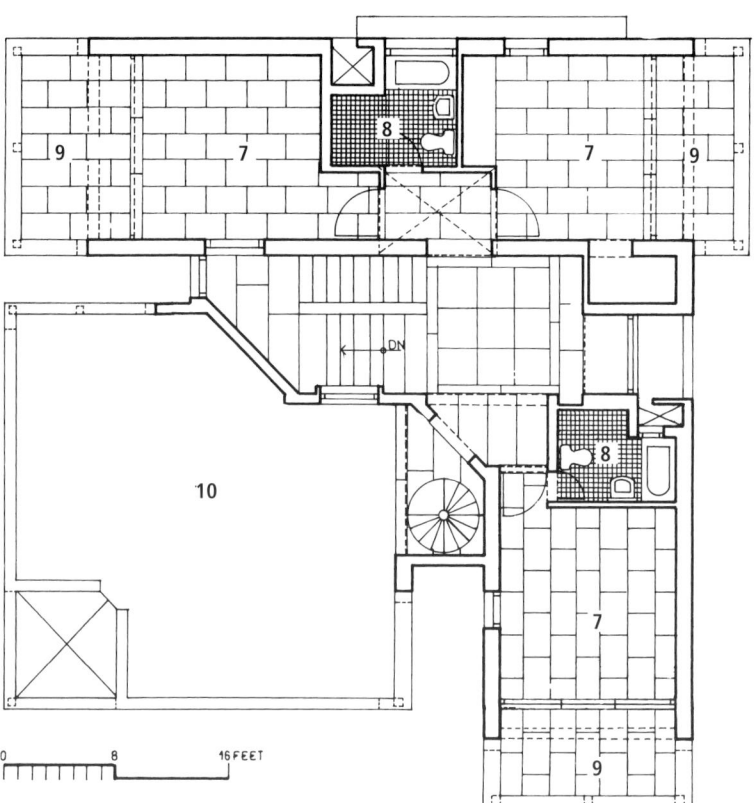

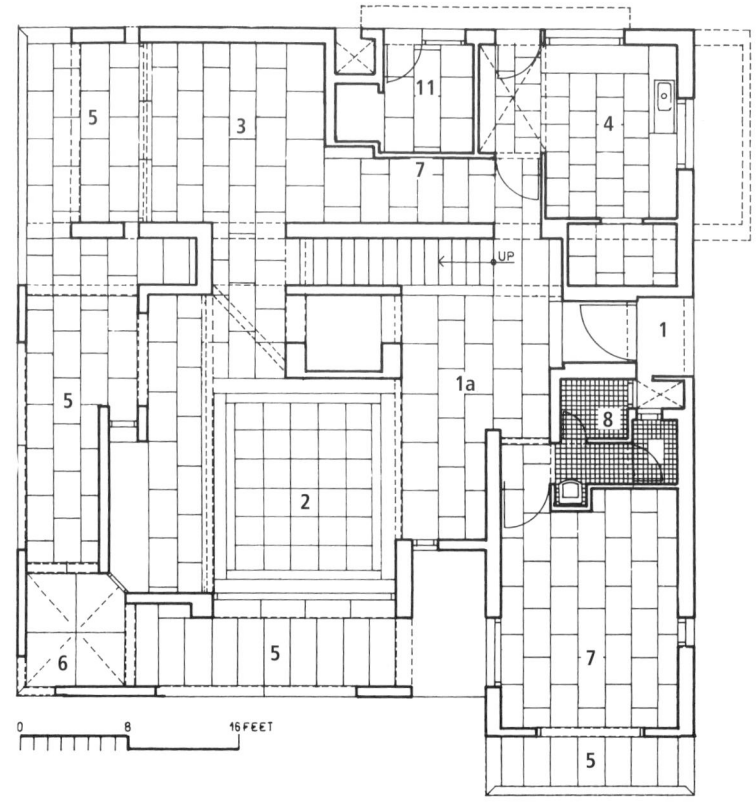

> Street side elevation study, April 1986.

∨ Garden side elevation study, April 1986.

RAJE
API '86
Thursday.

93

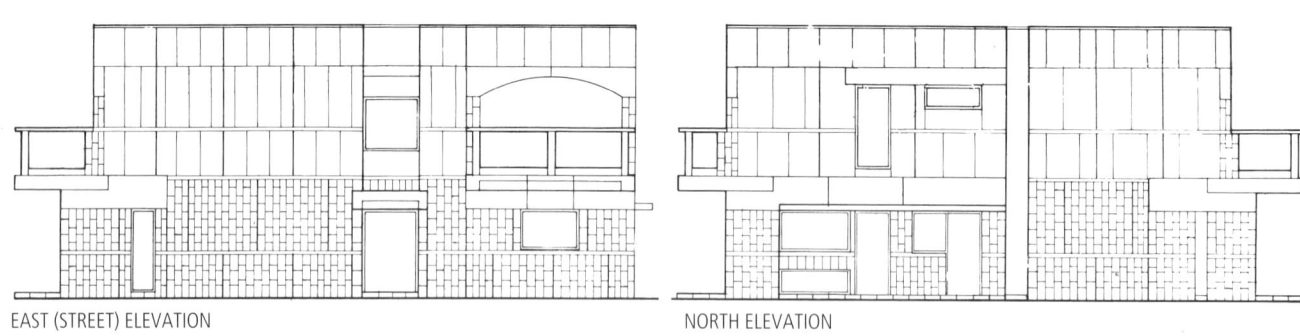

EAST (STREET) ELEVATION

NORTH ELEVATION

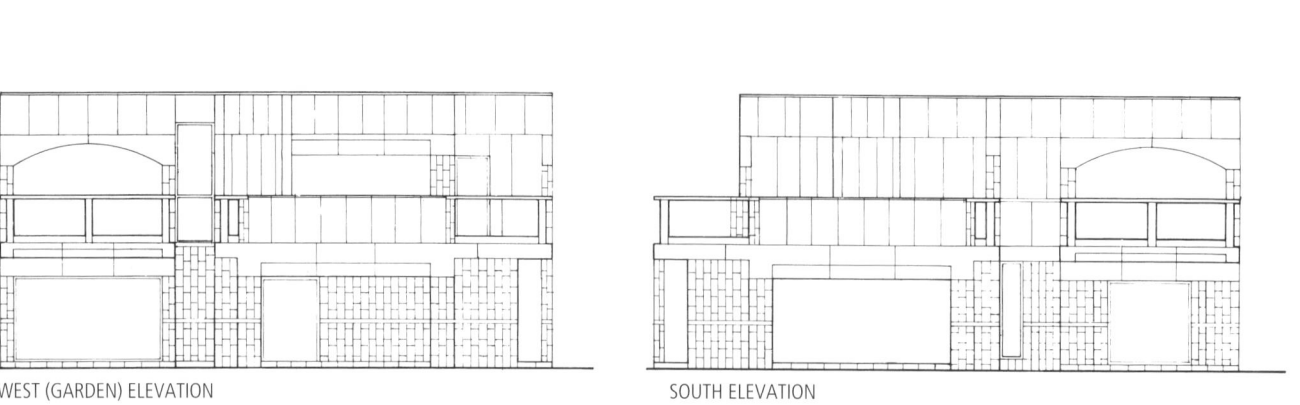

WEST (GARDEN) ELEVATION

SOUTH ELEVATION

The corner is emphasized and is razor-sharp. When the stone is razor-sharp, it results in shadows that are very crisp. Where the shadows are crisp, the material begins to tell its own story.

The verandahs: some project, some recede, depending upon what the situation of the landscape is. Out of the lintel comes out a balcony, giving a wonderful proportion to the verandah. When I started to develop these elements and detail them out, I found that it is true in a way – that one can make a wonderful thing out of a beam, out of an apron, out of the railings, and bring them into certain compositions as a sculpture.

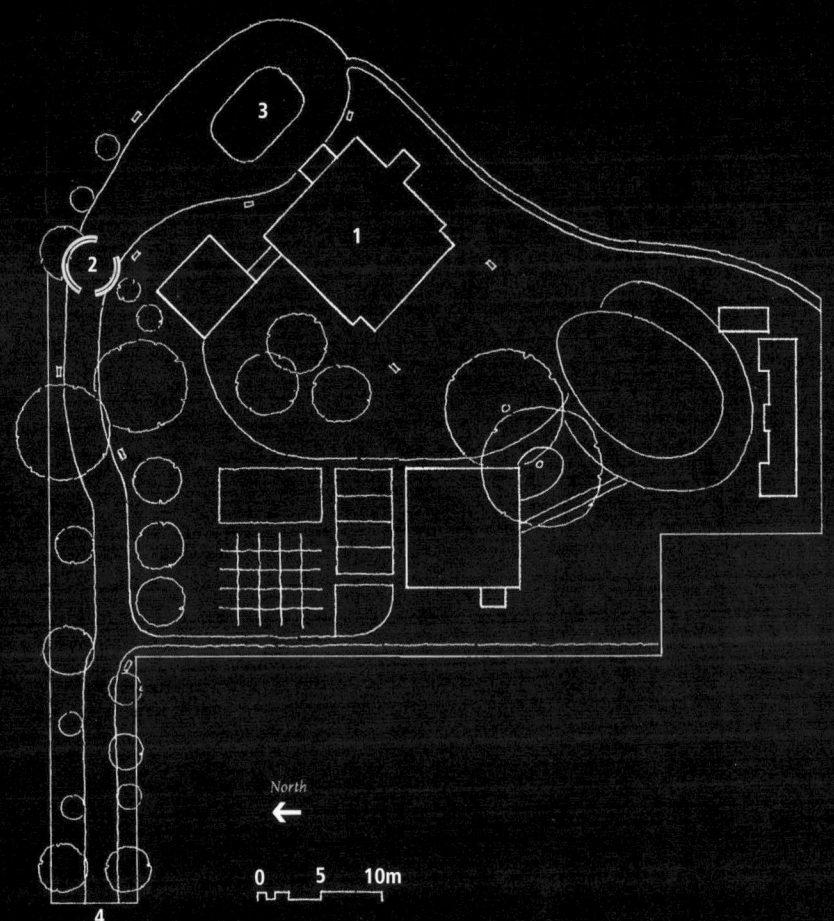

^ Wedding wall against the backdrop of Villa Shodhan.

> Location plan.
  1 Villa Shodhan, by Le Corbusier
  2 Wedding wall
  3 Wedding 'mandap' (pavilion)
  4 Site entrance

North

0   5   10m

Wedding Wall
Villa Shodhan, Ahmedabad, 1990

The bride's family, in a traditional Hindu wedding cere-
mony, receives the bridegroom. This was to be located in the com-
pound of Shodhan Villa, designed by Le Corbusier. We pondered
over this structure, the entry point for marriage vows, and felt that
it must be in an aesthetic vocabulary of the platonic solids that
Corbusier thought of in his language as the cube, the cone, the
cylinder...

The cube already existed (as the house), and we decided
to bring in a cylinder. We made the cylinder about 8 feet high. The
two parts of the cylinder (walls) were made in sundried brick. They
are asymmetrical – one side is smaller than the other in terms of its
perimeter. The cylindrical shape also gave stability to the masonry walls, which we made as though they came from the stepped
foundations – broader at the base, narrower at the top, to give them
stability without having to make foundations which would have
destroyed the existing concrete driveway.

In our folk culture, everything is done through singing
and storytelling. For this event, then, the walls were constructed,
not by regular contractors and labourers, but by women from the
villages. They came with sundried bricks, mud plaster and started
to sing at the same time. The members of the family also joined in,
making it one big event!

We introduced alcoves (niches in the walls) and embel-
lished them with 'abhalas' (mirrors) – you find these on the textiles of the region. There is a great art about these 'abhalas' and
we started to make some abstractions of trees, and also tried to
accentuate the steps by having the simple 'abhalas' pressed into
the mud plaster.

The canopy for the wall structure was a huge mango
tree. During the day – the magnificence of the shadows cast on
the wall and the mirrors! In the evening, every member of the family placed an oil lamp in the alcoves, marking the wedding event.

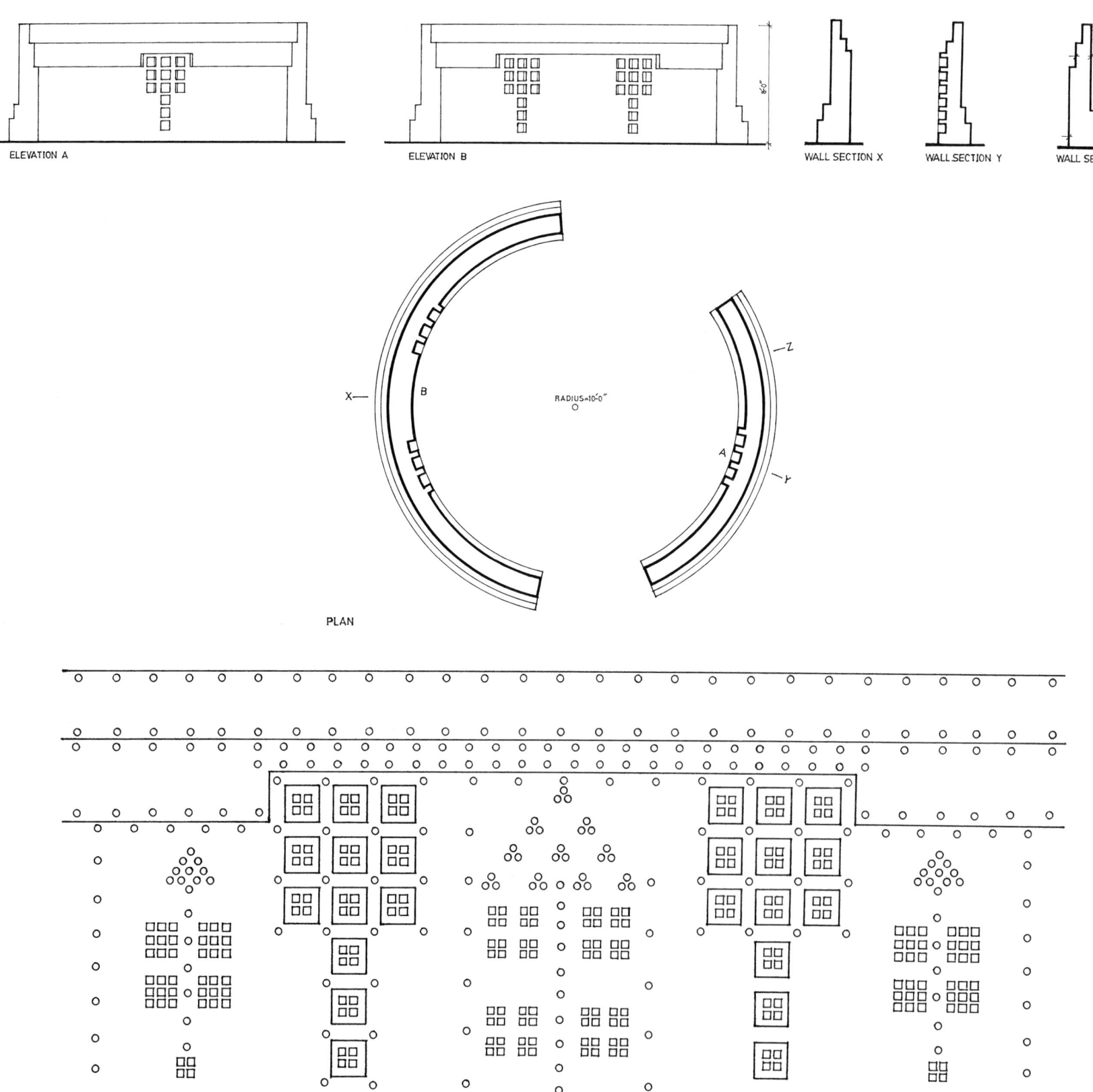

ELEVATION A

ELEVATION B

WALL SECTION X

WALL SECTION Y

WALL SECTION Z

RADIUS=10'-0"

PLAN

< Elevations | Sections
  Plan
  Detail elevation of adobe wall with niches and mirrors

∨ Women applying mirrors in the adobe plaster of the wedding wall
  with the mango tree as a canopy.

Nandan Mehta house, April 1999.

Residence for Nandan Mehta
Ahmedabad, 2000

2000 sq. ft of house on a residual plot of land left over by constructing a *haveli*-type, thick-walled, large family house, displaying its 'manor' to the main street, formal gardens around it, and an ad-hoc way of building out of salvaged timber relics of old town houses which forms a strip, leaving a group of old trees between the two houses. The residual piece of land makes a dead corner on the entire site, similar to the cul-de-sac situation observed at the dead-end of the street in the *pol*s of the walled city of Ahmedabad. The new house 'form' is therefore a series of houses built with their own entrances, cemented together by a geometry of cul-de-sacs. This sac, a semi-circular shape of open-to-sky court, is flanked by two entrance porches made of exposed concrete post and beam construction elements, also indicating sequences of lifts needed to pour concrete into steel moulds, making a 'memory connection' between elements made by concrete and those made by wood in traditional buildings.

The two porches make the semi-circular court an indivisible element of the house with the porches subordinate to it. The composition of the plan made by two identical elements of architecture has been an important revelation throughout the history of architecture. It has given a new notion to the 'freedom of disposition of symmetry'. Deeply set openings allow the mass to be characteristic of bearing wall construction, and in turn create shadow pockets and set the window openings as the space behind them demand.

The stretched circulation connects the living–dining–kitchen behind the curved wall, having a sieve of square openings to the bedrooms. This circulation with light filtering through the openings having stained glass adds a new dimension to the enclosed spaces. The bedrooms have sleeping areas, as also the sitting next to the large openings to the outside courts. The curved circulation connects the upper floor through the stairs with the roof decks.

This is a home without a facade. It offers simultaneous interior and exterior experiences with isolated and connected parts of the house, independently and together, as the occasion demands. There are various events in the Indian calendar year, which have their own significance for an individual and for a group. They carry their own rituals, their ceremonies; they bring their own memories of past events and record the same so that these events continue through the present into the future. The house and the user have this kinship, which if allowed to grow unhindered and unbiased, invariably presents a richer relationship. This relationship is a major contributory factor in creating and sustaining a meaningful environment within the neighbourhood. Like the *pol*s of Ahmedabad, this house is an example of residences that have become an institution.

> Definitive model in wood, showing the heart of the house (the arrival court) flanked by two hollow columns (the pavilions).

> Views of the court and pavilions.

∨ Site plan.
1 Existing haveli
2 Existing music pavilion and guest house
3 New house
4 Semi-circular court

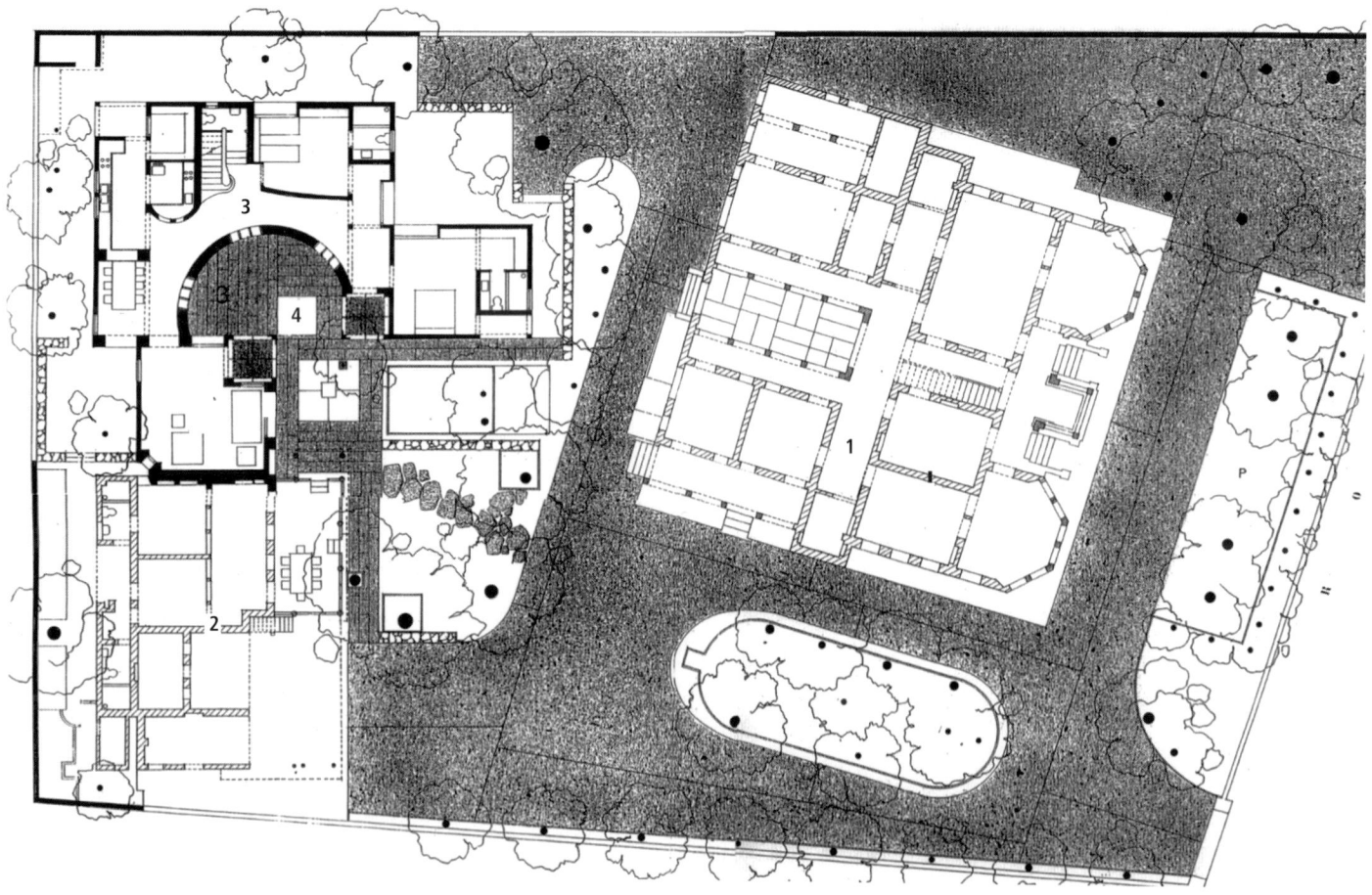

You arrive between two buildings and the first thing you experience is the pocket of opening with the two pavilions in two corners, around which the whole house swings. It is a good experience.

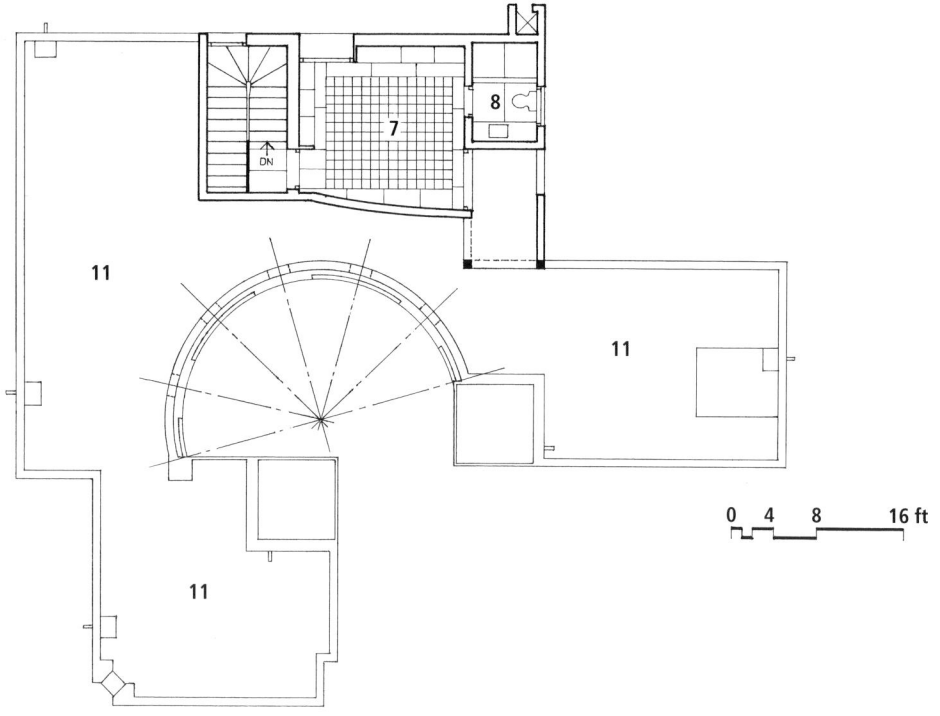

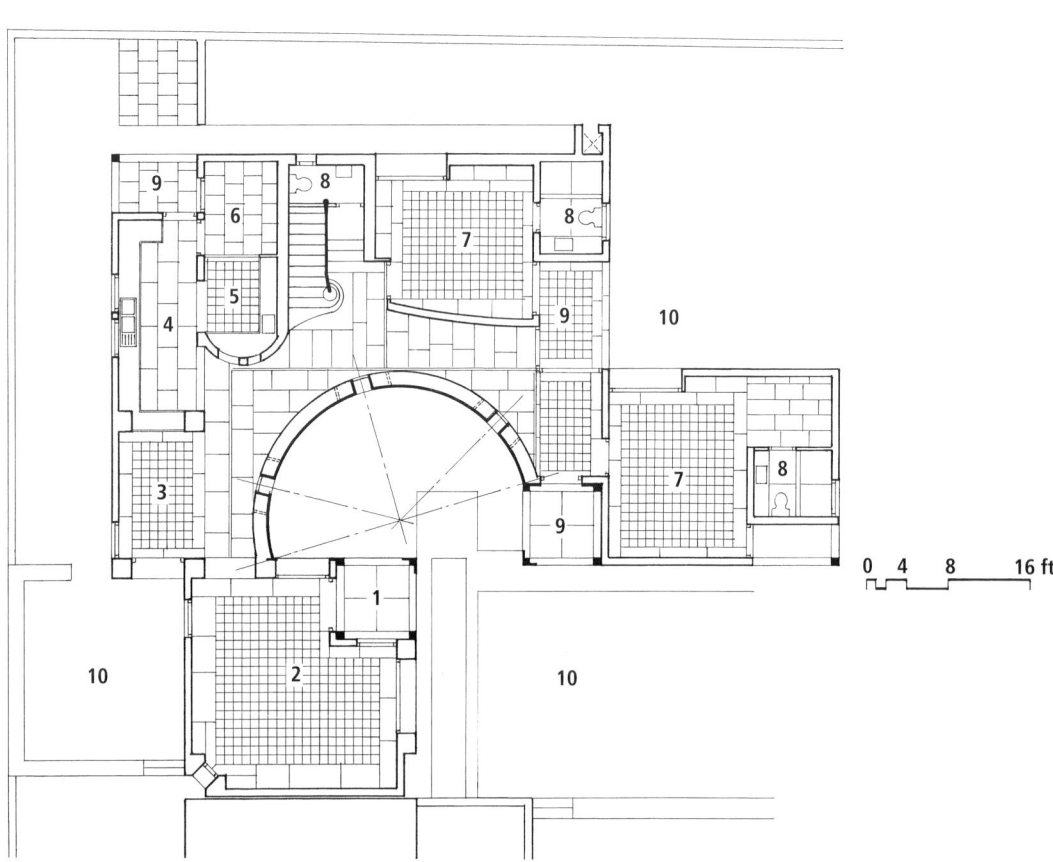

< Ground floor plan | First floor plan.
1 Entry
2 Living
3 Dining
4 Kitchen
5 Pantry
6 Store
7 Bedroom
8 Bathroom
9 Verandah
10 Garden
11 Terrace

Detail of porch column. I jokingly started to call it 'Rambo' as I liked the muscularity.

∧ Definitive model in wood.

> View of court and entrance pavilion.

> View of bedroom pavilion from the entrance pavilion.

> Interior circulation around the court.

∨ Exterior elevations.

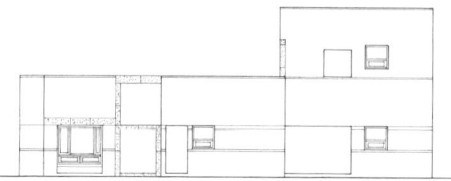
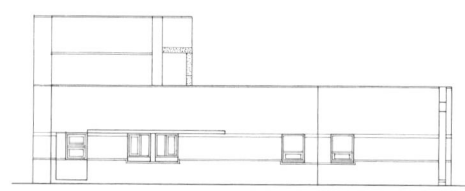

The two porches, which came naturally to me to be able to enclose and define the space of the court, I started to call 'Navara–Navari' (husband–wife). So the house is really the home of the Navara–Navari. The two porches look at each other amidst the Asopalav trees.

When you arrive, the porch columns and beams are connected together. I like to do this so that the construction can be expressed. There is a narrow shaft of the column at the top, broader at the bottom with two flanges that receive the beam. The circular, plastered wall gives the backdrop. It is not a very hard wall because it has no corners, except for some punctuation (through the openings) that give a sense of a 'jaali' (screen) on a larger scale. Inside, the light that comes through these windows with the stained glass is marvellous!

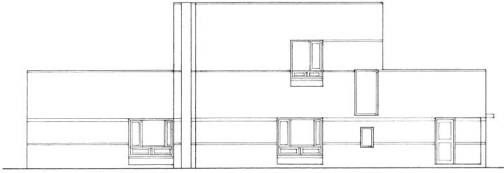

> 'Mogra' (newel post) stair parapet termination.

∨ Studies of newel cap over stair parapet, June 2000.

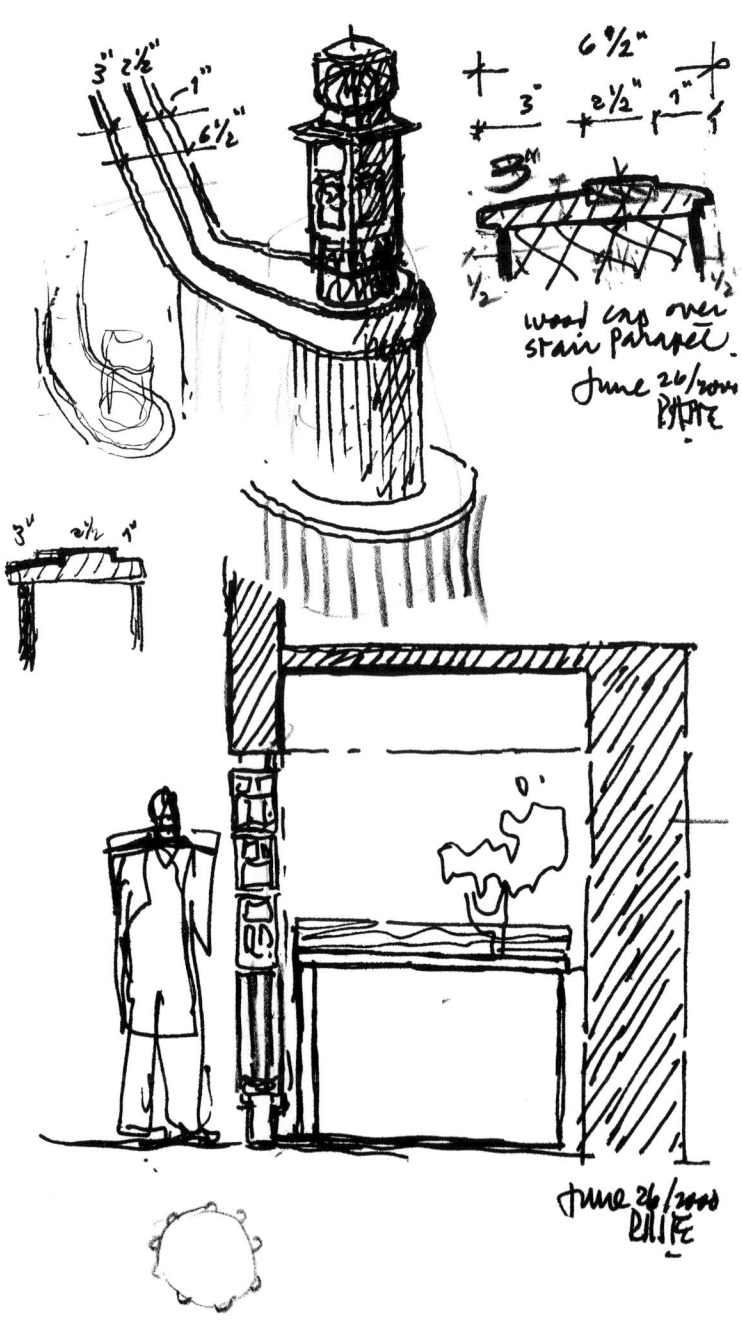

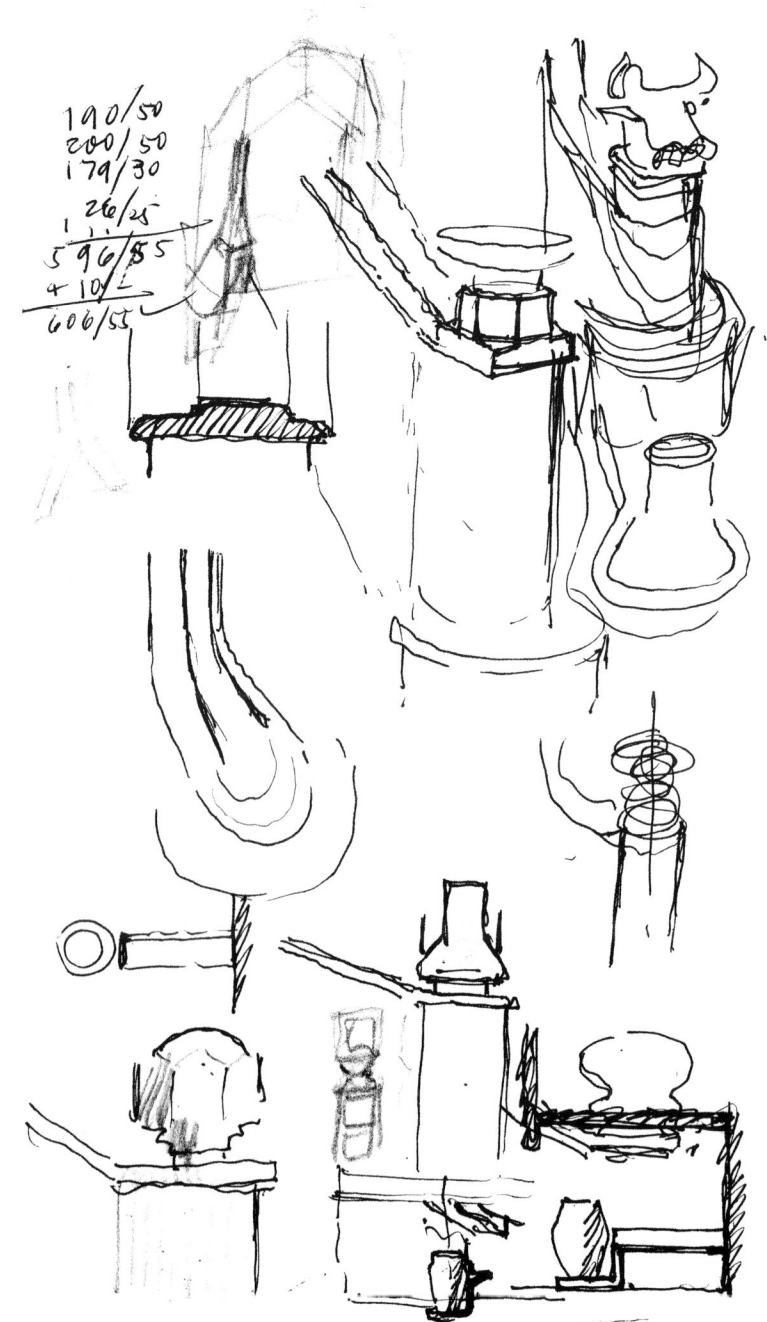

Public Institutions

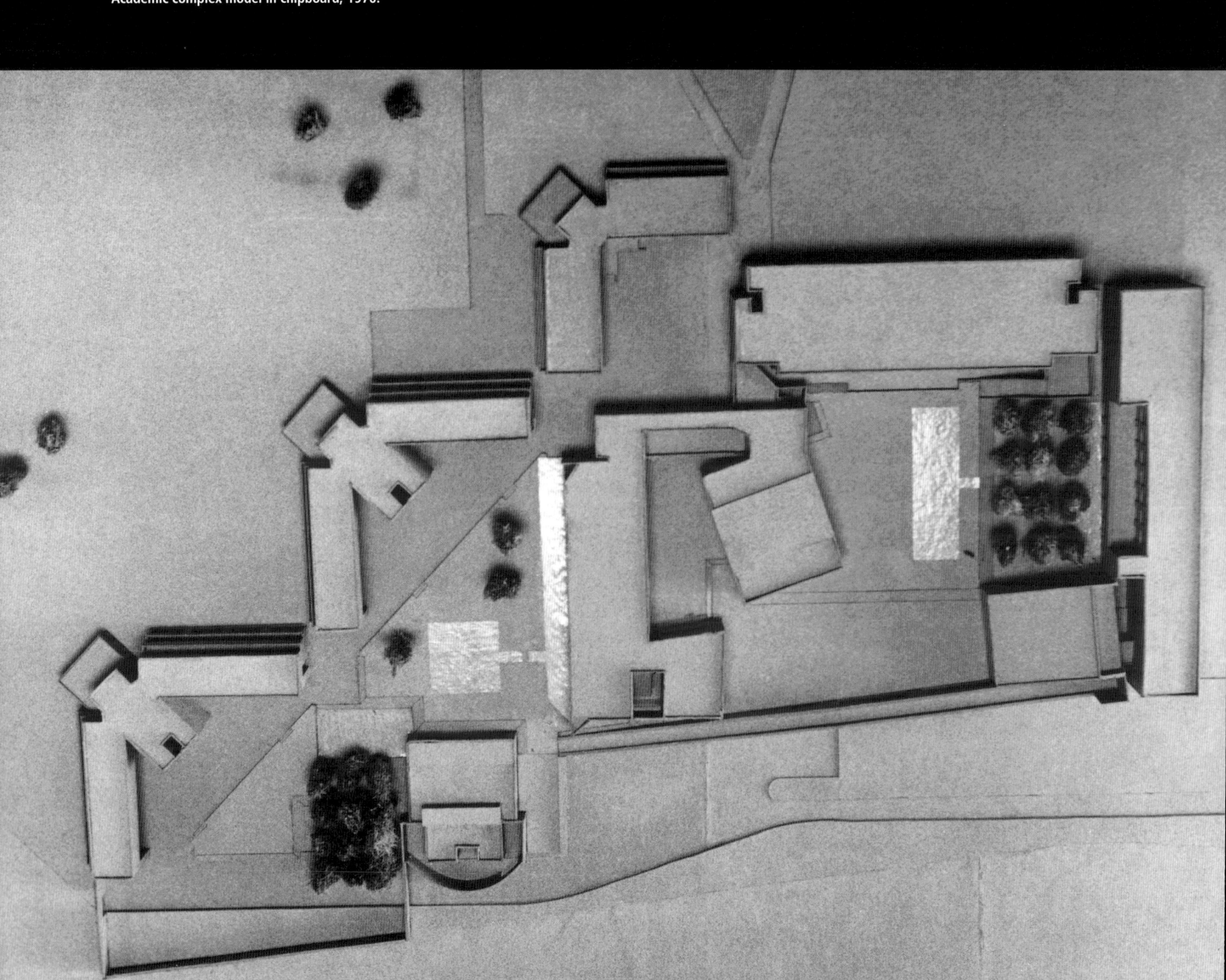

Academic complex model in chipboard, 1976.

Indian Statistical Institute
**Planning Commission of India, New Delhi, 1975
(in collaboration with Kanvinde & Rai Architects,
New Delhi)**

Any institution of learning has two inseparable parts –
one, the library; and two, the rooms in which teaching happens.

The Indian Statistical Institute in New Delhi is located on
a 15-acre site on the side of a creek, adjoining the main road on
the broad side with the backdrop of the Qutab Minar and the
ruins. The buildings are grouped around an entrance court, lead-
ing to other courts around which the dormitories and dining halls
are grouped.

The programme called for an institute with a library, lecture halls, research offices for the faculty, student dormitories and
dining halls in the first phase, to be followed by an auditorium,
staff and faculty housing in the second phase.

The principal element of construction is brick, with reinforced concrete as the spanning element at lintels as well as slabs.
The entire vertical dimensioning system is based on the unit of a
brick, such that the material that makes the mass and forms the
void is answerable to it.

> Model views of the campus.

∨ Layout plan.

Academic complex
1 Library
2 Classrooms and seminar rooms
3 Lecture theatre
4 Faculty offices
5 Auditorium
6 Project win
7 Research fellows' dormitories
8 Undergraduate students' dormitories
9 Dining

Housing
10 Housing 500 sq. ft
11 Housing 800 sq. ft
12 Housing 1000 sq. ft
13 Housing 1200 sq. ft
14 Housing 1850 sq. ft
15 Guest house
16 Recreation

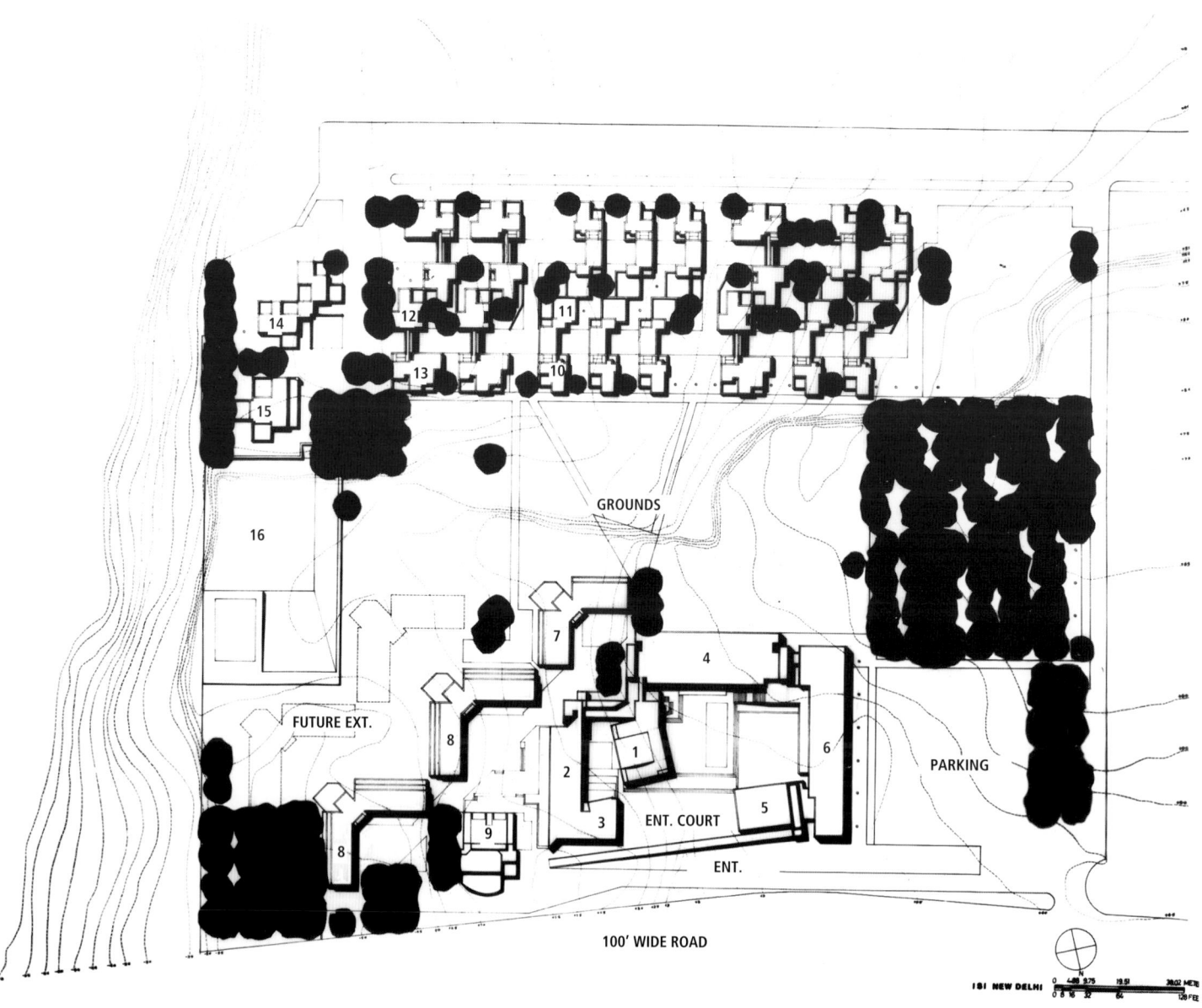

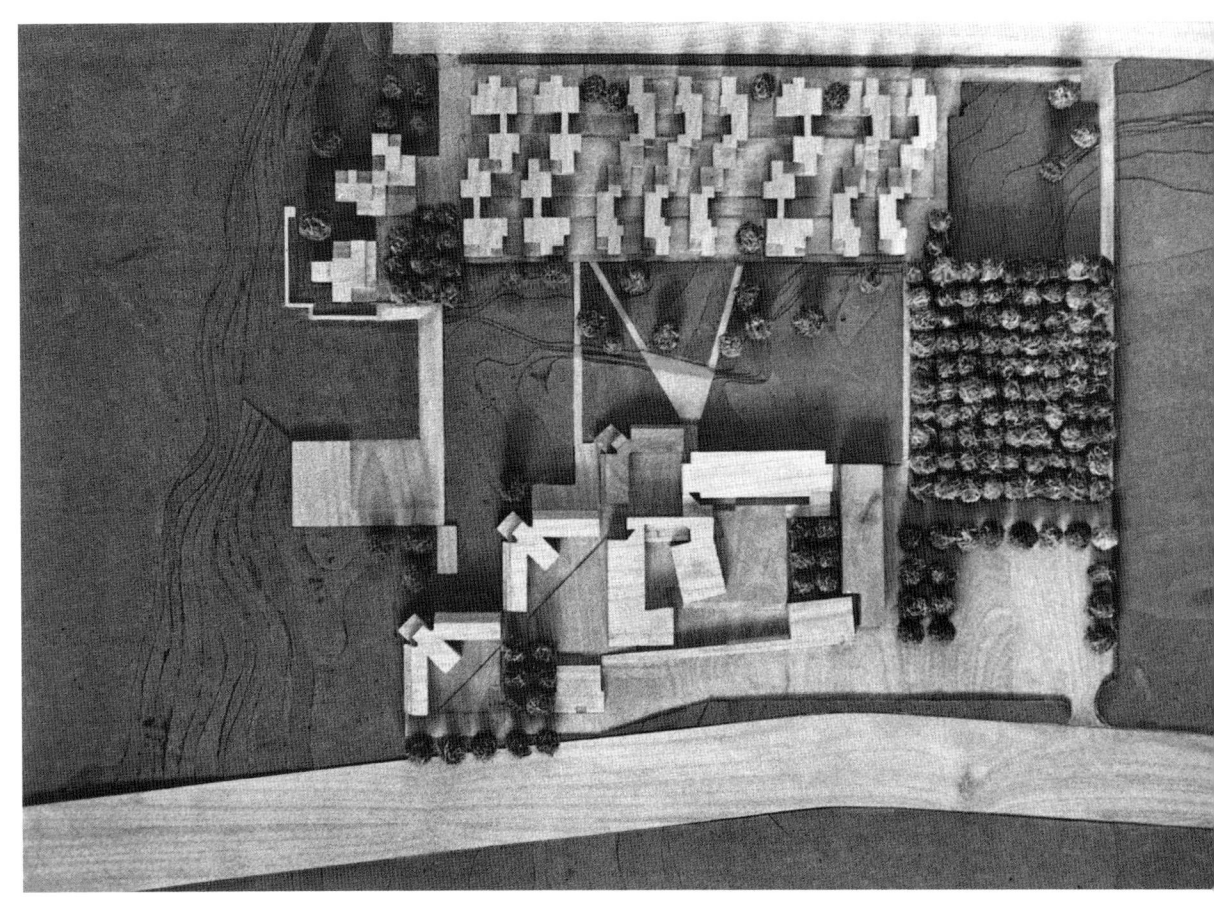

> Academic complex court facades and details.

v Academic complex plan, ground floor.

1 Library
2 Classrooms and seminar rooms
3 Lecture theatre
4 Faculty offices
5 Auditorium (future phase)
6 Project wing (future phase)
7 Research fellows' dormitories
8 Undergraduate students' dormitories
9 Dining
10 Entrance court
11 Amphitheatre
12 Court

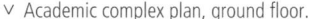

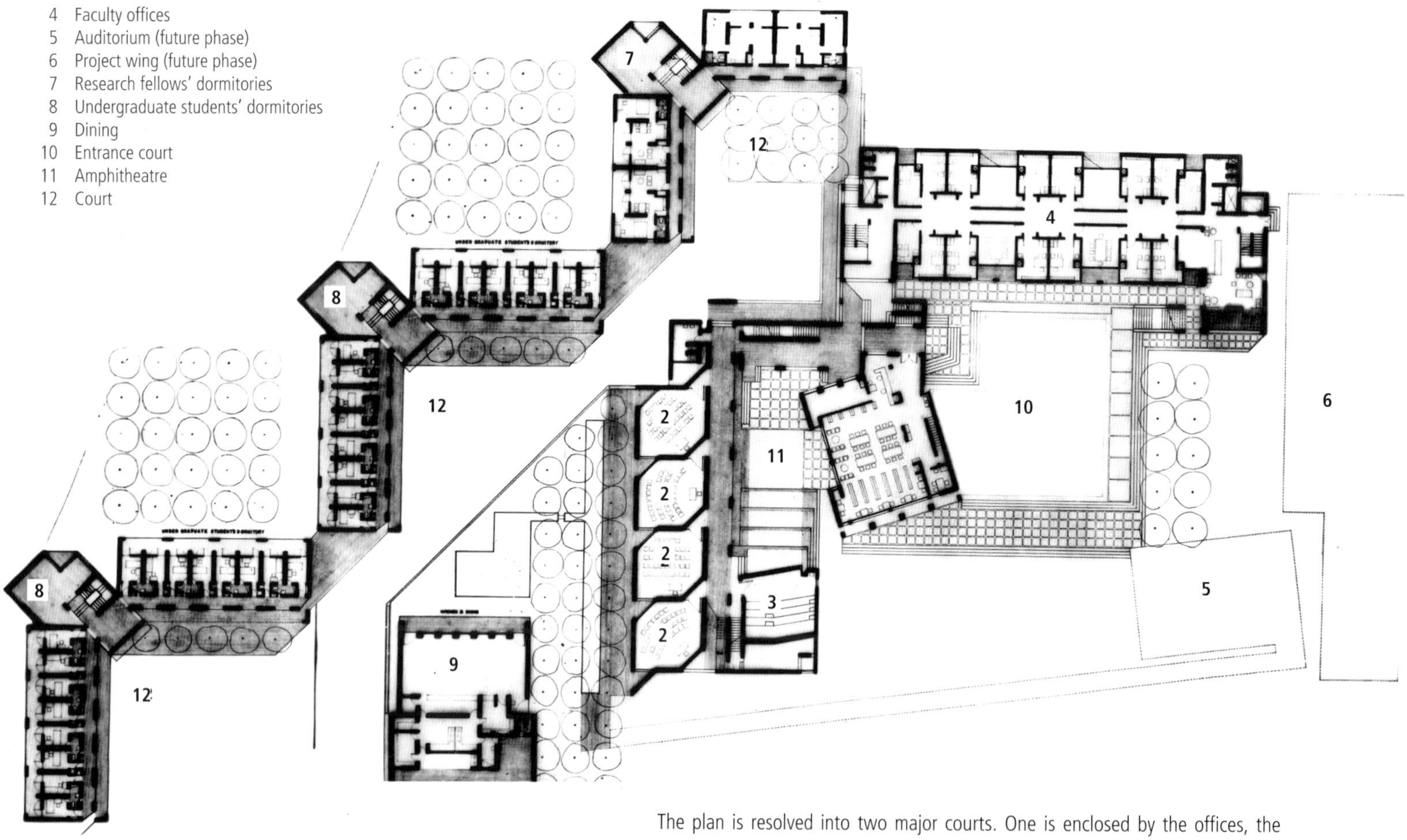

The plan is resolved into two major courts. One is enclosed by the offices, the library and the project wing (unbuilt), and the other by the student dormitories and student dining halls.

The first court is the arrival court, approached from the main road under the ramp (that connects the auditorium, unbuilt) with the student dining halls. The buildings that enclose this court are not on the court but a couple of steps below it, acknowledging the free spirit of the court.

The library and the classrooms enclose a smaller court, of the library. The classrooms form a buffer between the arrival court and the courts of the dormitories. This forms a distinct hierarchy amongst the outdoor spaces enclosed by buildings. Enclosures come out of the attitude towards room-making. Room-making is a philosophy and not design, and is central to architecture. A room lends itself to connection. Spaces enclosed by connection are as important as rooms.

< Inner court of the academic complex.

∨ Inner court and corridor of the academic complex.

Views and details of the dormitories.

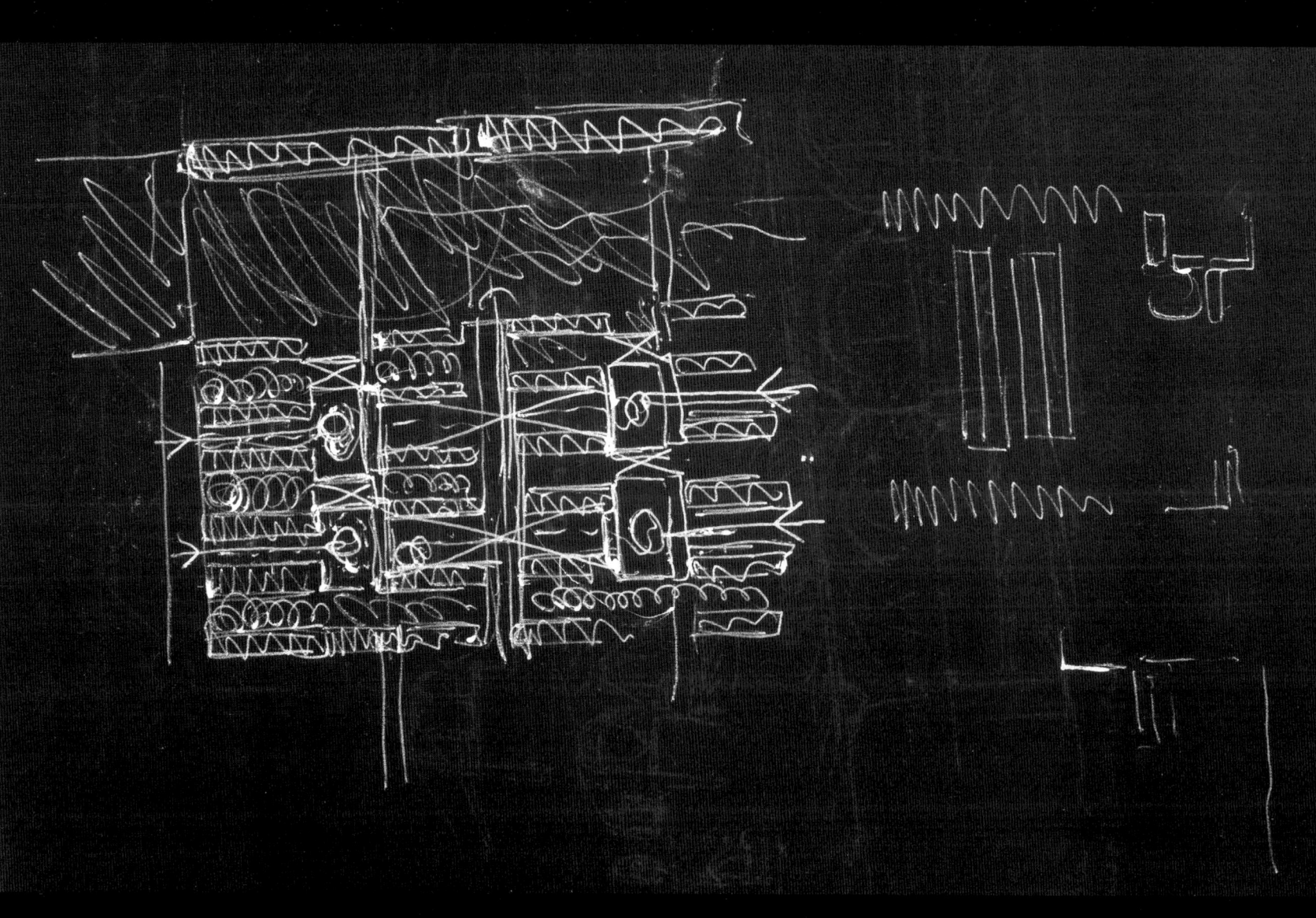

Agricultural Produce Wholesale Market Complex
New Bombay, 1973–76
(partially completed)

The site for the MAFCO wholesale market, extending up to the Vashi township Thana–Belapur Road, covers an area of approximately 11 hectares. Four trucking courts with auction halls mark the vehicular entry to the market. Behind the auction halls a wide inner pedestrian circulation path connects the two ends where the community functions for the traders are located. Bordering this pedestrian strip are the trading cells and the semi-wholesale market, with its shaded streets and courts defining the edges and the inner spaces of the market.

I started to explore, early in my career, an order which comes under the purview of a particular system. This I would develop, try to find out how many variations I can get using the order and the system, and test that against the overall forms and spaces both inside and out.

The major element that structures the plan is the 'street'. It is the covered, vaulted edge of various groups of buildings; elsewhere, it simply cuts through the body of buildings, forming a series of linked open-to-sky spaces. These streets turn inwards from the roads that border the market area, emphasizing the pedestrian nature of circulation. The market functions are designed to extend into the street as an integral part of it.

The first variation on the street is the auction hall, with a trucking court and a raised extended platform for the purposes of loading and unloading of goods on one side, linking one group of trading cells with the semi-wholesale market.

The second variation is the porch linked to a group of buildings or any specific building capable of extension, in order to link up with the adjacent streets.

> ∨ Overall preliminary site layout, views of model in wood, 1974.

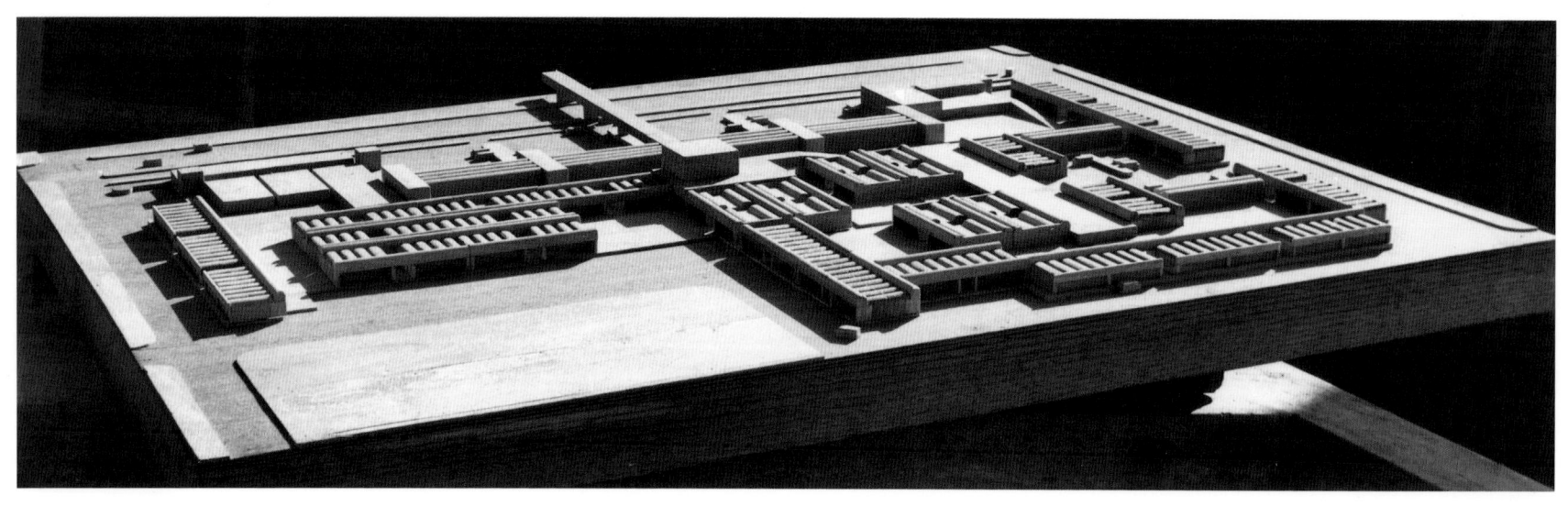

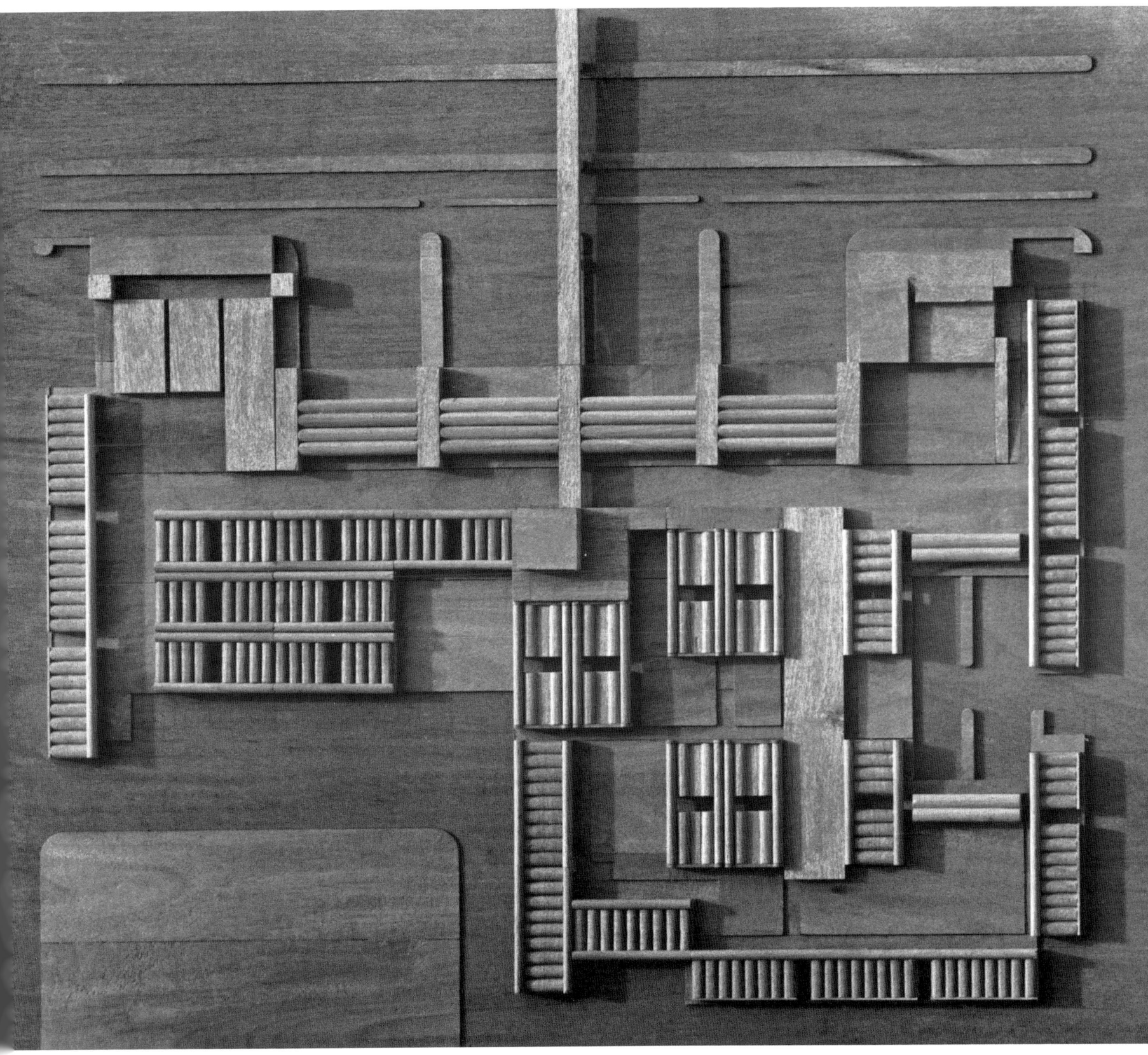

129

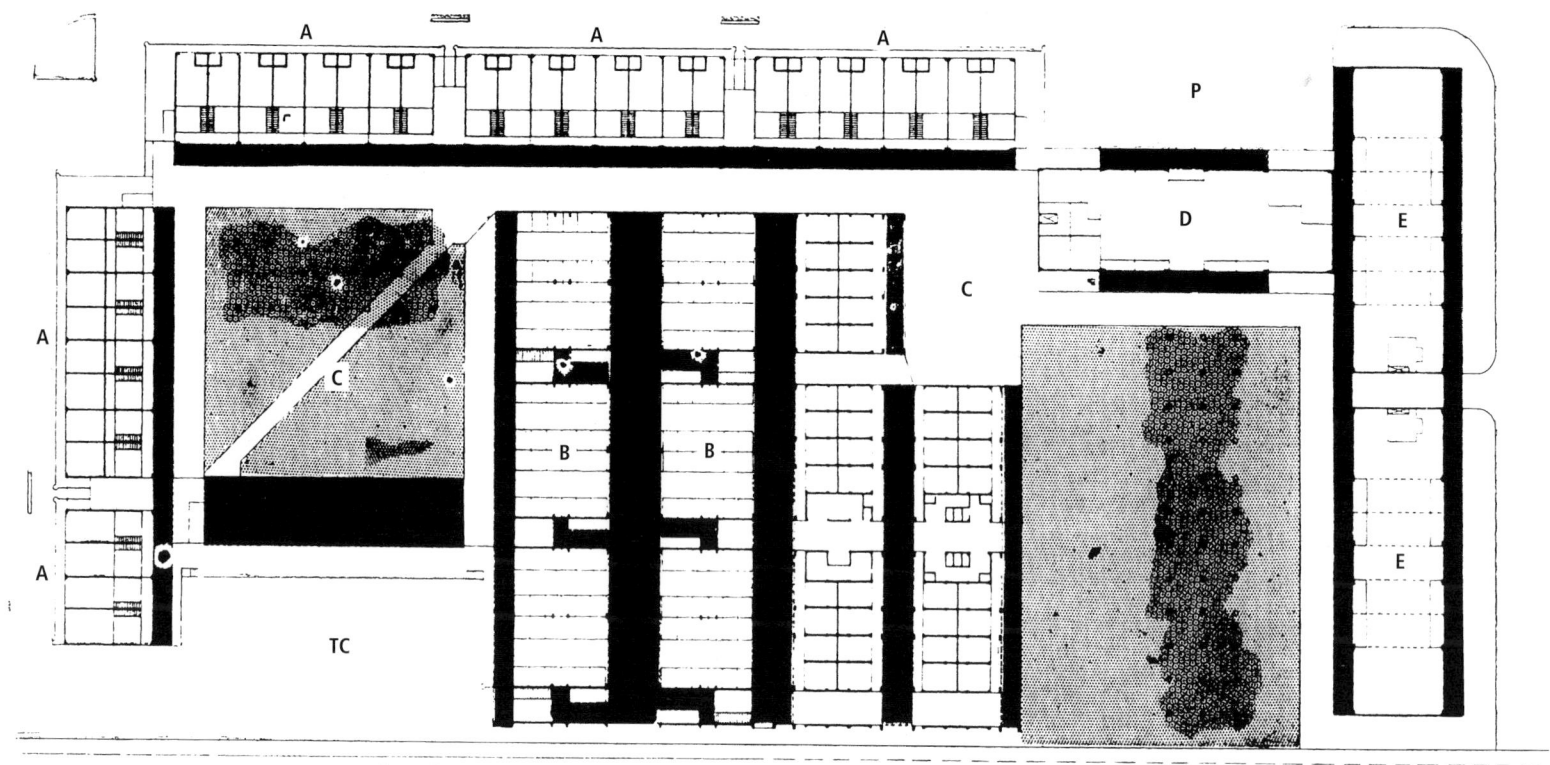

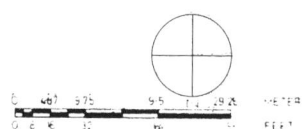

Trading cells

All trading cells are accommodated within a standard dimension of 18.29 m, divisible by numbers from 1 to 6. The dimensions chosen here are 18.29 m, 9.14 m, 4.57 m and 3.65 m. Each cell comprises three distinct spaces: (i) the office or 'pedhi', (ii) a godown, and (iii) sleeping space for overnight stay.

Auction hall

Each bay of the auction hall is 18.29 m long and 9.14 m wide. It is covered by an inclined concrete roof with gullies for the disposal of rainwater. This roof divides the auction hall into two bays, distinguishing the incoming and outgoing areas of auctioning material. A raised loading platform helps carry the spillover goods and materials from the covered auction hall.

The wholesale market

This market within a market consists of rows of raised platforms for selling activities with circulation aisles on the ground floor, and smaller offices on the first floor. Each small office has a platform for discussions at the window side. Four such 18.30 m x 13.10 m units make a cluster, and are connected by two pairs of staircases and an upper-level deck in a 4.57 m wide inner street that crosses the central hall. These can be extended in the future along the principal axis of the central halls.

Banks

Three branch banks are accommodated within the same structural bay that makes the trading cells. A central banking space is flanked by ancillary spaces on either side. The thin shell roof over the central five bays is cambered on the principal axis of the shell such that the space underneath becomes one vaulted space.

Structure

Each unit of the shell spans on its longer axis two reinforced concrete trusses. Each truss carries two units of shell on a concrete column grid of 9.14 m x 13.1 m. The presence of marine clay makes it necessary to have concentrated point loading for effective and economical foundations. The plinth beams carry the internal partition loads and the long spans permit flexibility in the arrangement of these partitions. The concrete work is exposed, while the rest of the construction is plastered and painted.

<   Market layout plan, 1975.
    A   Trading cells
    B   Wholesale market
    C   Court
    D   Branch banks
    E   Offices | Information
    F   Auction hall
    P   Parking
    TC Trucking court

>   Typical shaded street with
    entrances to trading cells
    (to the left).

∧ Wholesale market interior, construction photograph, 1976.

> Wholesale market roof studies in wood.

∨ Growth sequence. Wholesale market sectional studies, March 1973.

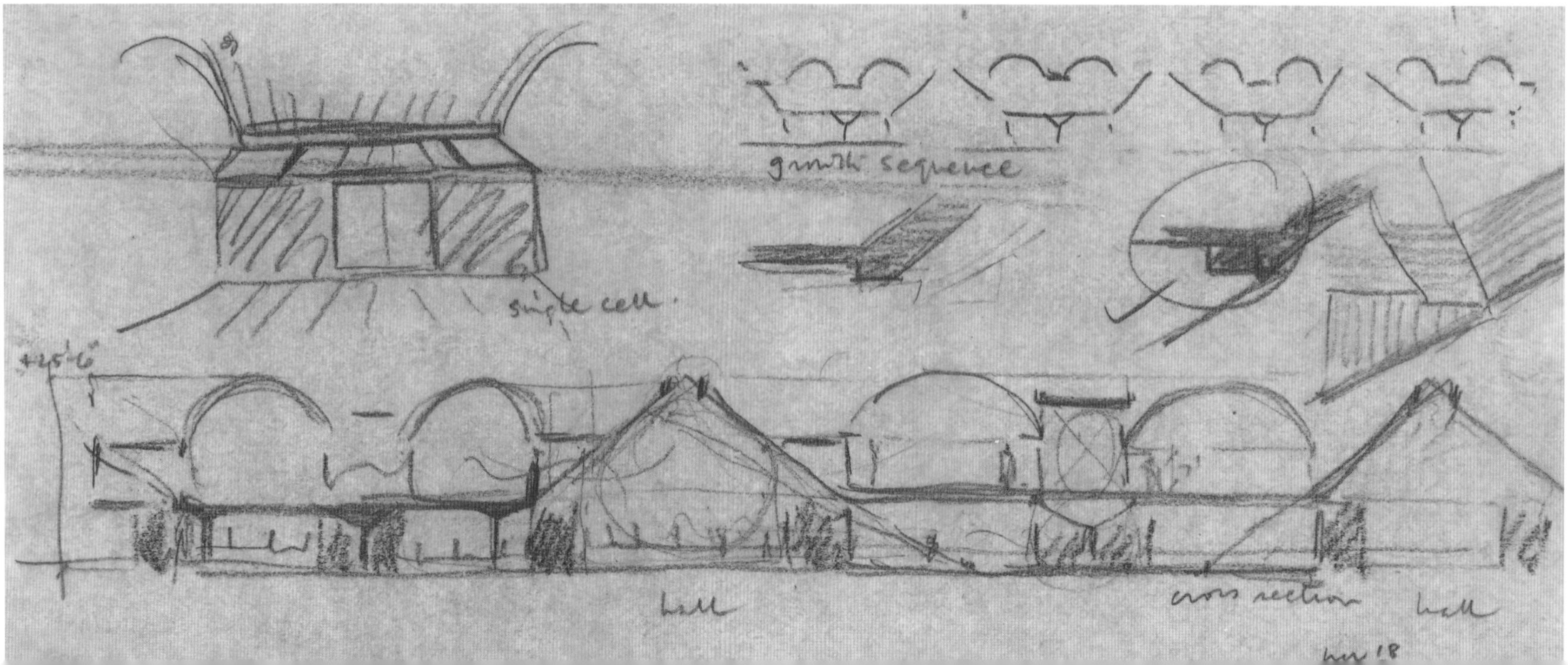

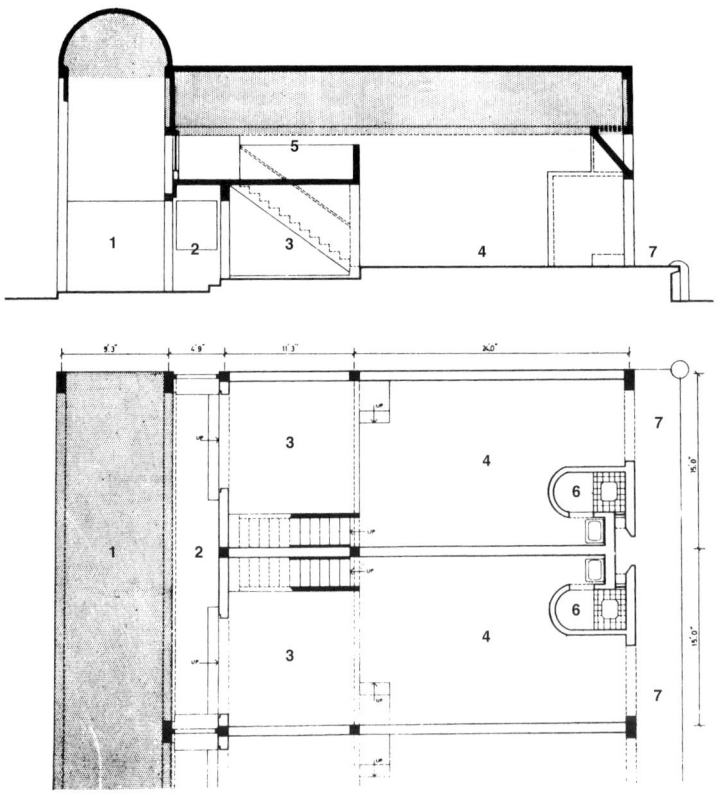

< Plan and section of trading cell.
  1 Street
  2 Porch
  3 'Pedhi'
  4 Godown
  5 Sleeping area
  6 Toilets
  7 Loading

> Construction photograph, trading cell cluster, 1976.

∨ Study of trading cell cluster in wood, 1973.

> Trading cell cluster, with shaded streets and entrances to the cells
  (to the left).

∨ Views of study model of trading cell in wood, 1973.

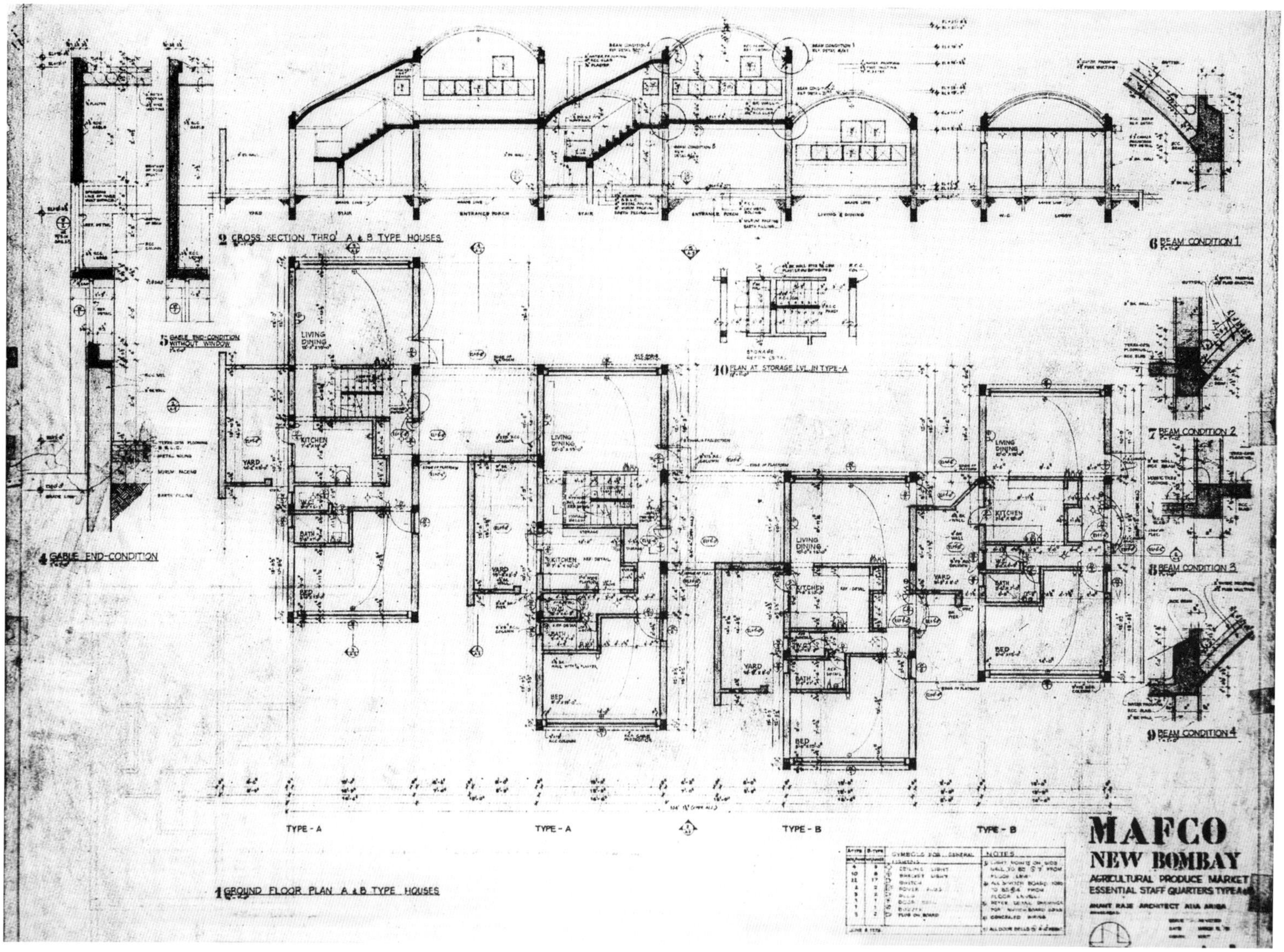

^ Ground floor plan and sections, staff quarters.

> Vault construction, staff quarters.

> Staff quarters cluster, construction photograph, 1976.

MAFCO Dairy
National Dairy Development Board (NDDB)
Bombay, 1977

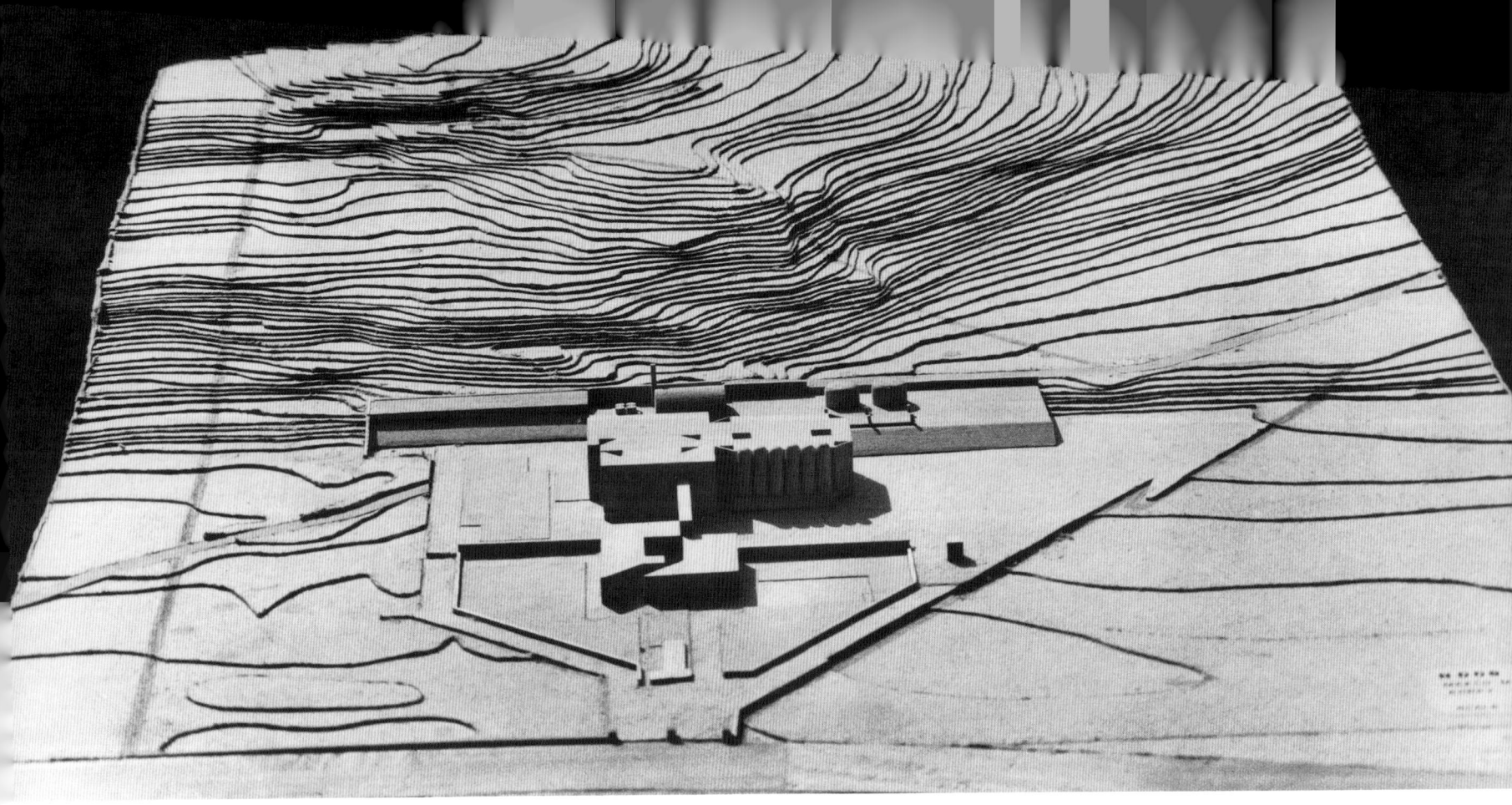

^ Block site model.

> Site plan.
1 Entrance court
2 Offices
3 Canteen and recreation
4 Parking
5 Garden
6 Empty crates reception
7 Tanker court
8 Pouch filling
9 Cold storage
10 Pouch dispatch
11 Milk reception
12 Processing plant
13 Refrigeration
14 Milk court van

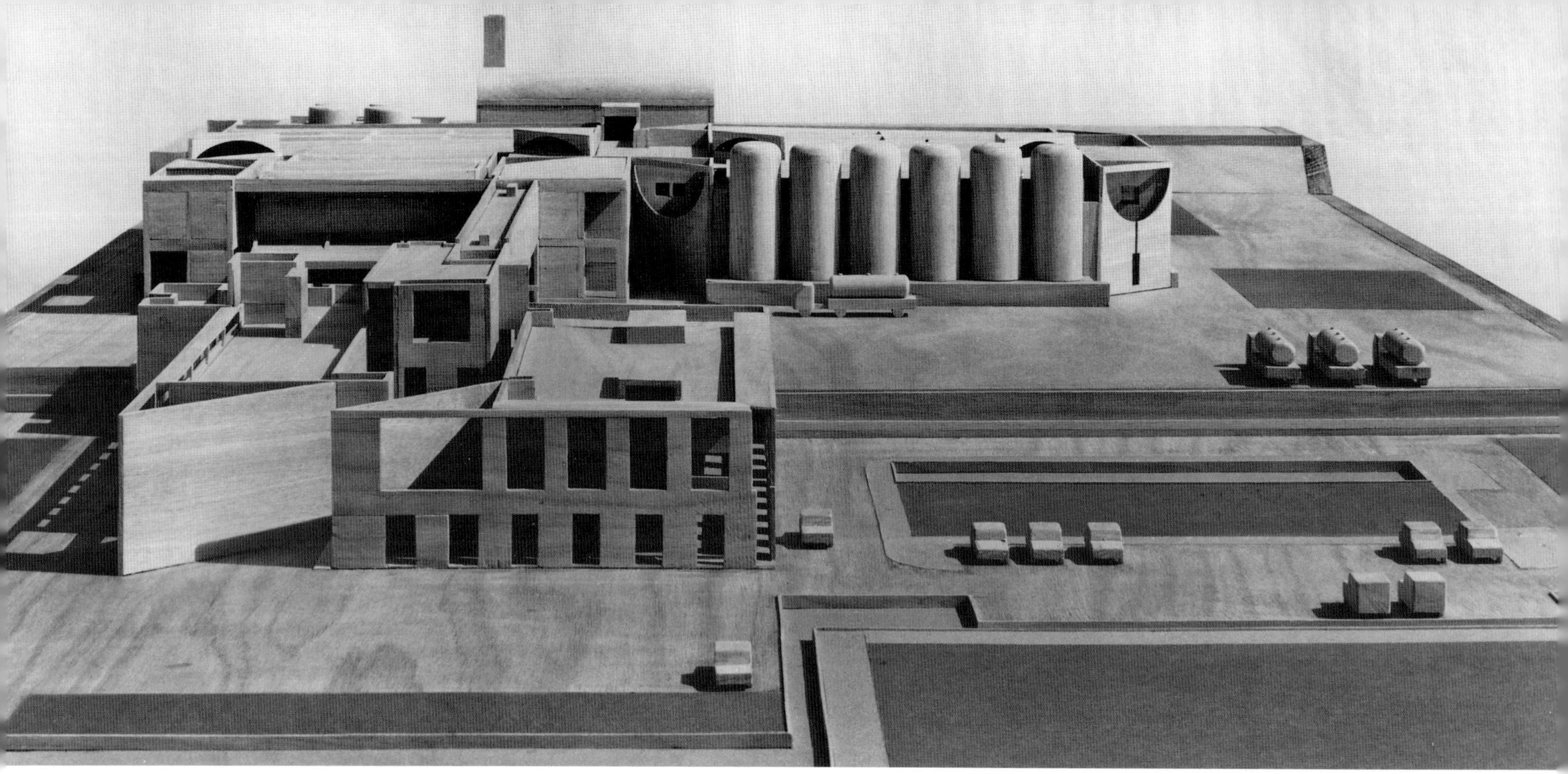

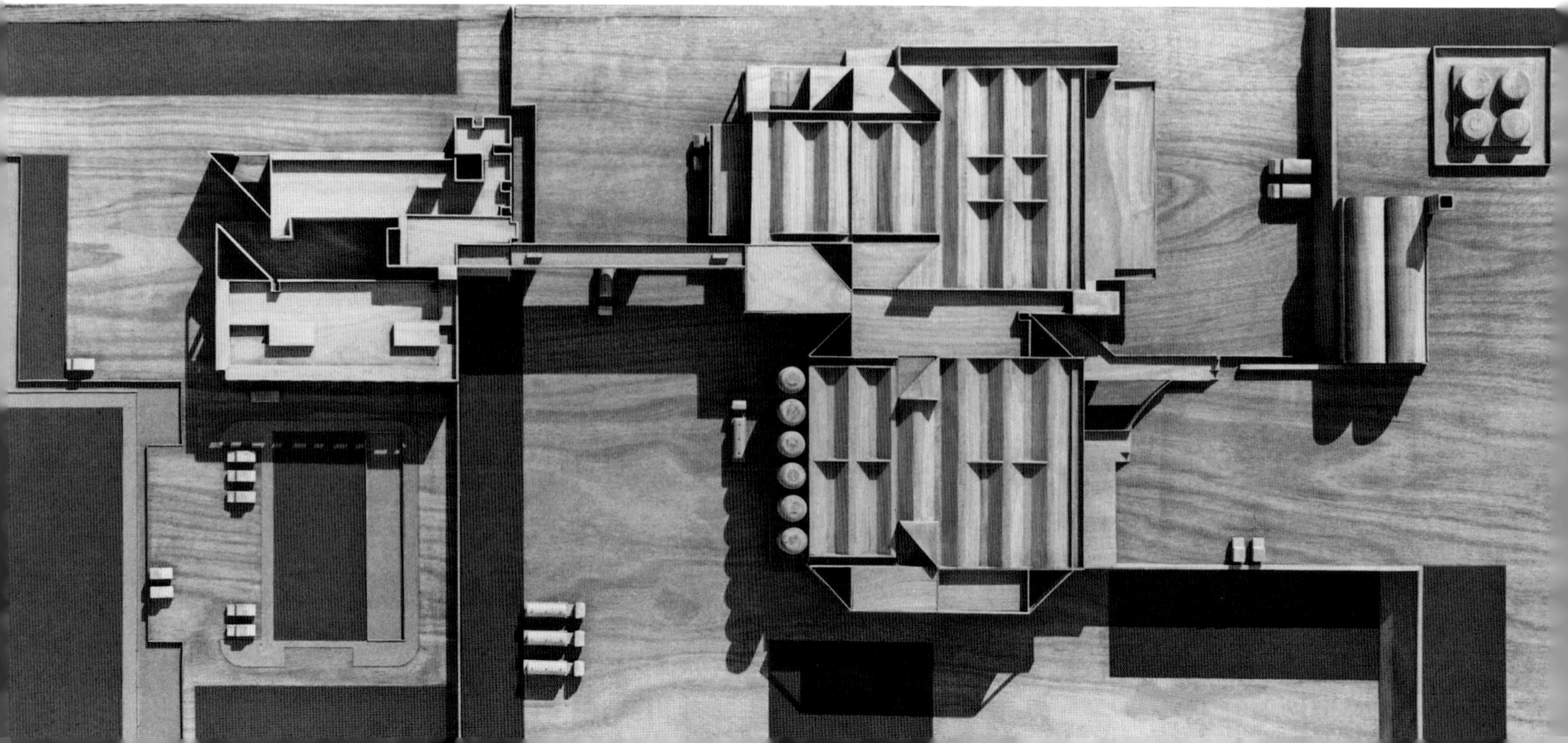

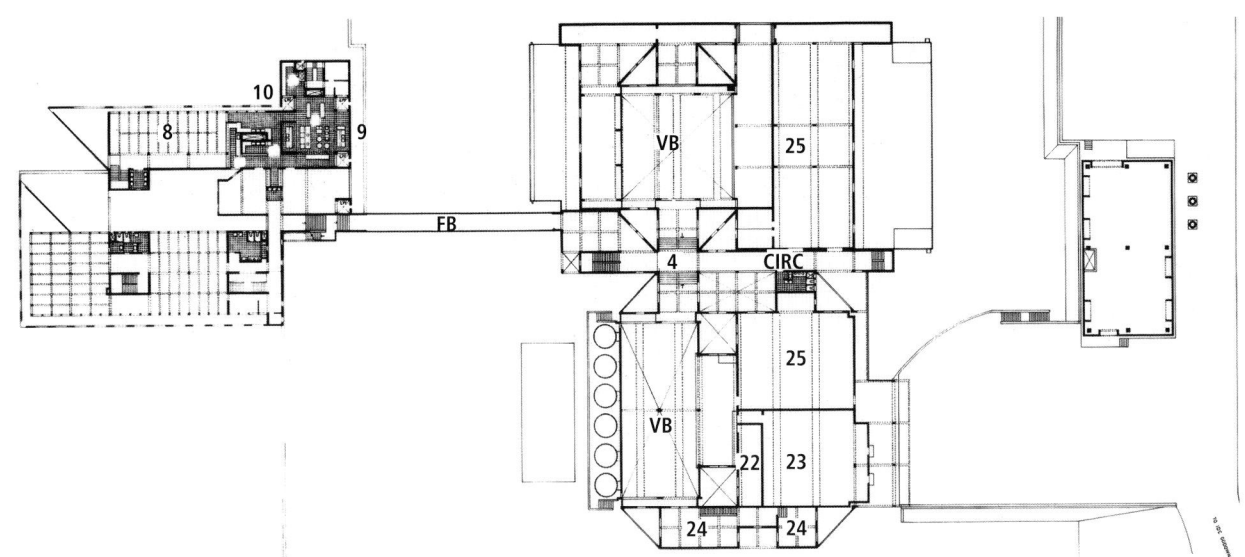

< Dairy model views

> First and ground floor plans.

OFFICES AND CANTEEN
1   Workers' Entry
2   Staff Entry
3   Visitors' Entry
4   Lobby
5   Reception
6   Exhibition Hall
7   Administration
8   Dining
9   Kitchen
10 Food Service
11 Changing/Prep
LW Light Well
C   Court
FB Footbridge
AP Apron
D   Dock
CIRC Circulation
VB Void to Below

PROCESSING–STORAGE
12 Receiving and Processing
13 Pouch Filling
14 Milk Cold Store
15 Air Lock
16 Milk Dispatch Dock
17 Silos
18 Processing
19 Recombination
20 Refrigeration
21 Laboratory
22 Butter Oil Heating
23 Butter Oil Cold Store
24 Supervision & Ancillary
25 Storage

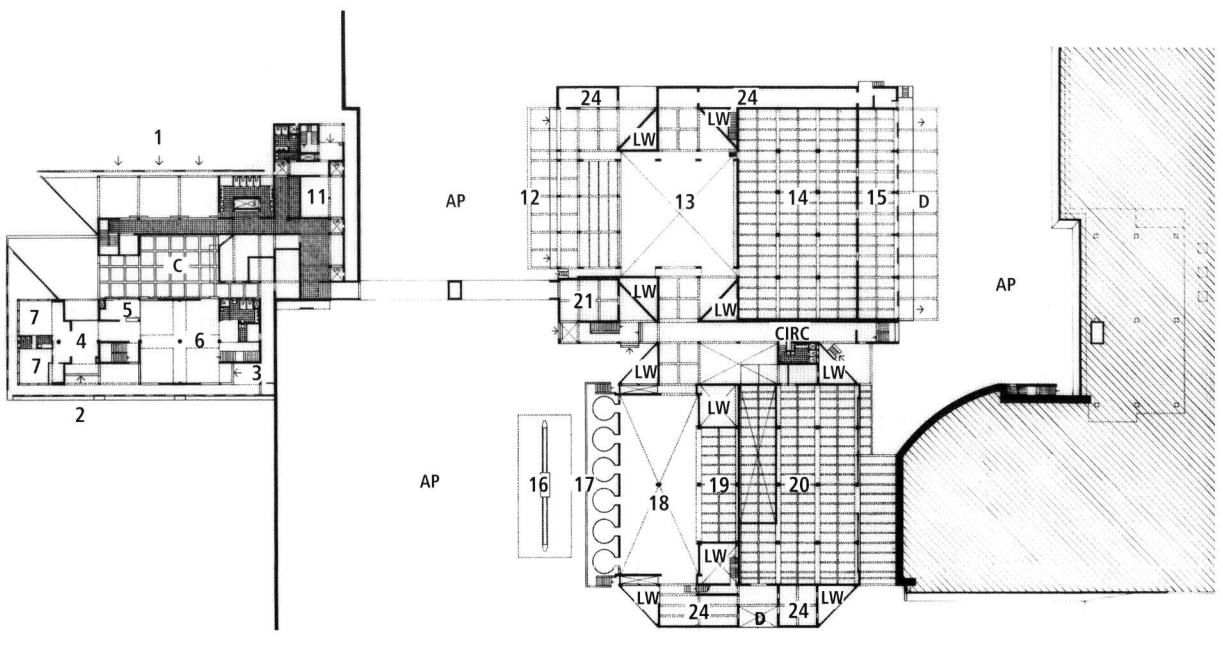

147

Goregaon Dairy
Goregaon, Mumbai, 1982

Banas Dairy
Banaskantha, Gujarat, 1978–82

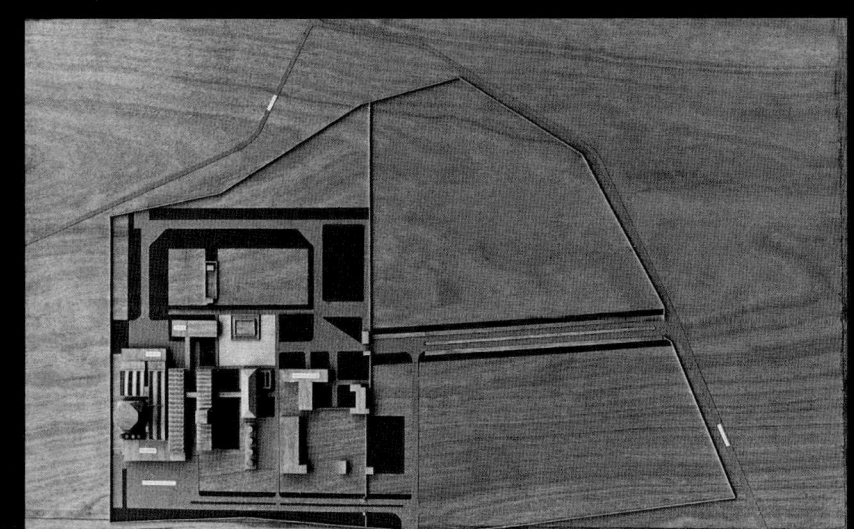

Mehsana Dairy
Mehsana, Gujarat, 1982

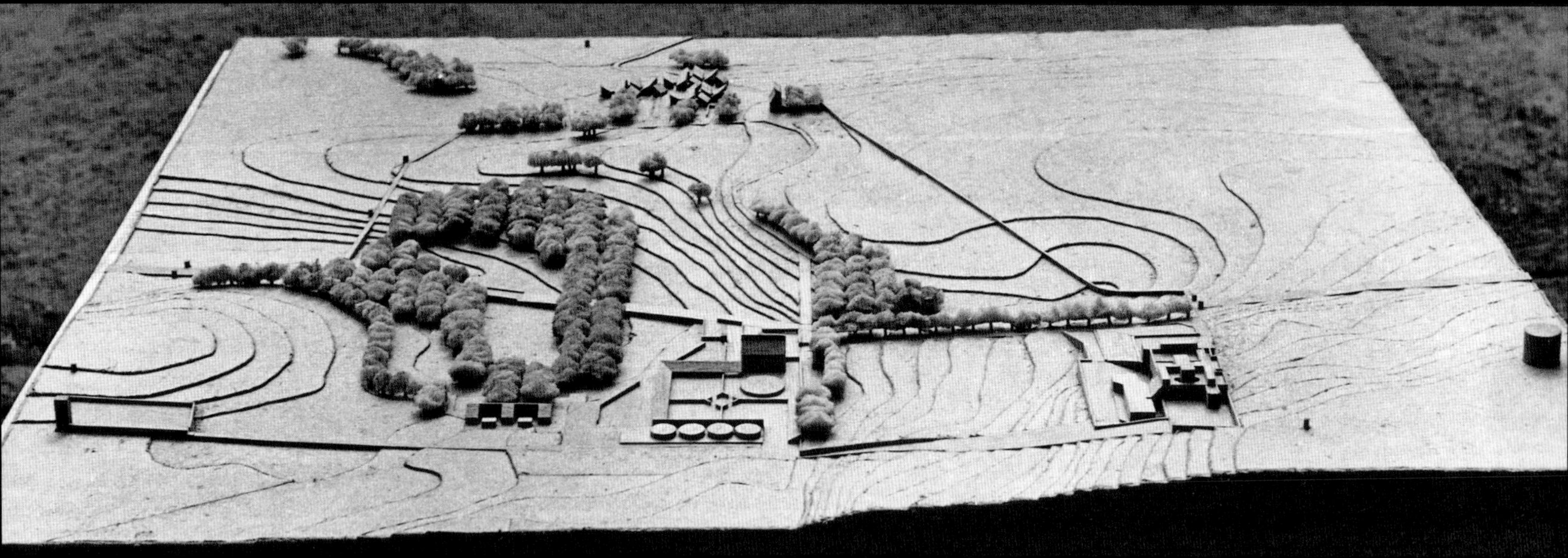

Central Godowns for the Indian Dairy Corporation
Nanded, Maharashtra, 1982

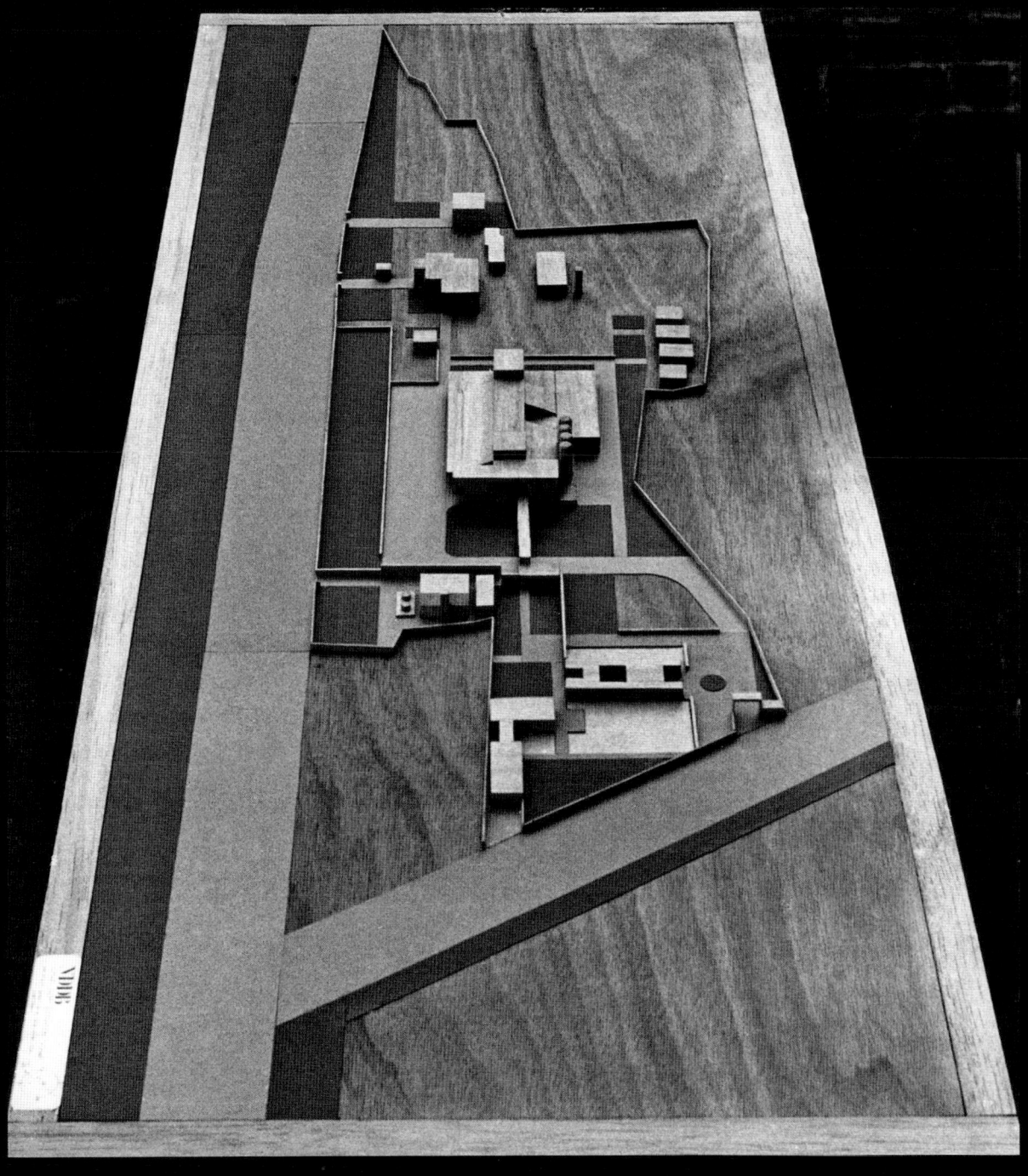

Galbabhai Farmers' Training Institute
National Dairy Development Board
Banaskantha, Gujarat, 1983

An institute set up for rural dairy farmers under a programme set up by the National Dairy Development Board (NDDB) in Palanpur, Gujarat, to impart basic training in cooperative dairy farming to villagers in surrounding districts. Set amidst wheatfields, the institute consists of a hierarchy of courtyards enclosed by stone walls.

The project includes two sets of classrooms with residential rooms for 24 students, dining and other facilities connected with a regular dairy plant.

The buildings are of load-bearing stone, quarried from nearby quarries. Openings are spanned by concrete lintels, and are deeply recessed to provide shade from the hot sun.

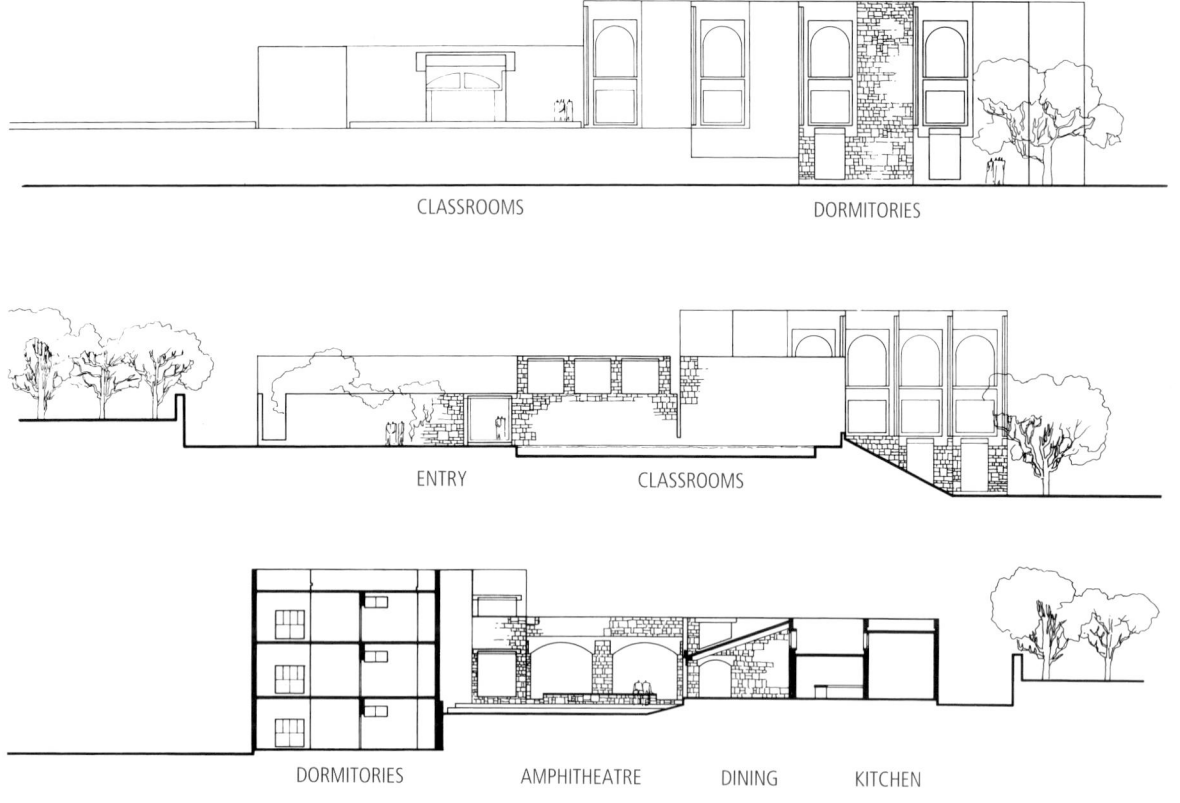

CLASSROOMS   DORMITORIES

ENTRY   CLASSROOMS

DORMITORIES   AMPHITHEATRE   DINING   KITCHEN

CLASSROOM   ENTRANCE COURT   AMPHITHEATRE

< West elevation.
  North elevation.
  Section through dormitories.
  Section through classroom.

> Entrance to training institute.

> Site plan.

TRAINING INSTITUTE
1   Arrival court
2   Court
3   Classroom
4   Kitchen–dining
5   Office
6   Dormitories
7   Amphitheatre
GUEST HOUSE
8   Existing guest house
9   Court
10 Dining
11 Guest room
SITE
12 Entry to existing dairy
13 Existing gate cabin
14 Pool

154

12
13
8
9
10
14
1
4
2
3
2
14
7
3
5
6

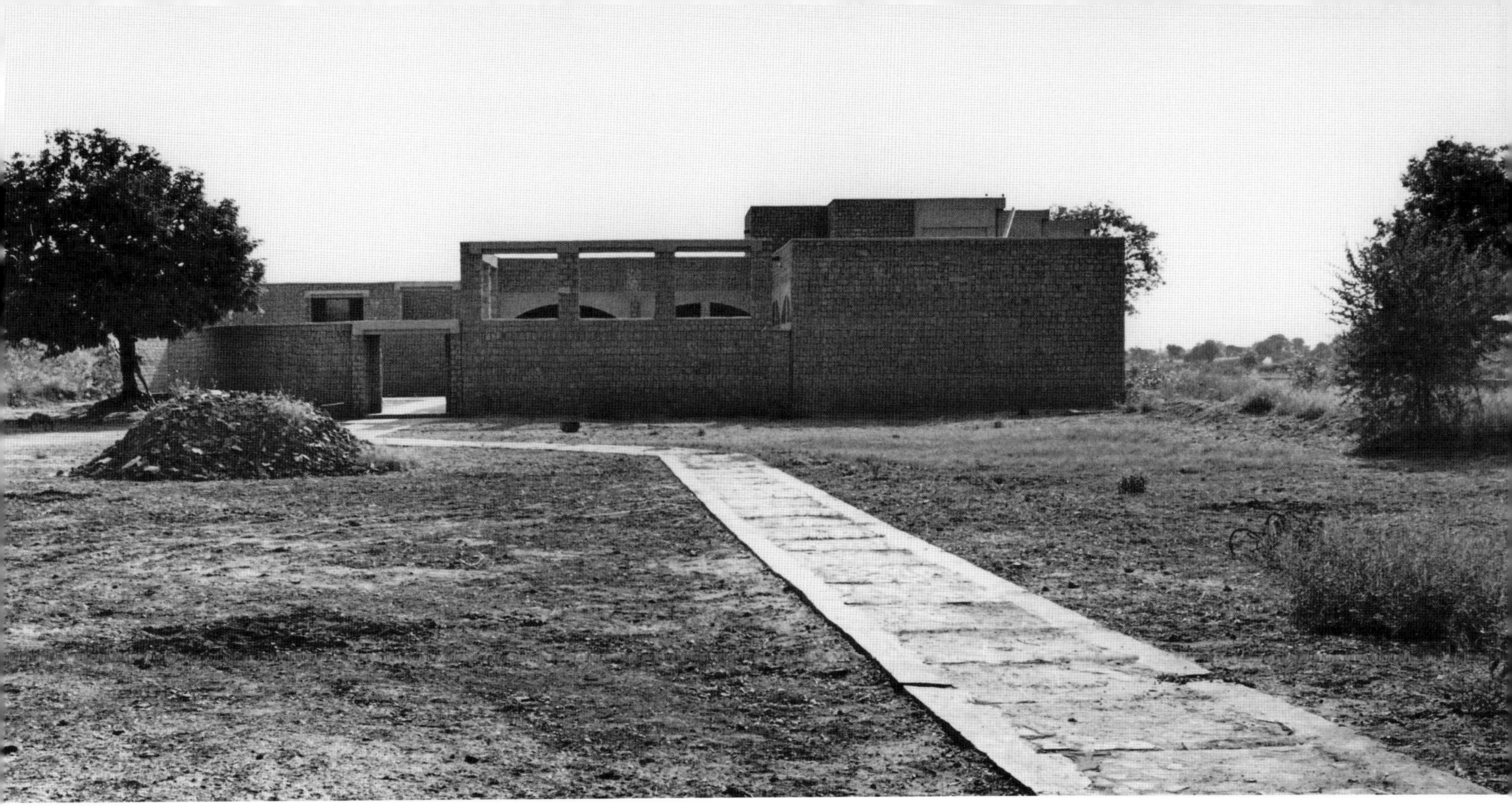

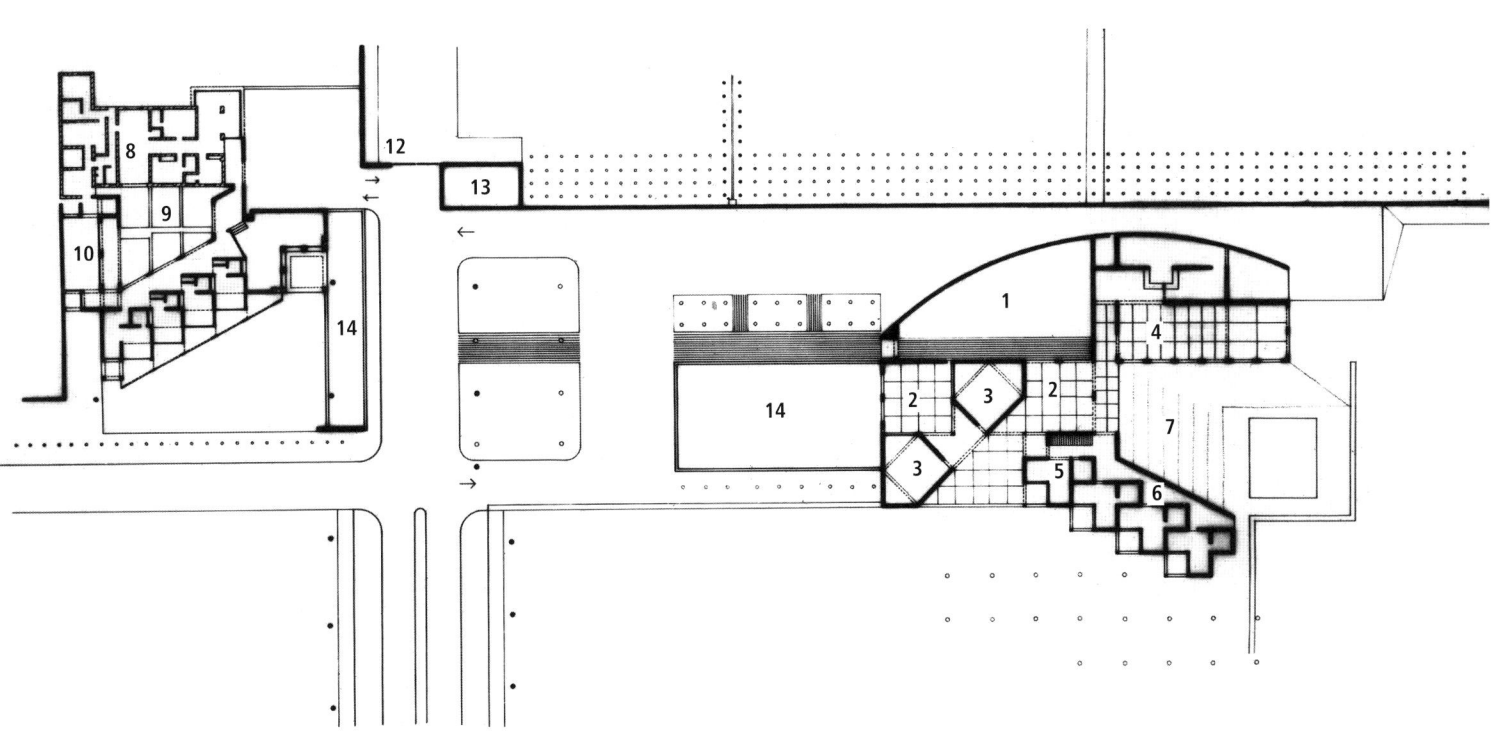

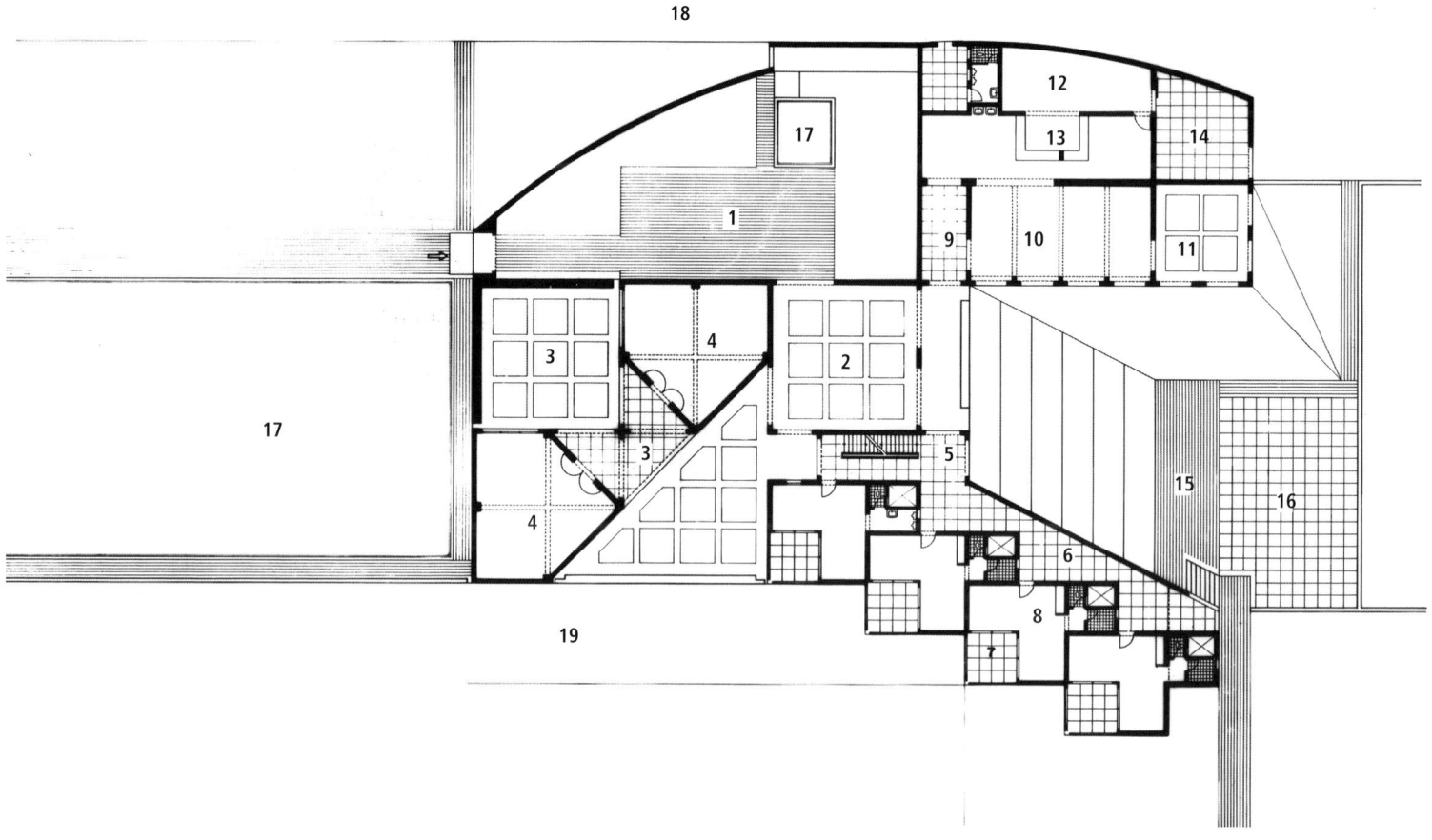

∧ Definitive models in wood.

< Institute floor plan.

1	Arrival court	11	Dining court
2	Entrance court	12	Kitchen
3	Classroom court	13	Service station
4	Classrooms	14	Yard
5	Entry to dormitory	15	Amphitheatre
6	Lobby	16	Raised platform
7	Light well	17	Water pool
8	Rooms	18	Service road
9	Entry to dining	19	Agriculture fields
10	Dining verandah		

Rough stone masonry wall and smooth exposed concrete
porches and lintels, used for elements of light, set against
the landscape of wheatfields and mango trees.

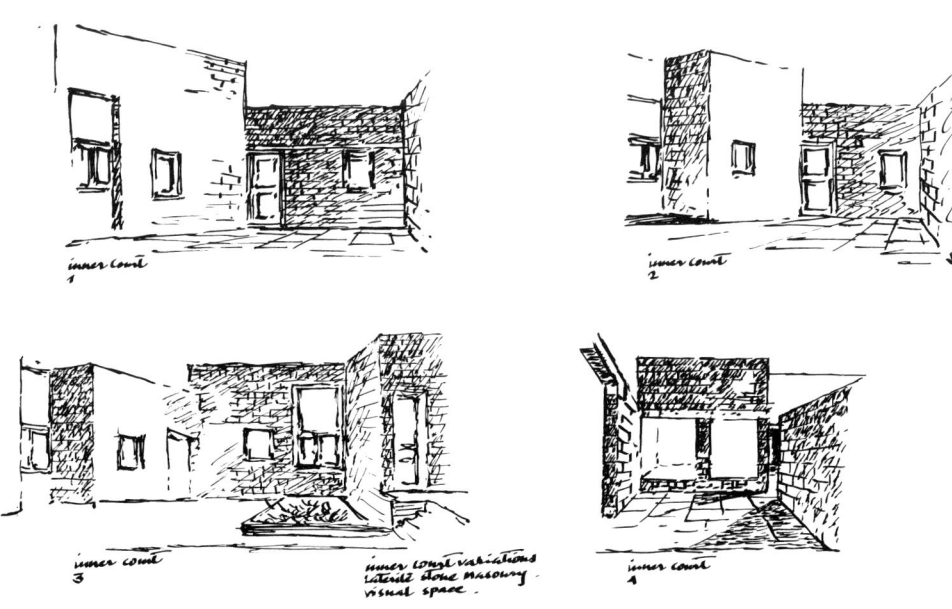

< ^ Photographs of buildings around the central courtyard.

∨ Inner court variations, April 1980.
Notes on the sketches:
'Inner court variations. Laterite stone masonry. Visual space.'

inner court
1

inner court
2

inner court
3

inner court variations
laterite stone masonry
visual space.

inner court
4

> Corridor beside the court.

∨ Dining verandah overlooking the court, and dormitories across.

I was trying to develop an element of span. This is not just a lintel, but a logical development in terms of the shear forces and their bending moments. Regardless what my engineers thought, it gave me a certain satisfaction that it is possible to express the stresses and the bending moments, not in the literal sense, but in the form of the kinds of spans where the actual 'hub' of load distribution is going to be.

The inside environment, where the element meets on a rectangular plane, one can fill it up with wall, or glass, or a window – the filler material; and on the outside it is left free for the environment. The space between is a little pocket to shade the filler material that came to be.

Lintel Development
Attitudes towards an Element of Span

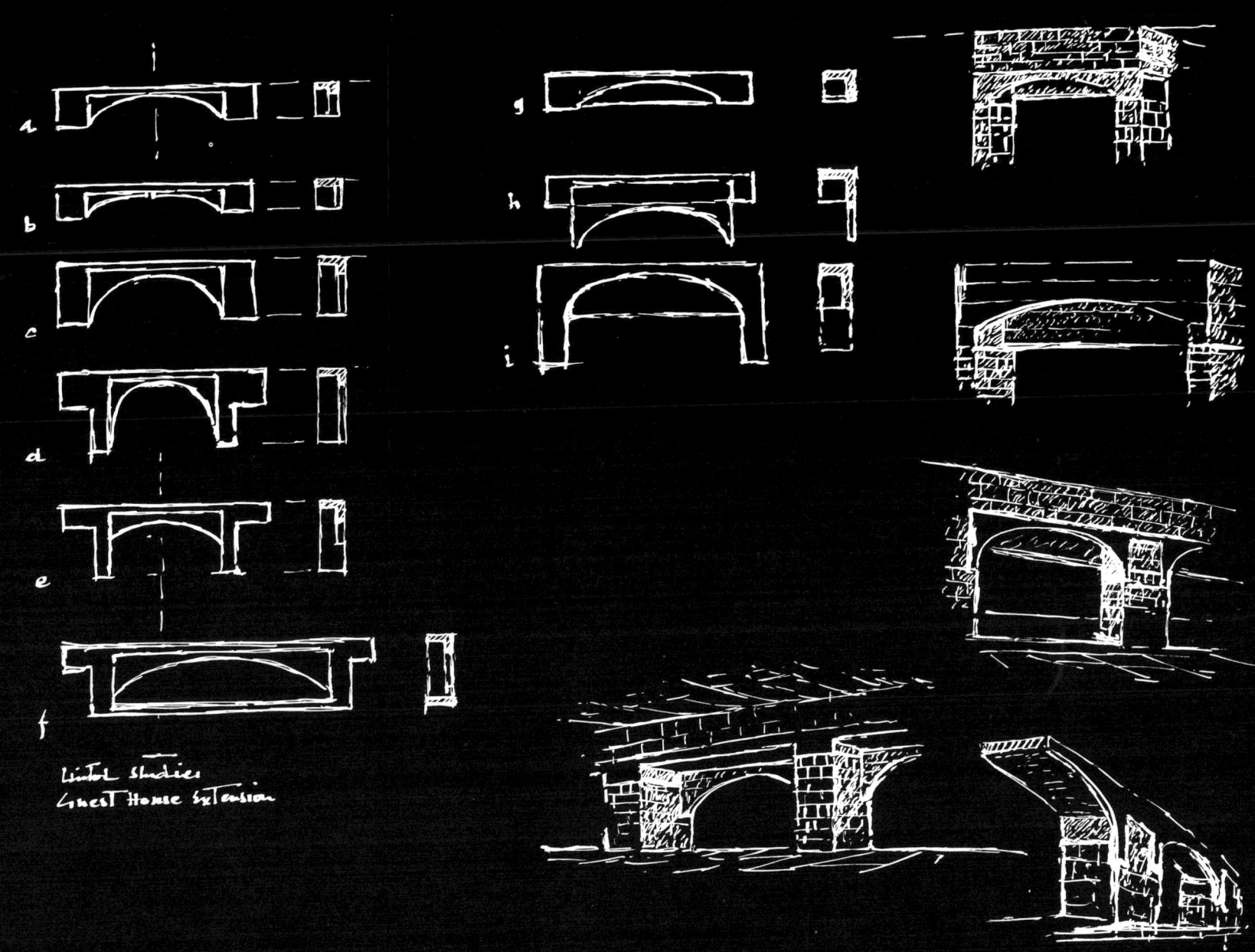

Lintel Studies
Guest House Extension

< Lecture hall, interior, October 1983.

⌄ Library, interior, October 1983.

Testing Board Offices and Science Museum
Madhya Pradesh State Testing Board
Bhopal, 1983–95
(Phase 1 completed)

Counselling students to take up higher education and go to college was the main intention behind developing the programme of this project. The programme was conceived almost single-handedly by the then chairman of 'Mandal', and called for a meeting place for the authorities, teachers and students: a place for information exchange and exhibition on the various aspects of higher education, and its implications on the future lives and careers of students. This place was identified through a lecture auditorium, exhibition galleries, a library, and facilities for multimedia programmes to be offered to both teachers and students.

A science museum with a science park for children is a part of the complex wherein the information facilities available through 'Mandal' can be used by children on study tours of the museum.

Supporting activities, such as a full secretariat with chairman's offices, seminar rooms, valuation rooms, bank and post office became a part of the programme. Residences for students and teachers in the form of dormitories and a guest house with dining facilities also became a part of the programme.

The plan is anchored by the library–auditorium buildings, and these became inseparable from the dormitories and the guest house. The association of the library with students and teachers realized the elevated open space in between, in the form of a soft court overlooking the lower gardens and connected through an elevated walkway.

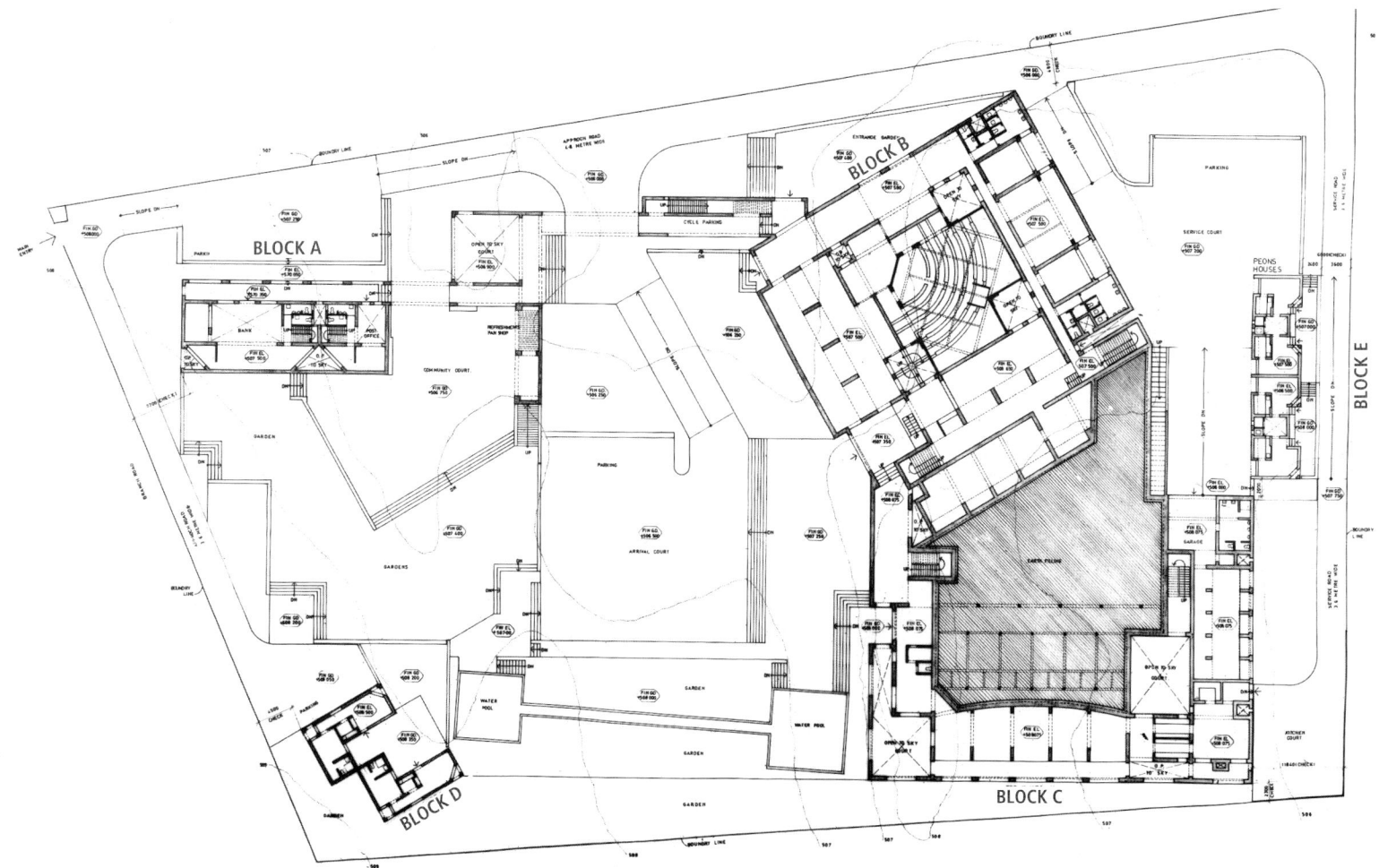

^ Site layout.

Block A   Science Museum

Block B   Auditorium, counselling halls, exhibition galleries, library

Block C   Kitchen–dining (lower floor), offices (upper floor)

Block D   Guest, transit housing

Block E   Staff housing

< Definitive site model in wood.

171

> Sketch of entrance pavilion to dining halls.

> Sections | Elevations.

∨ > Definitive model in wood.
  View from north | View from northwest

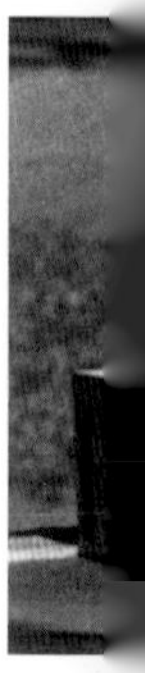

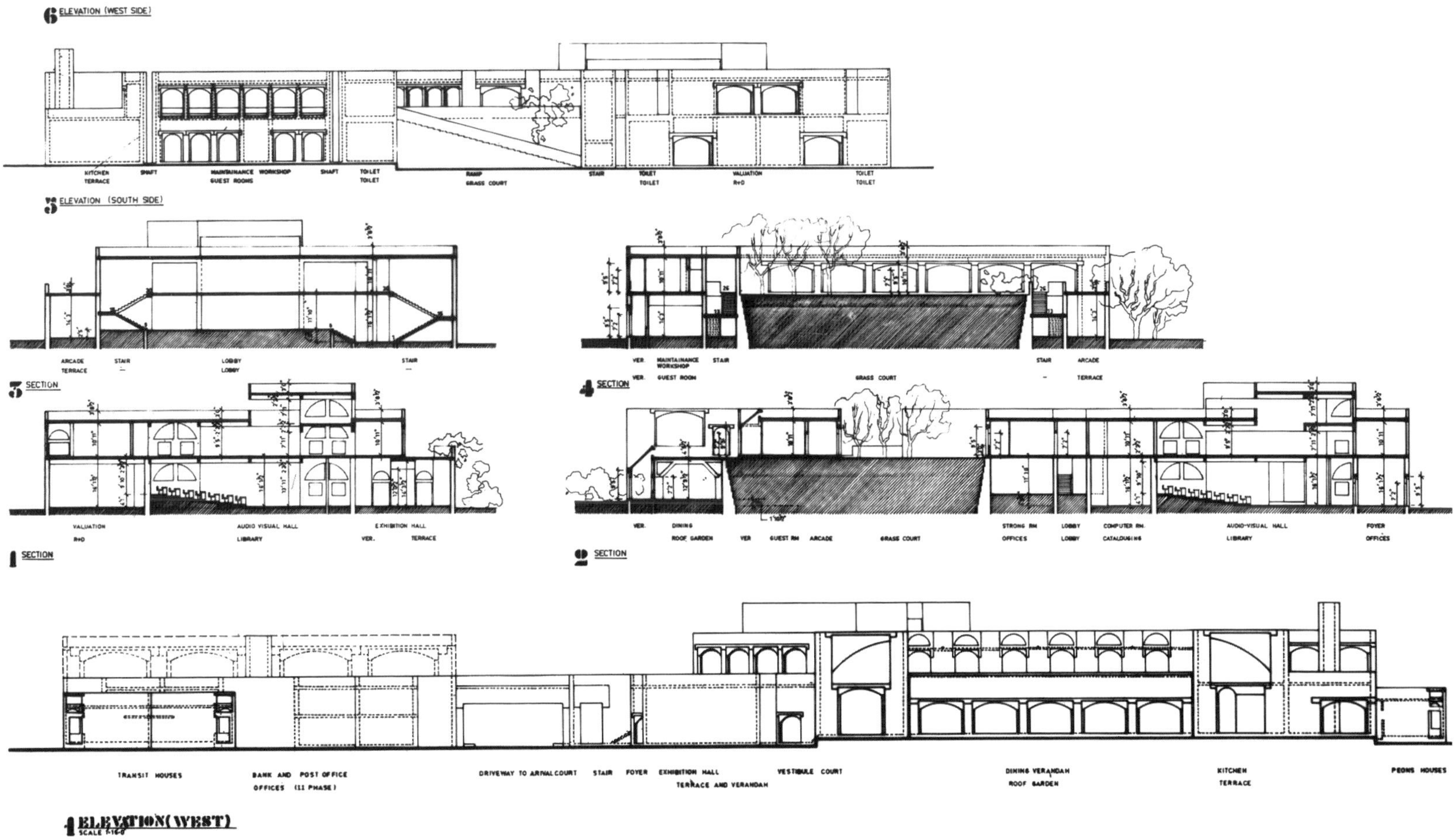
6 ELEVATION (WEST SIDE)
KITCHEN TERRACE
SHAFT
MAINTAINANCE WORKSHOP GUEST ROOMS
SHAFT
TOILET TOILET
RAMP GRASS COURT
STAIR
TOILET TOILET
VALUATION R+D
TOILET TOILET
5 ELEVATION (SOUTH SIDE)
ARCADE TERRACE
STAIR
LOBBY LOBBY
STAIR
3 SECTION
VER. MAINTAINANCE WORKSHOP
STAIR
VER. GUEST ROOM
GRASS COURT
STAIR
ARCADE TERRACE
4 SECTION
VALUATION R+D
AUDIO VISUAL HALL LIBRARY
EXHIBITION HALL
VER.
TERRACE
1 SECTION
VER.
DINING ROOF GARDEN
VER
GUEST RM
ARCADE
GRASS COURT
STRONG RM OFFICES
LOBBY LOBBY
COMPUTER RM. CATALOGUING
AUDIO-VISUAL HALL LIBRARY
FOYER OFFICES
2 SECTION
TRANSIT HOUSES
BANK AND POST OFFICE OFFICES (II PHASE)
DRIVEWAY TO ARIVAL COURT
STAIR
FOYER
EXHIBITION HALL TERRACE AND VERANDAH
VESTIBULE COURT
DINING VERANDAH ROOF GARDEN
KITCHEN TERRACE
PEONS HOUSES
1 ELEVATION (WEST)
SCALE 1'-16'-0"

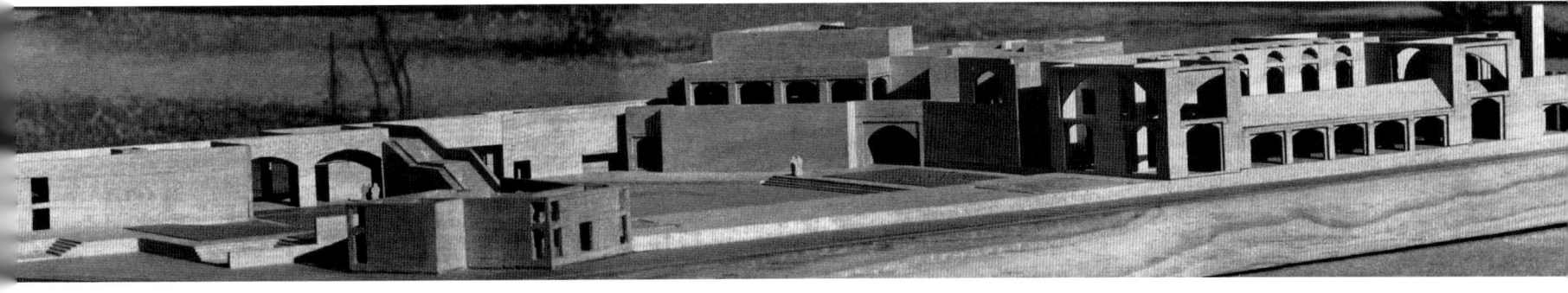

> Site model in wood. Buildings are parallel to the adjacent road. The Walmi Subcentre
is tilted and outside the axis of the main office building. The acute angle corner is used
for parking and service buildings, parking is in the opposite corner.
1 Commissioner's Office complex
2 Agricultural fields
3 Walmi Subcentre
4 Gardens
5 Playground
6 Parking

Commissioner's Office and
Walmi Subcentre

Morena, Madhya Pradesh
(under construction since 1985)

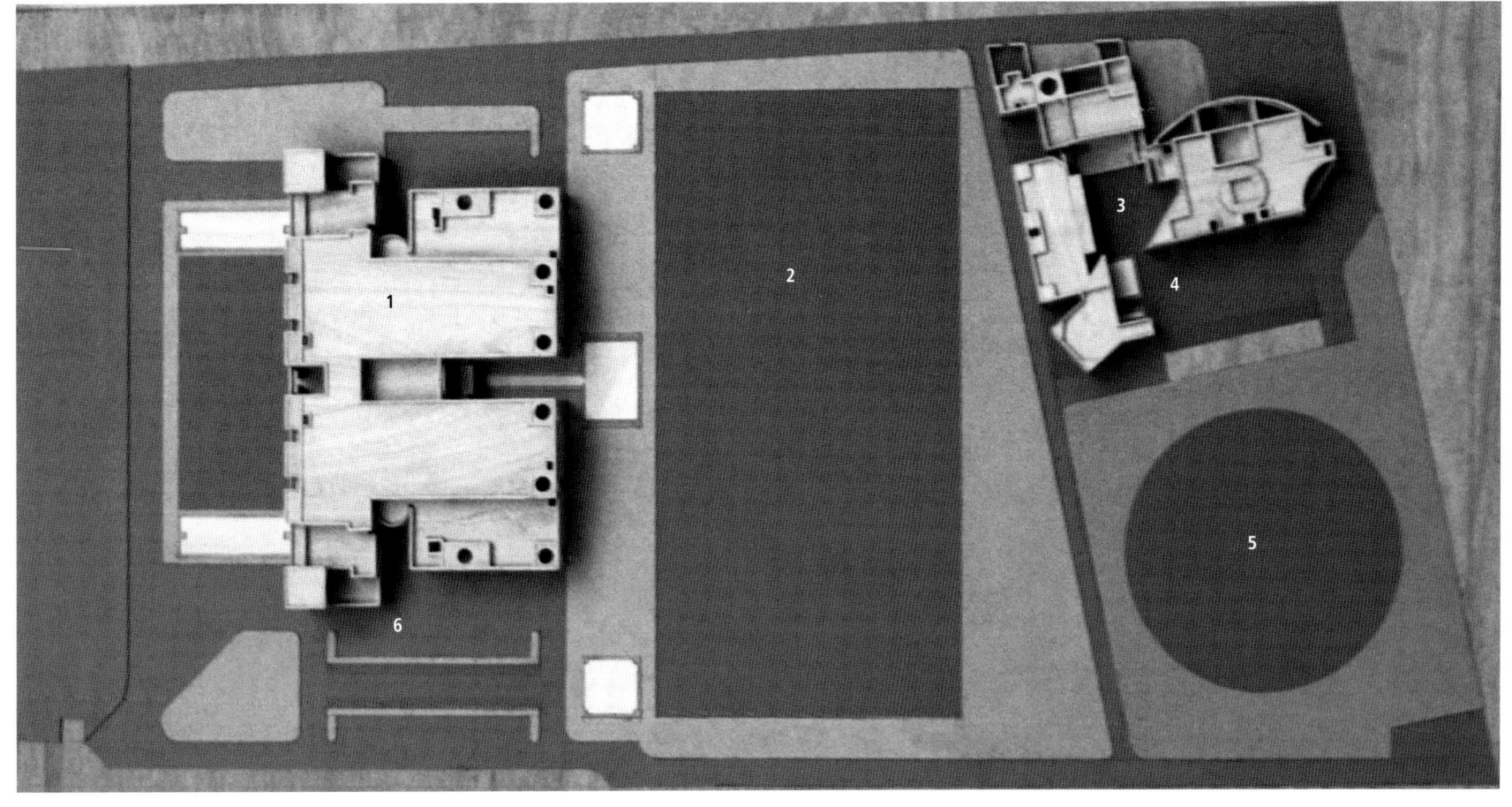

> Building elevations.

> Ground floor plan with the main assembly and public halls.
  1   Entrance / entrance porch
  2   Car porch
  3   Porch
  4   Guard room
  5   Lobby
  6   Hall
  7   Assembly hall
  8   Control room and project display
  9   Offices
  9a Open office / staff halls
  9b Commissioner's suite
  9c Lounge
  9d Court room
  10 Toilets
  11 Light well
  12 Open-to-Sky court
  13 Water pool

∨ Site plan, 1984 (without the Walmi Subcentre).

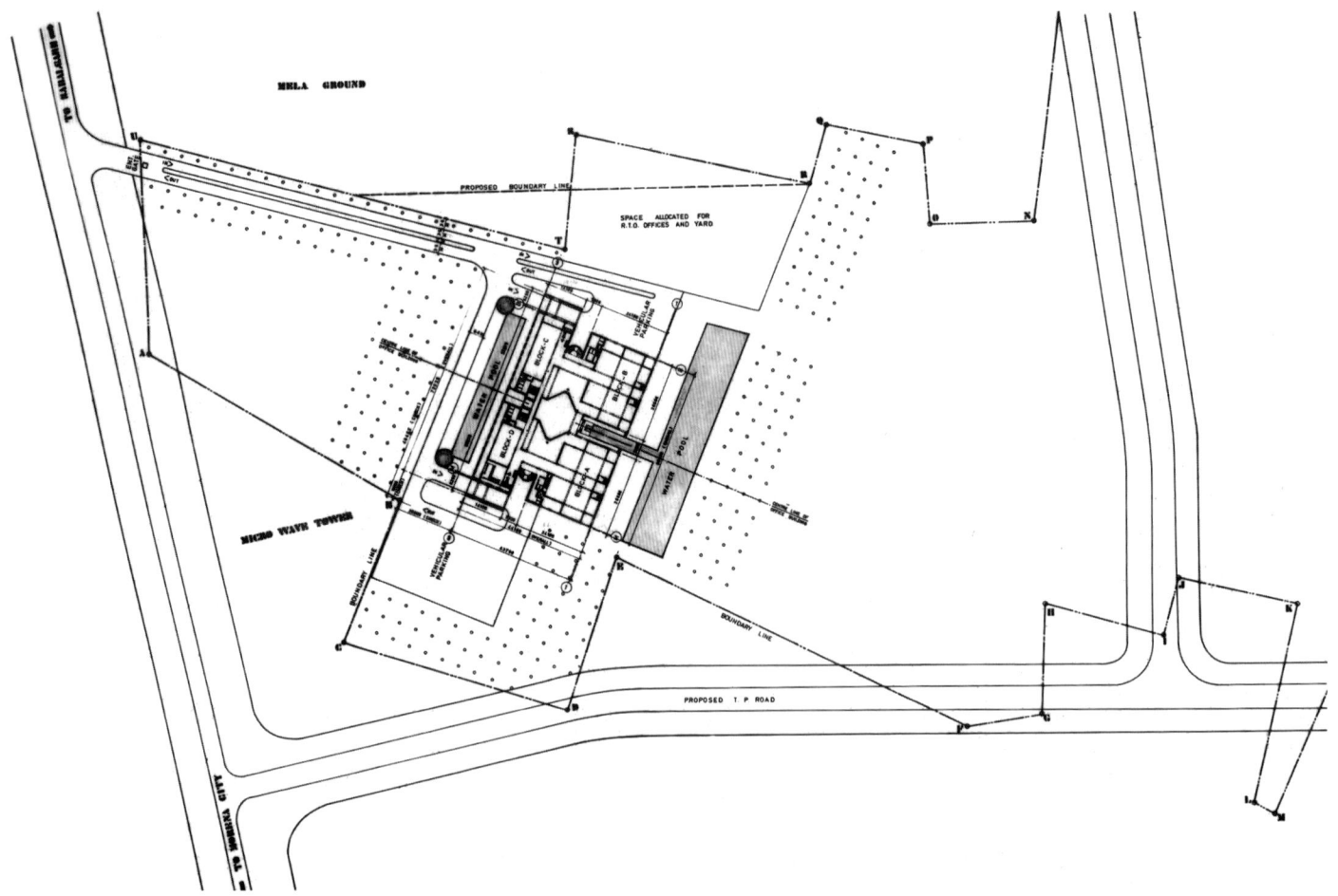

CAR PORCH DRIVE-WAY
L.W.2
OFFICES
L.W.3
OFFICES
L.W.4
ASSEMBLY HALL
L.W.7
OFFICES
L.W.8
OFFICES
L.W.9
CAR PORCH DRIVE-WAY
ELEVATION

CAR PORCH DRIVE-WAY
OFFICES
COURT
OFFICES
CAR PORCH DRIVE-WAY
ELEVATION

BLOCK A
BLOCK B
BLOCK C
BLOCK D
WATER POOL
ASSEMBLY HALL
HALL
HALL
LOBBY
PORCH
CAR PORCH
CAR PORCH
STAIR 1
STAIR 2
STAIR 3
TOILETS 1
TOILETS 2
IRRIGATION OFFICE
CONTROL ROOM AND PROJECT DISPLAY
GUARD ROOM
GROUND FLOOR PLAN

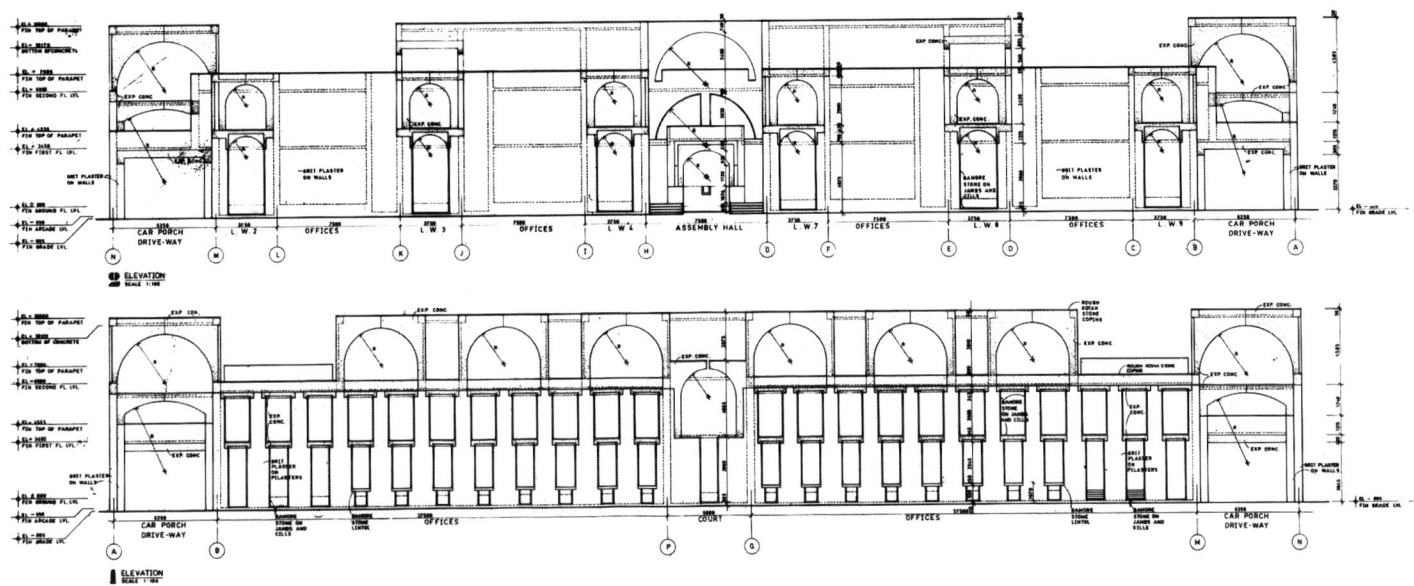

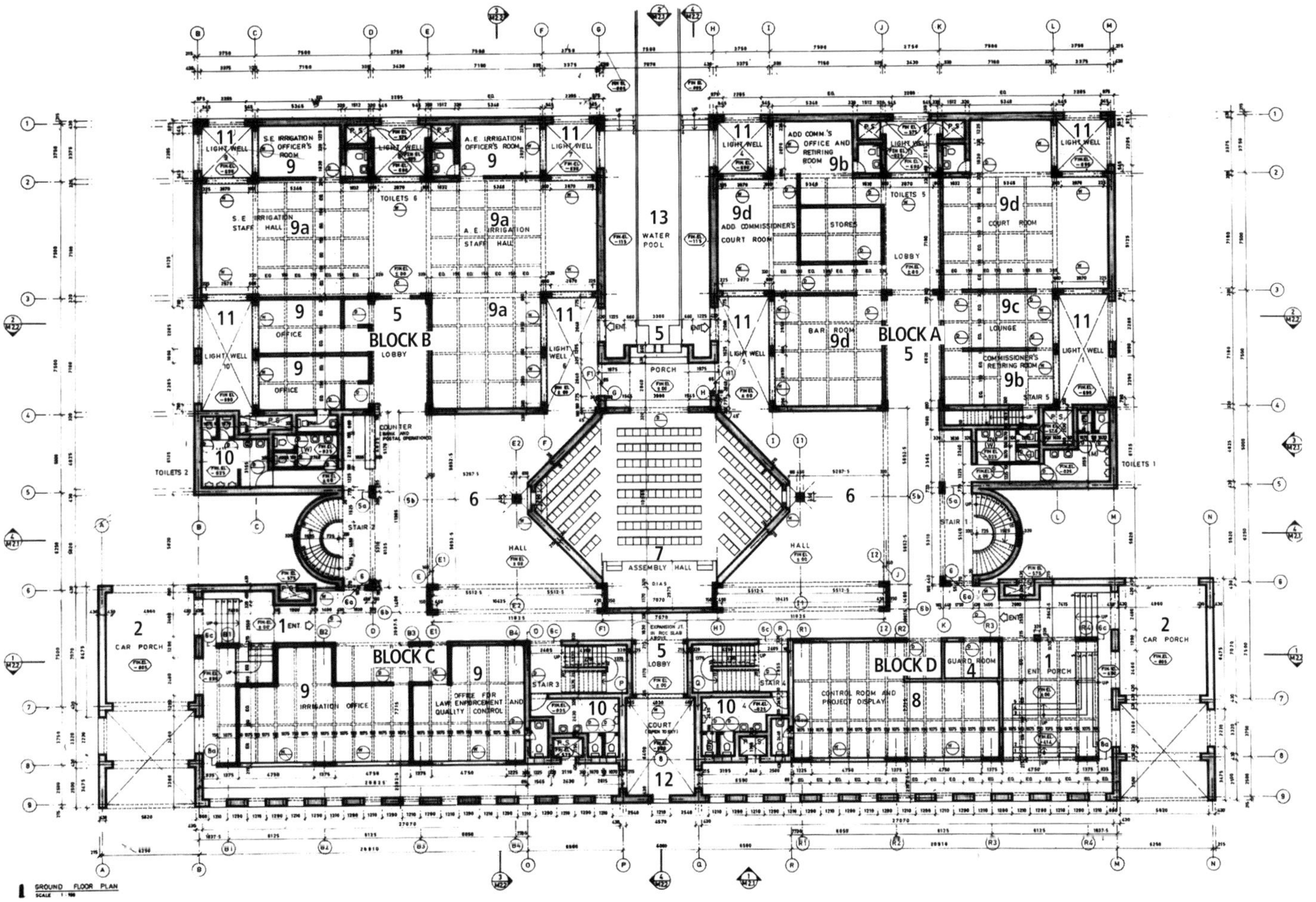

COMMISSIONER'S OFFICE AND WALMI SUBCENTRE, MORENA

Views of process model in wood.

179

^ Public hall, Commissioner's Office, looking from assembly hall across
   the public hall – sketch in pen and ink, September 1984.

> Public hall, Commissioner's Office, looking towards the assembly hall –
   sketch in pen and ink, September 1984.

180

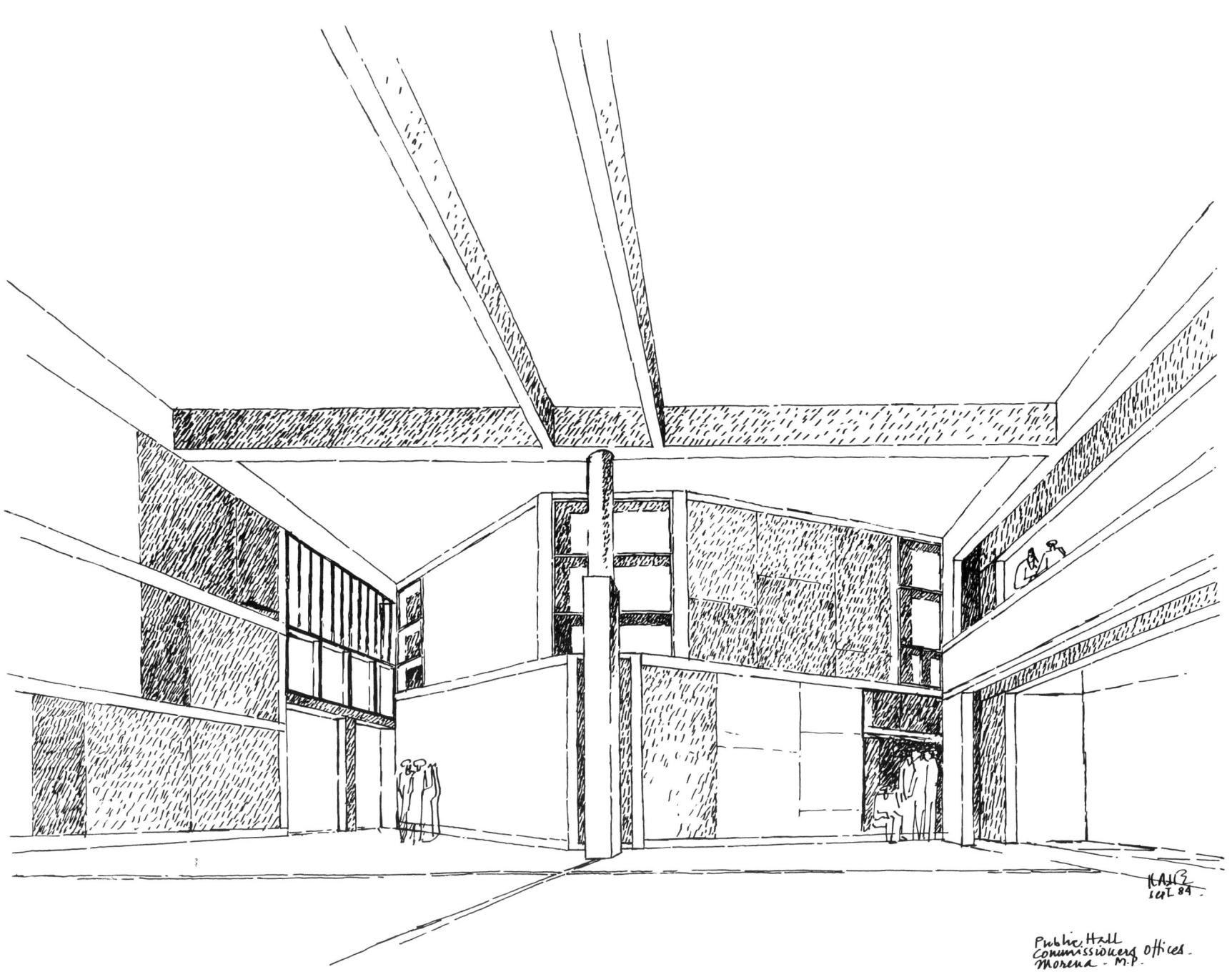

Public Hall
Commissioners Offices.
Morena - M.P.

181

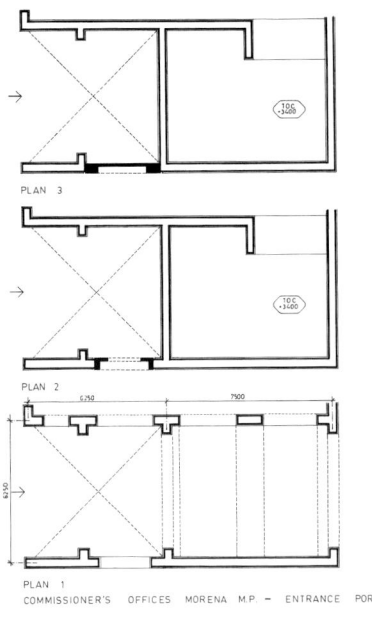

PLAN 3

PLAN 2

PLAN 1
COMMISSIONER'S OFFICES MORENA M.P. — ENTRANCE PORCH

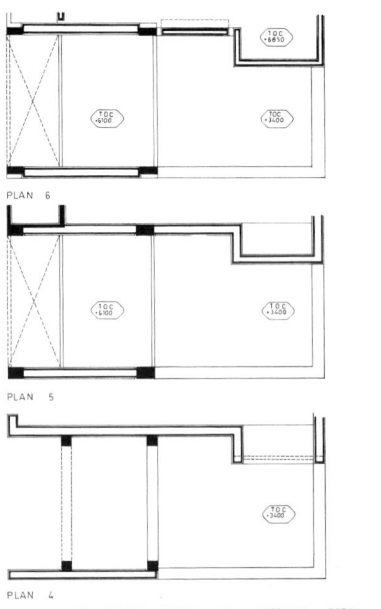

PLAN 6

PLAN 5

PLAN 4
COMMISSIONER'S OFFICES MORENA M.P. ENTRANCE PORCH

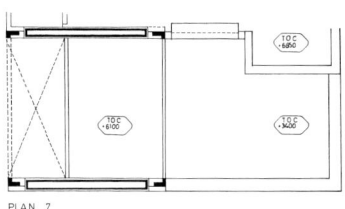

PLAN 7

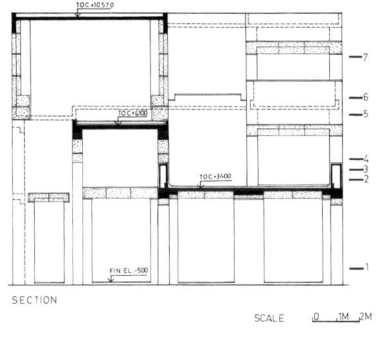

SECTION

SCALE 0 1M 2M

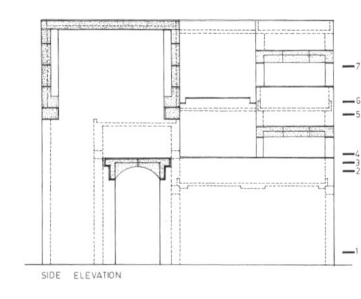

SIDE ELEVATION

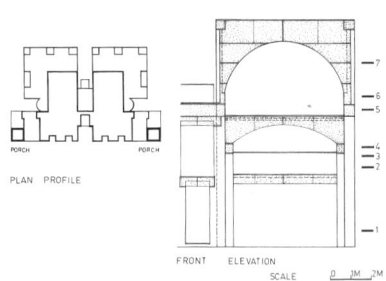

PLAN PROFILE

FRONT ELEVATION

SCALE 0 1M 2M

Development of the entrance porch.

< Plans | Sections | Elevations.

∨ > Study models in wood.

182

WALMI SUBCENTRE, MORENA

Scheme development.

A. Conceptual development, February 1990
Notes on the sketch:
'Very hot and dry in summer. Cold in winter. Impossible to look to the sky ... Hot air throughout night. Double loaded corridor for circulation makes a lot of sense. Screens – jaalis – on top and sides enclosing courts. Architecture of diffused light where sun will have strong light accent in generally diffused interior conditions. Desert cooling system. Sound of water. Moisture present throughout the day. Openings falling into court with screens. Hot air entry will be controlled and therefore entrances to main spaces of circulation – like fort entries – with baffles. Trees planted in groves. Water channels.

B. Proposal, January 1990
Notes on the sketch, from top:
'Living–Eating–Sports ... heavily panted plaza ... working–exhibition–PRO'
'Towards commissioner's offices'
1   Arrival Court
2   Dormitories
3   Lounges
4   Dining + Kitchen
5   Garden
6   Water Pool
7   Gallery
8   Administration
9   Classrooms
10 Museum

C. Proposal I, March 1990 (right)
Notes on the sketch:
'Single rooms for participants. Square classrooms. Smaller court blocked by stair to guest house. Smaller dining hall, stretched longer to kitchen and yard. Common toilets to dorms at the entry to dorms. Main garden isolated from court. Dorm and guest house connected through...'

D. Proposal II, May 1990 (left)
Notes on the sketch:
'Single rooms for participants changed to group dorms. Circular drum around stairs. Classroom low and high heights. Low wall with openings at the main entry. Water pool at guest house. Open to sky court and garden. Driveway along garden through a grove of trees. Court between dorms and school larger ... broader dining hall with veranda and garden.'

E. Central stair studies, March 1990

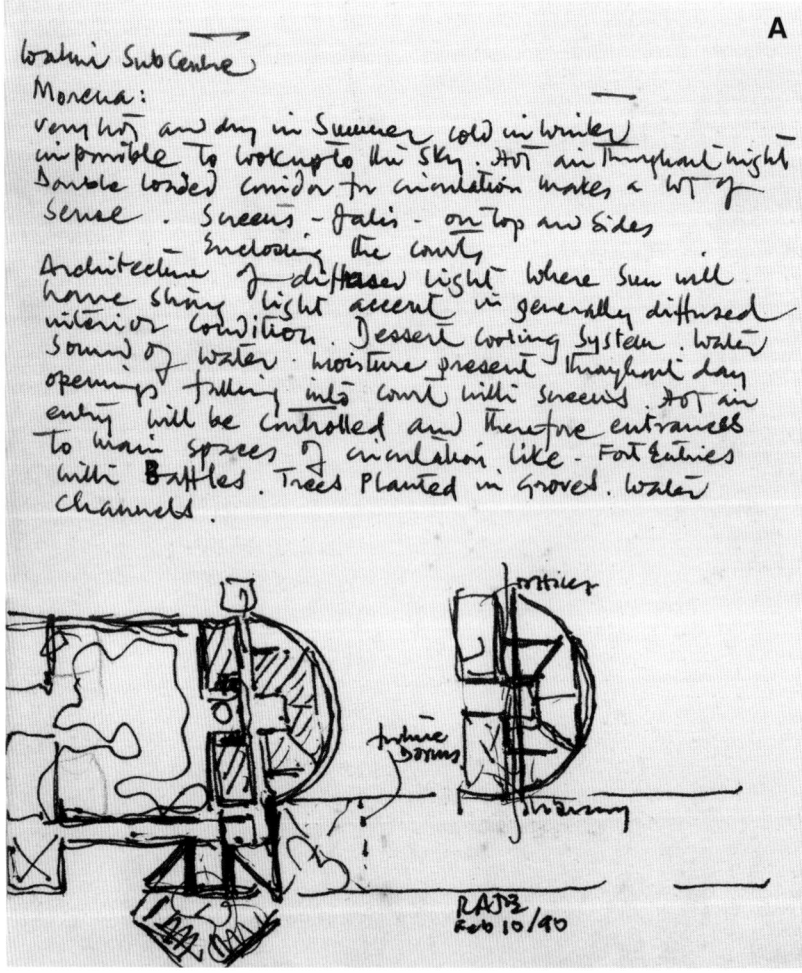

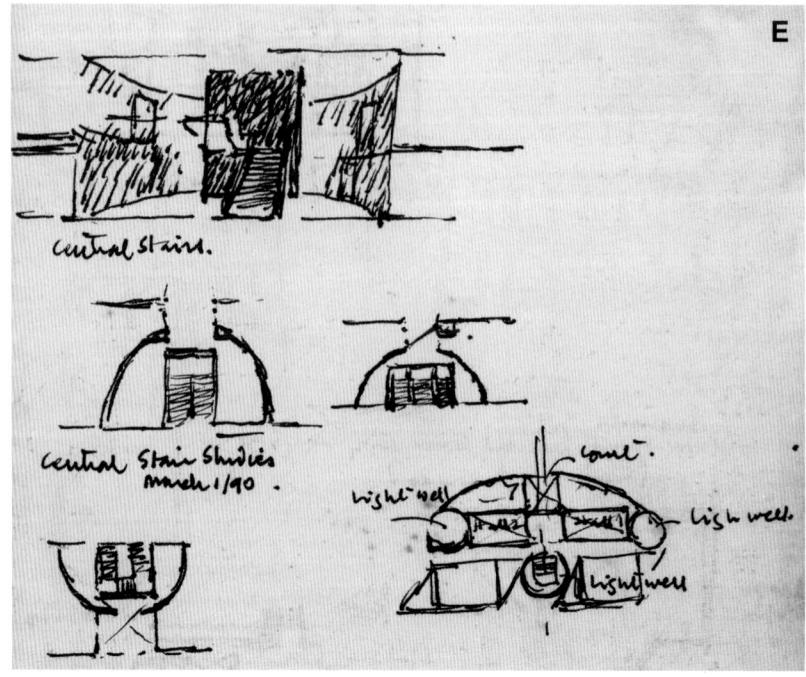

WALMI SUBCENTRE

A Note on the Concept (May 1990)

The plan of the Walmi Subcentre is organized in three segments around an inner courtyard:

Dormitories and Guest House

School and Offices

Dining Hall and Services.

This courtyard, besides helping to cross-ventilate the buildings, helps to keep the learning spaces a little detached from the living quarters. The rooms in the dormitories and guest house face north-northeast, away from the hot afternoon sun, whereas the offices and classrooms are protected and the natural light is filtered through the light wells used to cut the direct glare from the sun. An interior corridor links the main entry with the main court, and serves the classrooms as well as the offices on the ground floor, and the library and the museum on the first floor. The classrooms are designed to have square and rectangular spaces – the square space is double height, while the rectangular spaces are single height with flexible partitions inbetween to make, when required, a large rectangular space between two square spaces. This enlarged space can be used for presentations. An open-to-sky yard is proposed at the back of the classrooms for the cooling plant.

The dormitory is in two parts, one housing 12 beds (6 per floor) and the other housing 8 beds (4 per floor), with common toilets and baths. The beds are arranged to be away from the exterior walls which get heated in summer. The core to each dorm is given to storage, thus keeping natural light and ventilation for the habitable areas. The windows borrow daylight through light wells, cutting down the glare.

The dining hall, on the ground floor, extends on to a walled garden on one side, and on to the veranda on the other.

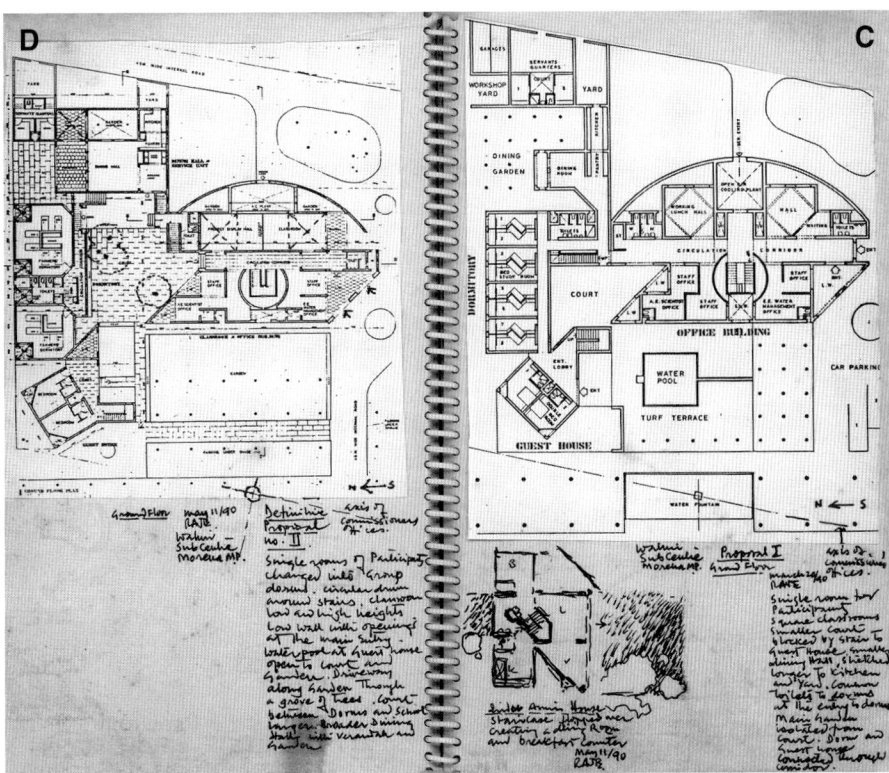

< Walmi Subcentre, external wall studies, February 1990.

> Definitive model in wood.

v Walmi Subcentre, typical dormitory rooms, February 1990.
Notes on the sketch, from top:
'Beds in centre of room to keep them away from walls which are likely to be hot in summer. Writing desks are close to the light.'
'Rooms are narrow and long, shorter side facing the exterior. Single seater for privacy and seclusion.'
'"Z" shape wall next to beds can be made of wooden partition boards to gain extra space. The width of the room to be 7'-6" clear.'

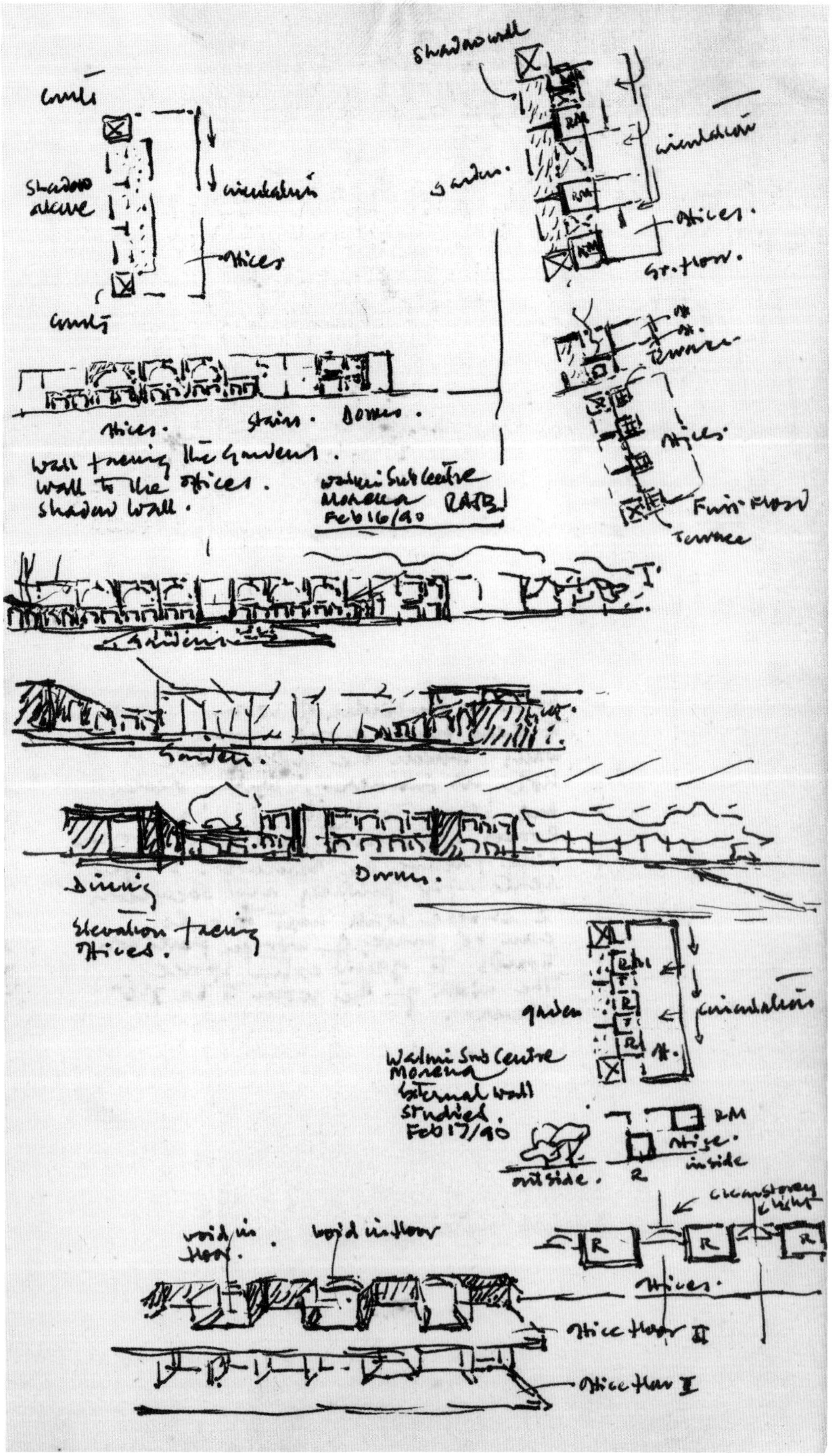

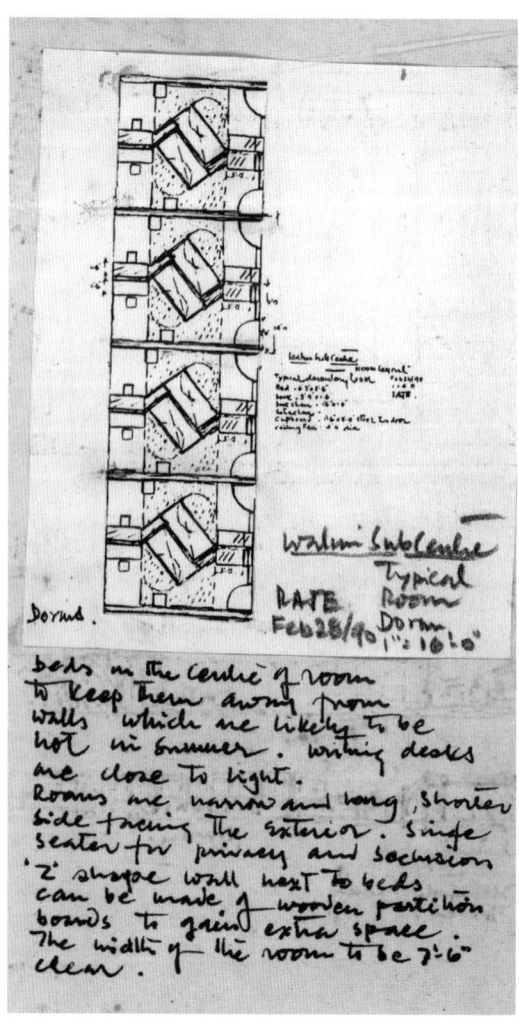

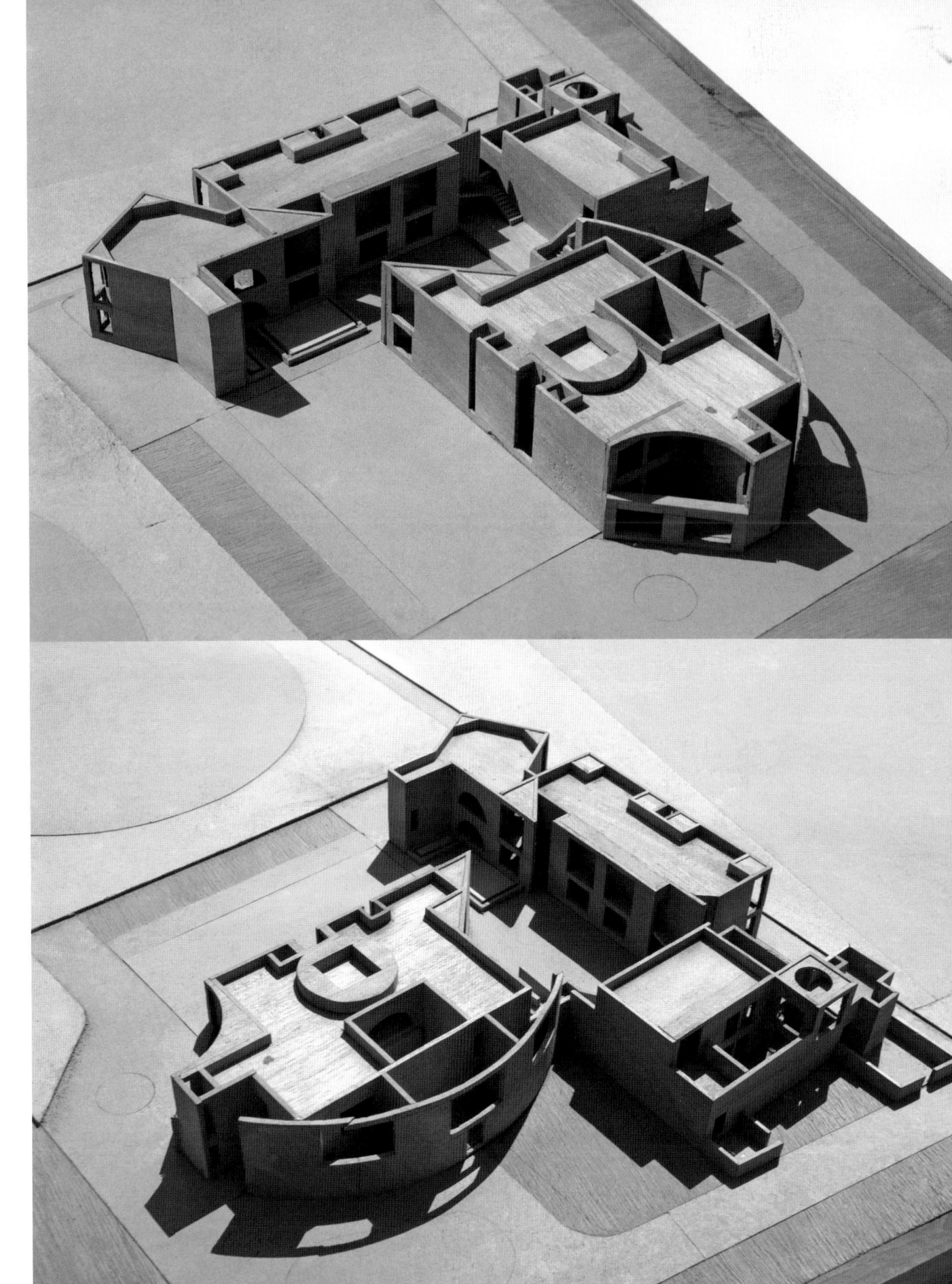

MDP, IIFM, Phase 2,
volume and site,
September 1989.

Indian Institute of Forest Management
Bhopal, Madhya Pradesh, 1988
(Phase 1 completion)

The design of the Indian Institute of Forest Management (IIFM) in Bhopal is inspired by the belief that institutions are self-contained entities whose growth is nurtured by a process of self-renewal through the various stages of their development.

The plan of the Institute depicts a set of space requirements for various activities. The complex should be architecturally interpreted as a homogenous entity rather than as separately identified buildings for specific functions on distinct territories. This perception of continuity mitigates isolationist tendencies and eases progress towards academic and social interactions, both of which are hallmarks of a successful and adaptive institute. To this end, the plan attempts to create a sense of community without contradicting the student's need for individuality.

The 65-hectare site is open and rises approximately 50 metres from the lower road level on a hill plateau, and is heavily contoured on the western and southern sides while the eastern side has gradual slopes.

The major axis runs north–south, and the main circulation spine is located on this axis. The plan of the academic area focuses on the academic and research offices that form the crucial inner core, located equidistant from administrative offices on one side and teaching spaces on the other. In place of a continuous narrow corridor, individual lobbies serve as 'stop-off' meeting spaces, opening towards the courts.

The hillside is crowned by the academic complex and is marked by the presence of a compact, cohesive group of buildings which constitute the working zone. This area flows along the flat contours providing a linear form capable of extensions along the other side of the promenade.

The buildings which form the academic court area contain large and small classrooms, and the library, auditorium and seminar rooms. No building other than the library is expected to be more than two storeys high. The library is a four-storeyed building, a strong focal point and a symbolic anchor of the academic court. The amphitheatre, with a capacity of 750, is planned for a multitude of activities: speeches, music performances or film screenings.

The living zone consists of dormitories, food service and dining, and other spaces for meetings and congregation. Student dormitories are located at the southern tip of the academic complex. Each unit consists of one house for ten students. Each house has a living room as a social centre at the terrace level, which captures the view of the distant lakes on the horizon; the bedroom–study areas provide privacy and individual space for each student.

All the dormitories are on the southern slopes, oriented towards the Bhopal lakes, in close proximity to the library within the academic complex. The rows of trees between the student dormitories and the academic complex create a buffer zone, besides providing shaded walkways connecting groups of dormitories.

The main features of the site are two hillocks with outcrops of slate stone. As a counterpoint to the natural features, deep bands of native trees are expected to shade the walkways and certain areas of the court, once fully grown. Water bodies, dispersed all over the site, carry water in narrow channels to the green areas. A water reservoir on top of one of the hillocks gives a strong focus to the landscape.

The entire campus is constructed of brick masonry load-bearing walls for the external enclosure of spaces, and reinforced concrete for the internal frame structure, offering inner flexibility for arrangement of desired layouts of furniture and equipment, and to relieve the external walls of heavy loads.

Shahi Mahal, Mandu, April 1986.

The openings that receive operable windows are recessed into shadow pockets and these pockets become the dominant architectural features, controlling and directing the scale and proportion throughout the complex. Reinforced concrete flat and arch lintels are standardized on the basis of how much they span, and are left exposed.

The areas around the light openings are clad in thin rough Kotah stone and thin slate, in bluish green to purple hues. The remaining part of the exterior masonry wall surfaces is plastered with stone-washed aggregate grit. The courts between buildings are paved with stone or landscaped to provide as much shade as possible.

The course-stone masonry retaining walls make either terraces or stairs as transfer points to circulate on various levels of courts. The open end of the courts face the prevailing southwest wind direction, so as to provide cross-ventilation through the interior spaces of the buildings.

In healing the land post-construction, it was observed that replanting was often not the best course of action; it was found more appropriate to leave it alone. This is the basis of the Bradley method of bio-aesthetic land rehabilitation, where little is done except for the removal of certain exotic weeds and the protection of land from disturbance. This was the basis for the landscaping of the entire site, interspersed on the slopes with earth bunds to capture rain water run-off.

191

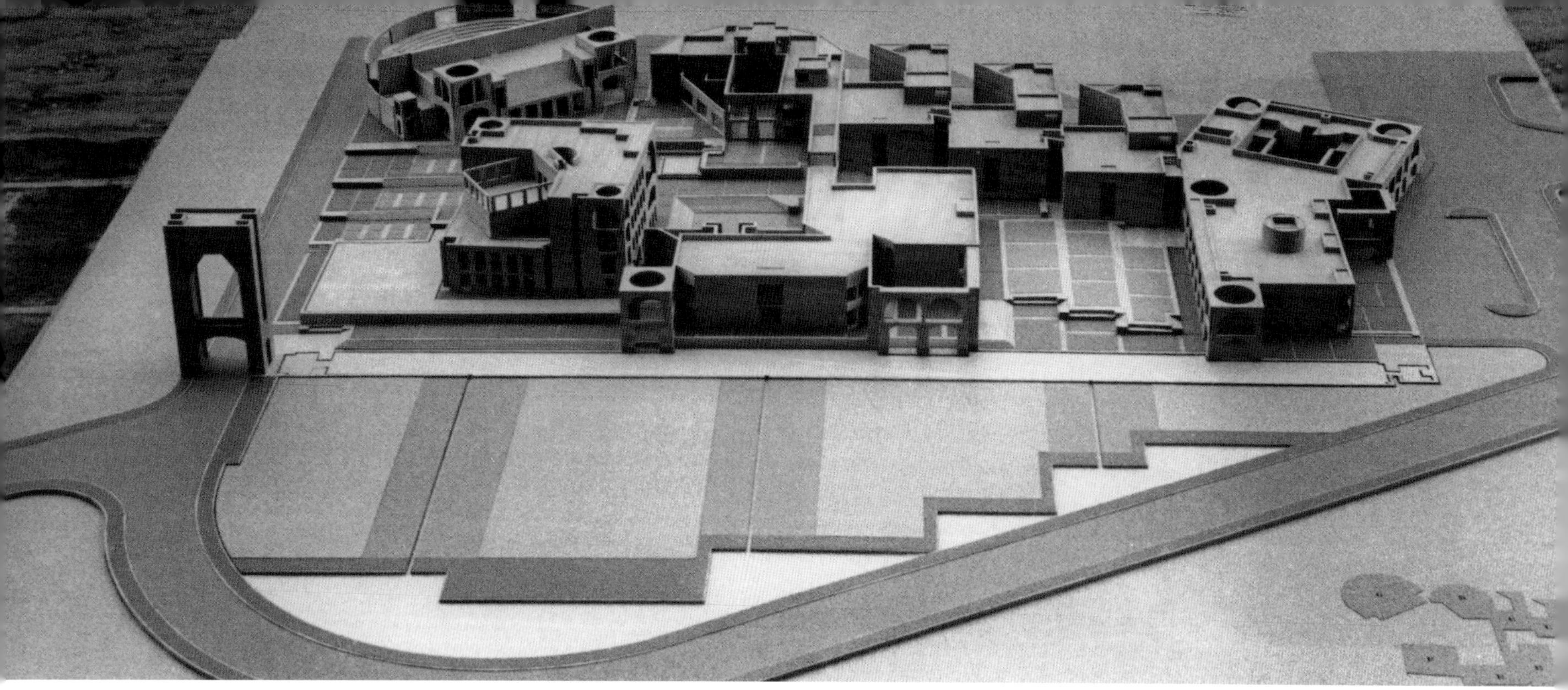

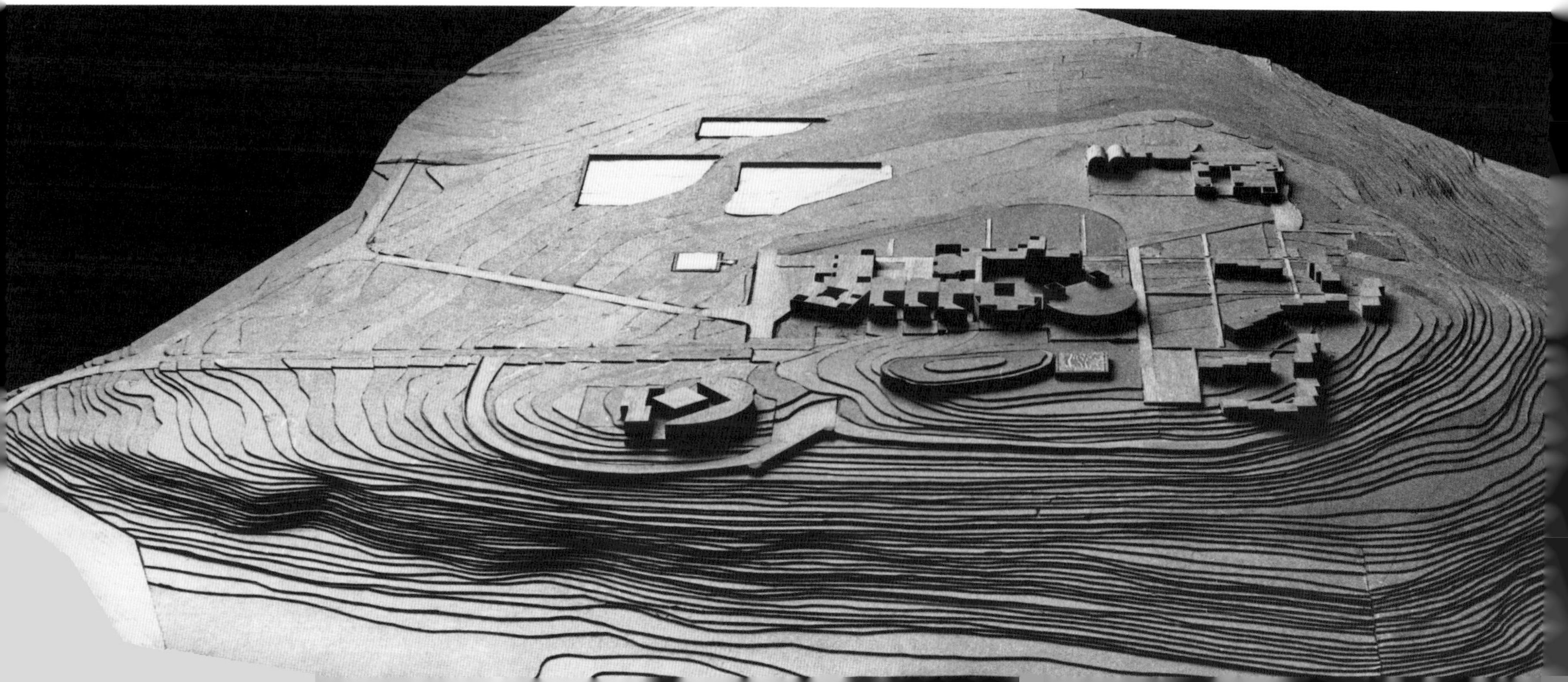

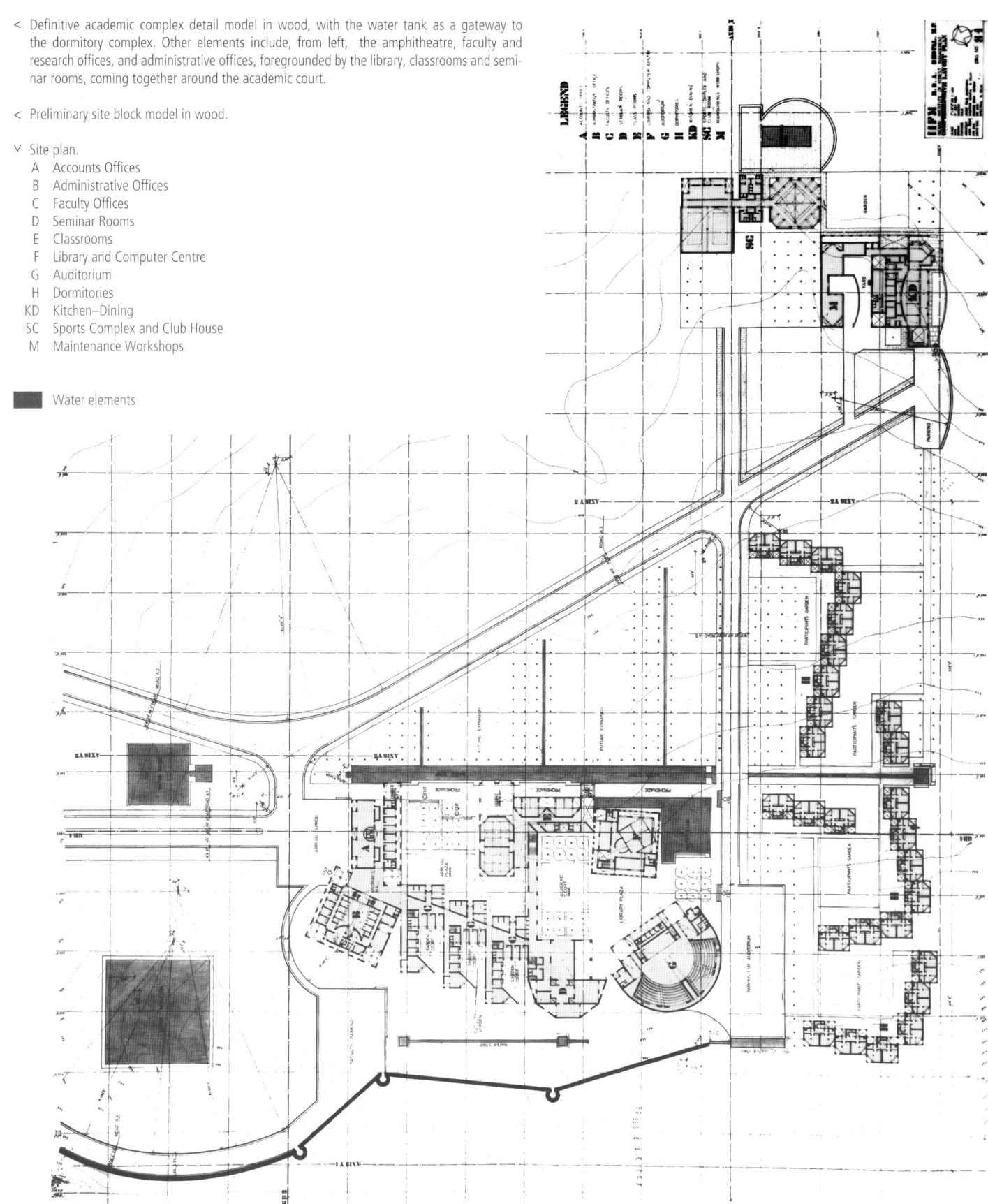

< Definitive academic complex detail model in wood, with the water tank as a gateway to the dormitory complex. Other elements include, from left, the amphitheatre, faculty and research offices, and administrative offices, foregrounded by the library, classrooms and seminar rooms, coming together around the academic court.

< Preliminary site block model in wood.

∨ Site plan.
A   Accounts Offices
B   Administrative Offices
C   Faculty Offices
D   Seminar Rooms
E   Classrooms
F   Library and Computer Centre
G   Auditorium
H   Dormitories
KD Kitchen–Dining
SC Sports Complex and Club House
M   Maintenance Workshops

Water elements

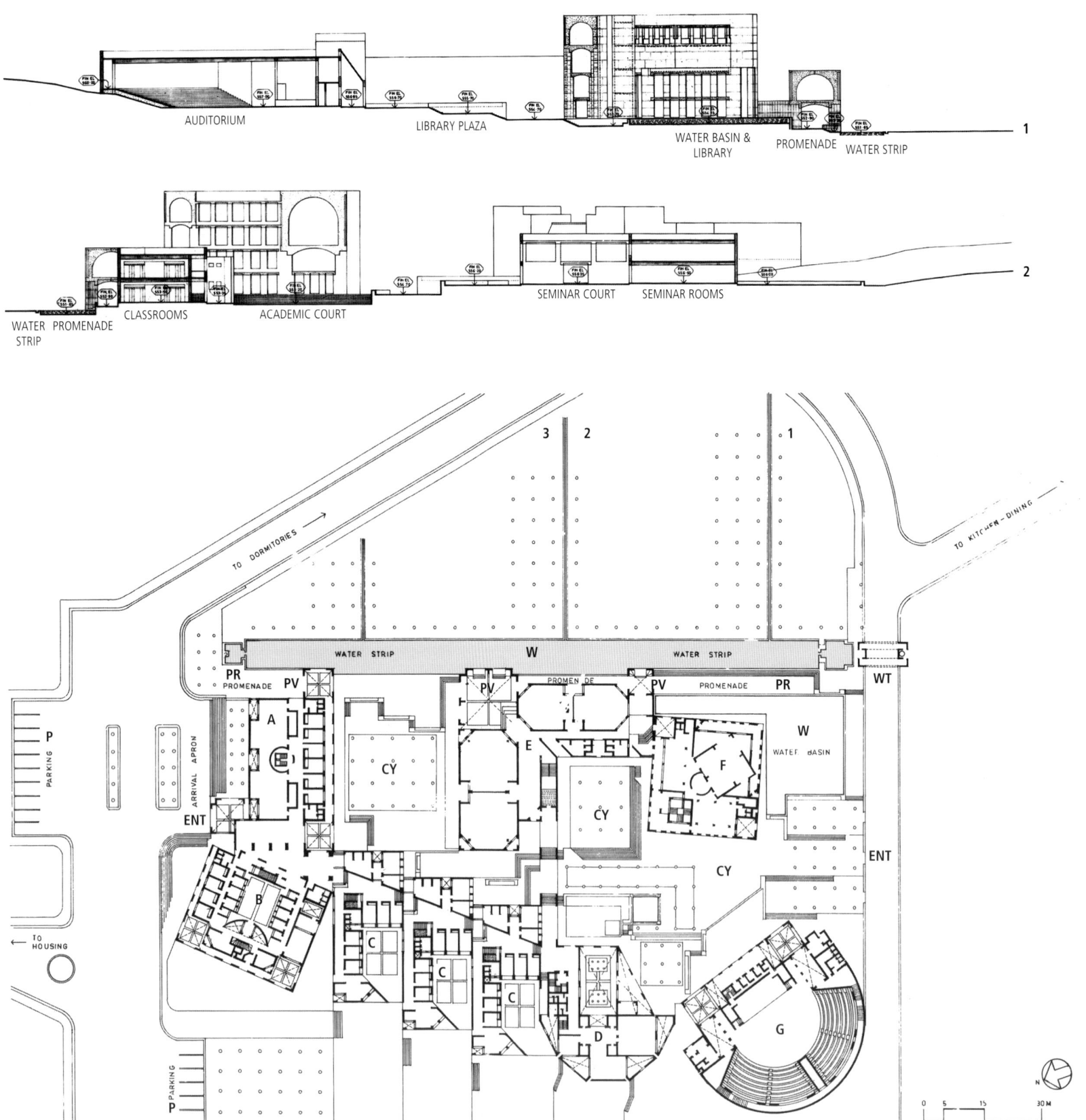

AUDITORIUM   LIBRARY PLAZA   WATER BASIN &   PROMENADE   WATER STRIP   1
                                                         LIBRARY

WATER PROMENADE   CLASSROOMS   ACADEMIC COURT   SEMINAR COURT   SEMINAR ROOMS   2
STRIP

< Sections, academic complex.

< Ground floor plan, academic
complex.
- A   Accounts offices
- B   Administrative offices
- C   Faculty offices
- D   Seminar rooms
- E   Classrooms
- F   Library and computer centre
- G   Auditorium
- ENT   Entry
- CY   Courtyard/Plaza
- PV   Pavilion
- PR   Promenade
- W   Water
- WT   Water tank
- P   Parking

> Promenade and water strip from the
water tank.

The promenade and pavilions along the
water is a major feature from where
the land slopes down. The rain water is
collected at the promenade water strip,
and the overflows go down the hill into
the native vegetation.

Entrance Court To Auditorium - Library from
Dormitories

Indian Institute of forest Management
Bhopal MP.

RAJE
AUG 84

∧ Promenade porches and pavilions, with exposed concrete and slate used for elements of light. Retaining walls of rough Kotah stone.

> Entrances from the pedestrian promenade along the water strip. Pen and ink sketch, August 1984.

Indian Institute of forest Management
Bhopal M.P.
Entrances from the Pedestrian
Promenade

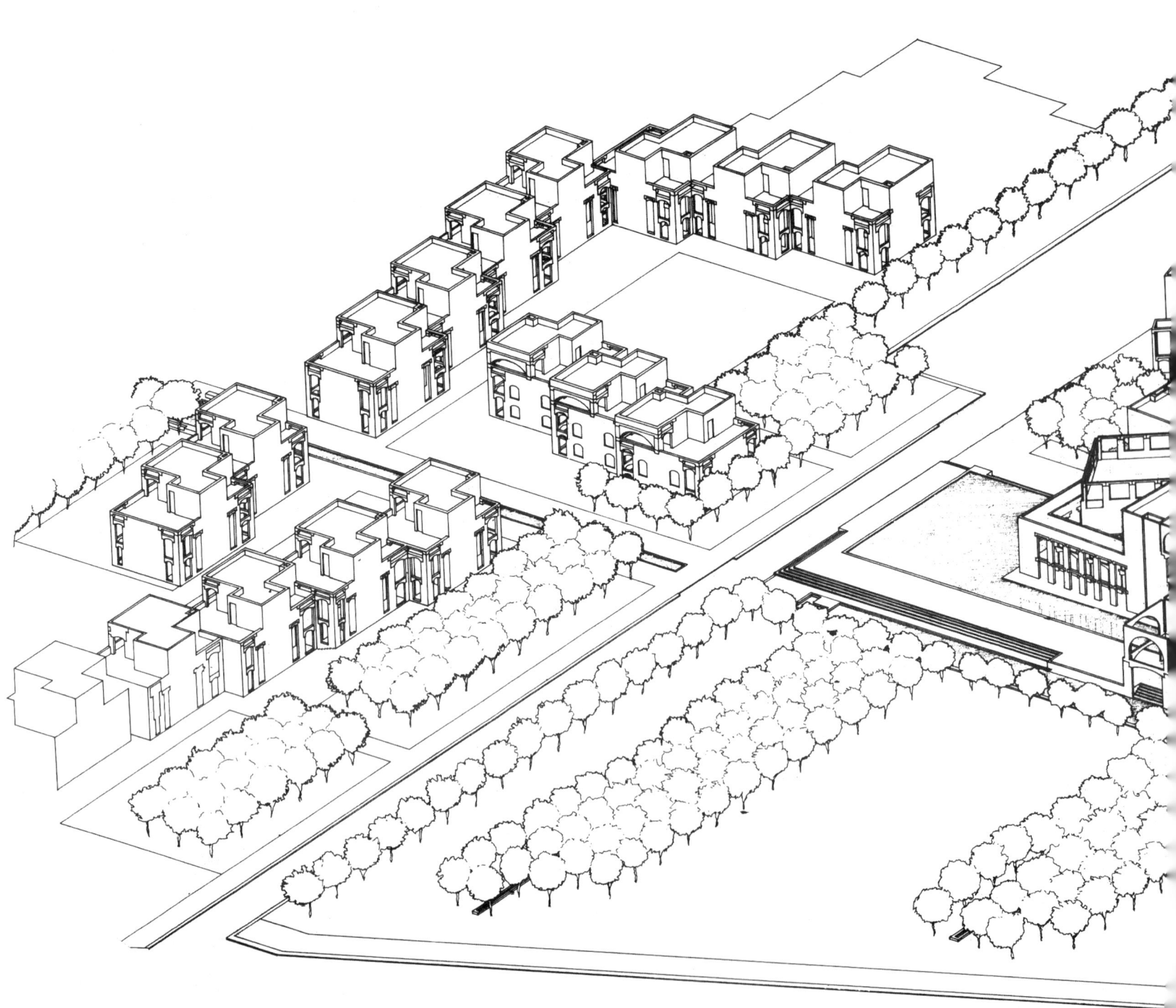

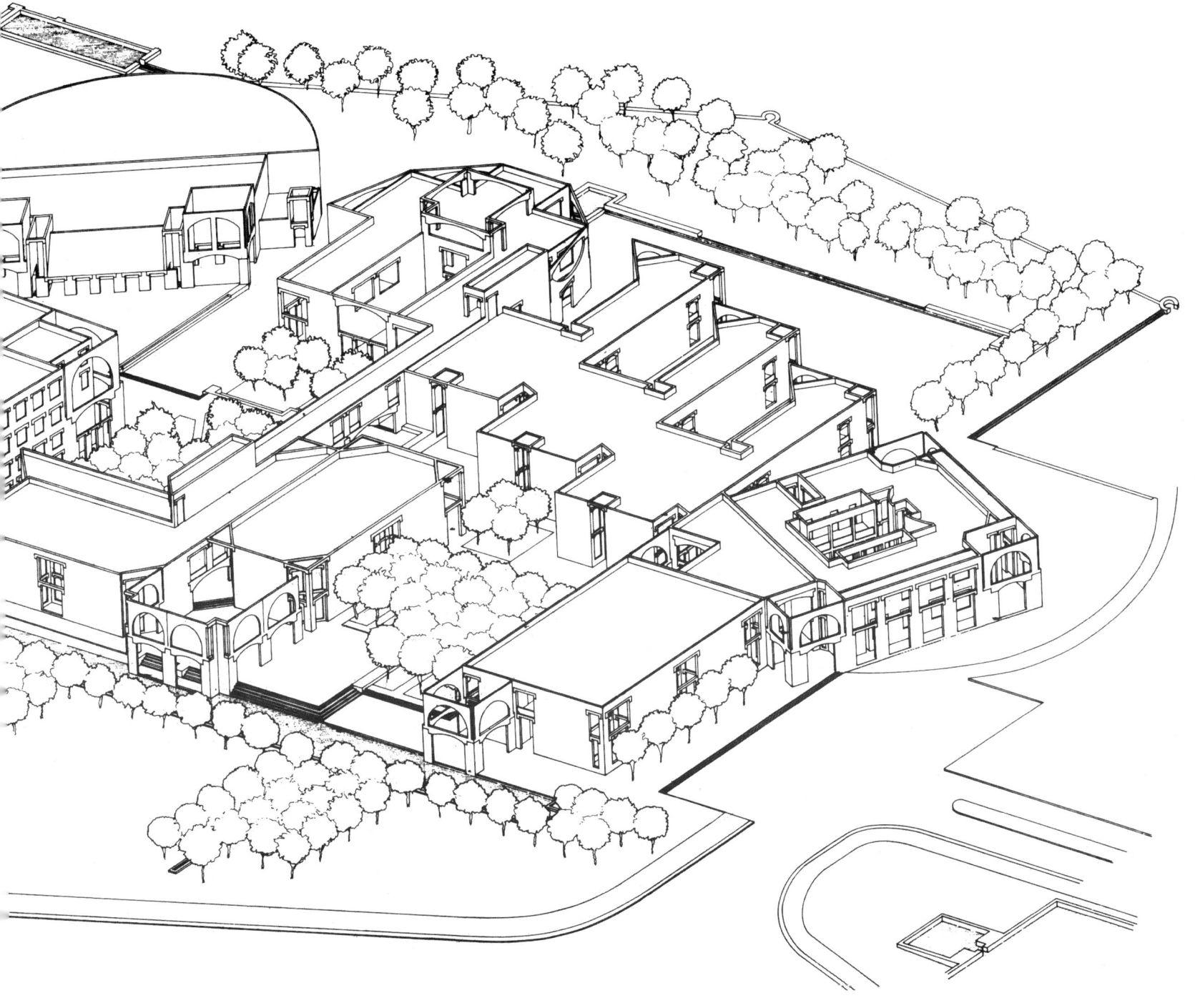

Southwest view of academic buildings from regenerated landscape.

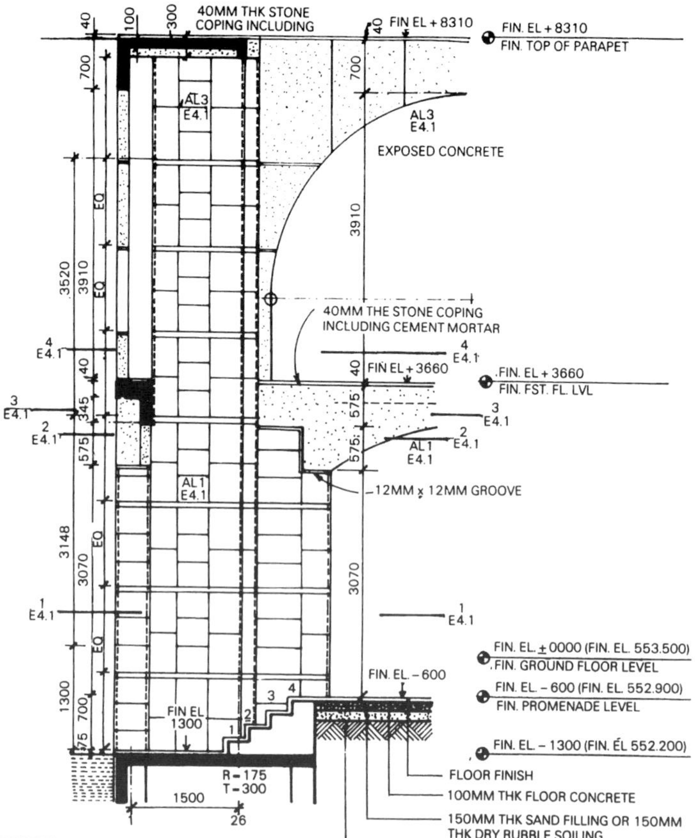

SECTION

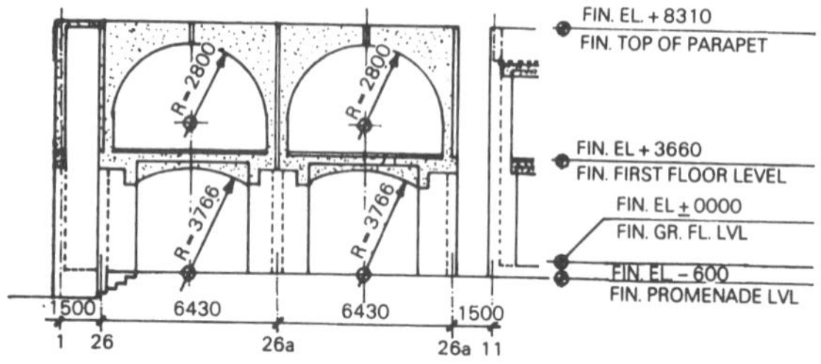

40MM THK STONE COPING INCLUDING

FIN EL + 8310

FIN. EL + 8310
FIN. TOP OF PARAPET

AL3
E4.1

AL3
E4.1

EXPOSED CONCRETE

40MM THE STONE COPING INCLUDING CEMENT MORTAR

4
E4.1

FIN EL + 3660

FIN. EL + 3660
FIN. FST. FL. LVL

3
E4.1

2
E4.1

AL1
E4.1

12MM x 12MM GROOVE

AL1
E4.1

1
E4.1

1
E4.1

FIN. EL ± 0000 (FIN. EL. 553.500)
FIN. GROUND FLOOR LEVEL

FIN. EL – 600

FIN. EL – 600 (FIN. EL. 552.900)
FIN. PROMENADE LEVEL

FIN EL 1300

FIN. EL – 1300 (FIN. EL 552.200)

FLOOR FINISH

100MM THK FLOOR CONCRETE

150MM THK SAND FILLING OR 150MM THK DRY RUBBLE SOILING

EARTH FILLING

R – 175
T – 300

1500

26

SECTION

ELEVATION

R – 2800
R – 2800
R – 3766
R – 3766

FIN. EL. + 8310
FIN. TOP OF PARAPET

FIN. EL + 3660
FIN. FIRST FLOOR LEVEL

FIN. EL ± 0000
FIN. GR. FL. LVL

FIN. EL – 600
FIN. PROMENADE LVL

1500   6430   6430   1500
1 26   26a   26a 11

ELEVATION

ELEVATION

R – 2800
R – 2800
R – 3766
R – 3766

FIN. EL. + 8310
FIN. TOP OF PARAPET

FIN. EL + 3660
FIN. FST FL LVL

FIN. EL ± 0000
FIN. GR. FL. LVL

FIN. EL – 600
FIN. PROMENADE LVL

EL – 1300

1500   6430   6430   1500
L K3   K2   K1 K

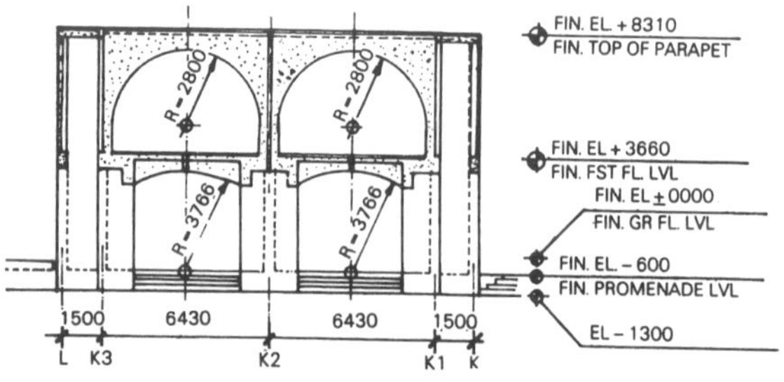

ELEVATION

PLAN GROUND FLOOR PAVILION – 2

8
E4.1

K K1   6430   K2   6430   K3 L

1500   1500

DN   DN

AL1
E4.1

27   27

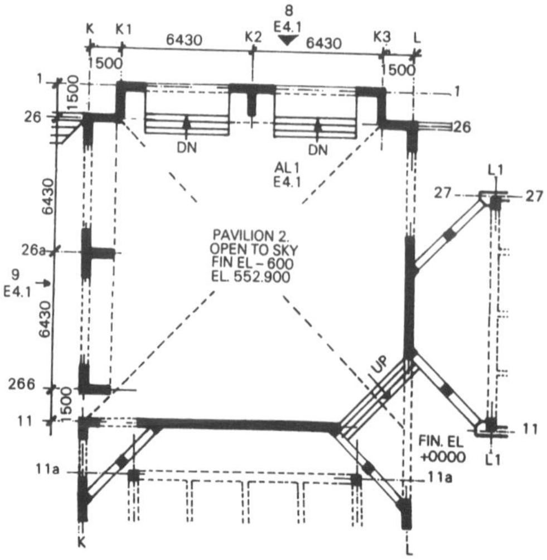

PAVILION 2.
OPEN TO SKY
FIN EL – 600
EL. 552.900

UP

FIN. EL
+0000

11   11

PLAN GROUND FLOOR PAVILION – 2

204

< Construction details at the arch and the finishing materials used in the spatial compositions of the Institute.

∨ Promenade pavilions silhouetted against the openness of the valley.

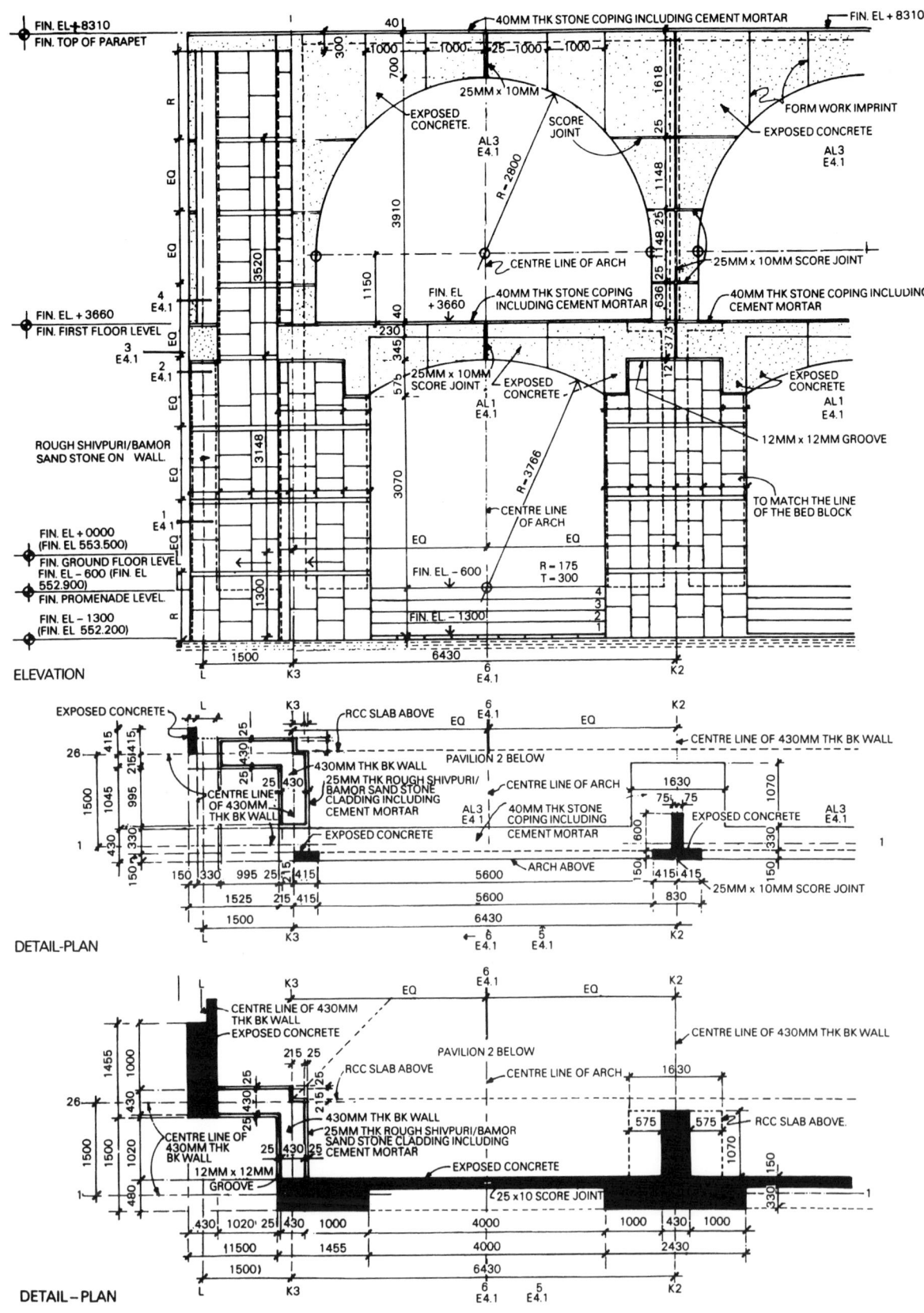

ELEVATION

DETAIL-PLAN

DETAIL-PLAN

∧ The meeting of two sides of the pavilion, and the making of a corner.

< Details at typical pavilion corner.

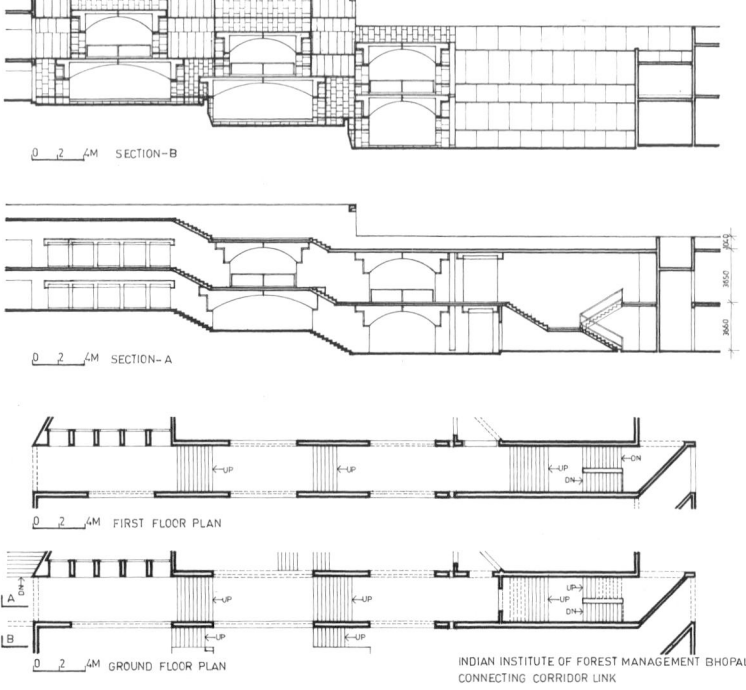

^ Entrance to main foyer from entrance court.

< Drawings of the bridge connecting different parts of the campus.

> Detail at the meeting of the bridge and adjacent building.

0 2 4M   SECTION-B

0 2 4M   SECTION-A

0 2 4M   FIRST FLOOR PLAN

0 2 4M   GROUND FLOOR PLAN

INDIAN INSTITUTE OF FOREST MANAGEMENT BHOPAL(M.P.)
CONNECTING CORRIDOR LINK

> Corner of the library, showing the transition of the structure from the top to the bottom. There is a certain amount of weight that one finds at the bottom and an attempt to shed that weight as one ascends.

∨ Construction drawings, library.
Ground floor plan | First floor plan.

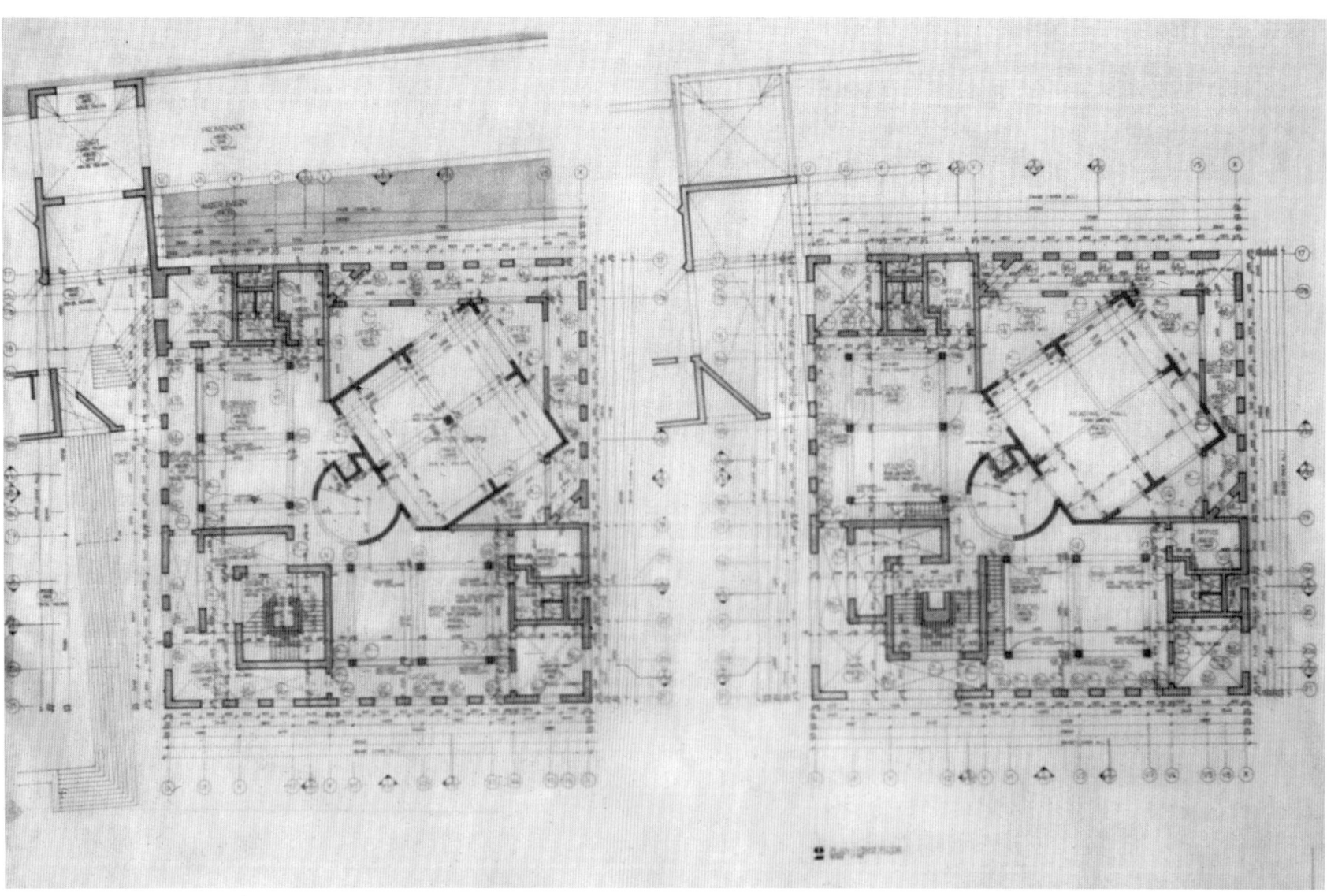

> Large rectangular frames define the pavilions located on either end of the dining hall verandah. The circulation is juxtaposed by experiences and the forms.

> Views of the dining halls and verandah overlooking the valley.

∨ Construction drawings, kitchen–dining.
Ground floor plan | First floor plan.

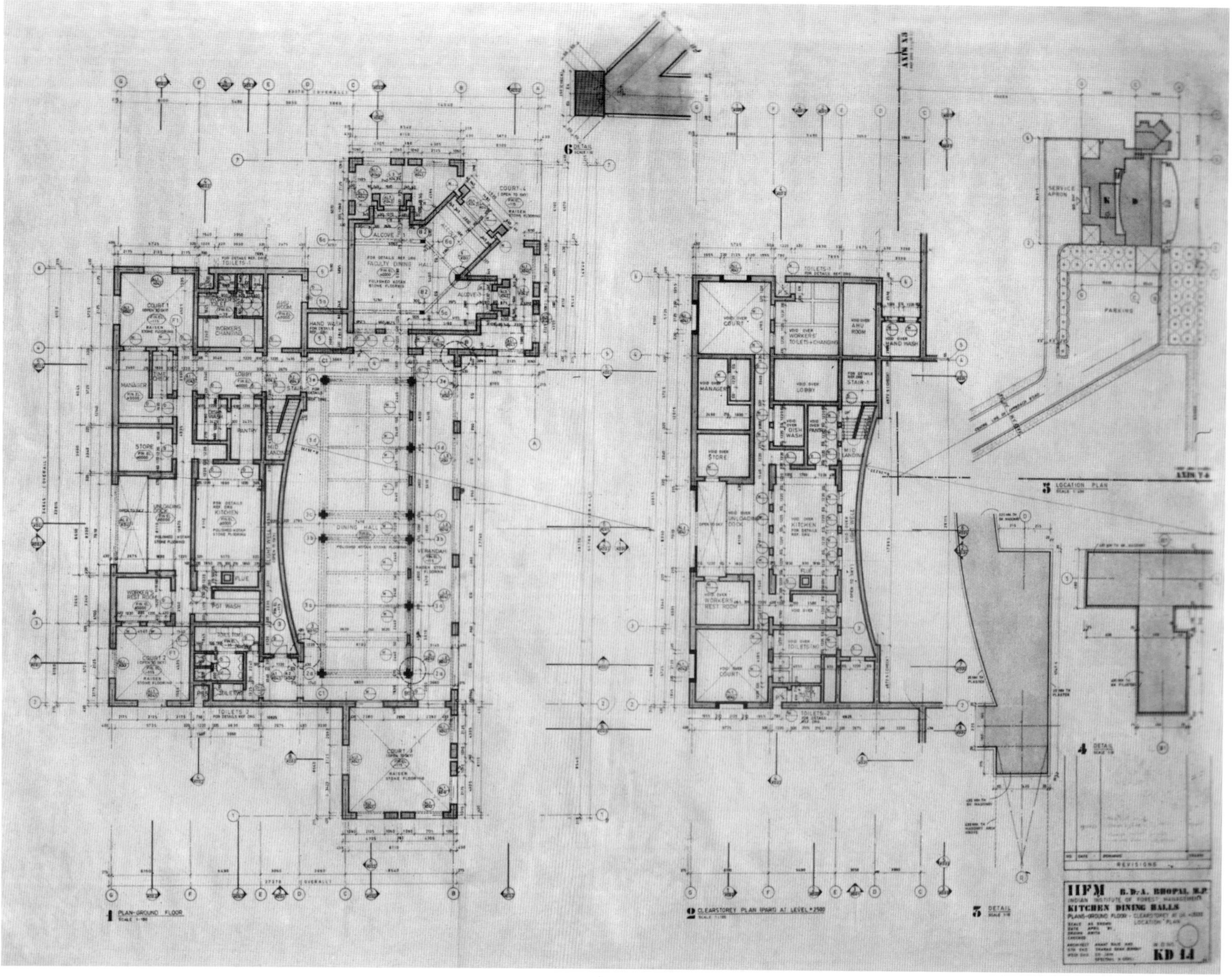

> Student dormitories.

∨ Construction drawings. Student dormitories.

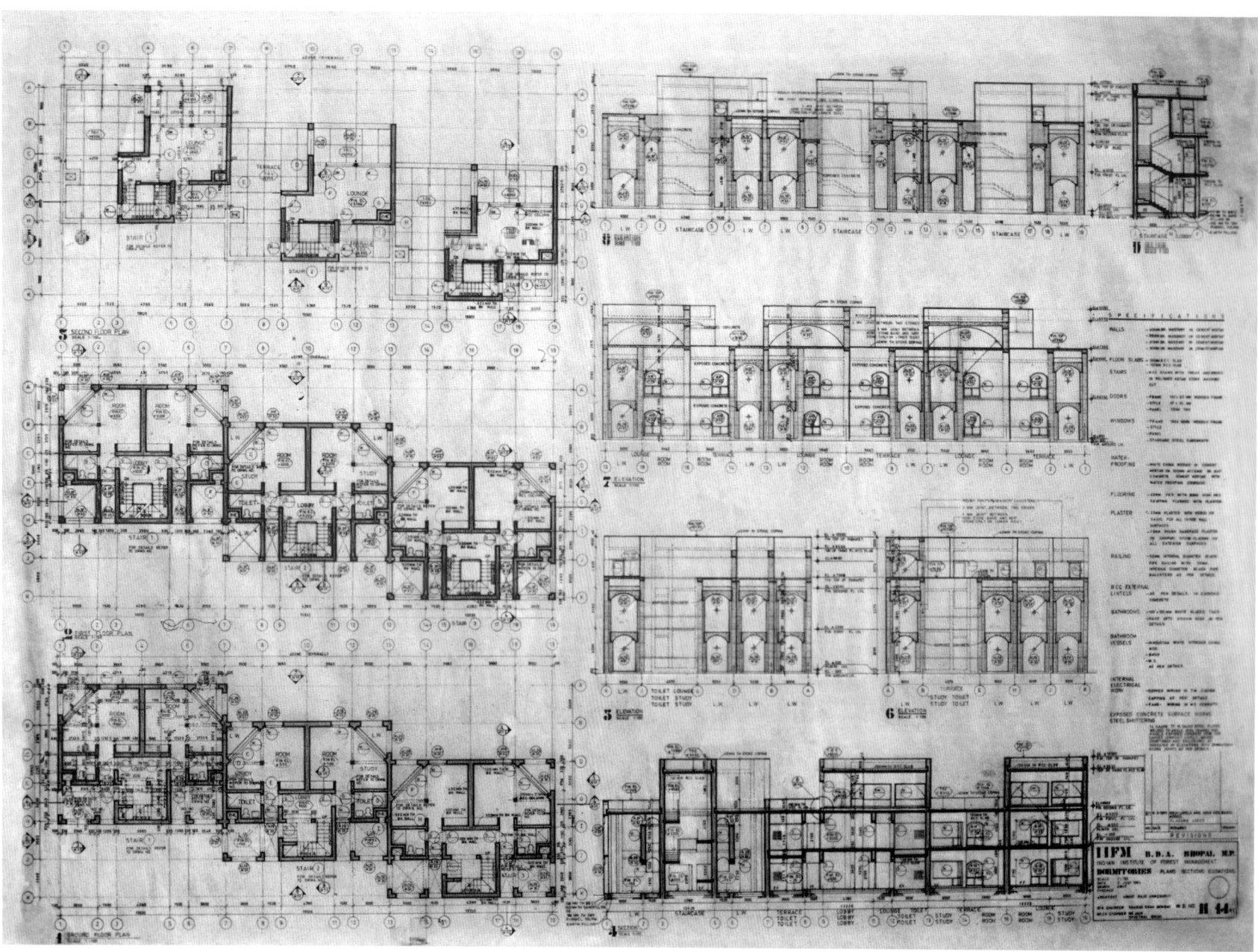

> Court within the student dormitories.

∨ Student dormitories.

Gas Tragedy Victims Memorial
Bhopal, Madhya Pradesh
(unbuilt)

The memorial is not in the form of a solid mass of a structure, but is an open, three-sided, walled pavilion overlooking the Bada Talav lake and Bhopal. The whole idea was to intentionally move away from the site of the tragedy at the Union Carbide factories on to a more serene hilltop that would be a fitting setting to contemplate and reflect.

The memorial site extends to two relationships: the ramp that ascends to the pavilion is in axis with a Shiva temple on the lake. As you turn around to enter the pavilion chamber, the axis shifts in the direction of Mecca, acknowledging the majority of the victims who were Muslim. I dedicated this particular place to them, even though it is a place that belongs to everybody. By rotating it, I brought about an acknowledgment of the religious sentiments of a particular community.

The other parts of the site were left untouched intentionally; water flows down the rocky hill in the monsoons and the mosses that form on these rocks change colour seasonally, making for a wonderful landscape for the site.

Within the interior of the pavilion chamber is a podium with white flowering trees, as a memorial not only to the people, but also to the birds and insects. Everyone should participate. The sense of white is acceptable in many communities.

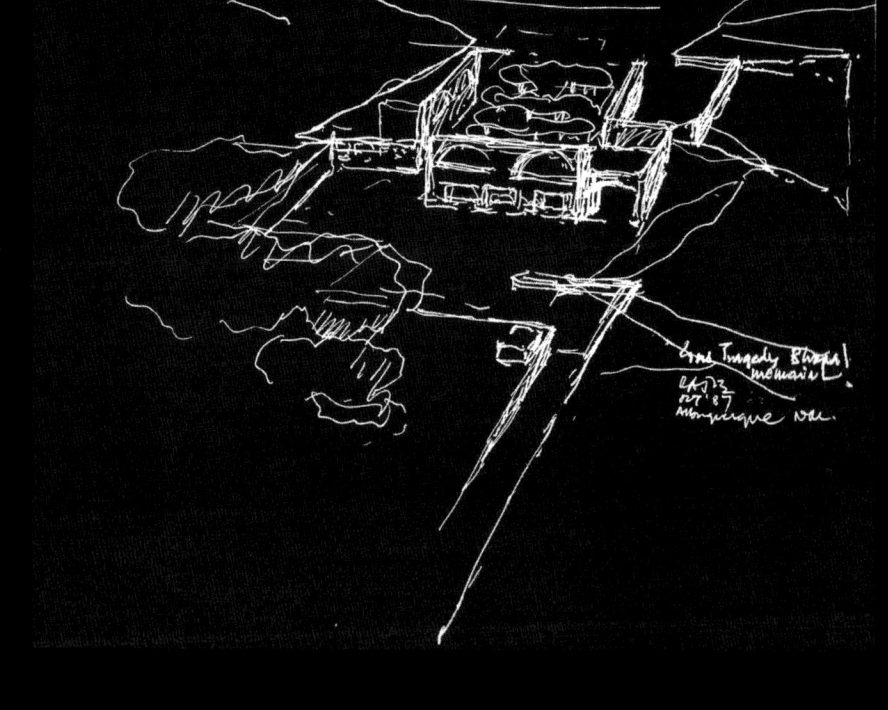

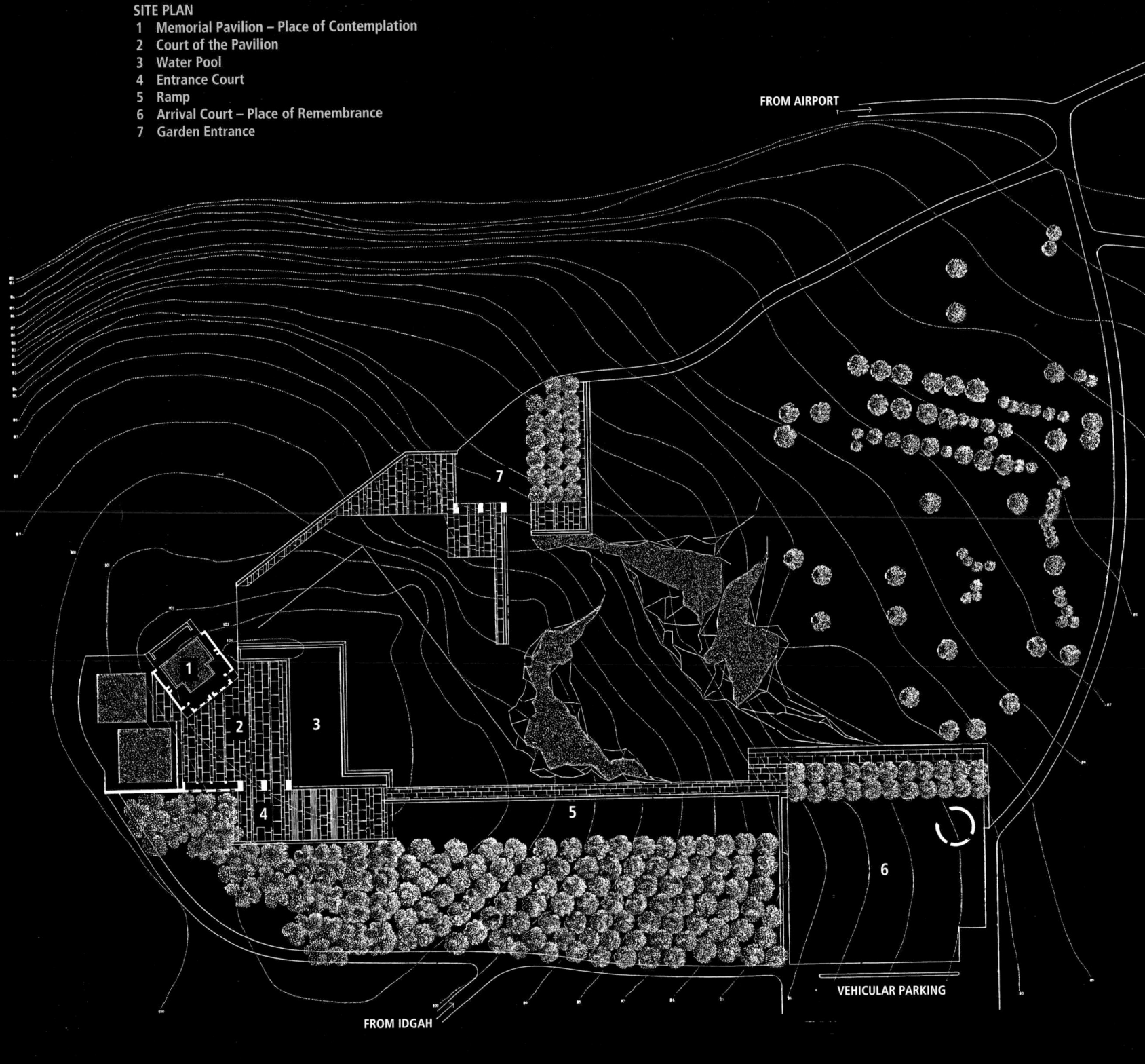

SITE PLAN
1   Memorial Pavilion – Place of Contemplation
2   Court of the Pavilion
3   Water Pool
4   Entrance Court
5   Ramp
6   Arrival Court – Place of Remembrance
7   Garden Entrance

FROM AIRPORT

7

1

2   3

4

5

6

VEHICULAR PARKING

FROM IDGAH

Amphitheatre
and the wall
Gandhagiri Memorial

Sketches describing the interior space of the pavilion chamber.

< Amphitheatre and the Wall, Gas Tragedy Memorial, October 1987.

∨ The Temple of Trees, Gas Tragedy Memorial, June 1987.

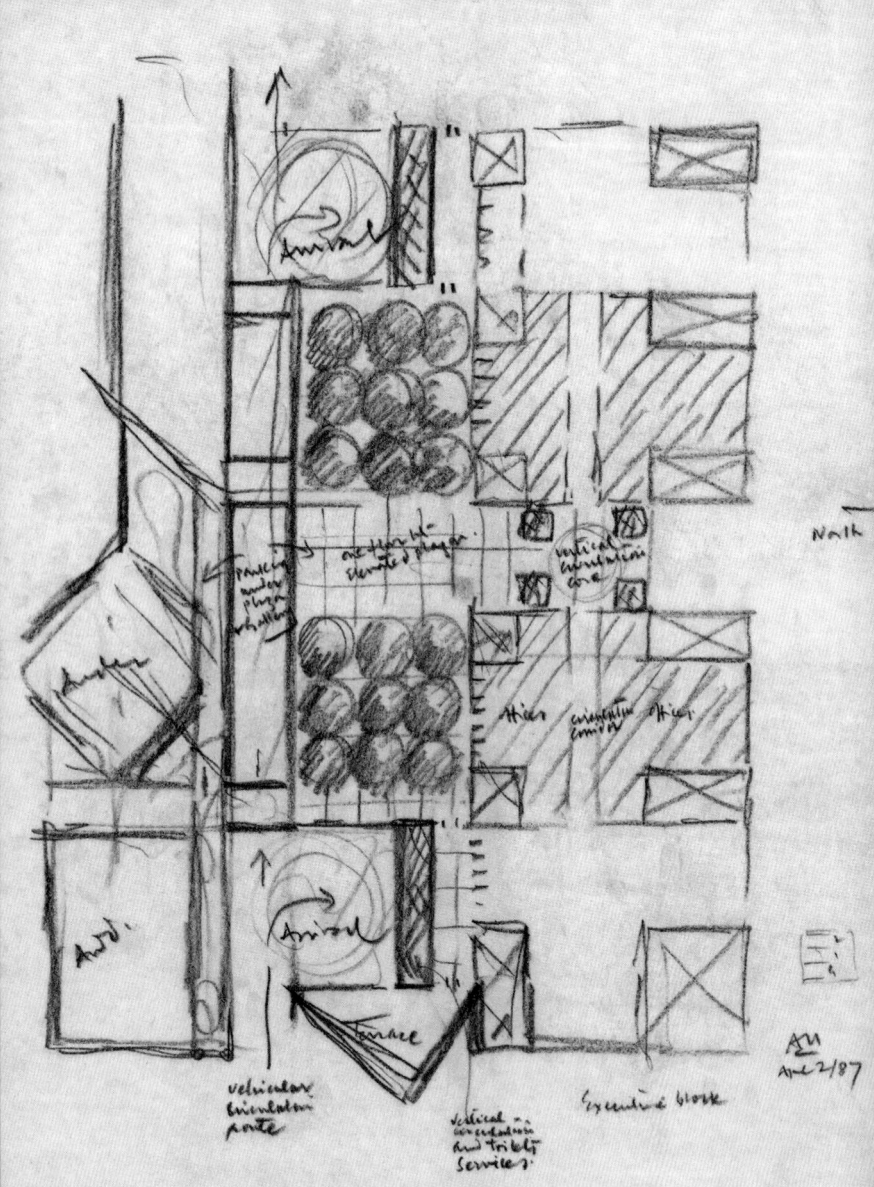

Headquarters for the
Bhopal Development Authority
Bhopal, Madhya Pradesh, 1990

The proposed buildings for the Bhopal Development Authority (BDA) are organized on the site taking into consideration access from three sides, corresponding to the three entrance hierarchies: (1) the VIP and executive staff entrances with parking; (2) the office staff and service entrance; and (3) the public entrance for the auction hall, offices and auditorium.

The building group, in correspondence, is divided into offices, auction hall for auctioning land parcels, and auditorium and kitchen and dining services.

The offices, on the ground floor and three upper floors, are organized with a main circulation corridor giving access to individual cabins on the south side, and general offices on the north. The corridor at the two ends links up with staircases and service spaces. The general offices are so structured in the plan as to allow flexible arrangement to partition any particular office space, if so desired, and give access to the attached record rooms.

The chairman-secretariat is at a vantage point on the first floor, at the northwest corner, with a porch underneath. The access to the secretariat is directly from this porch. This gives the building the image of authority, necessary to mark it as a distinctive headquarters within a growing metropolis.

Both the auditorium and the two-storeyed auction hall are situated on the ground floor. The two halls are connected internally, even though they have distinct entrances. The buildings help create an elevated, landscaped plaza between the offices and the halls. This is an important feature in the plan, as it creates approaches to all the programme elements of the complex, as well as a meeting point. Sitting under the trees, elevated from the traffic below, is a relaxing experience, especially in the winter sun. The plaza is expected to create cooling conditions on the ground floor, circulating the wind updraft through the light wells on the plaza side to all the floors, which are planned for cross-ventilation.

The plaza is also an urban feature. The elevated plaza demonstrates the linking of building groups in a comprehensive planning programme, bringing three-dimensionality to the urban fabric. BDA will be the first to introduce this important aspect of urban development, which is absent in most of our urban planning where vehicular and pedestrian traffic movement are in constant conflict with each other.

The food services–workshops–stores form the third side of the elevated plaza. The ground floor is given to workshops and stores, while the food services, spilling out on to the plaza, are on the first floor. The second floor houses records and inventory.

The buildings have crushed Kotah and crushed red sandstone grit plaster, expressed in the form of regulated panels with exposed concrete lintels and floor bands on the exterior. The same materials also cover the surfaces in the public lobbies, staircase enclosures, and the interiors of light wells and porches. The elevated plaza, as well as lobbies and corridors, have rough yellow sandstone paving, to give warmth inside the building.

A very close and compact plan not only ensures economy in space utilization, in structural design and in overall building expenditure, but also a meaningful solution to building in a hot and dry climate. The volumes of the buildings in this complex progressively grow in height in direct response to their functional needs and the forms of buildings expressing their wilful character. This, then, is a summary of the architecture of place-making, in this case the headquarters of the Bhopal Development Authority.

There is an attempt to bring the breeze in: cross-ventilation that traverses the building and courtyards. The building is oriented on the north–south axis, limiting east–west exposure.

The principal porch is in the same language as the other porches, except the dimensions are different. The roof integrates the elements that have a certain role to play in the composition of the complex.

Definitive model of building in wood, rear side.

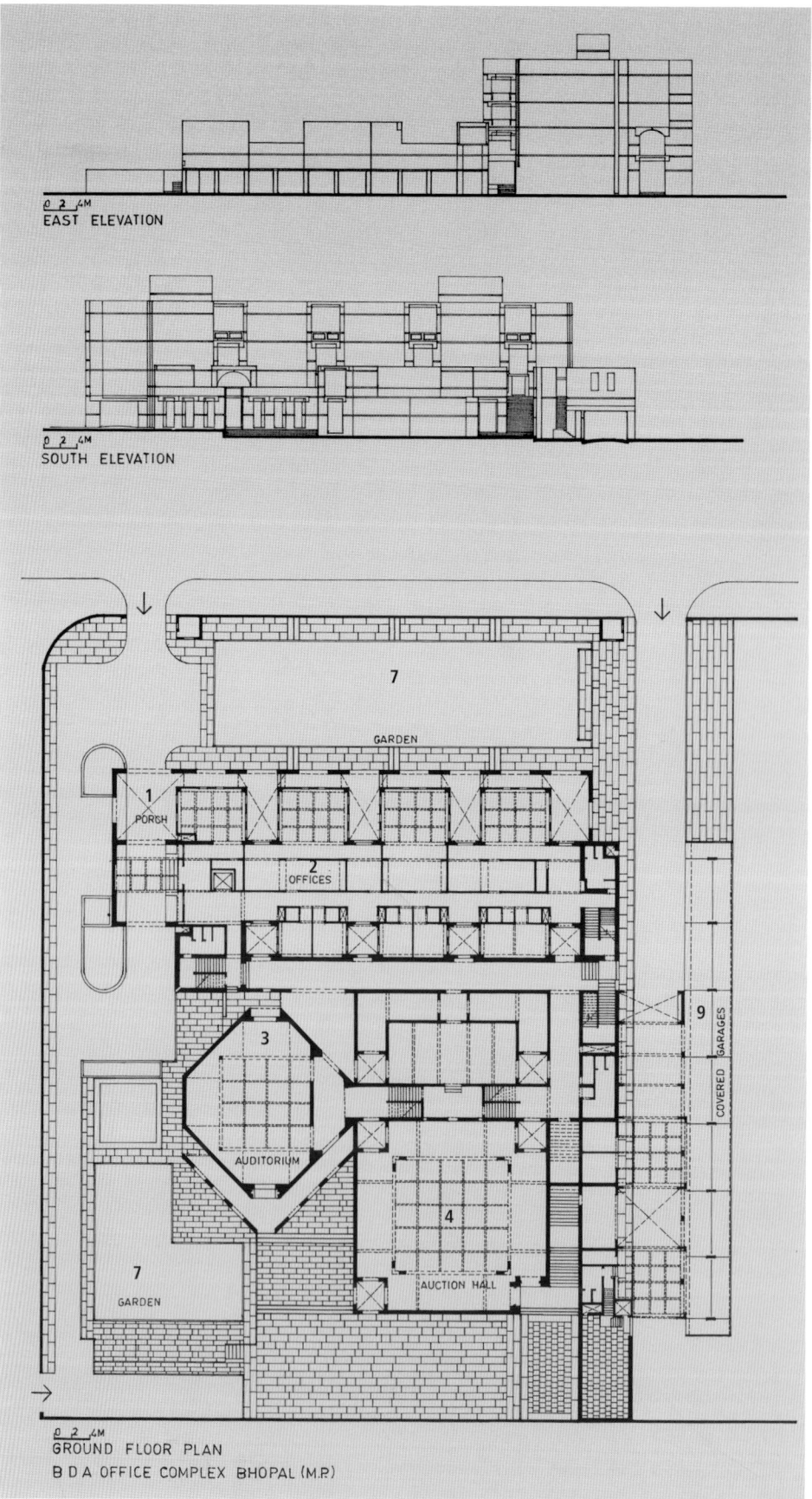

> East elevation | South elevation.

> North elevation | West elevation.

> Ground floor plan | First floor plan.
> 1 Porch
> 2 Offices
> 3 Auditorium
> 4 Auction hall
> 5 Kitchen
> 6 Dining
> 7 Garden
> 8 Plaza
> 9 Parking
> 10 Terrace
> 11 Roof over auction hall

EAST ELEVATION

SOUTH ELEVATION

GROUND FLOOR PLAN
B D A OFFICE COMPLEX BHOPAL (M.P.)

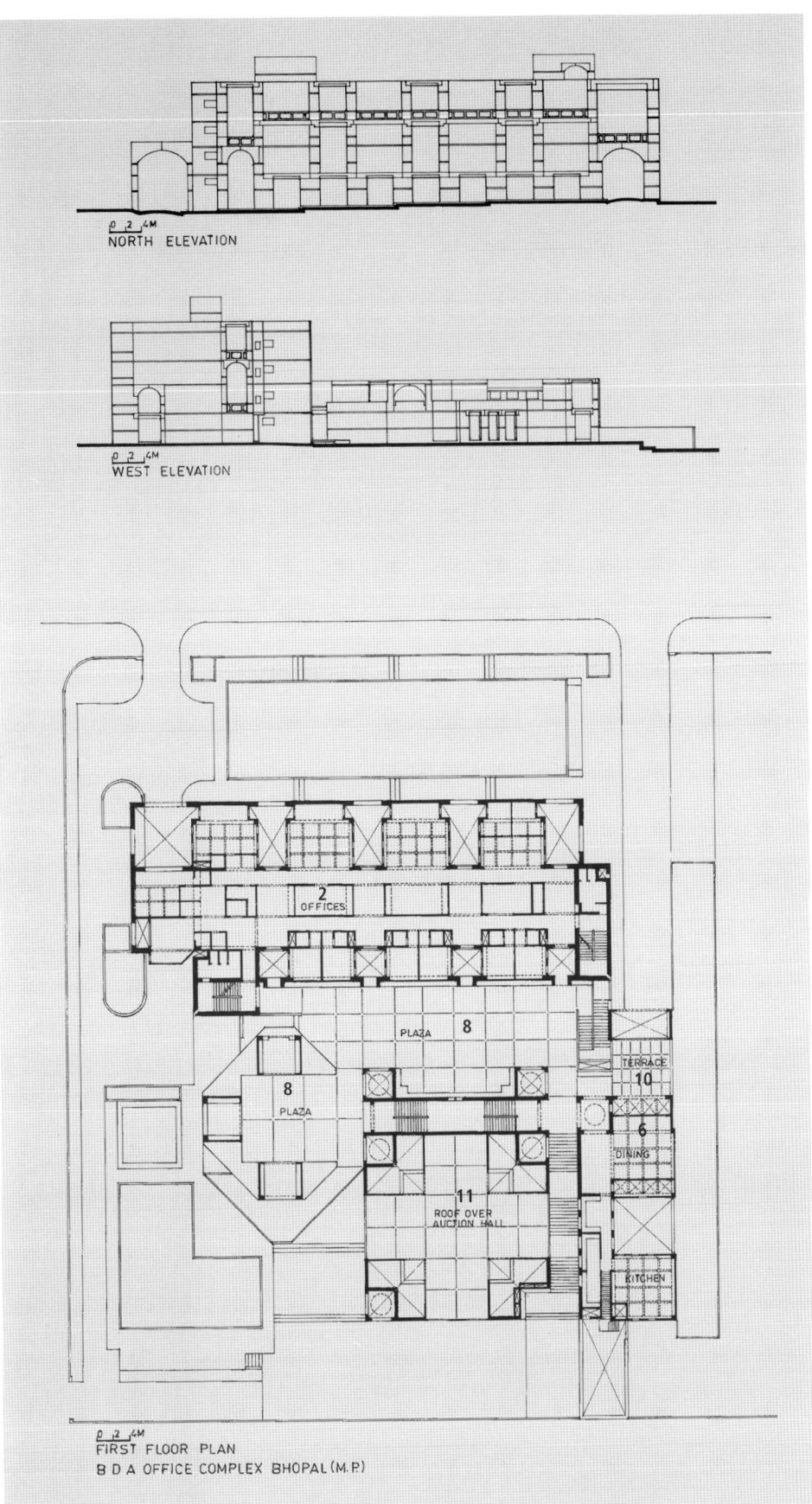

NORTH ELEVATION

WEST ELEVATION

2
OFFICES

PLAZA 8

TERRACE
10

8
PLAZA

6
DINING

11
ROOF OVER
AUCTION HALL

KITCHEN

FIRST FLOOR PLAN
B D A OFFICE COMPLEX BHOPAL (M.P.)

> Formal (principal) entrance porch with a terrace within on top, and the major offices around the two-storeyed terrace.

> Sections.

Crushed red sandstone and crushed Kotah stone, which is grey. So the composition moves from grey to light grey (which is the concrete), to something which also becomes a part of the traditional architecture – Bhopal has a lot of it – with the red sandstone. The photograph also shows the termination of the pockets of light at the top.

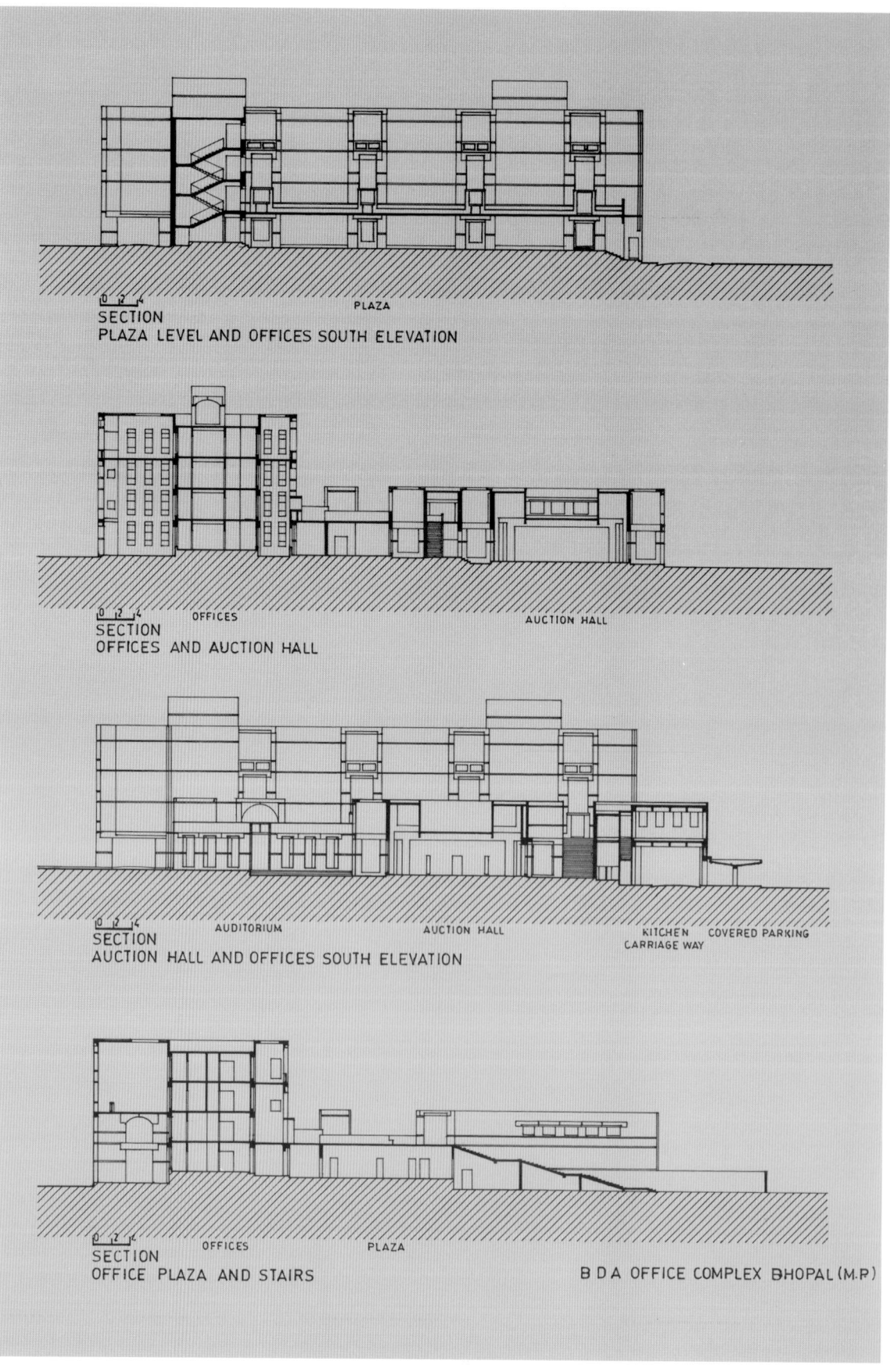

SECTION
PLAZA LEVEL AND OFFICES SOUTH ELEVATION

SECTION
OFFICES AND AUCTION HALL

SECTION
AUCTION HALL AND OFFICES SOUTH ELEVATION

SECTION
OFFICE PLAZA AND STAIRS

B D A OFFICE COMPLEX BHOPAL (M.P.)

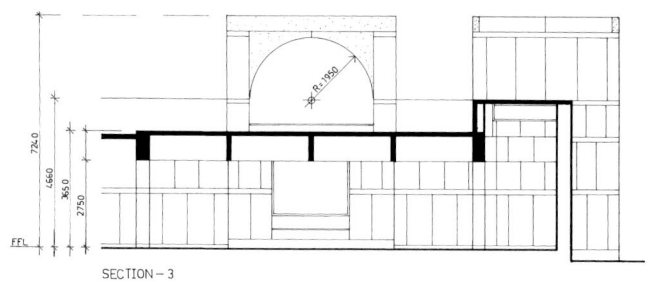

SECTION - 3

ELEVATION

> Public entry to the office building by a large flight of steps. All porches terminate at the top into elevated terraces that open up to the sky.

> ∨ Details of the assembly hall.

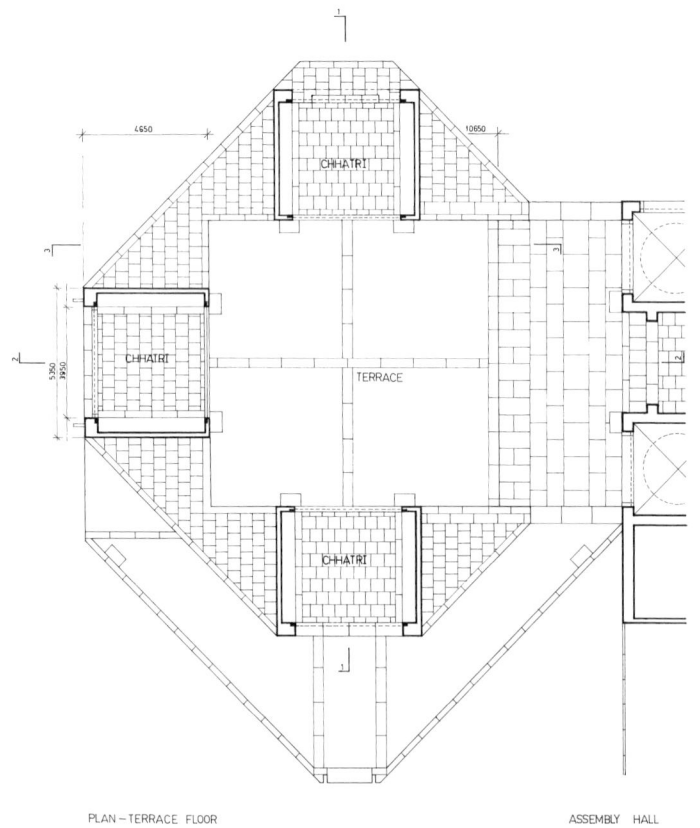

PLAN - TERRACE FLOOR

ASSEMBLY HALL
BDA OFFICE COMPLEX
BHOPAL   SCALE 1:100

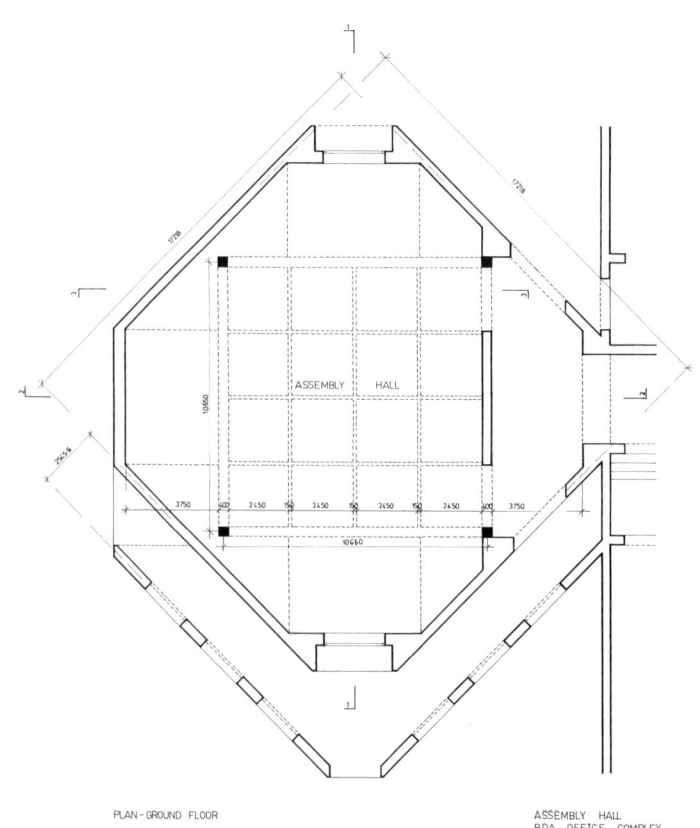

PLAN - GROUND FLOOR

ASSEMBLY HALL
BDA OFFICE COMPLEX
BHOPAL   SCALE 1:100

One begins to get a sense of the light and breezeways. There is also no glass on the periphery. These are very hot places, and as far as possible, I like to make elements in such a way that the glass is pushed as far inside as possible; that in the experience of the building, you recede from the light, and you create the kind of shadows that are the most welcoming part, giving a sense of shelter.

> View from the road. Offices, with arcade below.

> Part facade, north side.

234

Rear view of meeting halls, auction halls
and office block.

An extension to an adjacent housing complex (MOG Lines, left) near the city centre, the design accommodates the development of a total area of approximately 16,500 sq. metres. Of this, 5,800 sq. metres are allocated to housing, the rest being offices, shopping arcades, etc. The project is a major urban design statement in Indore which could extend its limits to integrate within itself a transport terminal for inter-state buses, and transform existing shopping streets and most of the unrelated planning efforts that have resulted in truncated urban design development. It is therefore just the beginning of an effort to bring in large-scale pedestrianization which links to major surface transport centres and parking lots within and around the periphery of this section of the city.

∧ MOG Lines overall layout in wood.

∨ Commercial complex, definitive model in wood.

Commercial Complex at MOG Lines
Indore, Madhya Pradesh, 1990–96

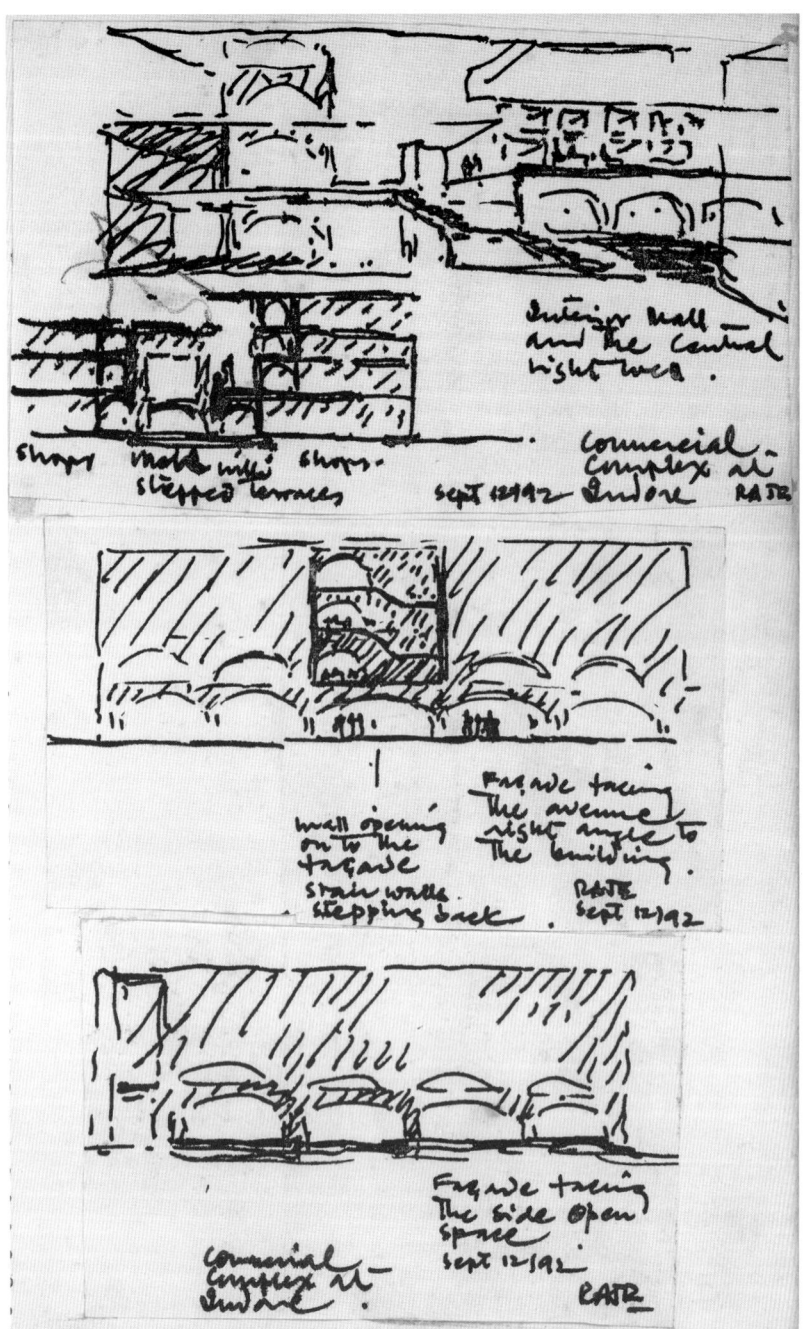

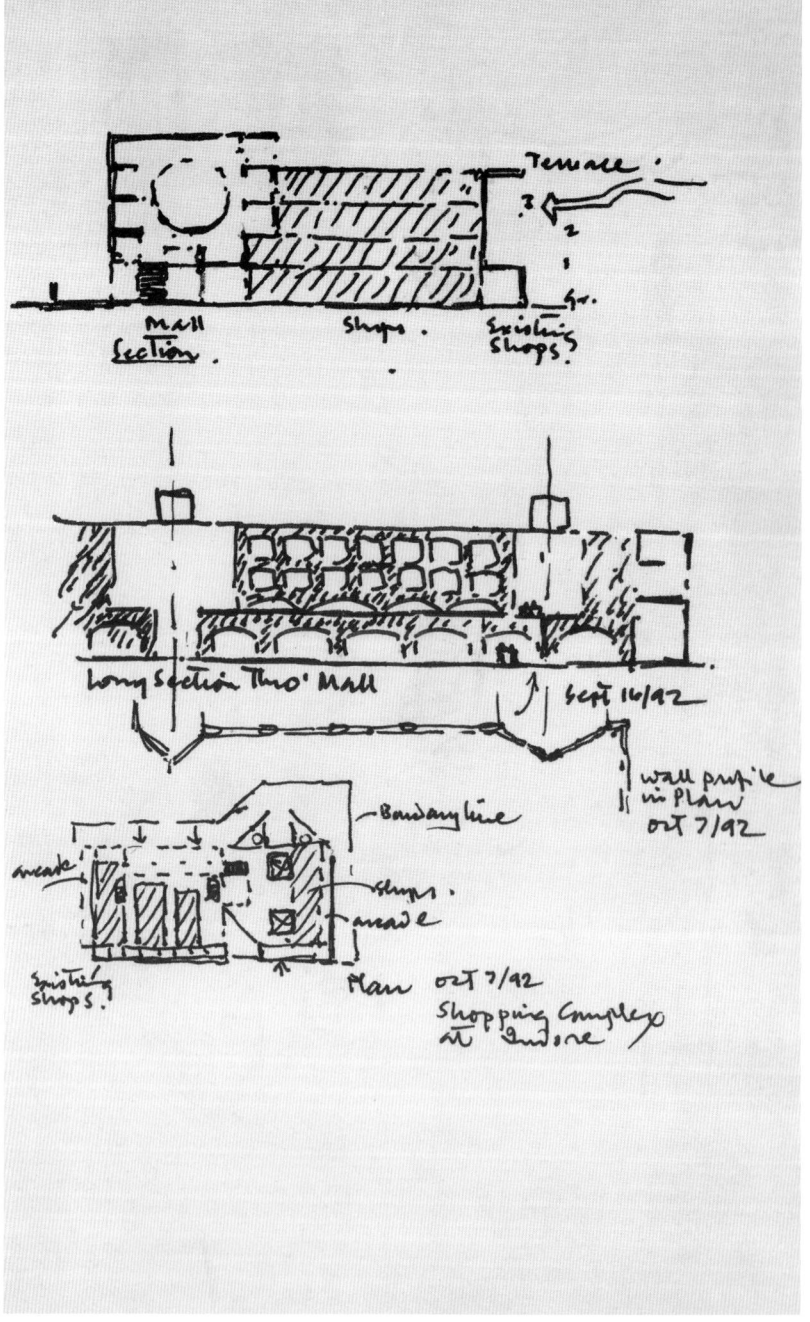

Development sketches, September 1992.
Notes on the sketches, from the top:
'Interior hall and the central light well'
'Shops – mall with stepped terraces – shops'
'Wall opening on the facade – stair walls stepping back'
'Facade facing the avenue right angle to the building'
'Facade facing the side open space'

Development Sketches, shopping complex, October 1992.
Notes on the sketches, from the top:
'Mall section – shops – existing shops – terrace'
'Long section through mall – wall profile in plan'
'Plan: building line – shops – arcade – existing shops'

> North elevation at shops and offices.

∨ Site plan at the first floor level.
1 Courtyards/landscaped courts at ground floor
2 Offices
3 Shops
4 Housing units
5 Parking
6 Elevated concourse/terraces at first floor

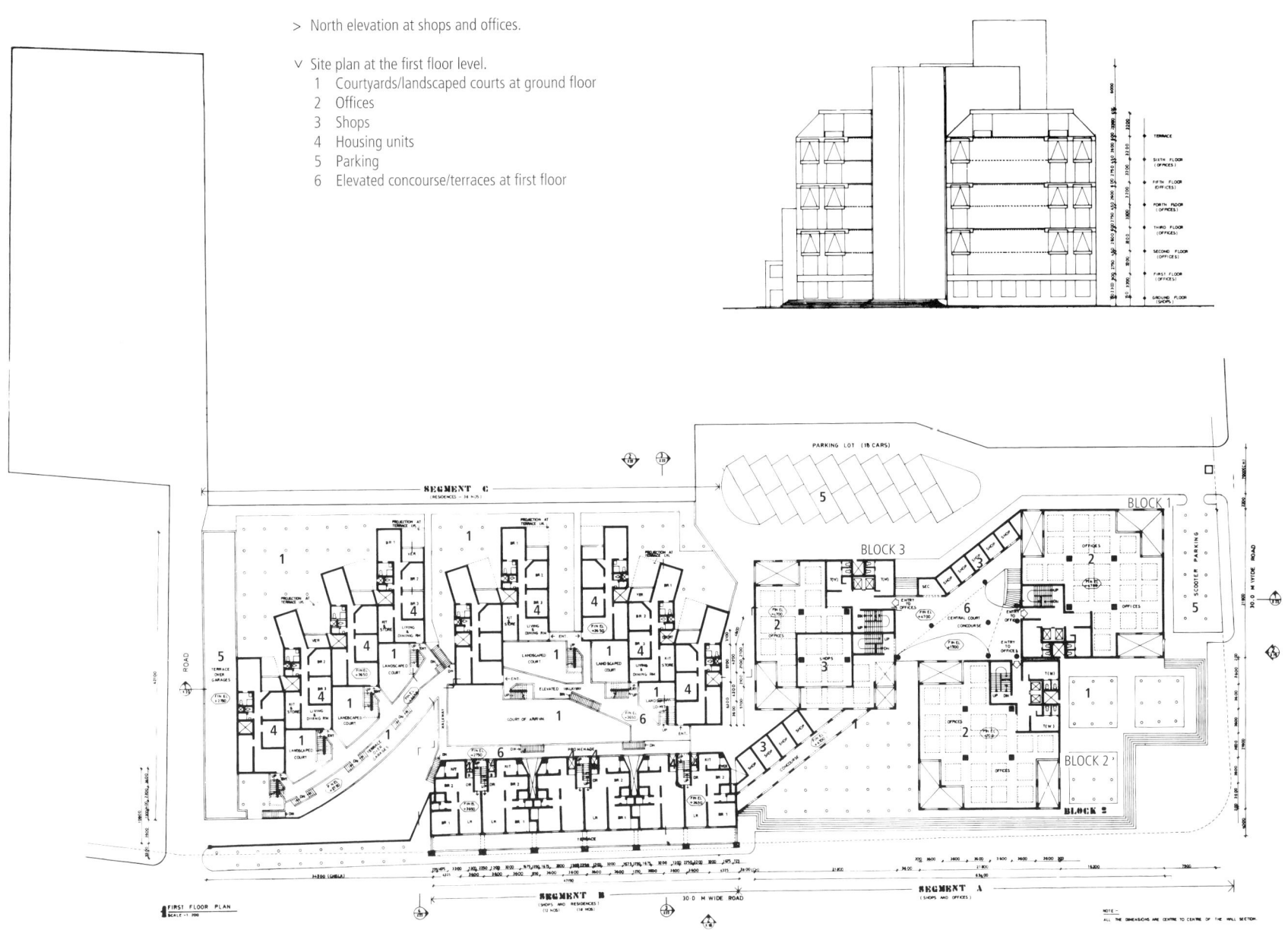

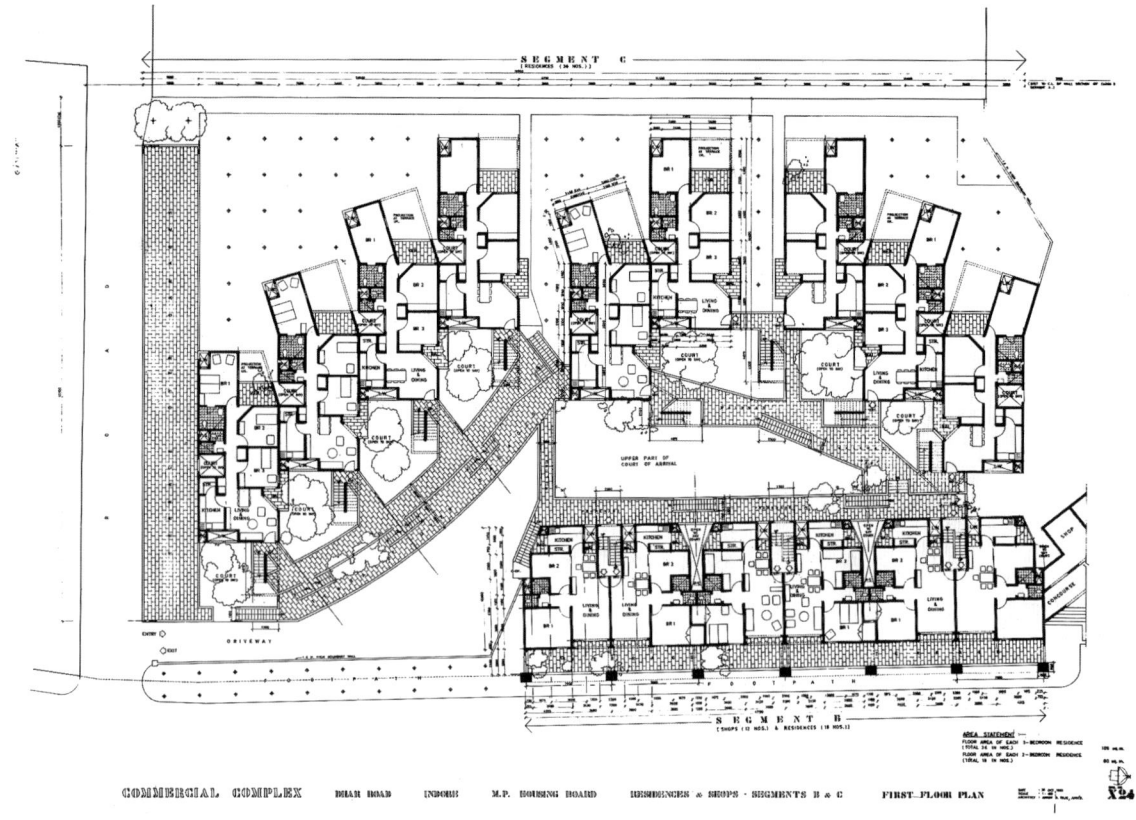

COMMERCIAL COMPLEX   BHAR ROAD   INDORE   M.P. HOUSING BOARD   RESIDENCES & SHOPS - SEGMENTS B & C   FIRST FLOOR PLAN

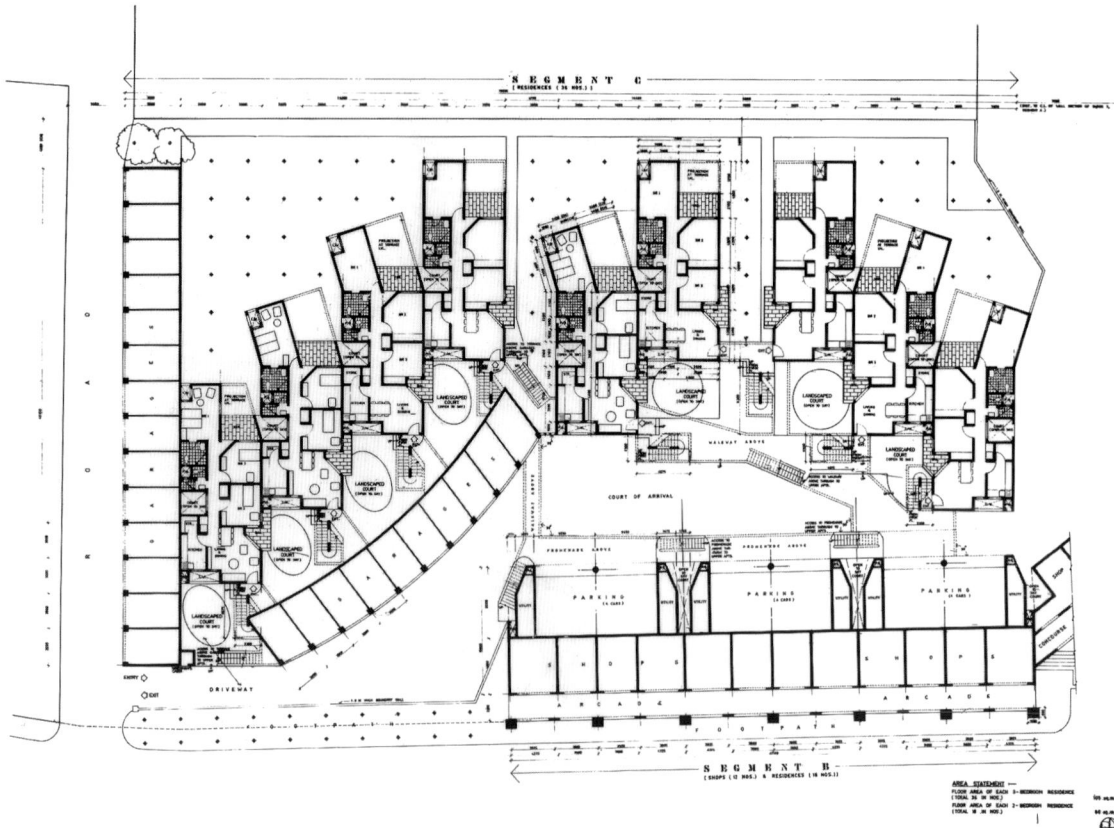

COMMERCIAL COMPLEX   BHAR ROAD   INDORE   M.P. HOUSING BOARD   RESIDENCES & SHOPS - SEGMENTS B & C   GROUND FLOOR PLAN

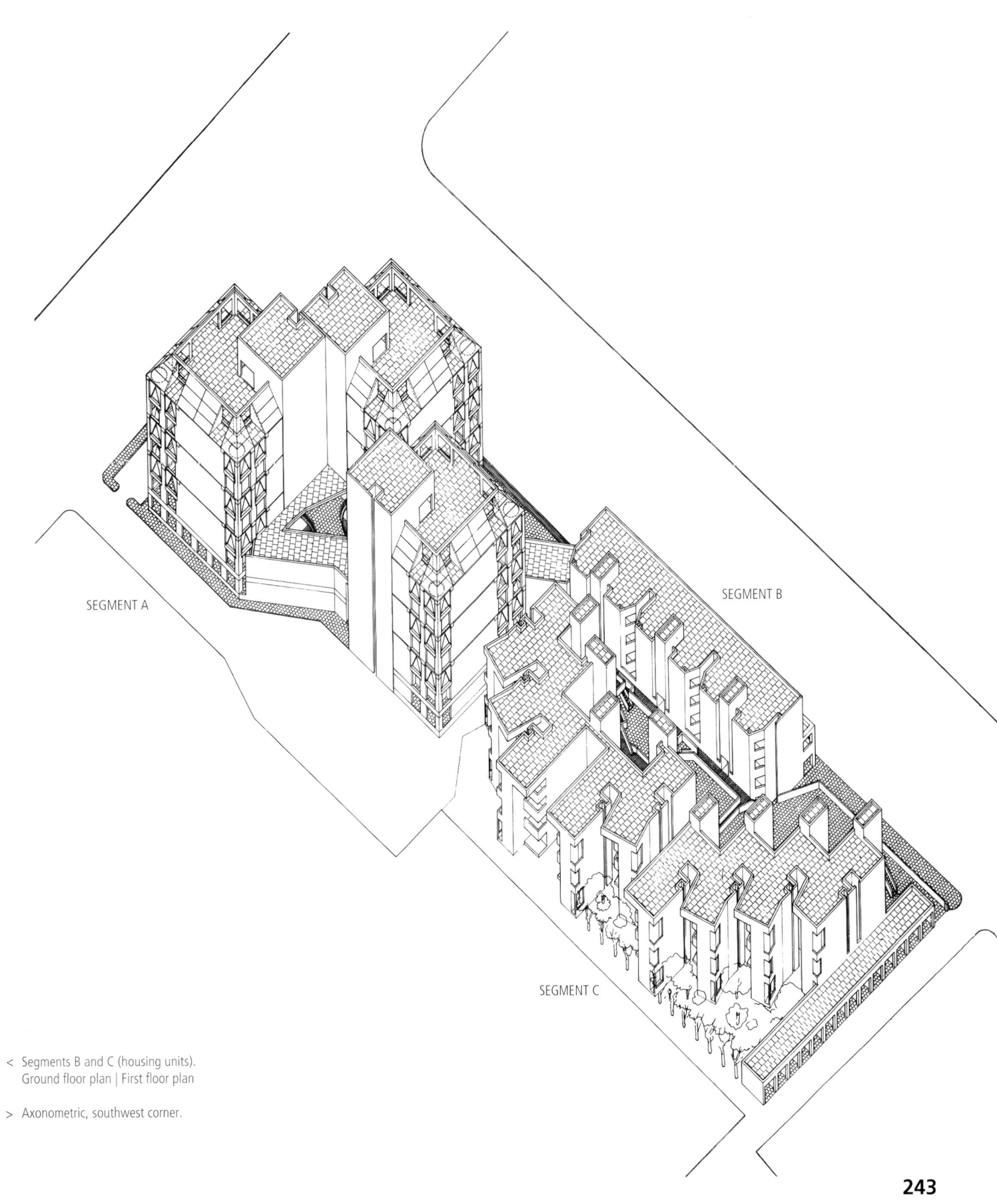

SEGMENT A

SEGMENT B

SEGMENT C

< Segments B and C (housing units).
Ground floor plan | First floor plan

> Axonometric, southwest corner.

243

27 Oct '93

27 Oct '93
Entry thru' Plaza
27 Oct '93

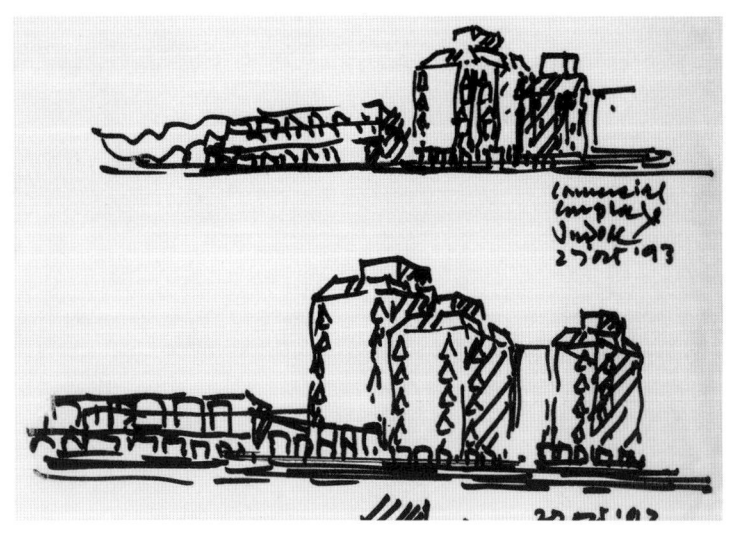

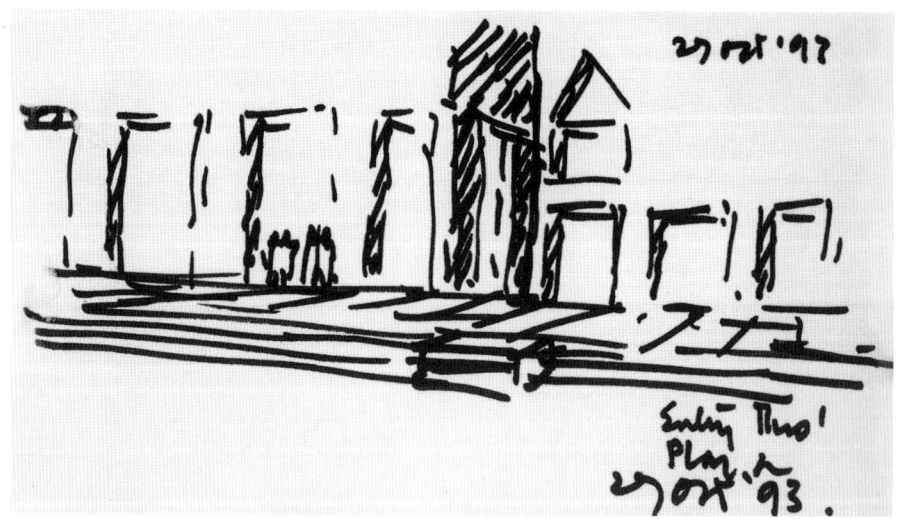

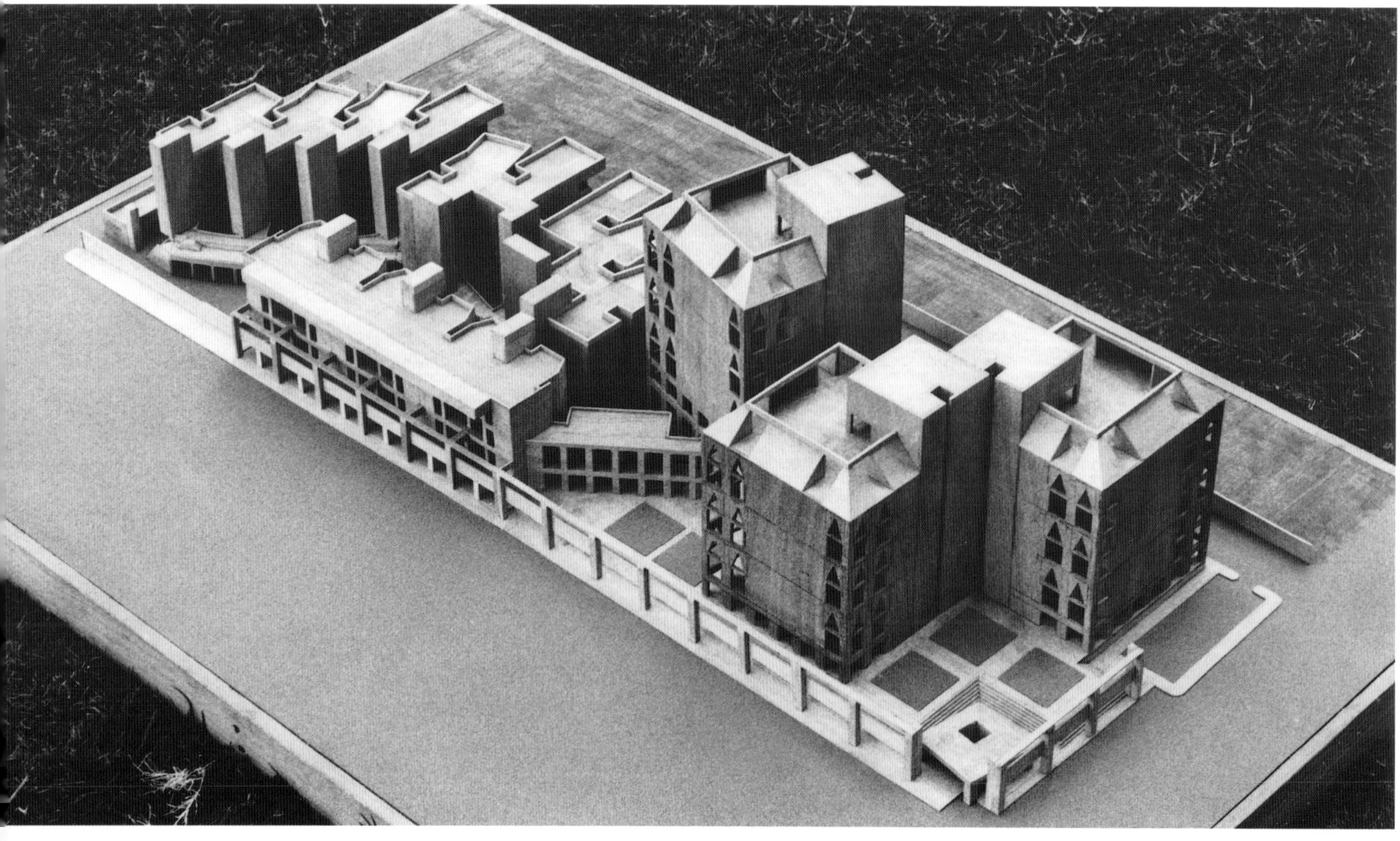

< Form studies, segment A, commercial
complex, October 1993.

< Entry through plaza, October 1993.

< Definitive model in wood.

> Segment A, floor plans.
Ground floor plan | First floor plan

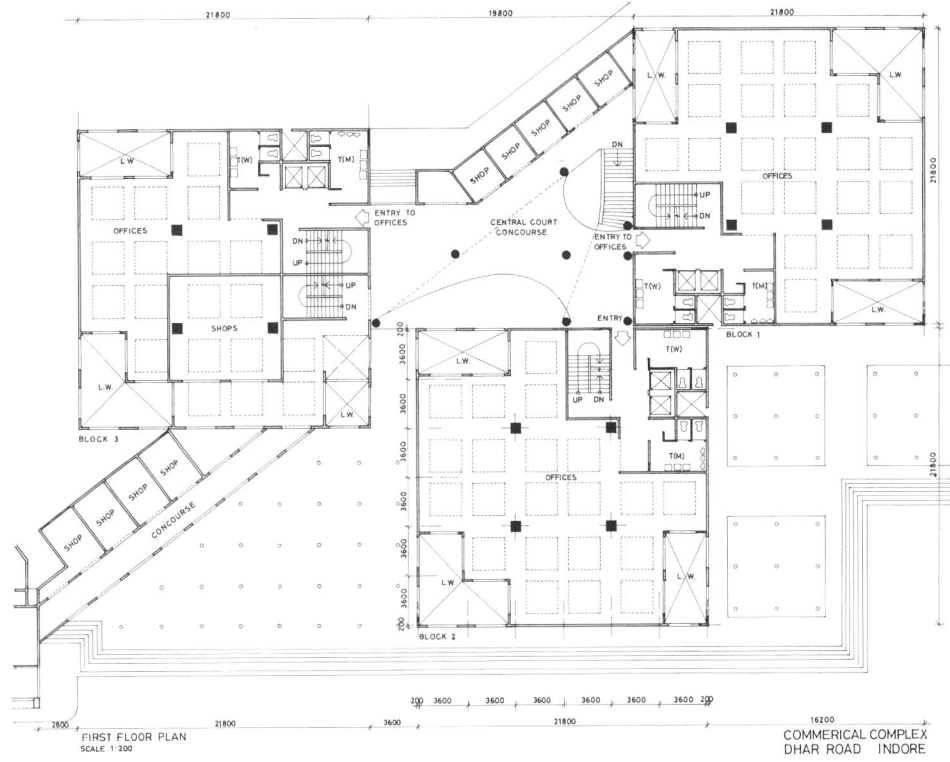

FIRST FLOOR PLAN
SCALE 1:200

COMMERICAL COMPLEX
DHAR ROAD INDORE

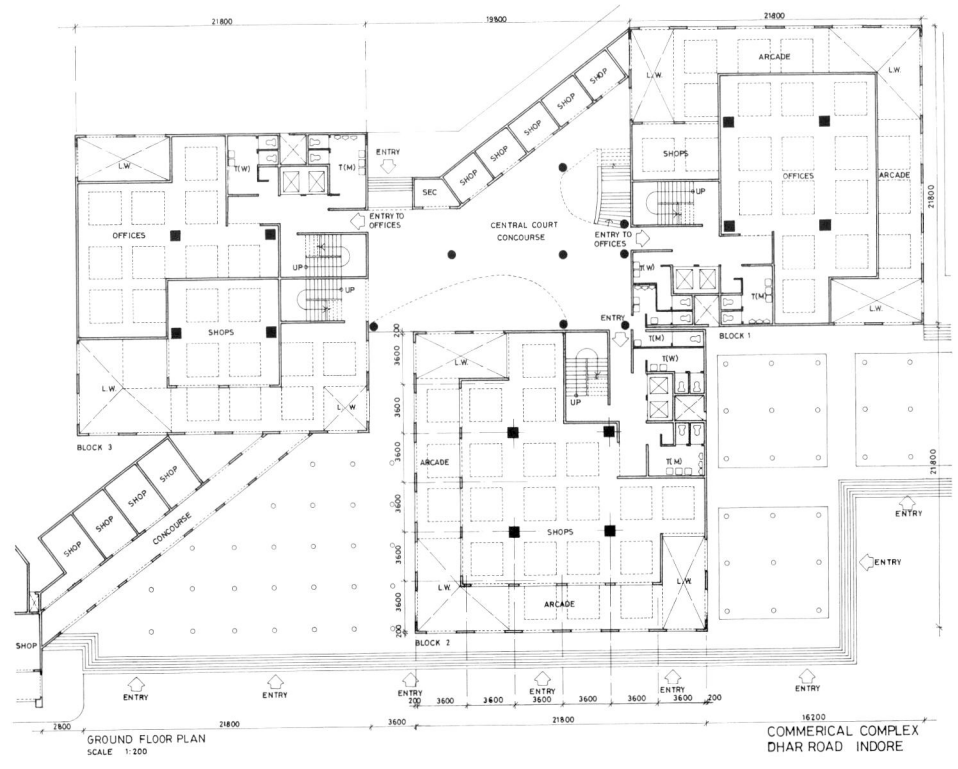

GROUND FLOOR PLAN
SCALE 1:200

COMMERICAL COMPLEX
DHAR ROAD INDORE

Birds eye view
MCA Layout.
Feb 21/91

Mudra Institute of Communications
Ahmedabad, 1990

The Institute to train students in all aspects of advertising sits on a 10-acre site along one of the branches of the Narmada canal, on the outskirts of Ahmedabad. The programmatic elements include faculty offices, studio workshops, dining halls, student dormitories and a teaching block with a 200-seat assembly hall. Built with an exposed brick and concrete vocabulary, the campus is designed as a low-rise development, extending the profiles to the broad vistas of the horizon on all sides.

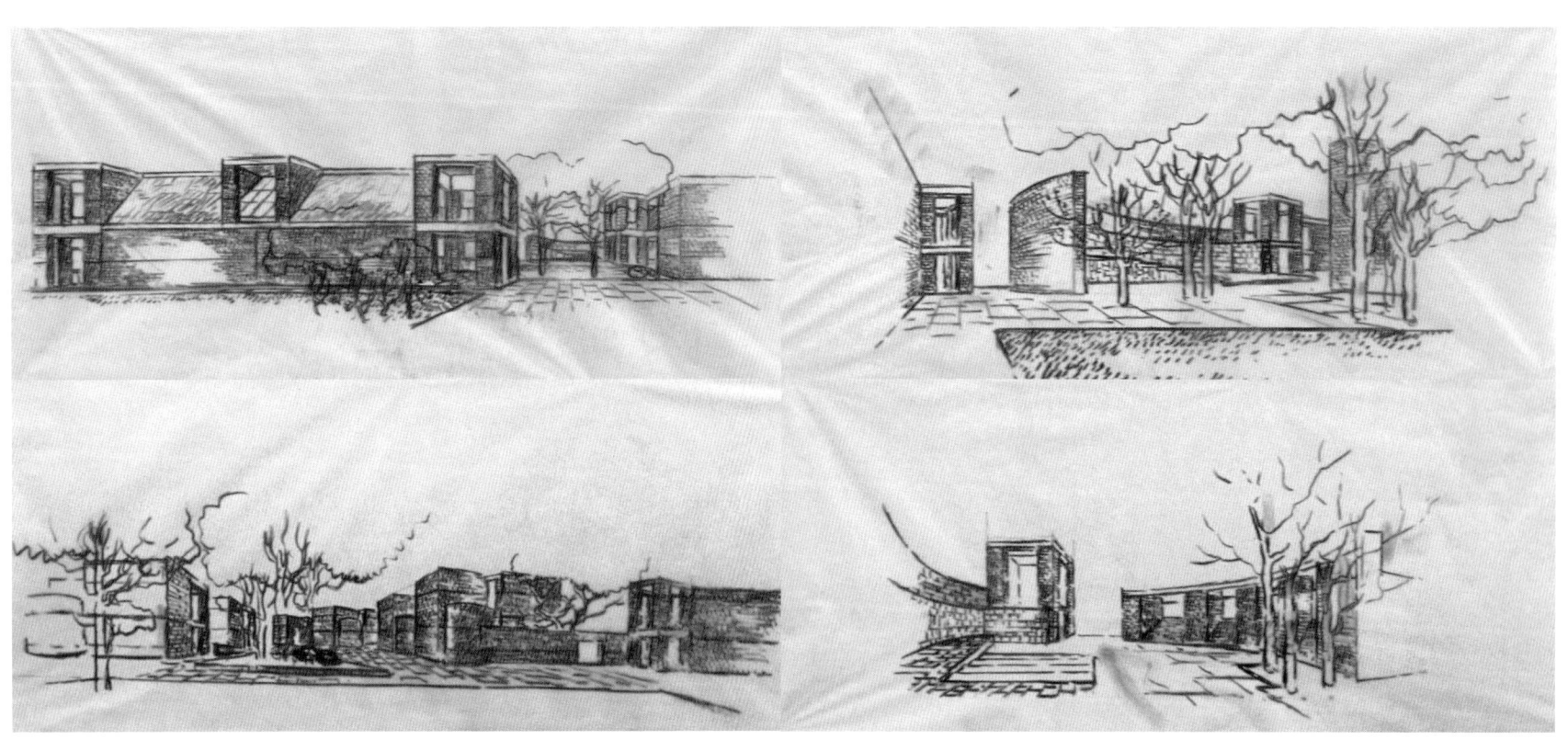

248

< Preliminary charcoal sketches, making compositions through elements, to make them into elements of participation.

∨ Preliminary site model, with the Narmada canal on the top left corner of the image. The circular element of the wedding wall and the court in the Nandan Mehta house is expressed here as the arrival point with the major classrooms and administration of the Institute. A small 'village' in the form of a village street articulates the dormitories with dining and other facilities.

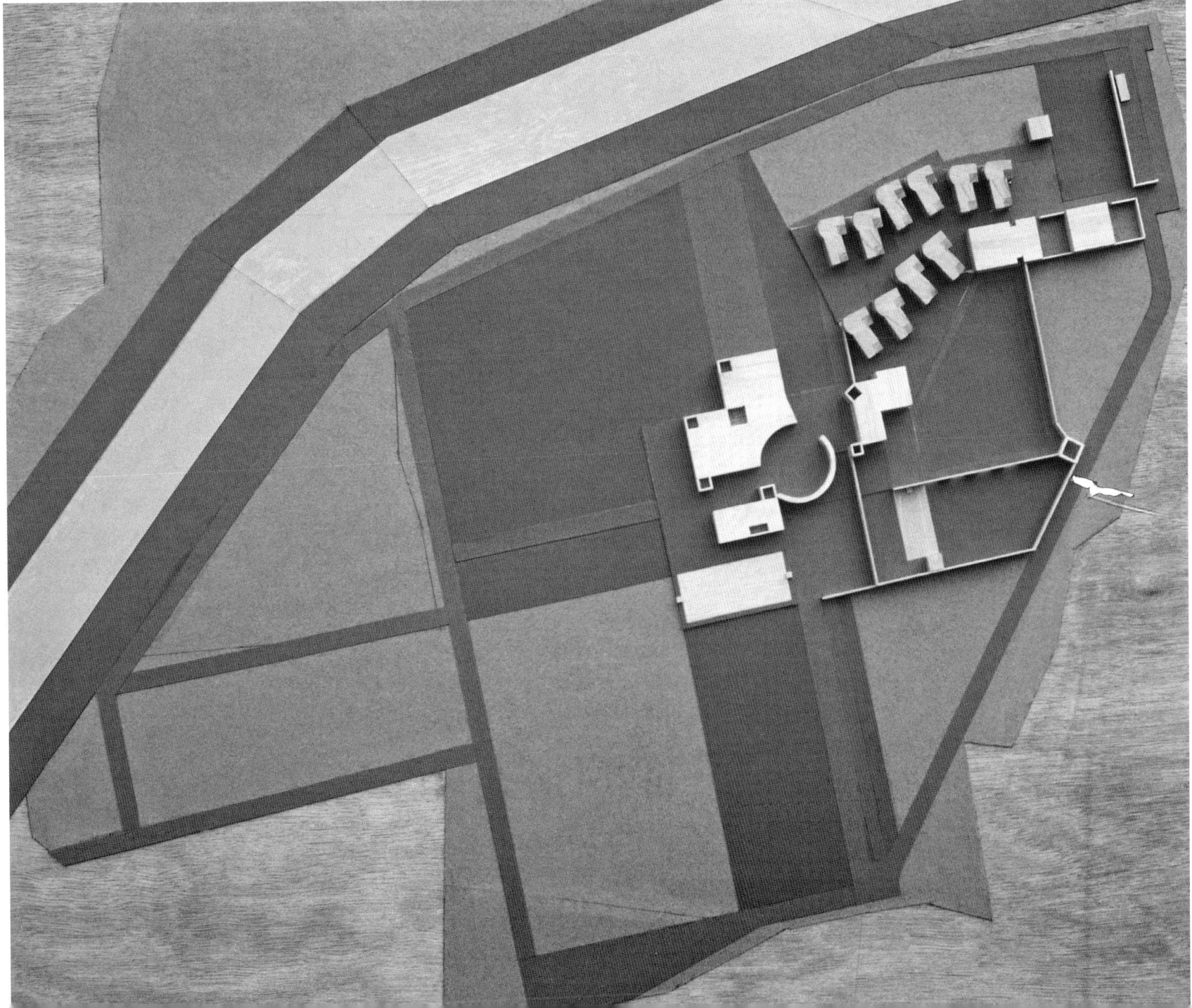

< Definitive model in wood showing all phases. Phase 1 consisting of the main building, with classrooms, administrative offices and the auditorium, which was the central part of the building, is completed.

 1   Teaching and training areas
 2   Administration
 3   Studios and workshops
 4   Library
 5   Dormitories
 6   Clubhouse
 7   Amphitheatre
 8   Dining halls
 9   Maintenance workshops
10   Water pool
11   Entry
12   Parking

> Site plan.

∨ Entrance promenade to the classroom building.

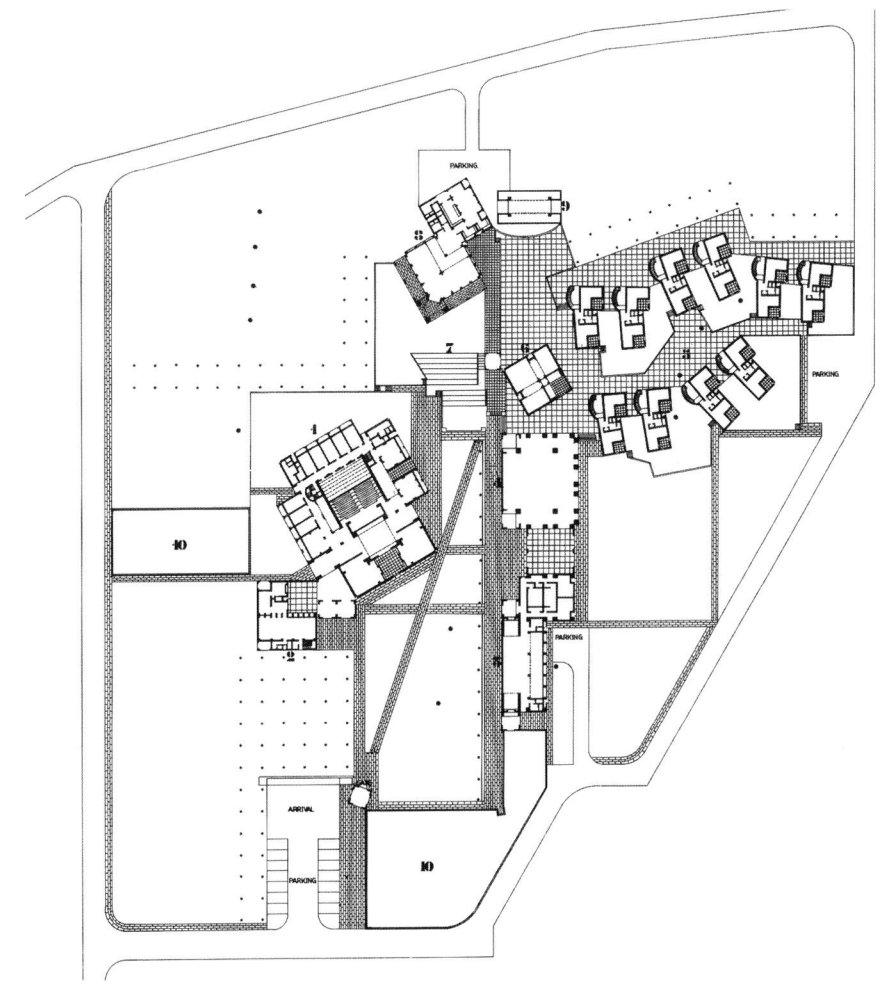

Exterior, on axis, with the court between the classrooms and the exhibition foyer.

< Classroom building, exterior.

∨ Floor plan, classroom building.
  1 Entrance porch
  2 Classroom
  3 Office
  4 Auditorium
  5 Exhibition foyer / Gathering space
  6 Court
  7 Toilets

∨ Sectional model of the auditorium. A study of the spaces from within, their relationships, their connections.

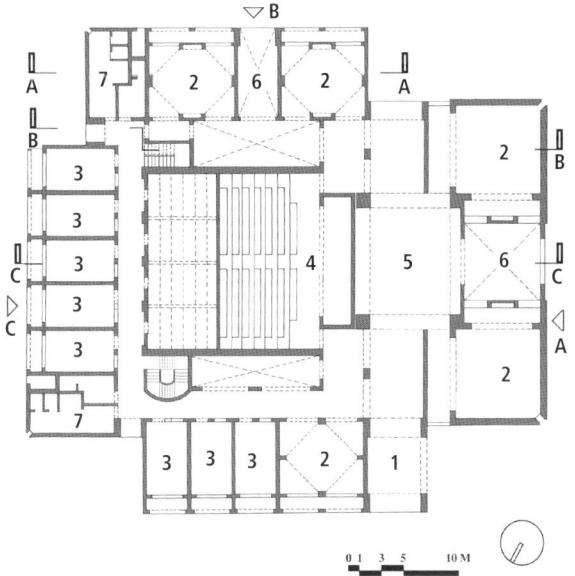

0 1 3 5   10 M

255

Exhibition foyer interior.

When we come to the centre there is a 'slot of light' which was a pyramid in the beginning, at the conceptual stage. I sliced that pyramid and pushed the two slices apart to get the slot of light between. There is a structural meaning to all this and the loads are brought down in terms of the setbacks on to the beams.

The light at the lower level of the 'slot' forms the axis between the outside court and the foyer, which is used to display and exhibit student work. It is a wonderful experience with diffused light coming from the top, and continuing as horizontal extensions into the landscape of beautiful mango trees.

< Interior, exhibition foyer.

> Axonometric of classroom building.

∨ Details of the light element.

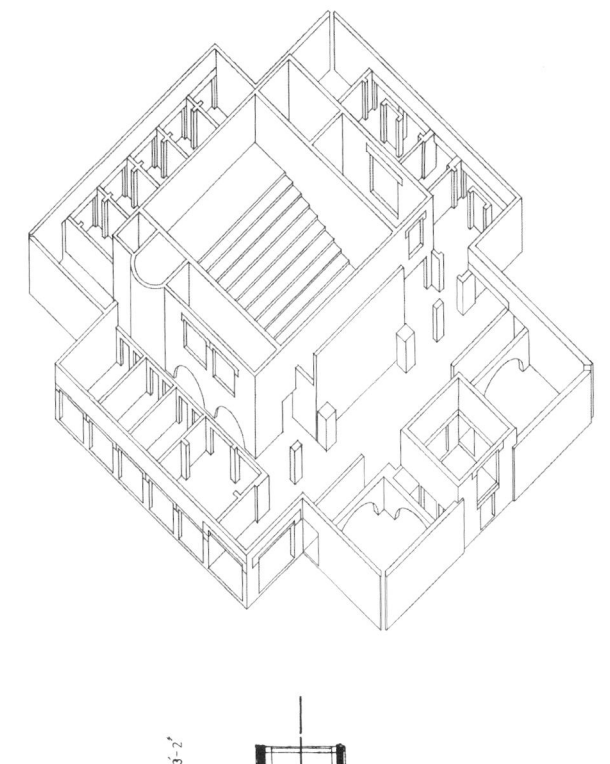

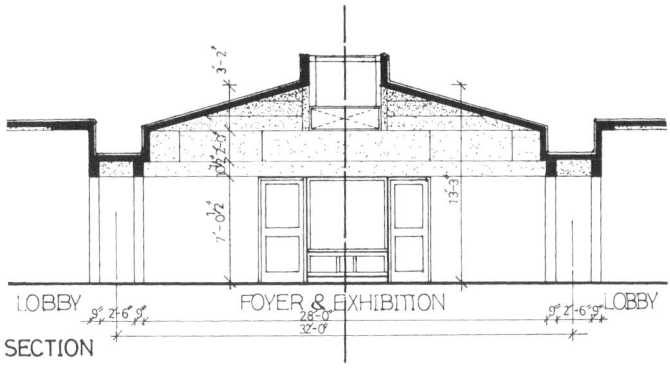

LOBBY   FOYER & EXHIBITION   LOBBY

SECTION

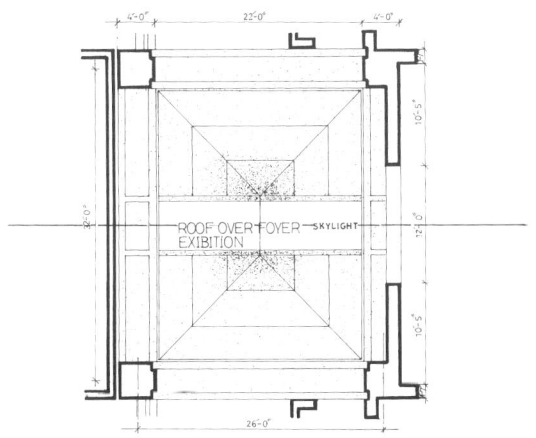

REFLECTED CEILING PLAN

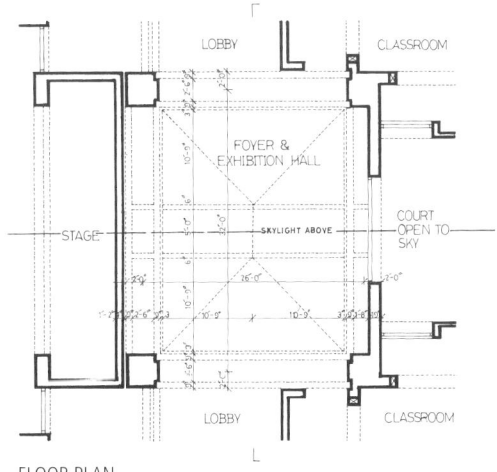

FLOOR PLAN

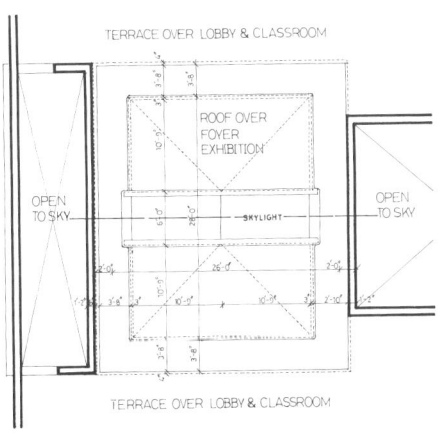

ROOF PLAN

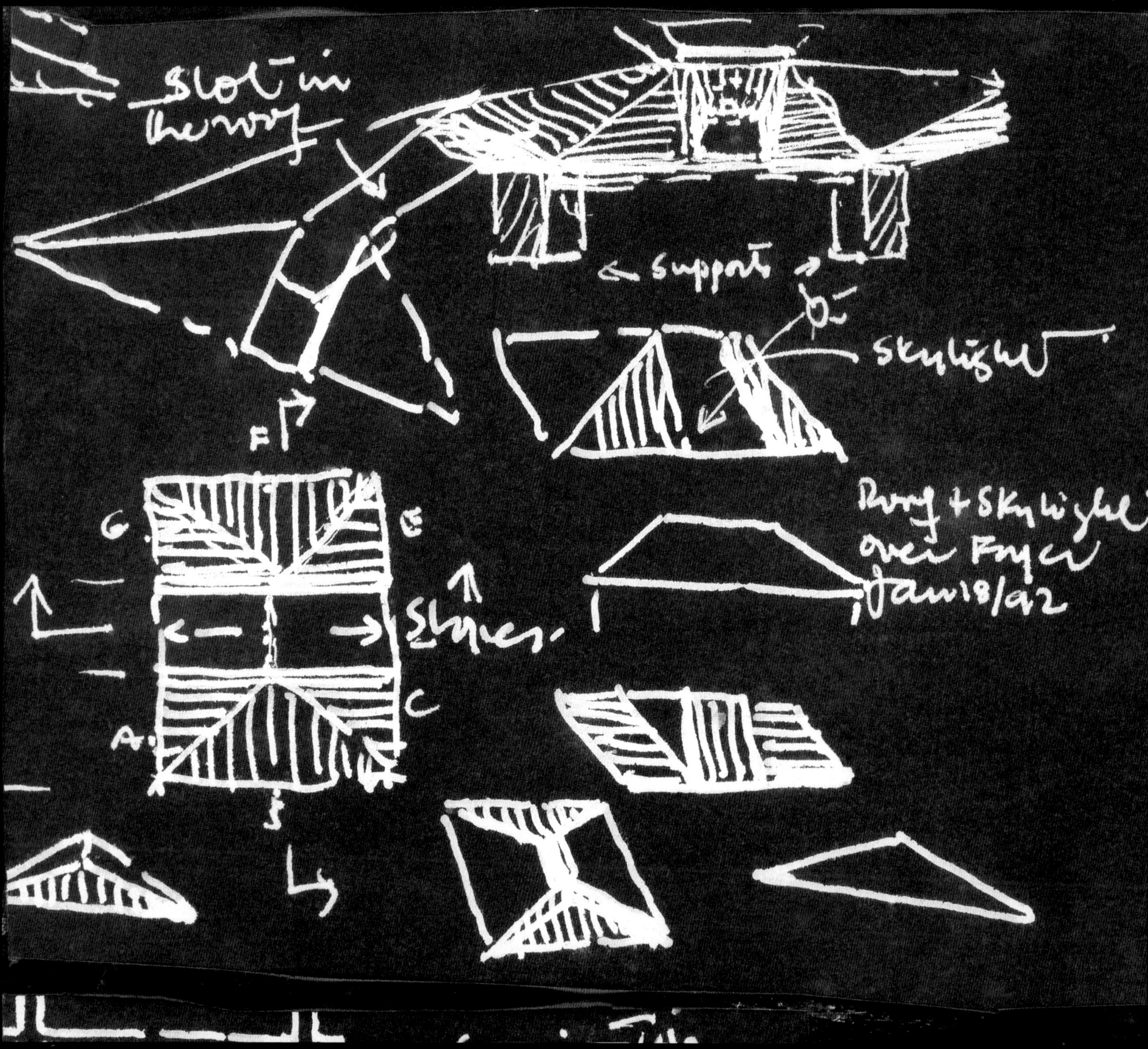
Slot in the roof
support
Skylight
Roof + Skylight over Foyer Jan 18/92
Stairs
G
E
C
A
F

> Roof and skylight over foyer, January 1992.
  Notes on the sketch read, from top:
  '8"x8" ceramic tile flooring – broad joints'
  'Section through ridge'
  'Rainwater flow'
  'glass skylight'
  'gutter'
  'bk [brick] pilaster'
  'inclined roof'
  'Two halves of the roof moved to make opening
  for light'
  'Gutter and bedblock over pilaster'
  'Mudra roof studies'
  'rainwater flow'
  'skylight across the roof raised'
  'Gutter and bedblock'
  'brick pilaster'

< Roof and skylight over foyer, January 1992.
  Notes on the sketch read, from top:
  'Slot in the roof'
  'supports'
  'skylight'
  'slopes'

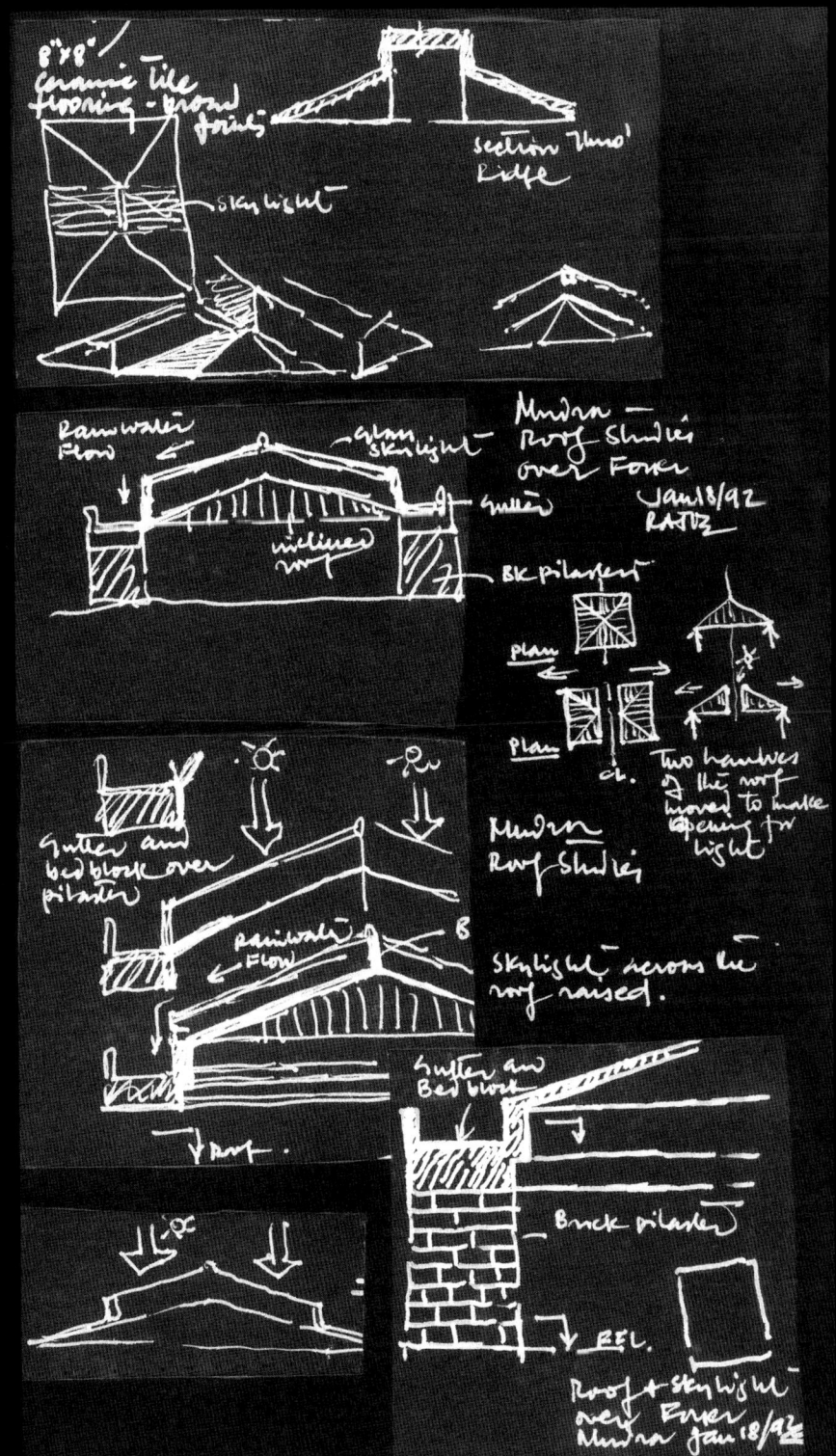

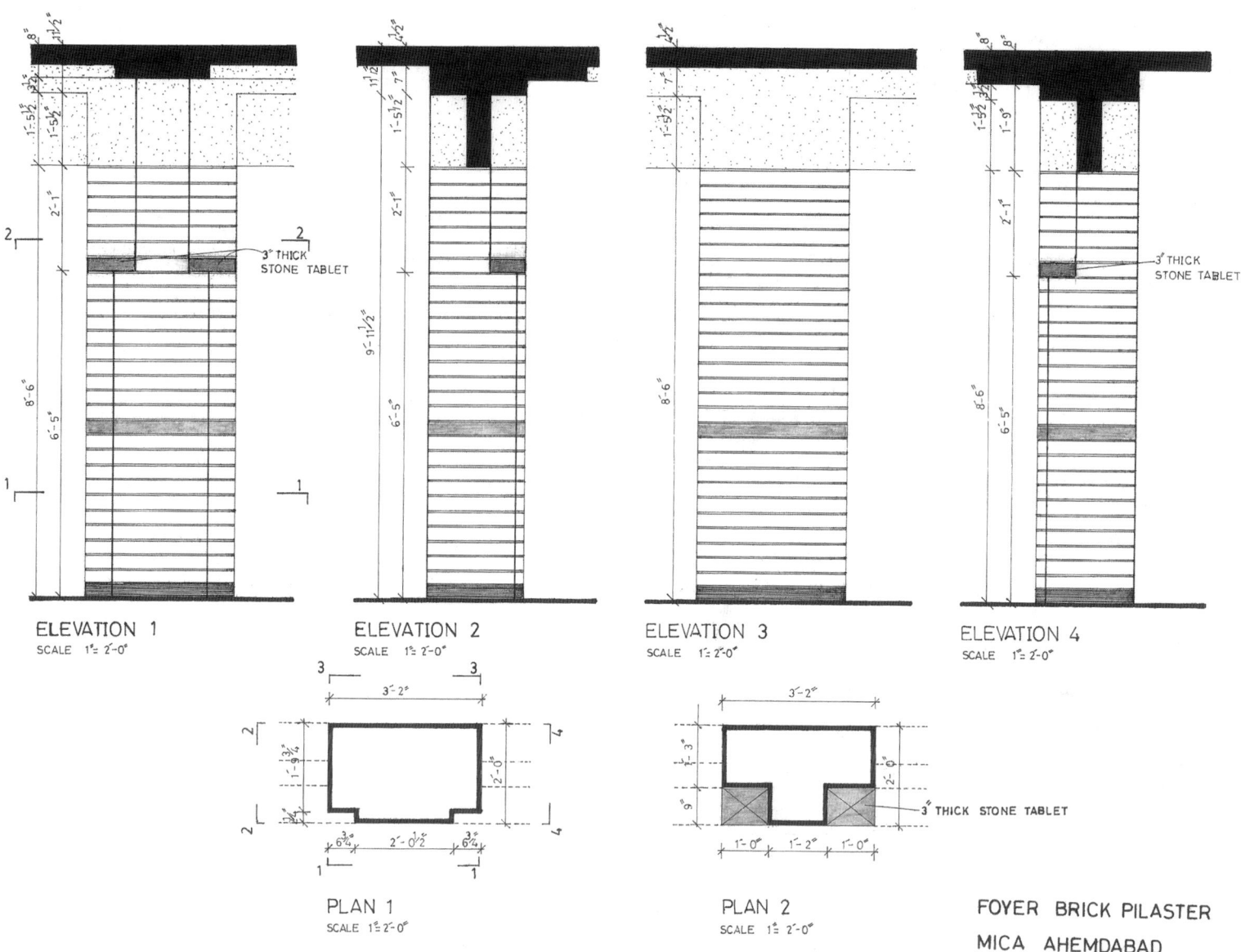

ELEVATION 1
SCALE 1"= 2'-0"

ELEVATION 2
SCALE 1"= 2'-0"

ELEVATION 3
SCALE 1"= 2'-0"

ELEVATION 4
SCALE 1"= 2'-0"

3" THICK
STONE TABLET

3" THICK
STONE TABLET

PLAN 1
SCALE 1"= 2'-0"

PLAN 2
SCALE 1"= 2'-0"

3" THICK STONE TABLET

FOYER BRICK PILASTER
MICA AHEMDABAD

^ Typical pilaster in the classroom building.

< Details of the pilaster.

When we started to use these pilasters, I was trying to be very anthropomorphic. These, I find, lend a tremendous quality to a very mundane pilaster. Something that receives the load on top, and in bringing the loads down you find corners and niches. A series of these are reminiscent of the temple pillars – there is a connection between the making of the pilasters and the temple pillars.

Foyer and exhibition hall in the classroom building.

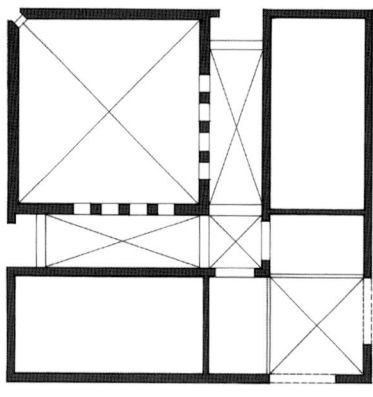
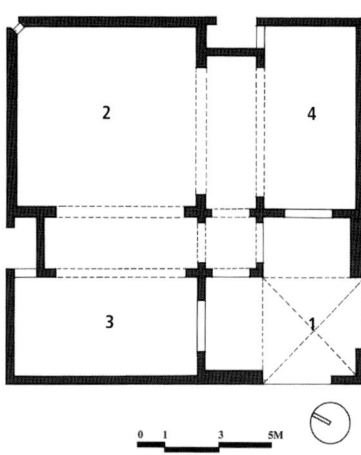

< Floor plan, club house (currently used as the library).
  1 Entrance court
  2 Reading area
  3 Library services / Administration
  4 Stacks

> View through entrance court to library.

∨ Reading area, interior view.

0   1   3   5M

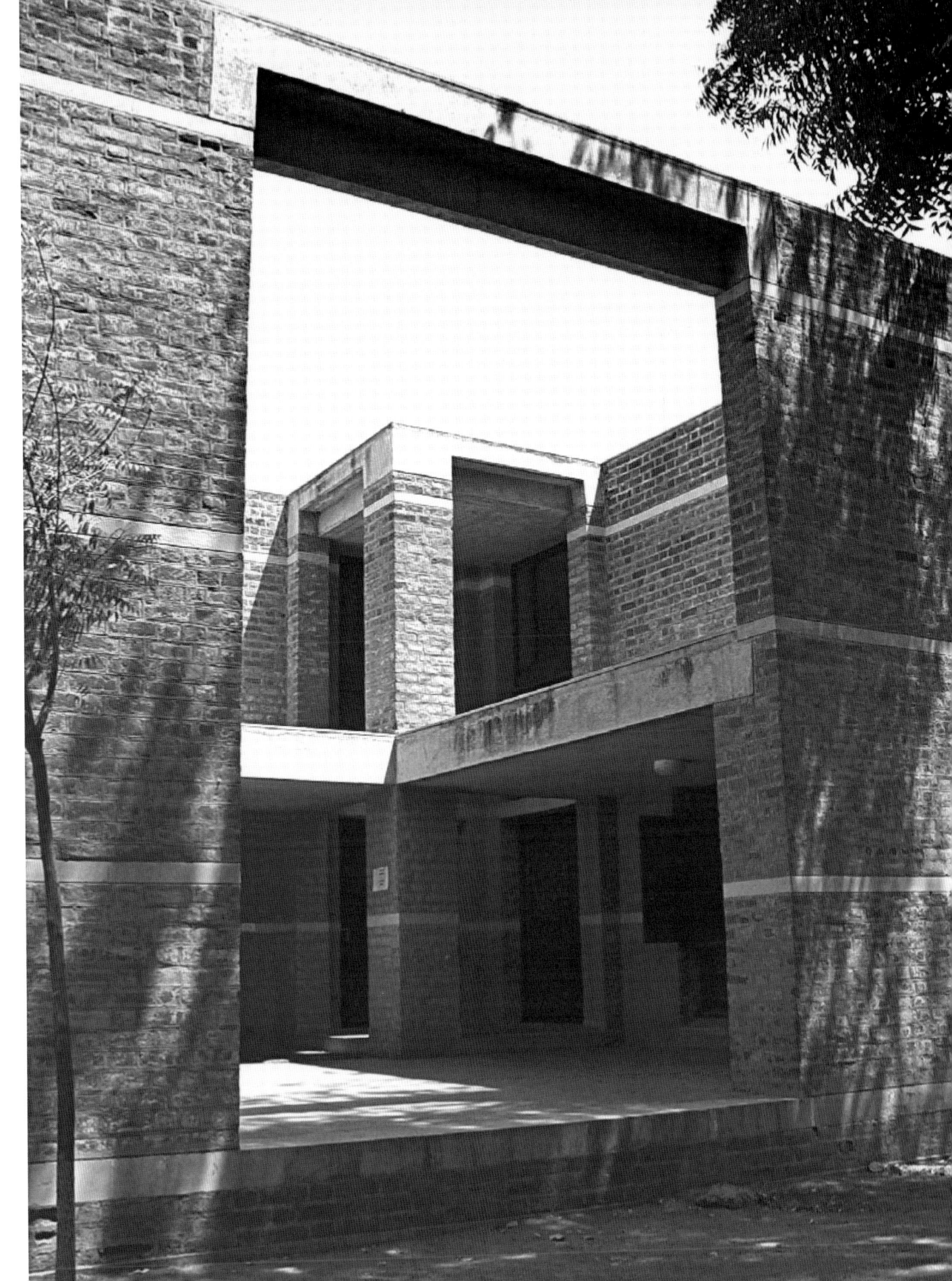

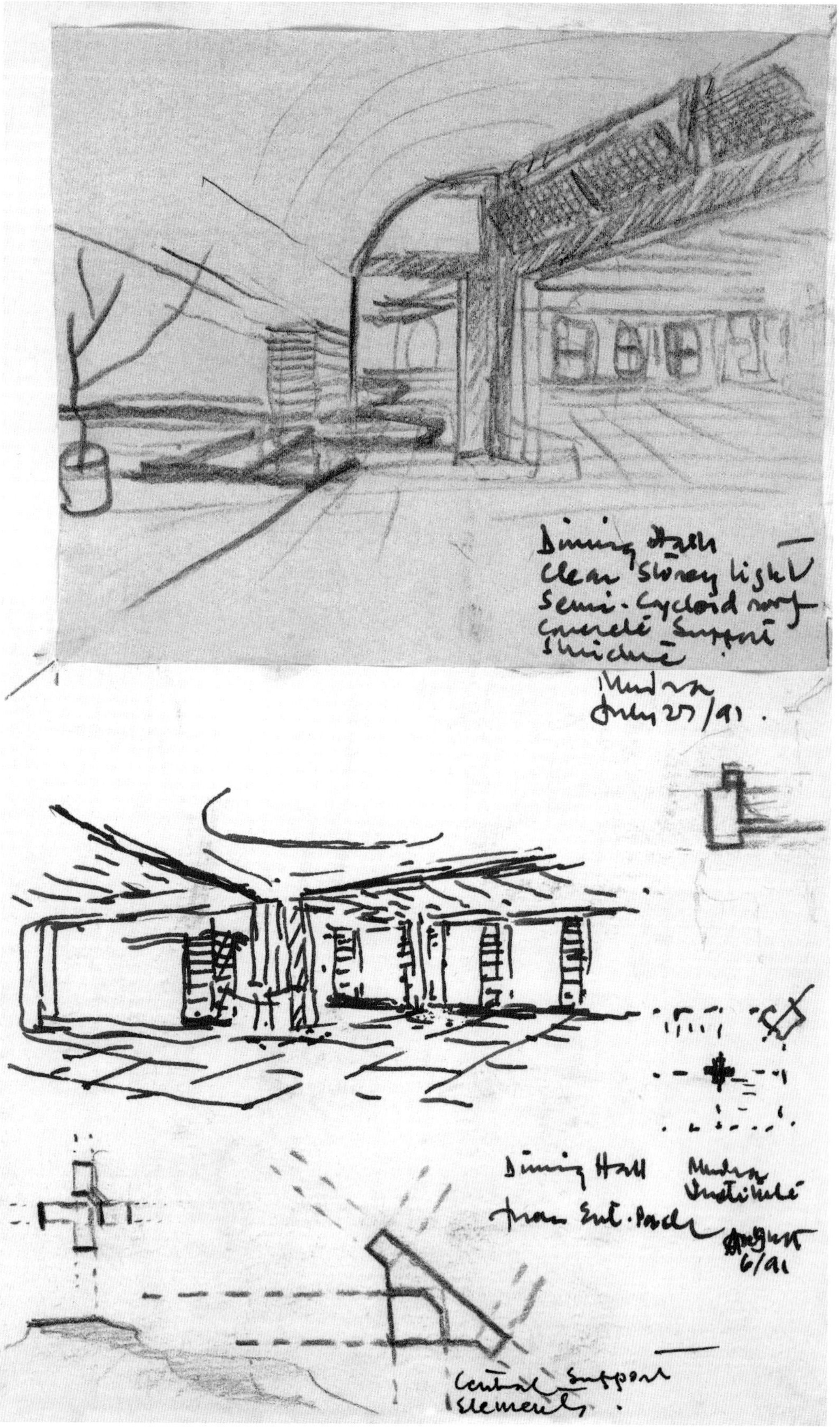

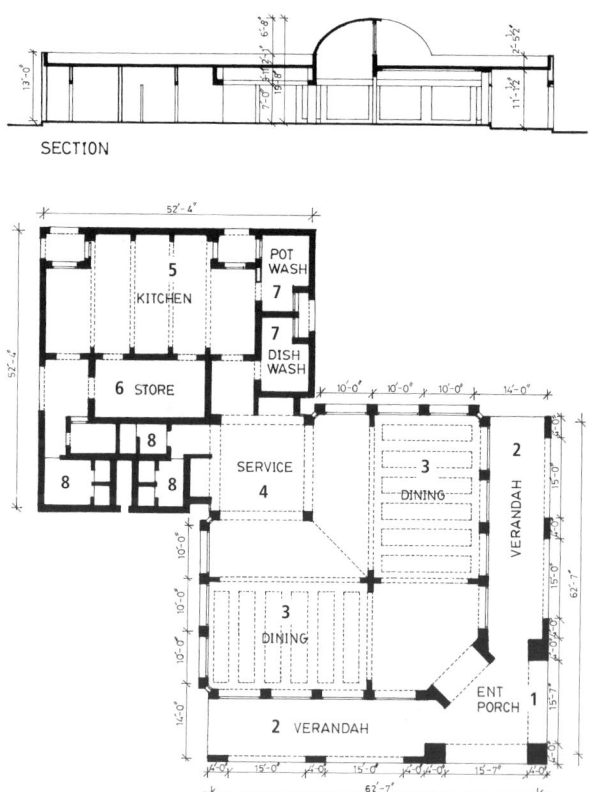

Dining Hall
Clear Storey light
Semi-Cycloid roof
Concrete Support
Structure
Madras
July 27/91.
Dining Hall
from Ent. Porch
Madras
Institute
August
6/91
Central Support
elements.

13'-0"
7'-0"
6'-8"
11'-1½"
2'-5½"

SECTION

52'-4"
5
KITCHEN
POT
WASH
7
7
DISH
WASH
6 STORE
8
8
8
SERVICE
4
3
DINING
3
DINING
2
VERANDAH
2 VERANDAH
ENT
PORCH
1
10'-0"
14'-0"
15'-0"
15'-7"
62'-7"

< Floor plan and section, kitchen–dining.
1 Entrance porch
2 Verandah
3 Dining
4 Food service
5 Kitchen
6 Store
7 Wash
8 Toilets

< Dining hall studies, June 1991.
Notes on the sketch, from top:
'Dining Hall, clerestorey light, semi-cycloid roof, concrete support structure'
'Dining Hall from Ent. Porch'

> Dining hall studies, June 1991.
Notes on the sketch, from top:
'Skylight in concrete with full half-circle gable at two ends, set back from parapet'
'Roof over dining'
'Parapet over pilasters'
'Gable set back'
'Dining Hall elevation studies'
'Verandah parapet set back'
'Verandah wall as a screen wall, lower height than the parapet over the dining hall to cut down the scale in relation to the outside turf and "sit-out"'
'Parapet over dining hall pilasters'
'Verandah space extending out to the turf outside'
'Dining hall openings layered behind verandah openings'
'Possible parapet height manipulations'

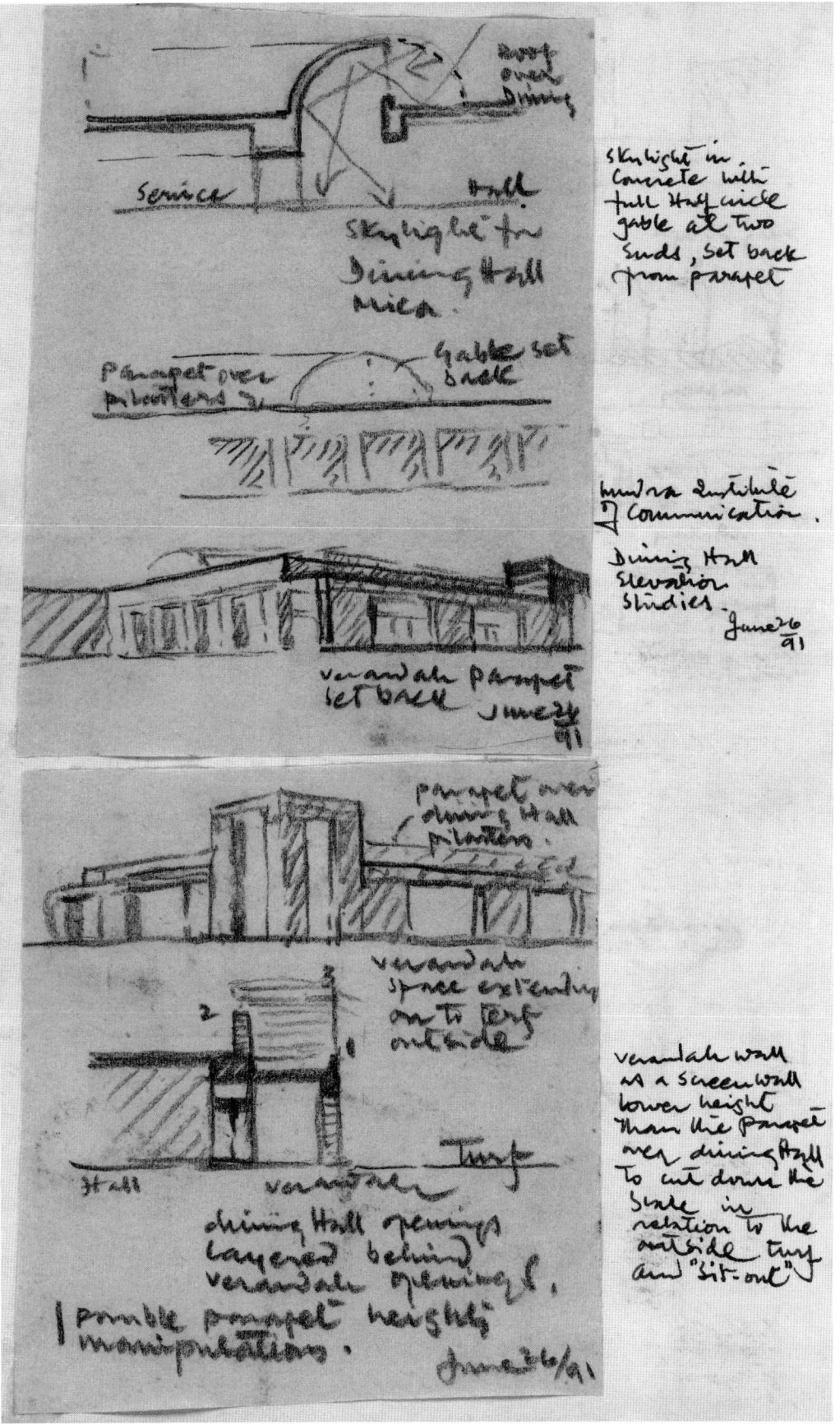

Student dormitory clusters, in the form of a village street with dining and club house facilities. Two dormitories making a court between. The entrance courts are articulated by the staircase turning inwards. Light wells at the corner, opening the rooms to the court.

< Dormitory cluster model in wood.

> Plan view, dormitory cluster model in wood.

> Mudra Institute dormitories, January 1991.
  Notes on the sketch read, from top:
  'Dormitory clusters'
  'two dorms making a court between'
  'light wells at the corner opening the room windows to the court'
  'Street approach to dorms'
  'dorms at ground and upper floor, 4 students – 8 students per cluster'
  'meeting spaces at street level'
  'Entrance court made by stairs turning inwards'

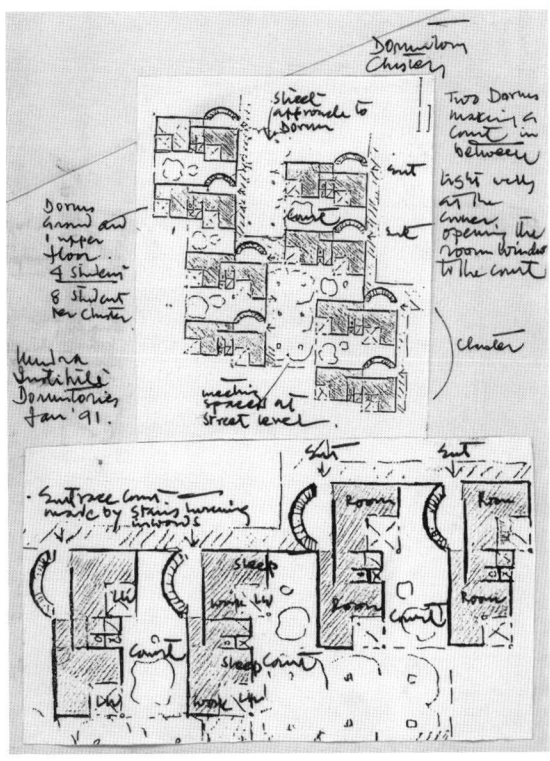

> Interior of the production plant. The vaults are made of corrugated metal sheets with fibreglass sheets in between to bring in light.

INTEC Polymer Factory and Laboratories
Silvassa, 1993–96

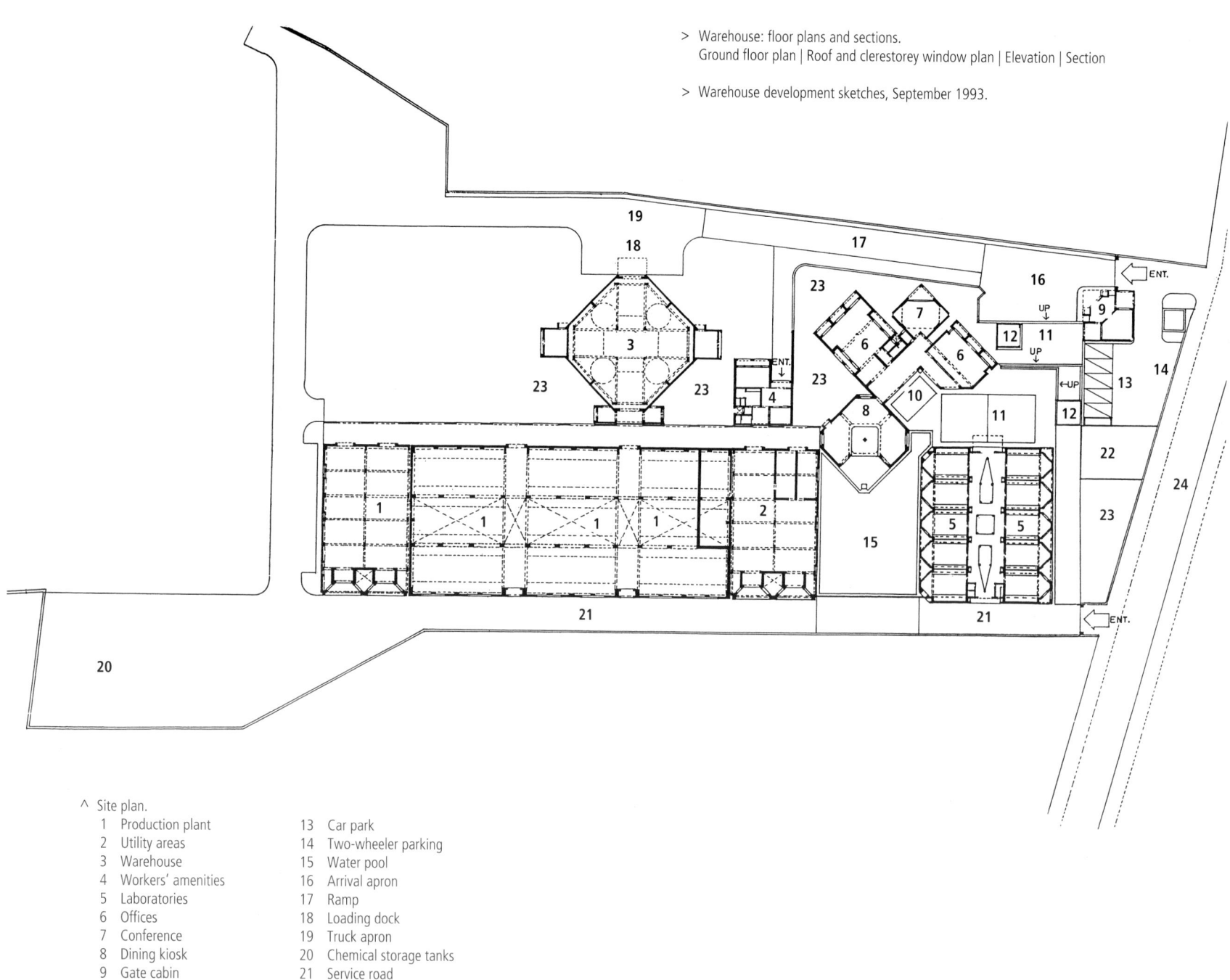

> Warehouse: floor plans and sections.
> Ground floor plan | Roof and clerestorey window plan | Elevation | Section

> Warehouse development sketches, September 1993.

∧ Site plan.

1	Production plant	13	Car park
2	Utility areas	14	Two-wheeler parking
3	Warehouse	15	Water pool
4	Workers' amenities	16	Arrival apron
5	Laboratories	17	Ramp
6	Offices	18	Loading dock
7	Conference	19	Truck apron
8	Dining kiosk	20	Chemical storage tanks
9	Gate cabin	21	Service road
10	Court of offices	22	Transformer space
11	Court of entrances	23	Garden
12	Planters	24	Access road

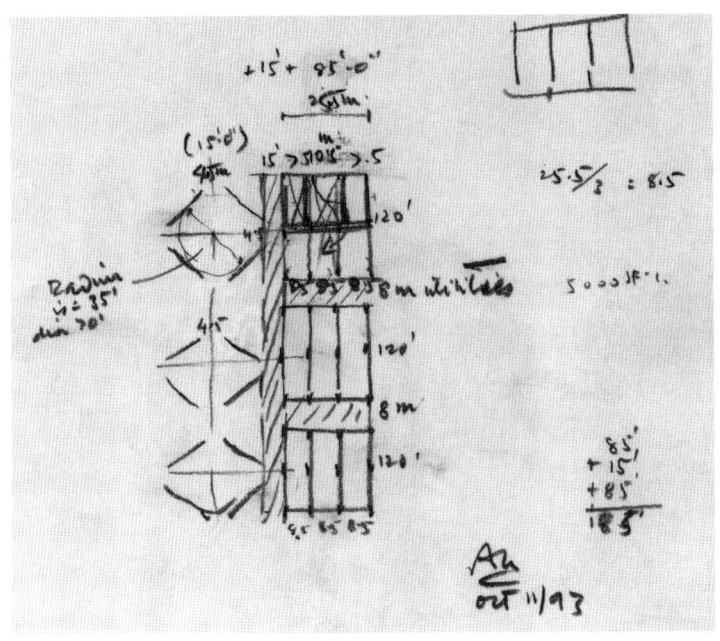

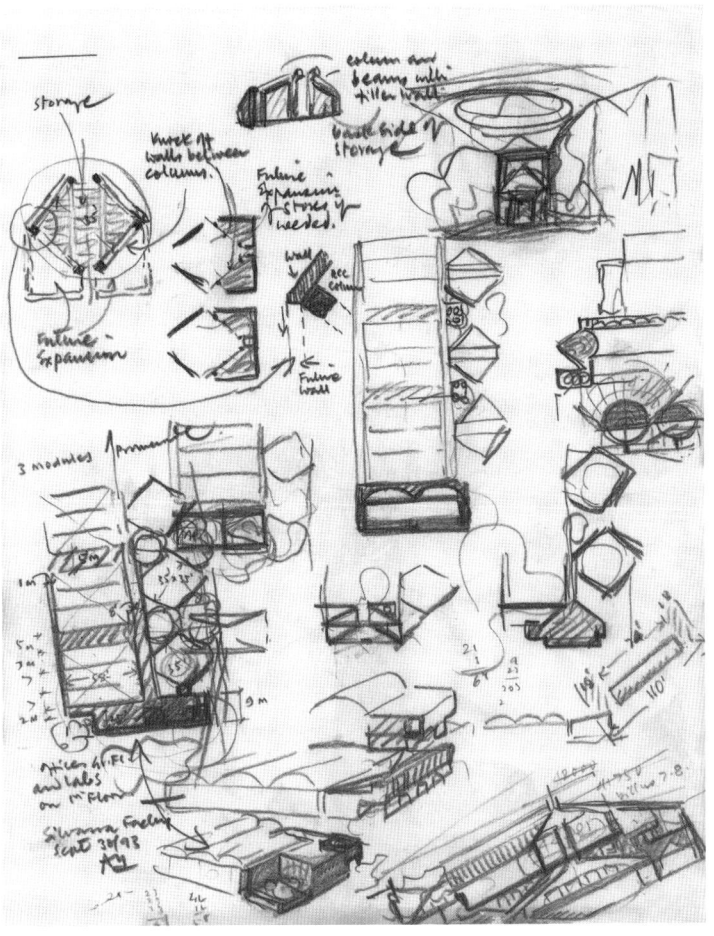

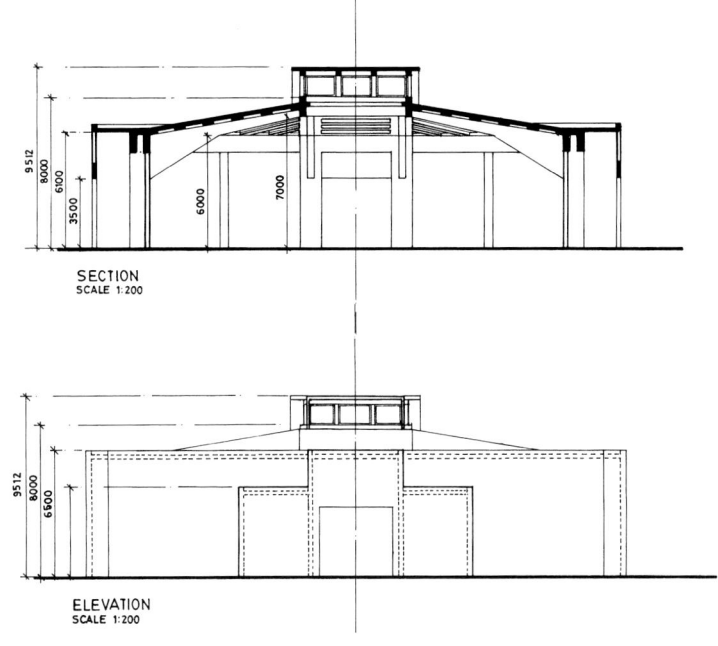

SECTION
SCALE 1:200

ELEVATION
SCALE 1:200

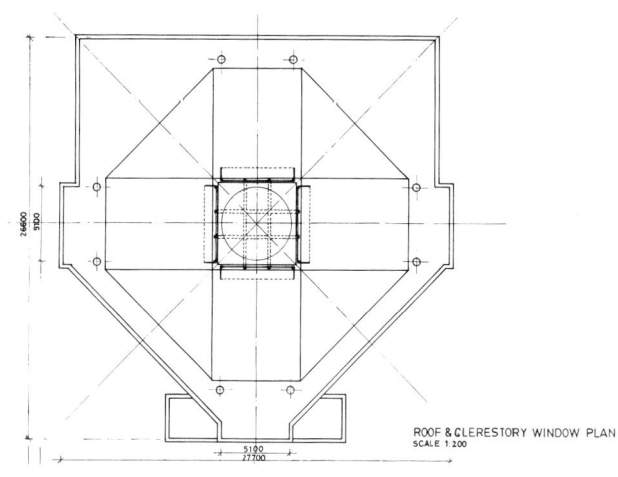

ROOF & CLERESTORY WINDOW PLAN
SCALE 1:200

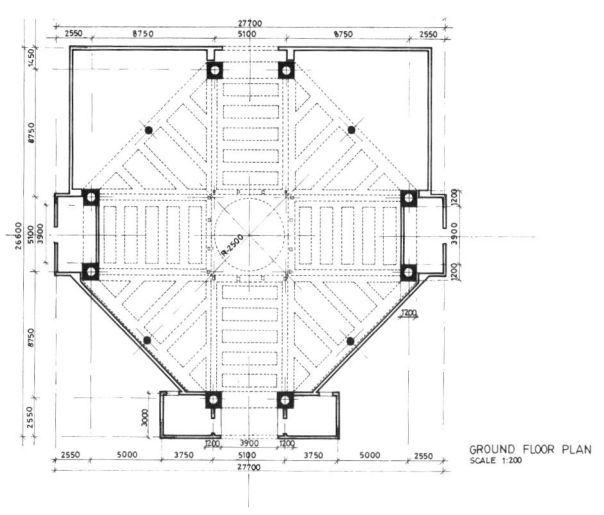

GROUND FLOOR PLAN
SCALE 1:200

> Production plant: interior view of clerestorey.

∨ Development of openings on exterior wall and front wall undulations to form solids–voids, June 1994.
   Notes on sketch include:
   'vault'
   'glass bricks continuous strip'
   'openable windows body ventilation'
   'Do not attach architecture to programme; assign programme to architecture. It is the reinterpretation of
   programme in response to architecture that results in spatial relationships"

∨ Development of openings and front wall modulations to form solids–voids, July 1993.

∨ Construction photograph of production plant (right) and warehouse (left).

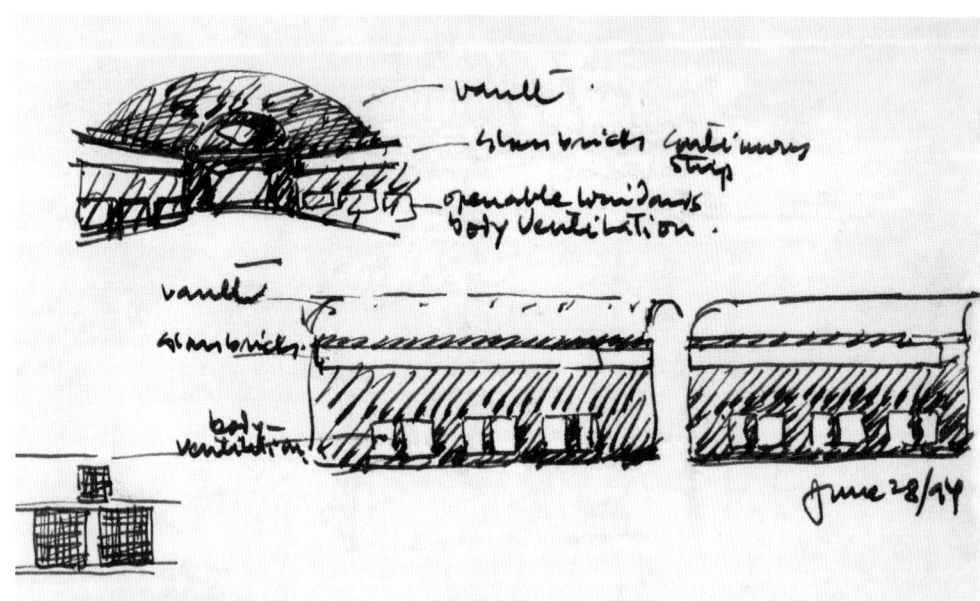

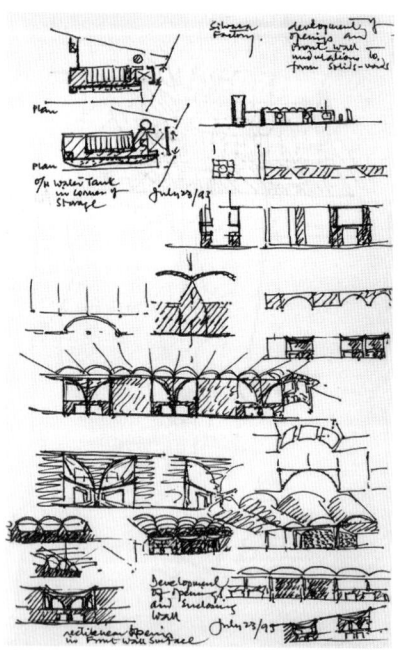

The laboratories, with a wide top-lit gallery – top-lit akin to the step-wells. This connecting gallery is a wonderful space with the top light bouncing off the plants underneath and the circulation around it. The exterior of this building is made by heavy, thick walls with perforations articulated to keep the sun out.

> Definitive plans and sections.

> Central top-lit gallery.

∨ Axonometric, with the central top-lit gallery, laboratory spaces and exterior wall.

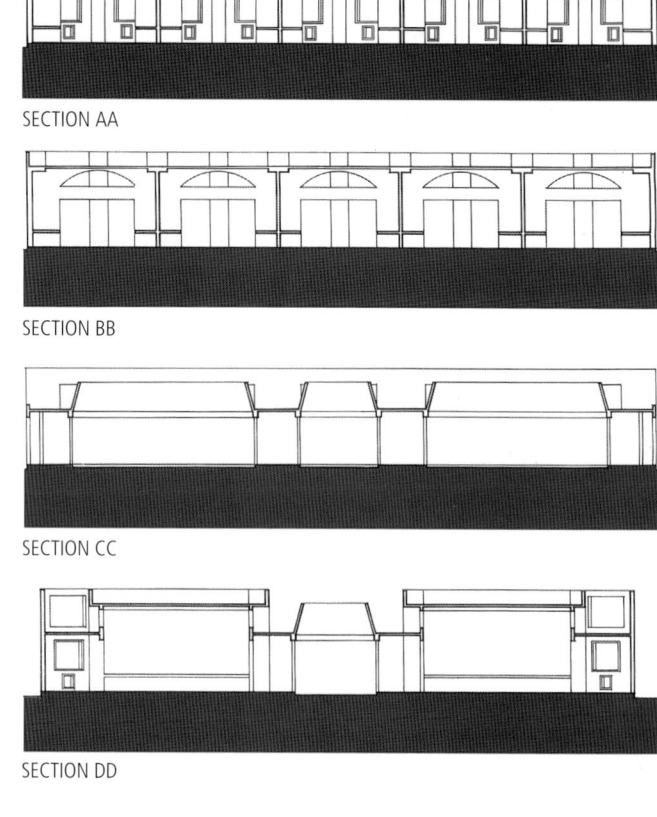

SECTION AA

SECTION BB

SECTION CC

SECTION DD

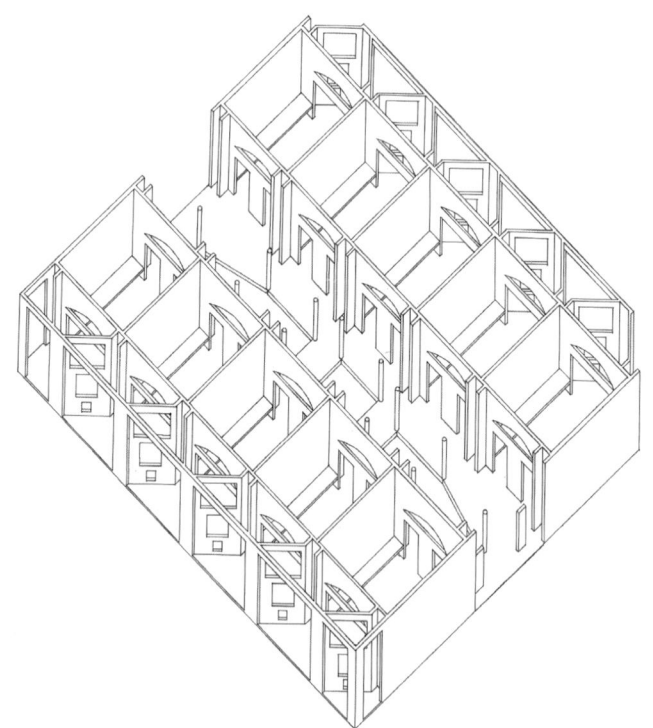

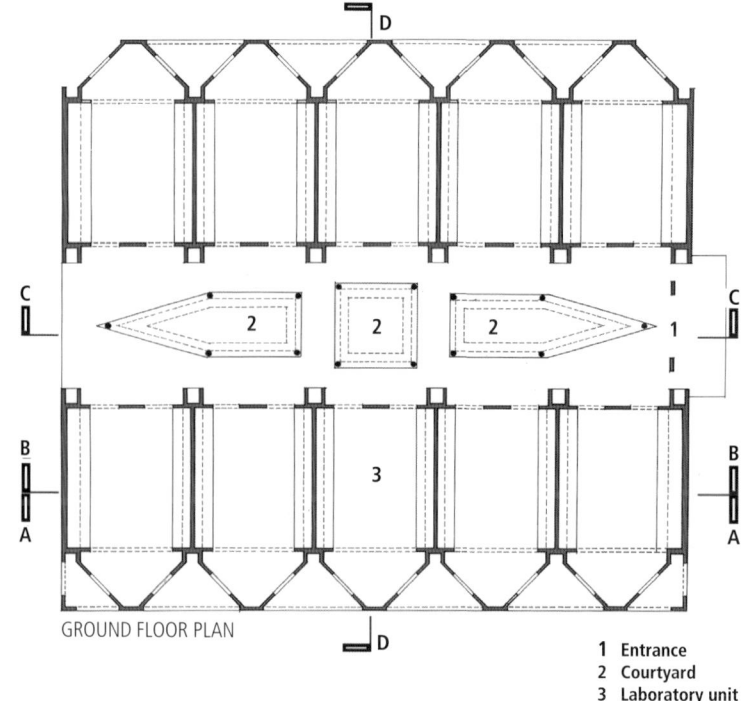

GROUND FLOOR PLAN

1 Entrance
2 Courtyard
3 Laboratory unit

278

The architecture at the periphery of the laboratory enclosure. The interior alcoves, with their clerestorey and windows, give the periphery a sense of a three-dimensional enclosure.

Museum of Minerals and Mines
Nagpur, Maharashtra, 1996
(in collaboration with the National Institute of Design)

The architecture of the museum, or for that matter any building, is expressed through space and material. Light, natural light, reveals the character of this space. The museum space is a special event in time. The past records passing through the present must direct towards the future which is unknown, yet predictable. Architecture of the museum must work for this backdrop, whatever may be its shape, size and form. It must create a kinship both for the objects and the spaces which enhance the true nature of these objects. Man is part of the entire record in which only the present is comprehensible for him. The true kinship between the spaces and the objects can accelerate and help encompass the full story of which he is a part.

The museum is realized in the form of a sequence of spaces stepping down from the grade on the northwest side to almost 24'-0" below on the southeast. The southwest side provides access to the auditorium, workshops, stores, the working of which is independent from the functioning of the exhibits in the museum.

The climate of Nagpur fluctuates between two extremes – very hot in the summer to very cold in the winter. To protect the exhibits from such fluctuating extremes, the museum exhibits are dug into the ground. We have, as a part of our cultural heritage, examples of such buildings in the step-wells of Gujarat and Rajasthan. The museum spaces and the exhibits are thus protected and at the same time isolated from other activities on the site. It also gives an opportunity to simulate the conditions which prevail in the underground mines, and the experience that is offered is that of participation and discovery. The various heights inside the museum lend a freedom to organize the exhibits, which have different scales and sizes.

The building which is linear with its major axis running northwest–southeast has one entry on the northwest side of the site, and another entry (to the auditorium) on the southeast side. The auditorium is located above grade and is connected through the foyer to the lower part of the museum by means of stairs and an elevator. It can function independently of the museum and is outside the main circulation to the museum. Both entrances have parking adjacent to them. Besides the vehicular parking, the AC plant and workshops can be approached directly from the auditorium side.

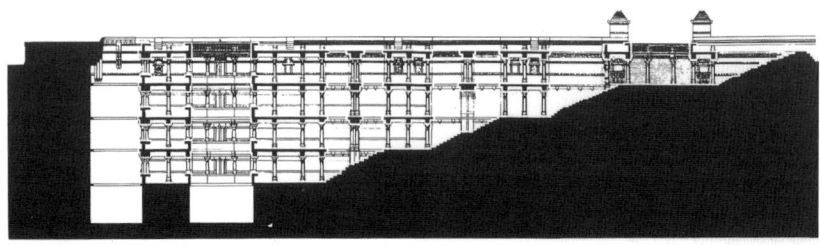

∧ Section through the Adalaj stepwell, Ahmedabad.

> Definitive model in wood.

∨ Site plan.
   1 Museum
   2 Workshops
   3 Auditorium
   4 Canteen

Adjacent to the site was a horrendous high-rise. With that building so close, what kind of a superstructure could I have designed for the museum? Also, the subject matter suggested that one would have to go deep into the ground. That may not sound convincing, but it helped me to push the entire building down into the ground.

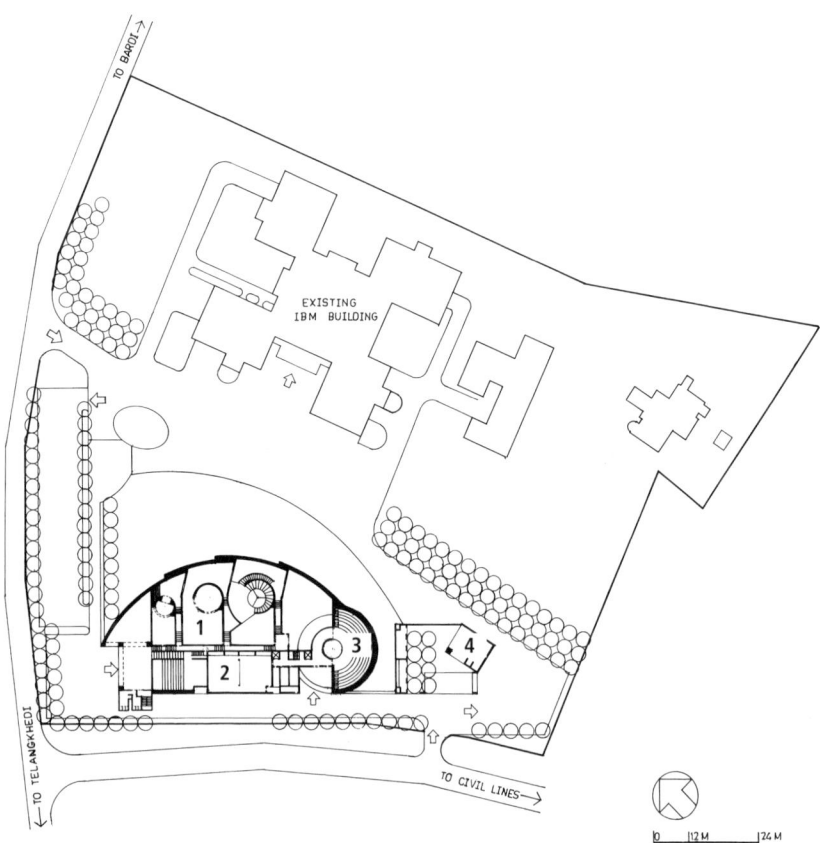

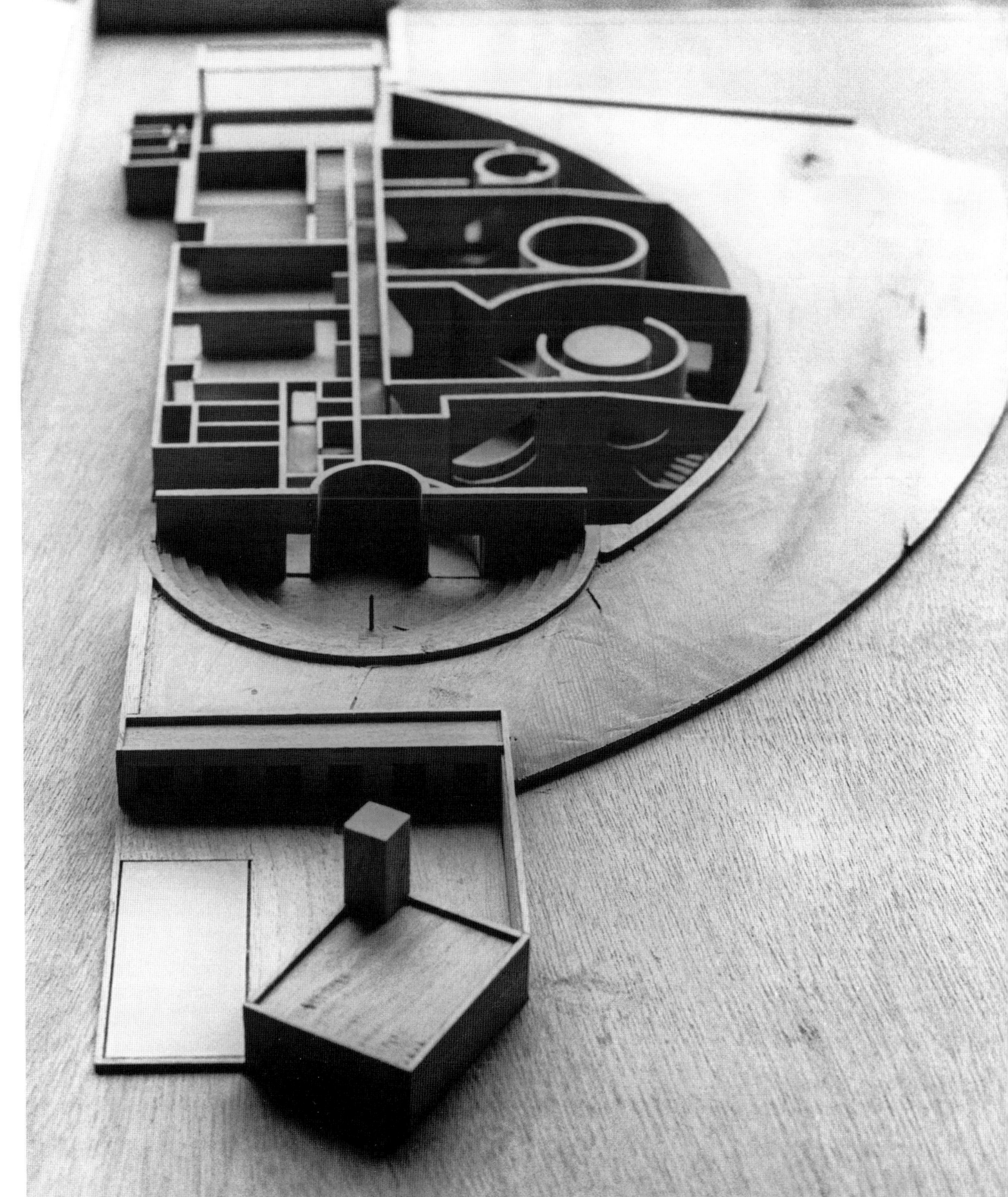

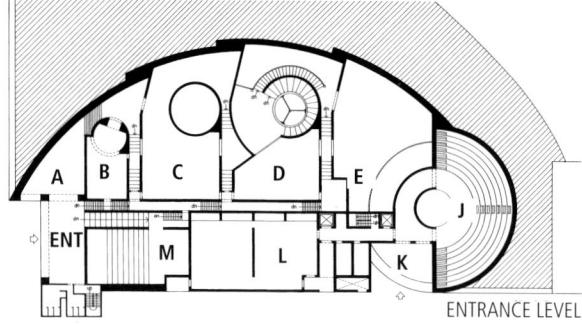

ENTRANCE LEVEL

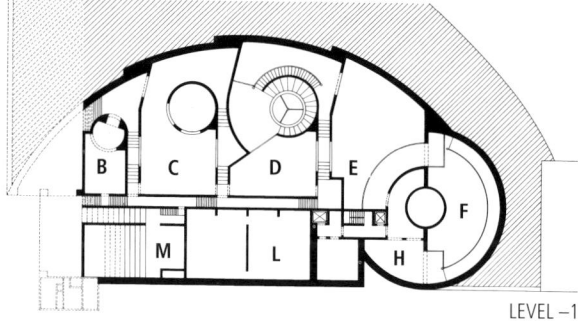

LEVEL −1

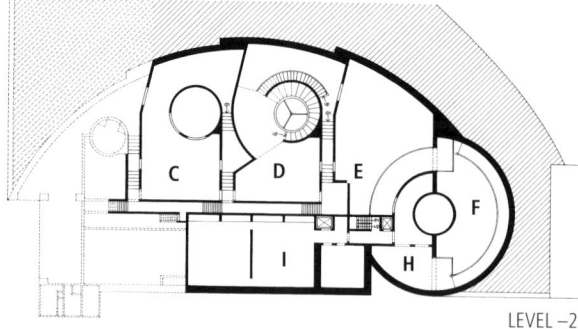

LEVEL −2

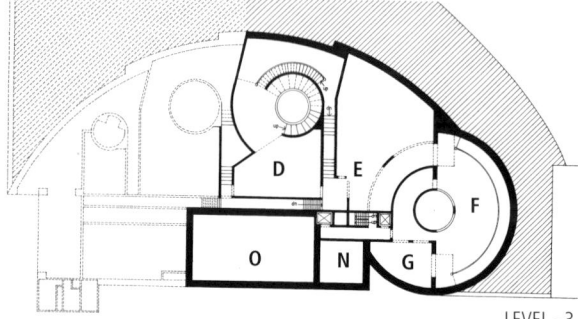

LEVEL −3

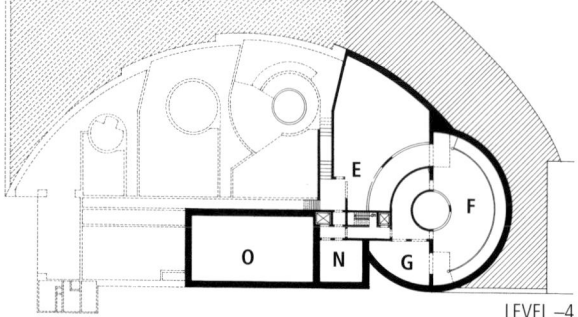

LEVEL −4

< Floor plans.
ENT Entrance foyer to museum (entrance level)
A Information and overview (entrance level)
B Birth of a mineral (level −1)
C Minerals and man (level −2)
D Mines and mining (level −3)
E From mineral to metal (level −4)
F Future options (level −4)
G Feedback arcade (level −4)
H Bookshop (level −2)
I Resource centre (level −2)
J Auditorium
K Entrance foyer to auditorium (entrance level)
L Workshops and design cell (entrance level)
M Audiovisual room (entrance level)
N AC plant for auditorium (level −4)
O AC plant and mechanical room for the museum (level −4)

> Wooden model showing the delineation of spaces (below)
and the form from above grade (top).

∨ The Pueblo Bonito, New Mexico.

Each floor is a horizontal section, where you go around the periphery to get an introduction to very large exhibition spaces. Inside there are chambers, which were being worked out in conjunction with the NID. The chambers are in the form of 'kivas' – the Anasazi chambers of initiation – recalling my experiences and observations of the Chaco Canyon in the American southwest.

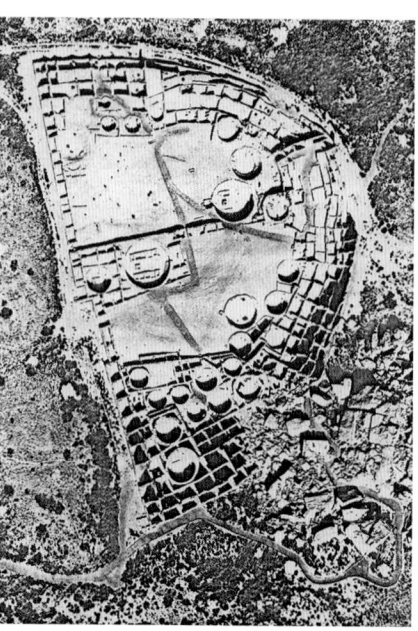

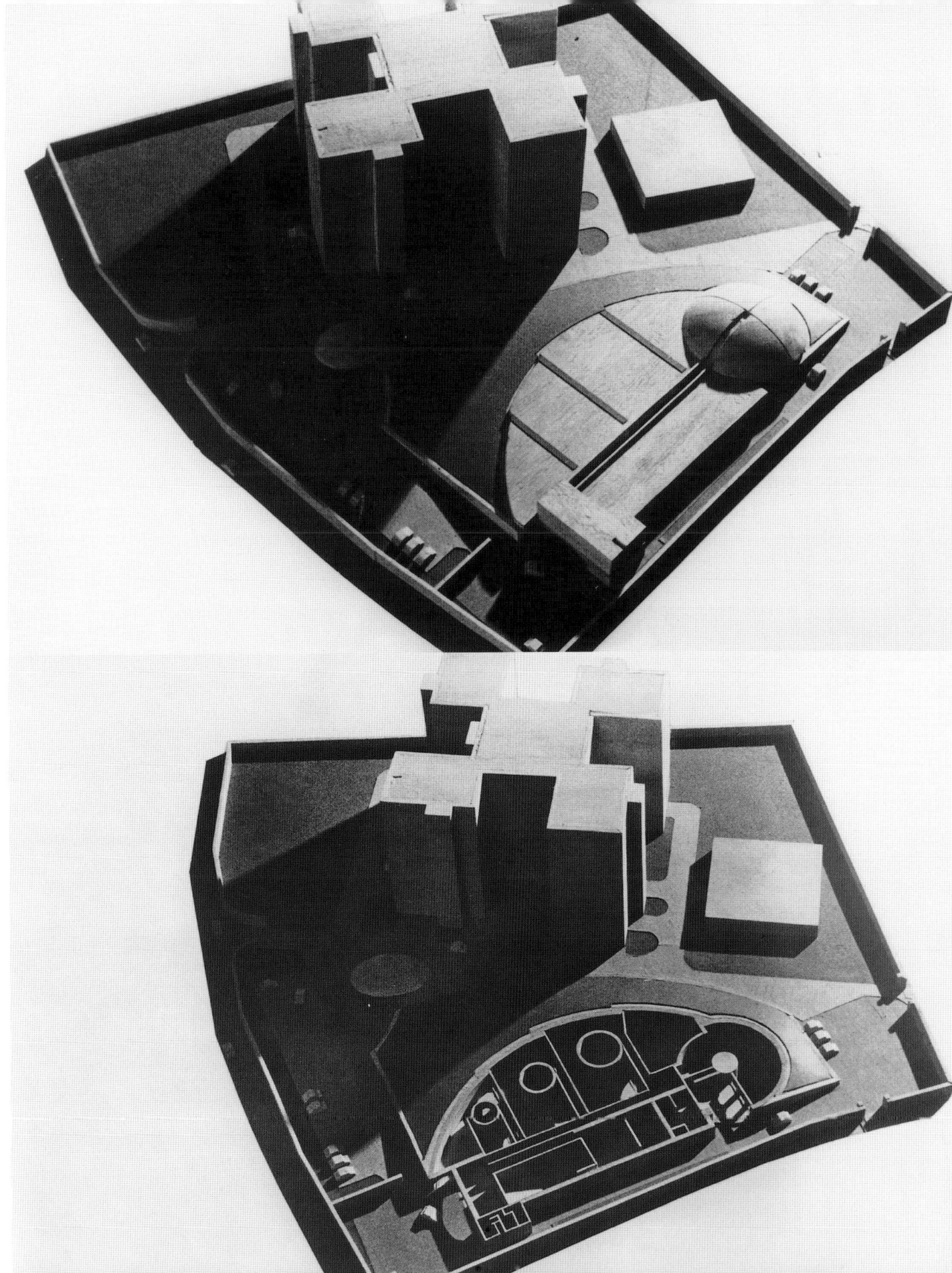

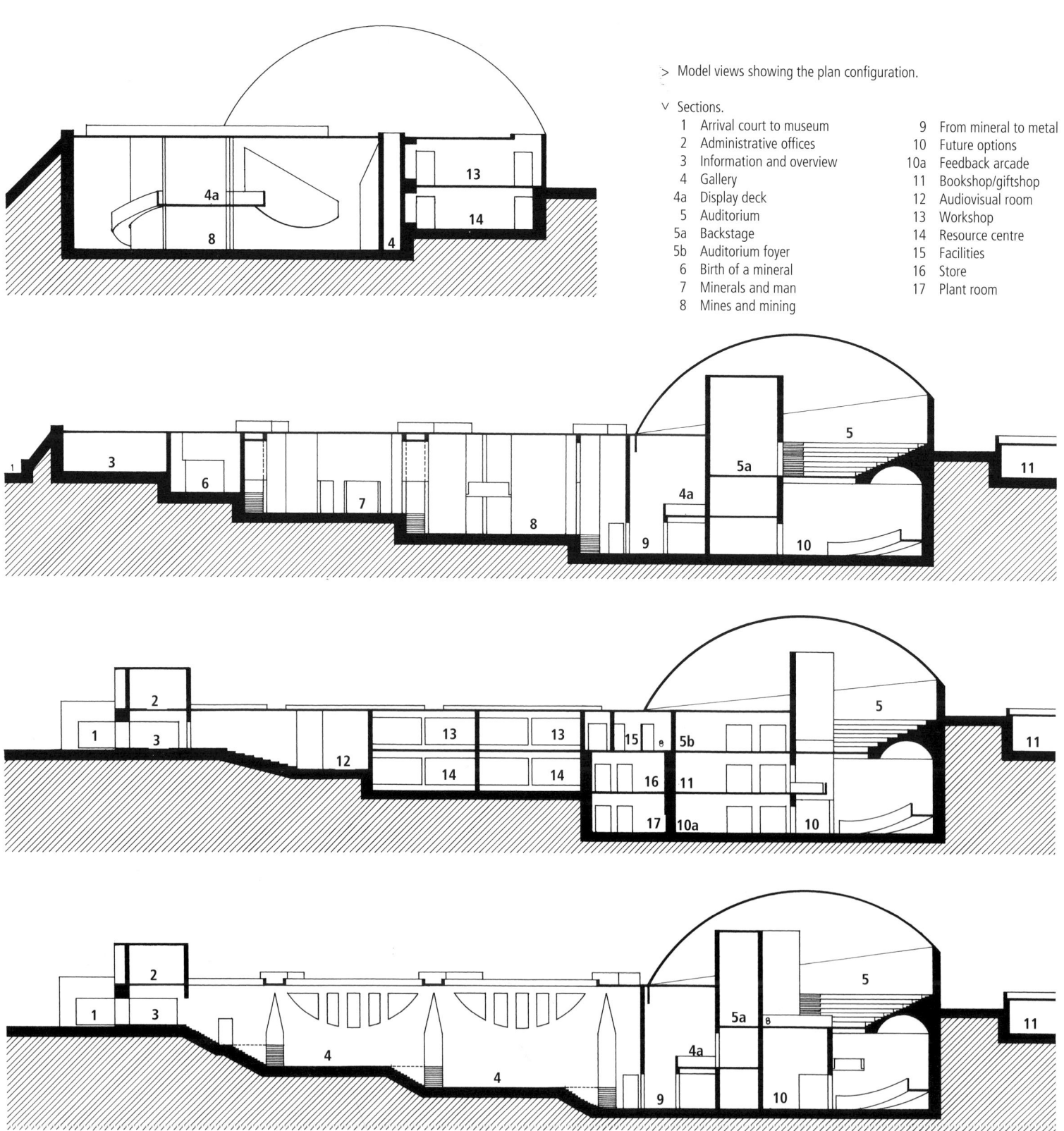

> Model views showing the plan configuration.

∨ Sections.
1   Arrival court to museum
2   Administrative offices
3   Information and overview
4   Gallery
4a Display deck
5   Auditorium
5a Backstage
5b Auditorium foyer
6   Birth of a mineral
7   Minerals and man
8   Mines and mining
9   From mineral to metal
10 Future options
10a Feedback arcade
11 Bookshop/giftshop
12 Audiovisual room
13 Workshop
14 Resource centre
15 Facilities
16 Store
17 Plant room

I have done a lot of competitions. Never have I won any competition in my life – I was always a finalist ... this is the reality of the situation; but boy, you keep doing them because there are so many things you learn out of making a competition where there is no real client, no budget, nobody behind you to push you to finish your drawings until you meet the deadline. These were certain challenges and certain happy moments in my life – by doing competitions and getting something out of it for yourself.

– Anant Raje, FEED Pune Lecture, 5 July 2003

Competitions

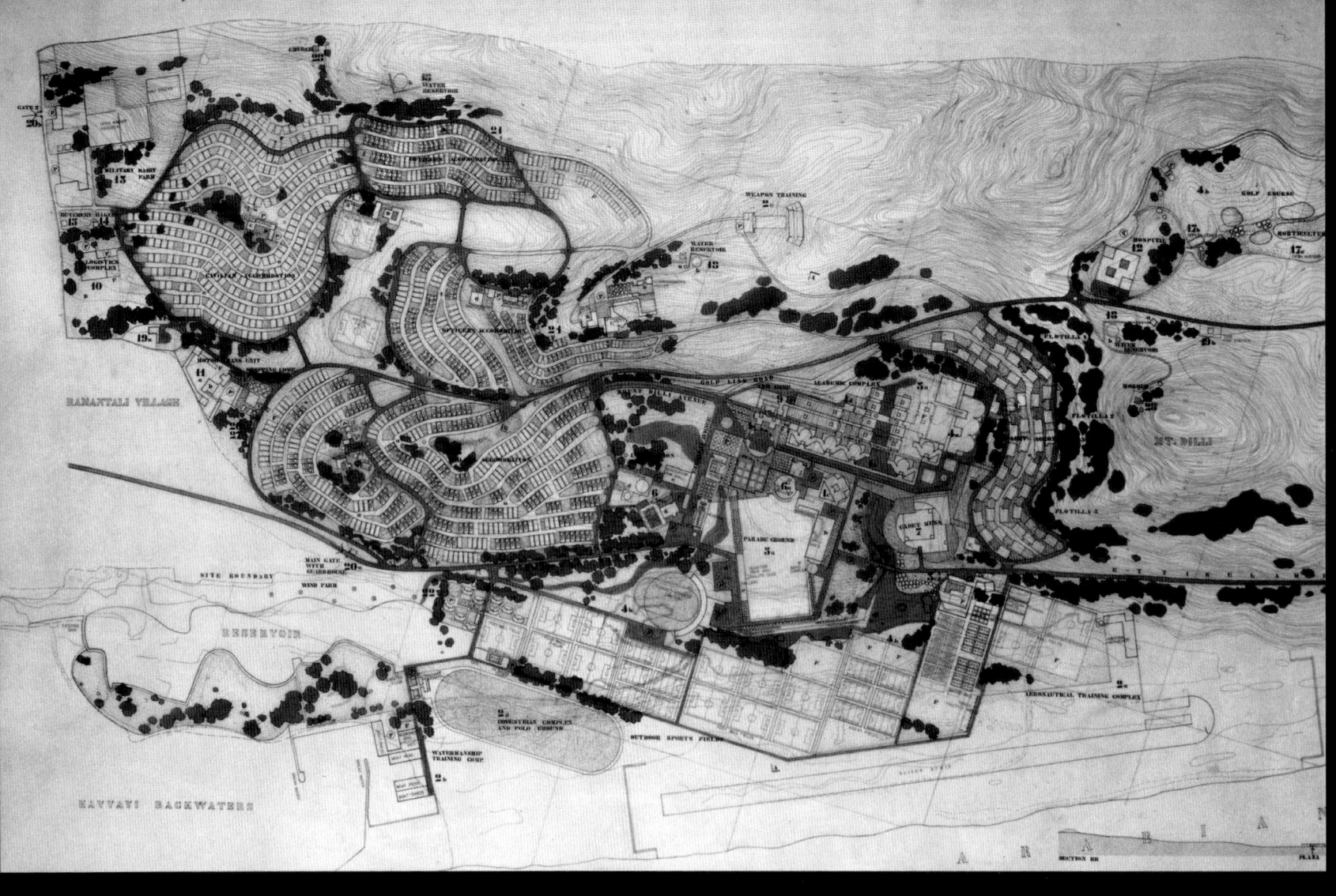

^ Overall site plan with the academic complex and housing.
  Original plate submitted for stage 1.

> Model of academic complex. Original submittal for stage 2.

The Naval Academy
Ezhimala, Kerala, 1988
(invited competition, finalist)

The programme was only one factor in the synthesis of our architectural composition. The master plan, the environments, the existing buildings on the site and the technical aspects of the various structures influenced the eventual design of the Academy.

Our proposal attempted the embodiment of a sense of history through architectural forms established at decisive places to reflect an association with a strong coastal history and coastal traditions. The library, mess halls and service buildings are round in exterior character with the connected walls, ramparts of the promenade and terraces being of strong coastal–historical traditions. From far out at sea, these buildings give the impression of the seaside edge of a city with its chapel situated on high ground, commanding a view from Mount Dilli on the backwaters and beyond. The headquarters (HQ) building takes its inspiration from domestic coastal architecture and is integrated with the arrival plaza. Within this environment, conducive to academic learning, a cadet finds his own identity.

The focus of the entire institution is the parade ground, both ceremonial and commemorative in nature. It occupies a central place in the layout on the flat plateau. Its major axis runs approximately in a north–east/south–west direction; the two open ends on this major axis face the sea and the slopes of the wooded ridge, bringing both elements of nature into one composition and giving it a monumental dimension under the shadow of Mount Dilli. The presence of Mount Dilli is further accentuated by two major circulation routes for vehicular traffic. One, at the bottom of the low ridge abutting the broad side of the parade ground forms a VIP entry and pavilion; and the other, at the bottom of the long ridge, gives access to administrative buildings as well as the academic buildings and library, all the way up to the cadets' mess halls and flotillas.

The second focal point is the area for the cadets' residences positioned in close proximity to the academic centre. Designed in a manner that reflects the local expression of residen-ces on the hillsides of Kerala, these provide a sense of community and belonging to a place.

Every squadron is identified with its hard-court provided for daily assembly. The hard-court and the landscape court allow a flexible adjustment of the cadets' blocks to the contours of the site. The courts offer connections between two blocks, their final shape depending on the twists and turns of the sloped surface underneath. The access to all cadets' housing is at three levels. These linear streets link each flotilla with stepped approaches across the contours to connect common amenities, indoor games and the gymnasium; as do the lower streets which pass by the cadets' mess halls through the valley to outdoor sport areas and the club house with swimming pool facilities.

The civil residences are located at the extreme edge, on the northern part of the site, in contrast to the rest of the housing which is in close proximity to the academic centre and the administrative group of buildings. The residences have loop roads as major circulation routes and at their higher levels reach the great upper bowl for sports such as golf, riding and trekking along the slopes of the hills. The row form of dwelling units accomplishes a high density per hectare, which is desirable from the point of view of land utilization.

(Text from Competition Entry)

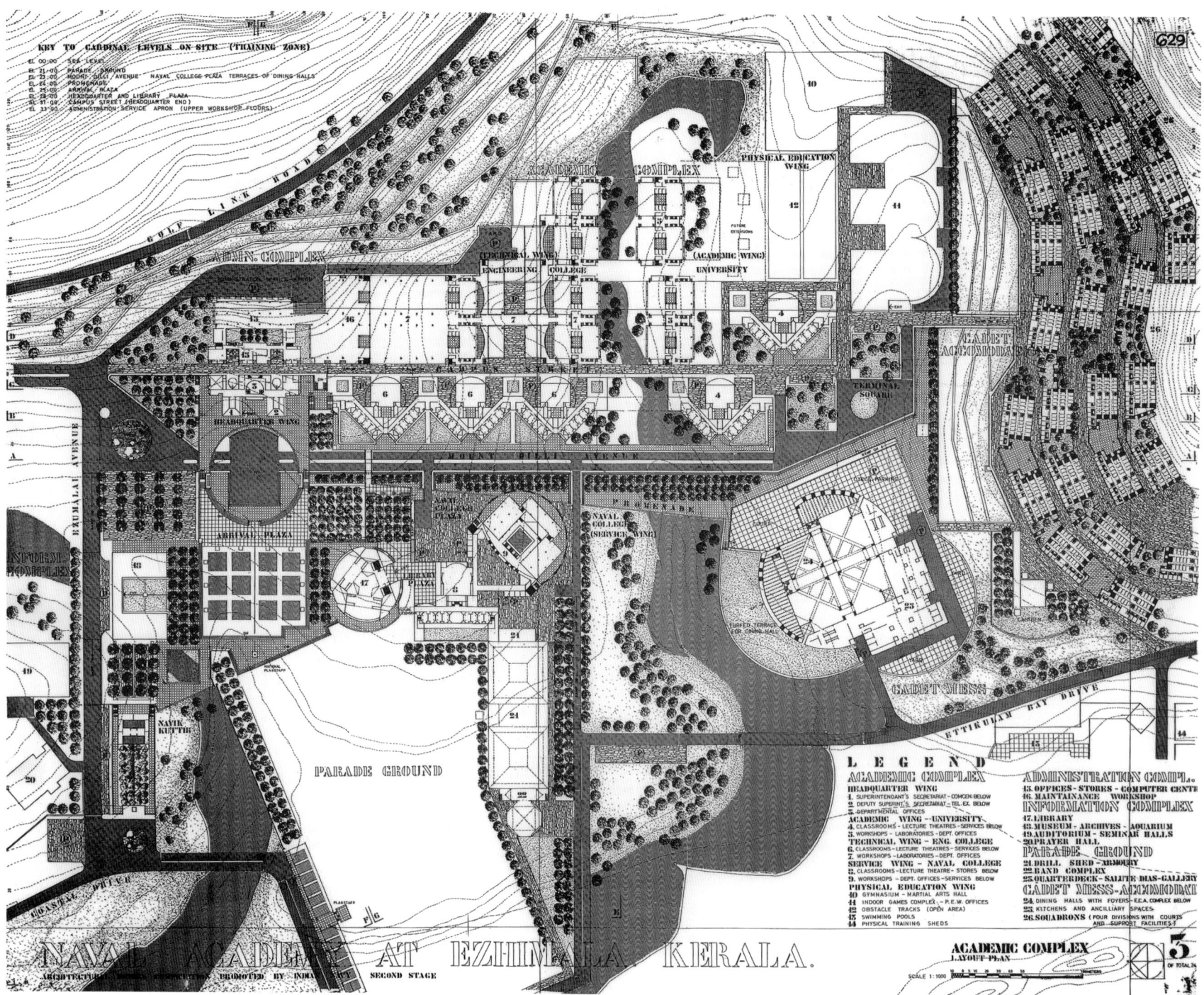

∧ Academic complex layout plan. Original plate submitted for stage 2.

> Headquarters wing. Original plate submitted for stage 2.

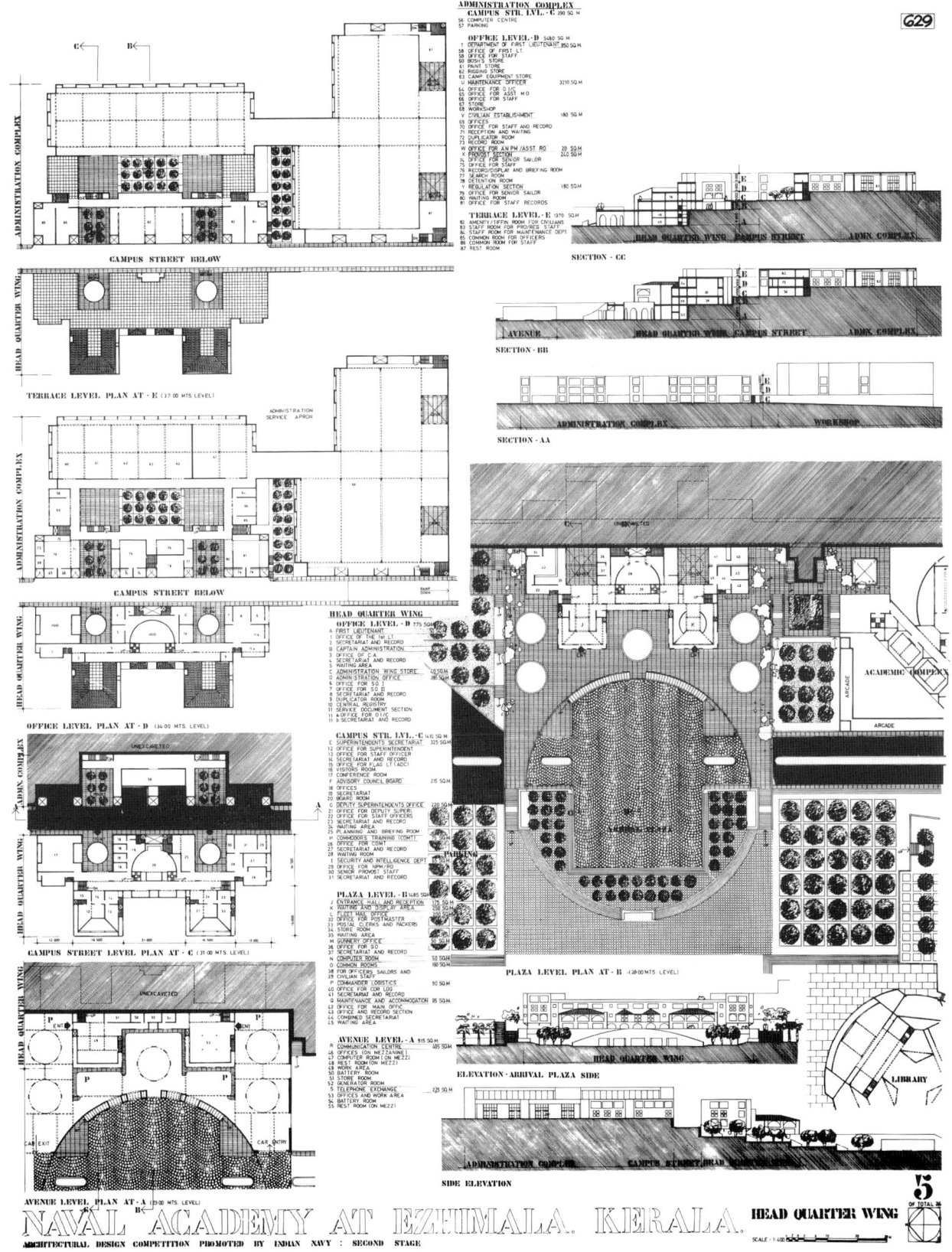

ADMINISTRATION COMPLEX
CAMPUS STR. LVL - C 390 SQ.M
56 COMPUTER CENTRE
57 PARKING

OFFICE LEVEL - D 5480 SQ.M
1 DEPARTMENT OF FIRST LT.
U DEPARTMENT OF FIRST LIEUTENANT 850 SQ.M
58 OFFICE OF FIRST LT.
59 OFFICE FOR STAFF
60 BOSN'S STORE
61 PAINT STORE
62 RIGGING STORE
63 CAMP EQUIPMENT STORE
U MAINTENANCE OFFICER 3210 SQ.M
64 OFFICE FOR O.I/C
65 OFFICE FOR ASST M.O
66 OFFICE FOR STAFF
67 STORE
68 WORKSHOP
V CIVILIAN ESTABLISHMENT 180 SQ.M
69 OFFICES
70 OFFICE FOR STAFF AND RECORD
71 RECEPTION AND WAITING
72 DUPLICATOR ROOM
73 RECORD ROOM
W OFFICE FOR AN PM /ASST RO 30 SQ.M
X PROVOST SECTION 240 SQ.M
74 OFFICE FOR SENIOR SAILOR
75 OFFICE FOR STAFF
76 RECORD/DISPLAY AND BRIEFING ROOM
77 SEARCH ROOM
78 DETENTION ROOM
Y REGULATION SECTION 180 SQ.M
79 OFFICE FOR SENIOR SAILOR
80 WAITING ROOM
81 OFFICE FOR STAFF RECORDS

TERRACE LEVEL - E 1370 SQ.M
82 AMENITY/TIFFIN ROOM FOR CIVILIANS
83 STAFF ROOM FOR PROVED STAFF
84 STAFF ROOM FOR MAINTENANCE DEPT.
85 COMMON ROOM FOR OFFICERS
86 COMMON ROOM FOR STAFF
87 REST ROOM

SECTION - CC

SECTION - BB

SECTION - AA

HEAD QUARTER WING
OFFICE LEVEL - D 775 SQ.M
A FIRST LIEUTENANT
1 OFFICE OF THE 1st LT
2 SECRETARIAT AND RECORD
B CAPTAIN ADMINISTRATION
3 OFFICE OF C.A.
4 SECRETARIAT AND RECORD
5 WAITING AREA
C ADMINISTRATION WING STORE 1050 SQ.M
D ADMINISTRATION OFFICE
6 OFFICE FOR SO D
7 OFFICE FOR SO II
8 SECRETARIAT AND RECORD
9 DUPLICATOR ROOM
10 CENTRAL REGISTRY
11 SERVICE DOCUMENT SECTION
11 a OFFICE FOR O I/C
11 b SECRETARIAT AND RECORD

CAMPUS STR. LVL - C 1410 SQ.M
E SUPERINTENDENTS SECRETARIAT 325 SQ.M
12 OFFICE FOR SUPERINTENDENT
13 OFFICE FOR STAFF OFFICER
14 SECRETARIAT AND RECORD
15 OFFICE FOR FLAG LT (ADC)
16 VISITORS ROOM
17 CONFERENCE ROOM
F ADVISORY COUNCIL BOARD 215 SQ.M
18 OFFICES
19 SECRETARIAT
20 BOARD ROOM
G DEPUTY SUPERINTENDENTS OFFICE 220 SQ.M
21 OFFICE FOR DEPUTY SUPERI
22 OFFICE FOR STAFF OFFICERS
23 SECRETARIAT AND RECORD
24 WAITING AREA
25 PLANNING AND BRIEFING ROOM
H COMMODORE TRAINING (CDMT)
26 OFFICE FOR COMDT
27 SECRETARIAT AND RECORD
28 WAITING ROOM
I SECURITY AND INTELLIGENCE DEPT
29 OFFICE FOR NPM/RO
30 SENIOR PROVOST STAFF
31 SECRETARIAT AND RECORD

PLAZA LEVEL - B 1485 SQ.M
J ENTRANCE HALL AND RECEPTION 175 SQ.M
K WAITING AND DISPLAY AREA 250 SQ.M
L FLEET MAIL OFFICE
32 OFFICE FOR POSTMASTER
33 POSTAL CLERKS AND PACKERS
34 STORE ROOM
35 WAITING AREA
M GUNNERY OFFICE
36 OFFICE FOR SO
37 SECRETARIAT AND RECORD
N COMPUTER ROOM 50 SQ.M
O COMMON ROOMS 180 SQ.M
38 FOR OFFICERS, SAILORS AND
39 CIVILIAN STAFF
P COMMANDER LOGISTICS 90 SQ.M
40 OFFICE FOR CDR LOG
41 SECRETARIAT AND RECORD
Q MAINTENANCE AND ACCOMMODATION 85 SQ.M
42 OFFICE FOR MAIN OFFIC
43 OFFICE AND RECORD SECTION
44 COMBINED SECRETARIAT
45 WAITING AREA

AVENUE LEVEL - A 915 SQ.M
R COMMUNICATION CENTRE 405 SQ.M
46 OFFICES (ON MEZZANINE)
47 COMPUTER ROOM (ON MEZZ)
48 REST ROOM (ON MEZZ)
49 WORK AREA
50 BATTERY ROOM
51 STORE ROOM
52 GENERATOR ROOM
S TELEPHONE EXCHANGE 225 SQ.M
53 OFFICES AND WORK AREA
54 BATTERY ROOM
55 REST ROOM (ON MEZZ)

CAMPUS STREET BELOW

TERRACE LEVEL PLAN AT - E (37.00 LEVEL)

CAMPUS STREET BELOW

OFFICE LEVEL PLAN AT - D (34.00 MTS. LEVEL)

CAMPUS STREET LEVEL PLAN AT - C (31.00 MTS. LEVEL)

AVENUE LEVEL PLAN AT - A (25.00 MTS. LEVEL)

PLAZA LEVEL PLAN AT - B (28.00 MTS LEVEL)

ELEVATION - ARRIVAL PLAZA SIDE

SIDE ELEVATION

ADMINISTRATION COMPLEX   CAMPUS STREET   HEAD

NAVAL ACADEMY AT EZHIMALA, KERALA.
ARCHITECTURAL DESIGN COMPETITION PROMOTED BY INDIAN NAVY : SECOND STAGE

HEAD QUARTER WING
SCALE - 1:400

5 OF TOTAL 26

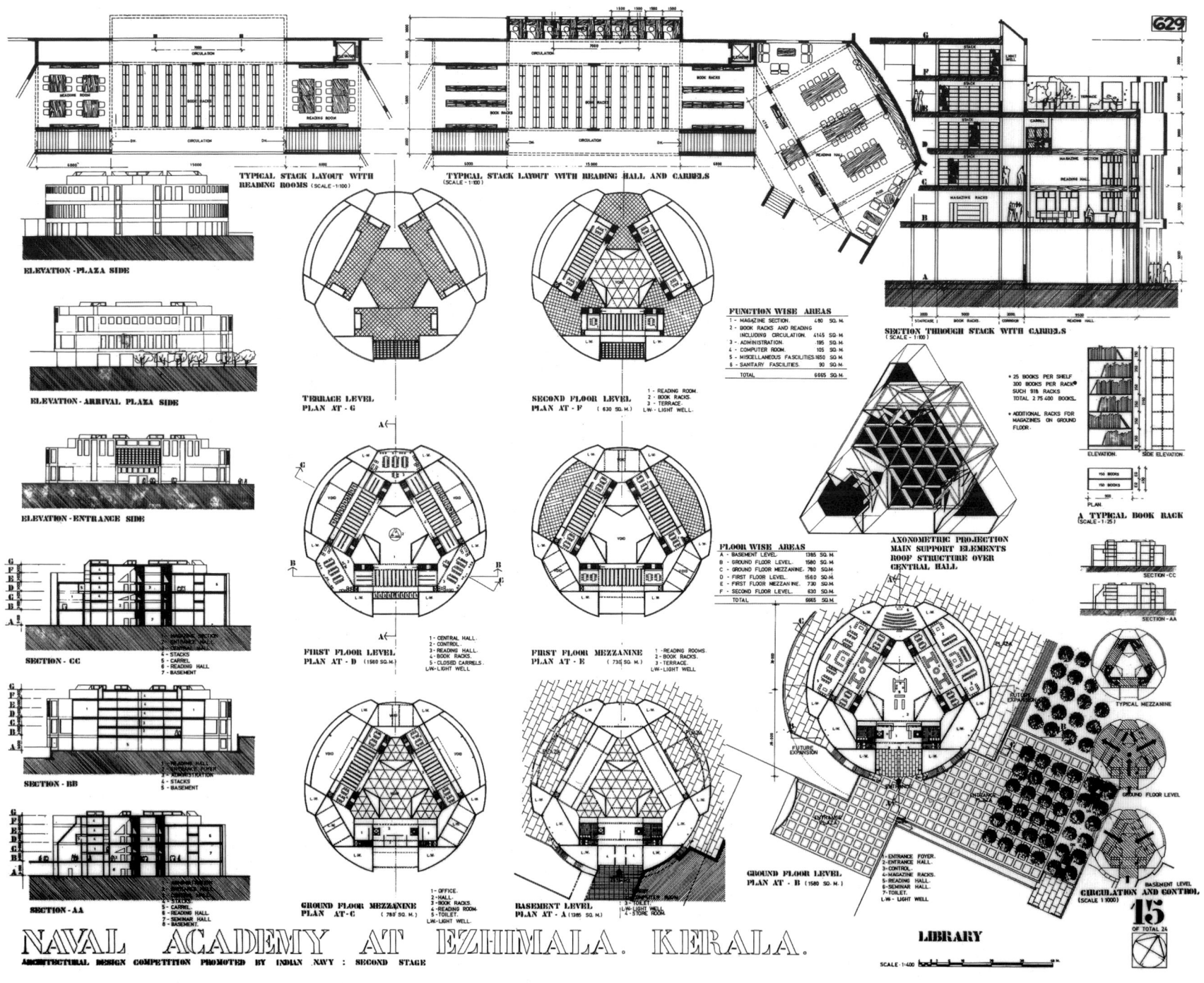

TYPICAL STACK LAYOUT WITH
READING ROOMS (SCALE 1:100)

TYPICAL STACK LAYOUT WITH READING HALL AND CARRELS
(SCALE 1:100)

SECTION THROUGH STACK WITH CARRELS
(SCALE 1:100)

ELEVATION - PLAZA SIDE

ELEVATION - ARRIVAL PLAZA SIDE

ELEVATION - ENTRANCE SIDE

SECTION - CC

SECTION - BB

SECTION - AA

TERRACE LEVEL
PLAN AT - G

SECOND FLOOR LEVEL
PLAN AT - F (630 SQ. M.)

1 - READING ROOM.
2 - BOOK RACKS.
3 - TERRACE.
LW - LIGHT WELL

FIRST FLOOR LEVEL
PLAN AT - D (1560 SQ. M.)

1 - CENTRAL HALL.
2 - CONTROL.
3 - READING HALL.
4 - BOOK RACKS.
5 - CLOSED CARRELS.
LW - LIGHT WELL.

FIRST FLOOR MEZZANINE
PLAN AT - E (730 SQ. M.)

1 - READING ROOMS.
2 - BOOK RACKS.
3 - TERRACE.
LW - LIGHT WELL

GROUND FLOOR MEZZANINE
PLAN AT - C (780 SQ. M.)

1 - OFFICE.
2 - HALL.
3 - BOOK RACKS.
4 - READING ROOM.
5 - TOILET.
LW - LIGHT WELL.

BASEMENT LEVEL
PLAN AT - A (1385 SQ. M.)

1 -
2 -
3 - TOILET.
4 - STORE ROOM.
LW - LIGHT WELL.

GROUND FLOOR LEVEL
PLAN AT - B (1580 SQ. M.)

1 - ENTRANCE FOYER.
2 - ENTRANCE HALL.
3 - CONTROL.
4 - MAGAZINE RACKS.
5 - READING HALL.
6 - SEMINAR HALL.
7 - TOILET.
LW - LIGHT WELL

FUNCTION WISE AREAS

1 - MAGAZINE SECTION.	480 SQ. M.	
2 - BOOK RACKS AND READING INCLUDING CIRCULATION.	4145 SQ. M.	
3 - ADMINISTRATION.	195 SQ. M.	
4 - COMPUTER ROOM.	105 SQ. M.	
5 - MISCELLANEOUS FACILITIES.	1650 SQ. M.	
6 - SANITARY FACILITIES.	90 SQ. M.	
TOTAL	6665 SQ. M.	

FLOOR WISE AREAS

A - BASEMENT LEVEL.	1385 SQ. M.	
B - GROUND FLOOR LEVEL.	1580 SQ. M.	
C - GROUND FLOOR MEZZANINE.	780 SQ. M.	
D - FIRST FLOOR LEVEL.	1560 SQ. M.	
E - FIRST FLOOR MEZZANINE.	730 SQ. M.	
F - SECOND FLOOR LEVEL.	630 SQ. M.	
TOTAL	6665 SQ. M.	

AXONOMETRIC PROJECTION
MAIN SUPPORT ELEMENTS
ROOF STRUCTURE OVER
CENTRAL HALL

* 25 BOOKS PER SHELF
  300 BOOKS PER RACK.
  SUCH 918 RACKS.
  TOTAL 2 75 400 BOOKS.

* ADDITIONAL RACKS FOR
  MAGAZINES ON GROUND
  FLOOR.

A TYPICAL BOOK RACK
(SCALE 1:25)

TYPICAL MEZZANINE

GROUND FLOOR LEVEL

CIRCULATION AND CONTROL
(SCALE 1:1000)

BASEMENT LEVEL

LIBRARY

SCALE 1:400

NAVAL ACADEMY AT EZHIMALA, KERALA.
ARCHITECTURAL DESIGN COMPETITION PROMOTED BY INDIAN NAVY : SECOND STAGE

15
OF TOTAL 24

Library. Original plate submitted for stage 2.

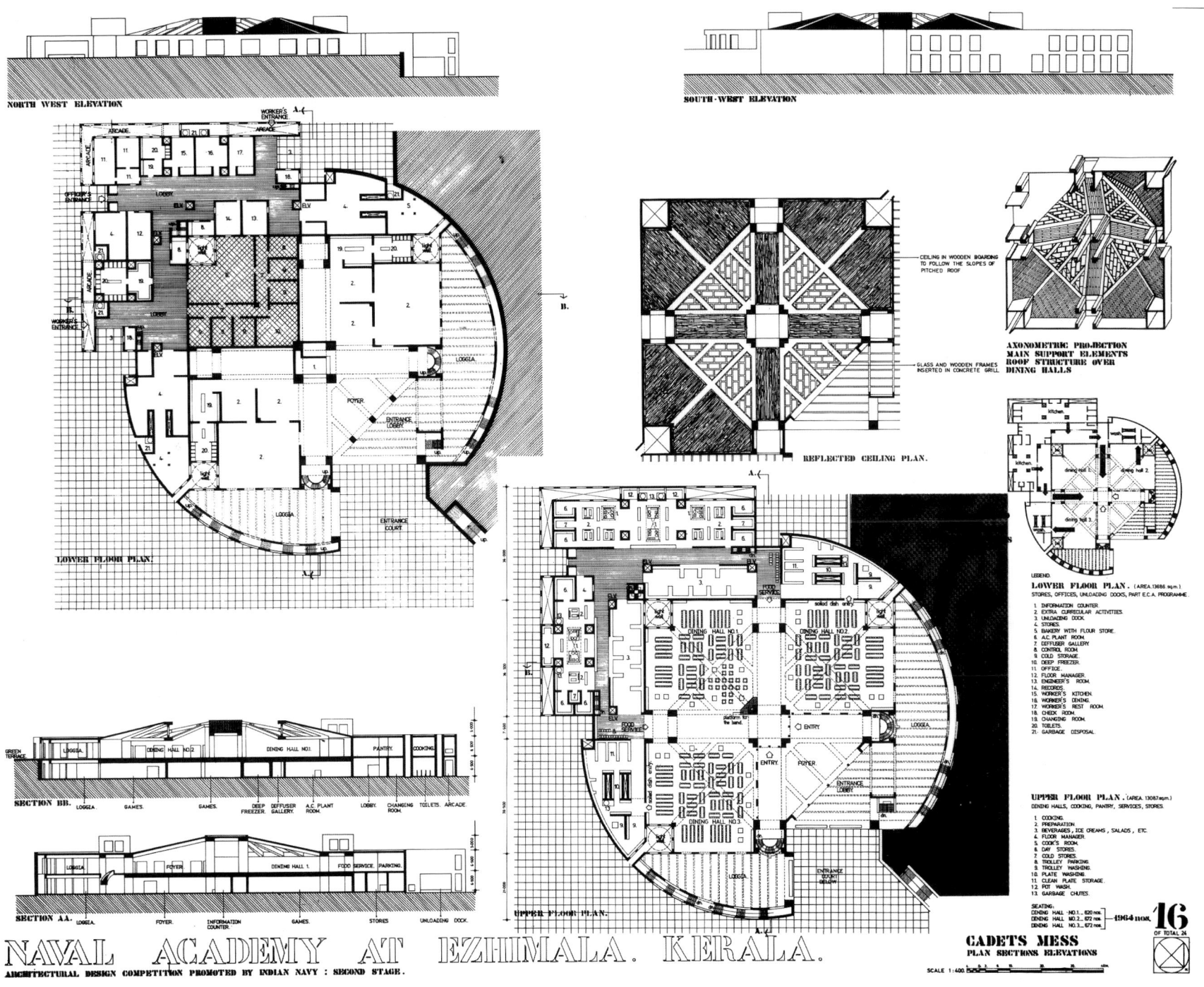

NORTH WEST ELEVATION

SOUTH WEST ELEVATION

LOWER FLOOR PLAN.

SECTION BB.
LOGGIA. GAMES. GAMES. DEEP DIFFUSER A.C. PLANT LOBBY. CHANGING TOILETS. ARCADE.
FREEZER. GALLERY. ROOM. ROOM.

SECTION AA.
LOGGIA. FOYER. INFORMATION GAMES. STORES. UNLOADING DOCK.
COUNTER.

CEILING IN WOODEN BOARDING
TO FOLLOW THE SLOPES OF
PITCHED ROOF

GLASS AND WOODEN FRAMES
INSERTED IN CONCRETE GRILL

REFLECTED CEILING PLAN.

AXONOMETRIC PROJECTION
MAIN SUPPORT ELEMENTS
ROOF STRUCTURE OVER
DINING HALLS

LOWER FLOOR PLAN. (AREA. 13686 sq.m.)
STORES, OFFICES, UNLOADING DOCKS, PART E.C.A. PROGRAMME.

1. INFORMATION COUNTER.
2. EXTRA CURRICULAR ACTIVITIES.
3. UNLOADING DOCK.
4. STORES.
5. BAKERY WITH FLOUR STORE.
6. A.C. PLANT ROOM.
7. DIFFUSER GALLERY.
8. CONTROL ROOM.
9. COLD STORAGE.
10. DEEP FREEZER.
11. OFFICE.
12. FLOOR MANAGER.
13. ENGINEER'S ROOM.
14. RECORDS.
15. WORKER'S KITCHEN.
16. WORKER'S DINING.
17. WORKER'S REST ROOM.
18. CHECK ROOM.
19. CHANGING ROOM.
20. TOILETS.
21. GARBAGE DISPOSAL.

UPPER FLOOR PLAN. (AREA. 13087 sq.m.)
DINING HALLS, COOKING, PANTRY, SERVICES, STORES.

1. COOKING.
2. PREPARATION.
3. BEVERAGES, ICE CREAMS, SALADS, ETC.
4. FLOOR MANAGER.
5. COOK'S ROOM.
6. DAY STORES.
7. COLD STORES.
8. TROLLEY PARKING.
9. PLATE WASHING.
10. PLATE WASHING.
11. CLEAN PLATE STORAGE.
12. POT WASH.
13. GARBAGE CHUTES.

SEATING:
DINING HALL NO.1. 620 nos.
DINING HALL NO.2. 672 nos.
DINING HALL NO.3. 672 nos. 1964 nos.

UPPER FLOOR PLAN.

NAVAL ACADEMY AT EZHIMALA. KERALA.
ARCHITECTURAL DESIGN COMPETITION PROMOTED BY INDIAN NAVY : SECOND STAGE.

CADETS MESS
PLAN SECTIONS ELEVATIONS
SCALE 1:400.

16
OF TOTAL 24

Cadets' mess halls. Original plate submitted for stage 2.

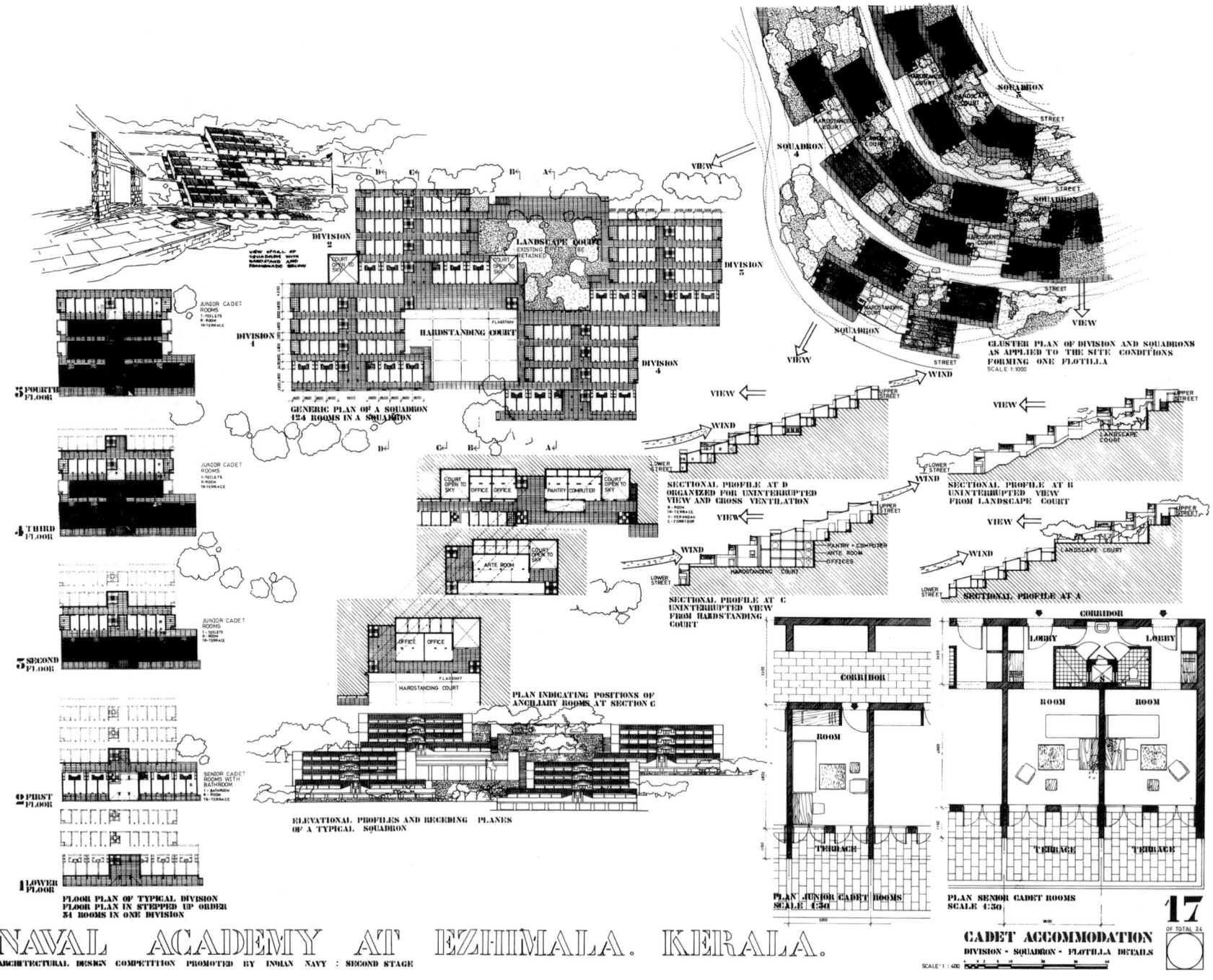

NAVAL ACADEMY AT EZHIMALA. KERALA.

ARCHITECTURAL DESIGN COMPETITION PROMOTED BY INDIAN NAVY : SECOND STAGE

CADET ACCOMMODATION
DIVISION · SQUADRON · FLOTILLA DETAILS

17 OF TOTAL 24

Cadets' accommodation – division, squadron and flotilla details. Original plate submitted for stage 2.

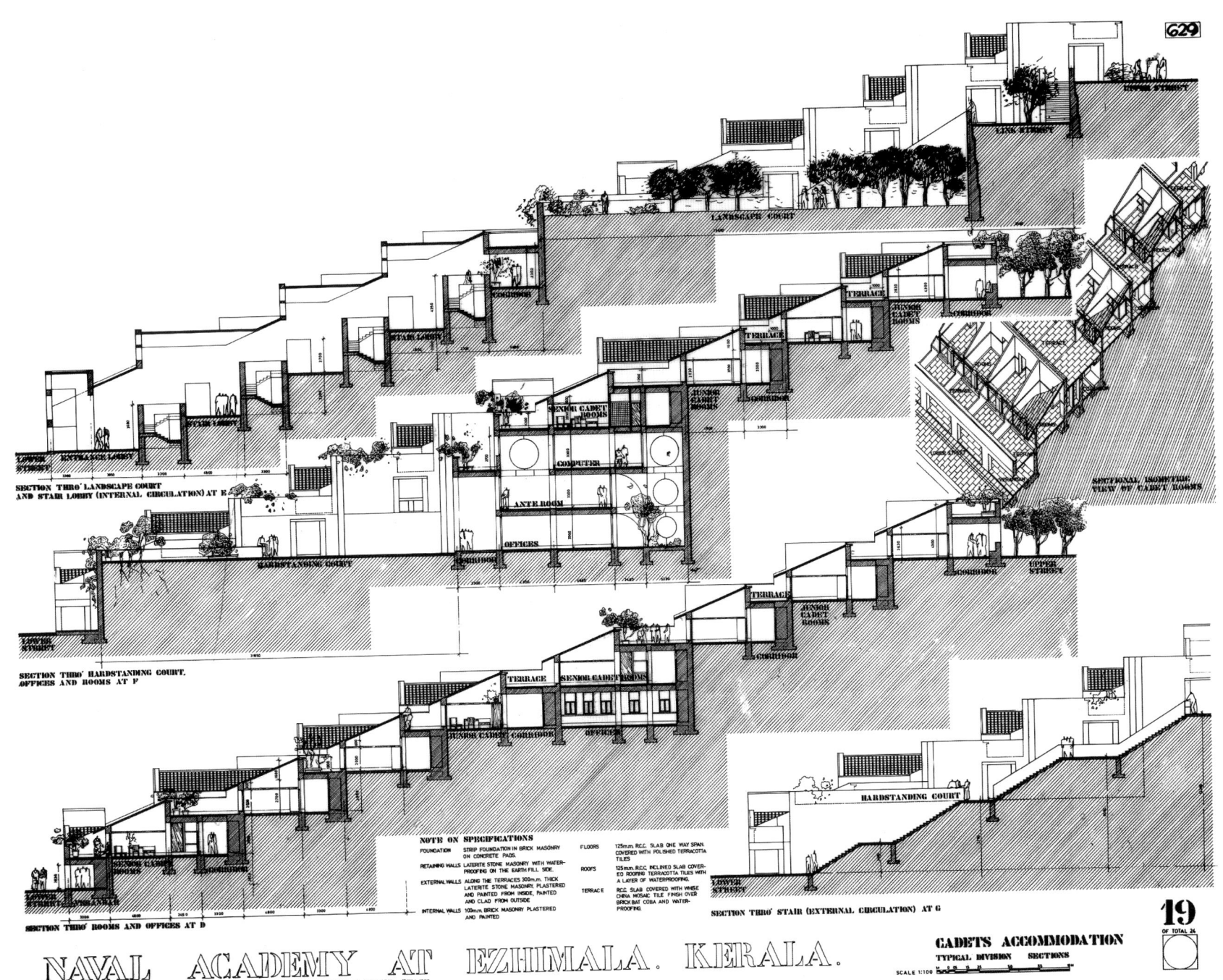

SECTION THRO' LANDSCAPE COURT AND STAIR LOBBY (INTERNAL CIRCULATION) AT E

SECTION THRO' HARDSTANDING COURT. OFFICES AND ROOMS AT F

SECTION THRO' ROOMS AND OFFICES AT D

SECTIONAL ISOMETRIC VIEW OF CADET ROOMS

SECTION THRO' STAIR (EXTERNAL CIRCULATION) AT G

NOTE ON SPECIFICATIONS

FOUNDATION	STRIP FOUNDATION IN BRICK MASONRY ON CONCRETE PADS.
RETAINING WALLS	LATERITE STONE MASONRY WITH WATER-PROOFING ON THE EARTH FILL SIDE.
EXTERNAL WALLS	ALONG THE TERRACES 300mm THICK LATERITE STONE MASONRY, PLASTERED AND PAINTED FROM INSIDE, PAINTED AND CLAD FROM OUTSIDE
INTERNAL WALLS	100mm BRICK MASONRY PLASTERED AND PAINTED
FLOORS	125mm. R.C.C. SLAB ONE WAY SPAN COVERED WITH POLISHED TERRACOTTA TILES
ROOFS	125mm. R.C.C. INCLINED SLAB COVER-ED ROOFING TERRACOTTA TILES WITH A LAYER OF WATERPROOFING
TERRACE	RCC SLAB COVERED WITH WHITE CHINA MOSAIC TILE FINISH OVER BRICK BAT COBA AND WATER-PROOFING

NAVAL ACADEMY AT EZHIMALA, KERALA.

ARCHITECTURAL DESIGN COMPETITION PROMOTED BY INDIAN NAVY : SECOND STAGE.

CADETS ACCOMMODATION
TYPICAL DIVISION SECTIONS
SCALE 1:100

Cadets' accommodation – typical division sections. Original plate submitted for stage 2.

It has been advocated and implemented in most parts of the world, developed and developing, that family culture and family life, full of desired interactions, are intimately connected with built forms related to the history of the site, climate, materials, and human relationships with them in isolation and in community. The way of life generated by the choice of material and forms of dwellings evolves under stricter accommodation to Nature, where the Laws of Nature and Human Nature find a common ground agreeable to one another, inspired by one another. The arguments of packing human life in packaged units assembled one on top of the other in the form of high-rises is not based on sociological or cultural terms, but purely and singularly on economic values. The relationship (contact) between the value of ground (contact) and the ascendance up in the sky are on diminishing returns when life is divorced from ground (earth), forcing an isolation in the life of community, one which inhabits the ground and other that inhabits the sky.

The other issue based on spatial considerations when families are put on top of each other, where, from the sky the sensations of space and the vista it offers to each dwelling is based on aesthetic value rather than social or cultural relevance. It is inevitable to the growth of community awareness and individual response to the immediate environment, where, man and nature are seen on equal terms. This offers a new and lasting aesthetic value stretching and encompassing the entire biosphere.

The principle on which the housing order is based at Ezhimala, revolves around a street and the experiences it offers, besides access to the dwelling units. A stepped section where each dwelling successively sets back from the road edge, revealing a terrace over the dwelling below and overlooks the distant vista and opens itself for cross ventilation guides the various categories of dwellings. Each family has either a partially covered terrace, or a garden and landscaped open space (existing one left undisturbed) in between the clusters except where a play space for games is created for both adults and children. The clusters are accommodating to changes in the direction of the contours so that no two open-to-sky spaces are identical. The structural system is based on a composite order of concrete frame and masonry retaining walls and filler walls. The dwellings are roughly plastered, and the concrete sloping roofs have terracota tiles. All the in-between courts are connected by stepped walkways lending a unique dimension to the scale of the cluster.

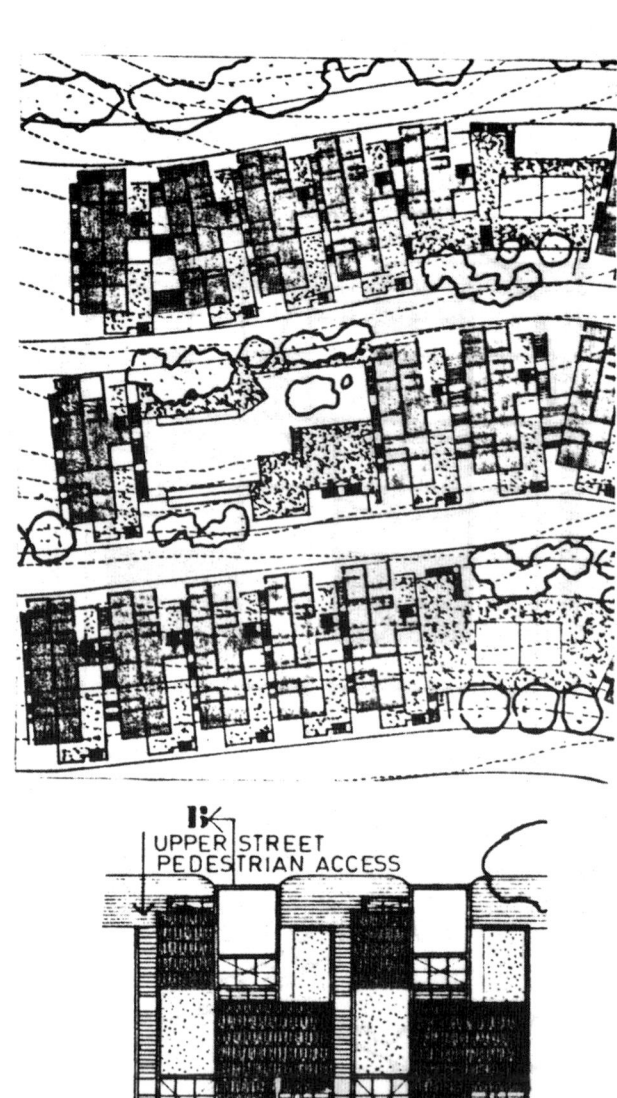

TERRACE PLAN

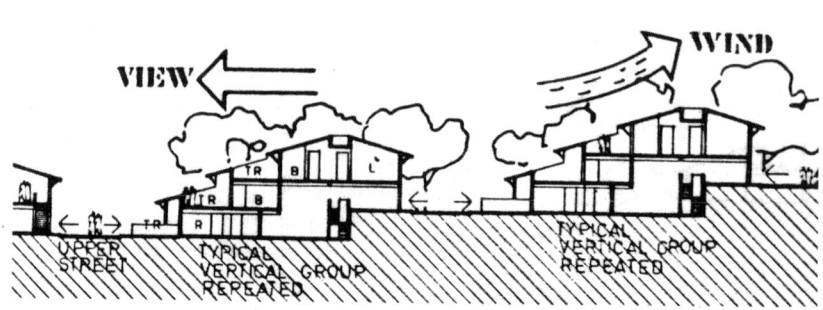

HOUSE TYPES

TYPE A-1 – LIEUTENANT COMMANDERS AND CIVILIAN OFFICERS(V)   **OVERALL AREA 190 SQ. M.** INCL. SER. PARKING AND STAIR·

TYPE A-2 – LIEUTENANTS AND CIVILIAN OFFICERS(IV)   **OVERALL AREA 150 SQ. M.** INCL. SER. PARKING AND STAIR

— **TYPE A-3** – CAPTAINS AND COMMANDERS   **OVERALL AREA 195 SQ. M.** INCL. SER. PARKING AND STAIR

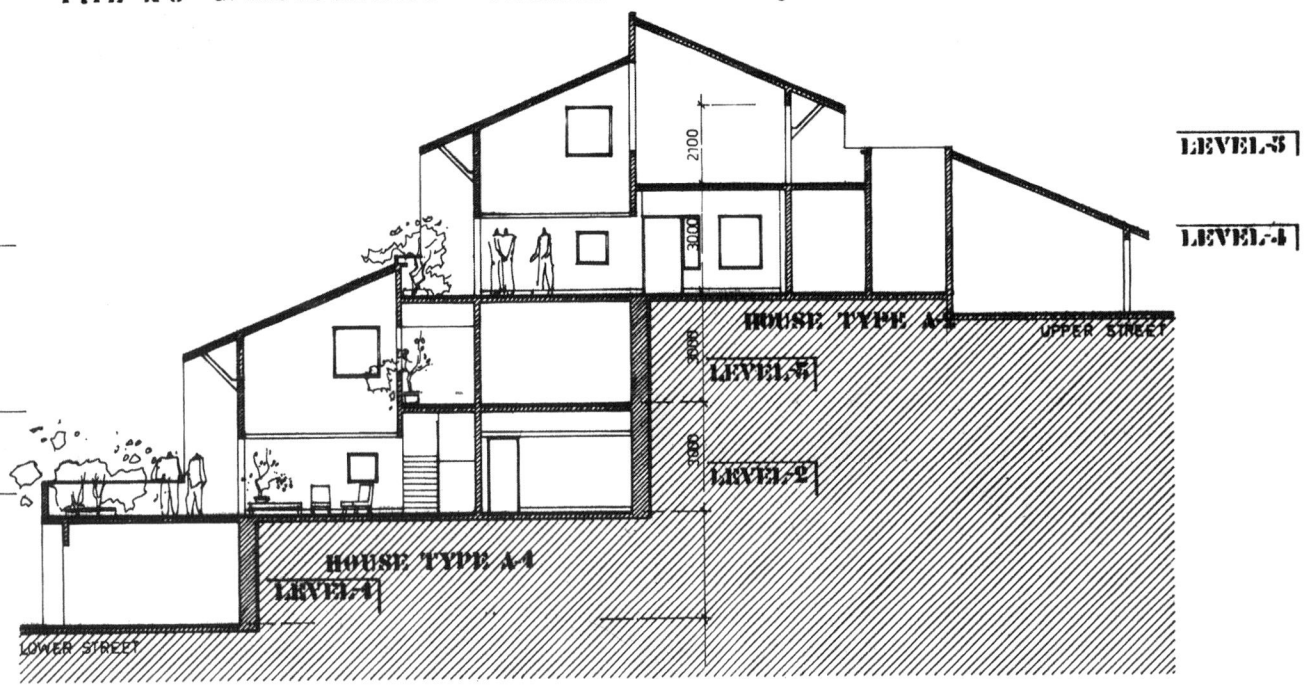

SECTION A-A (HOUSE TYPE A-1,A-2)

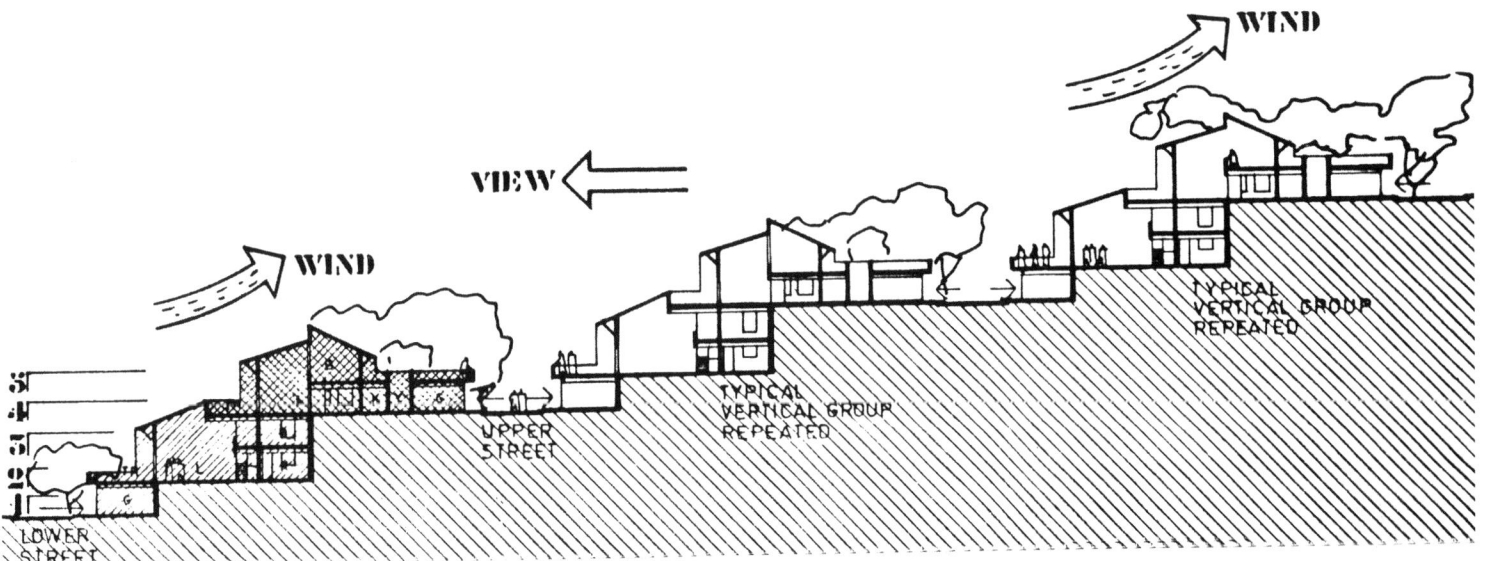

>   View from Rajpath (north). Garden entry.

>   View from Maulana Azad Road (south). Public entry.

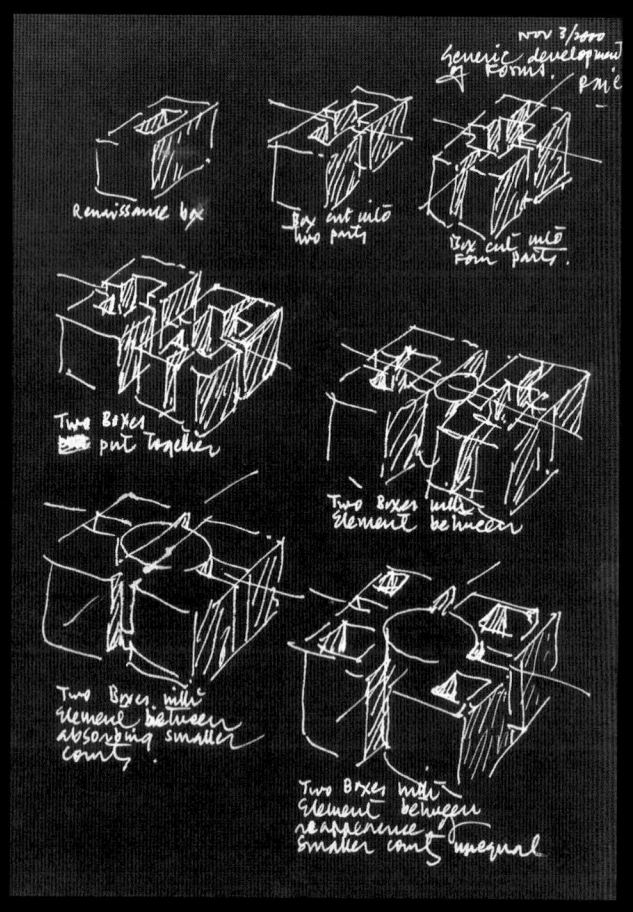

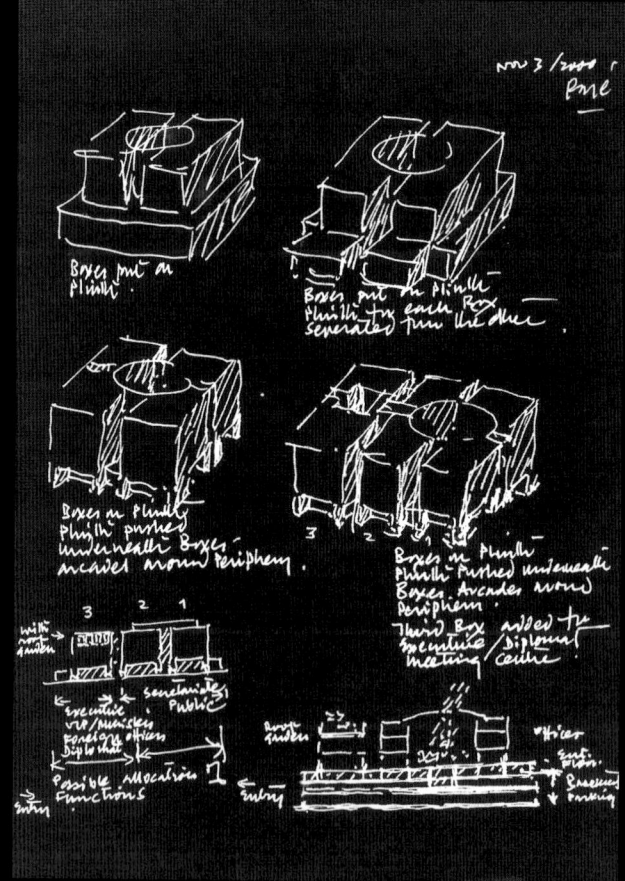

^   Generic development of forms, November 2000.
Notes on the sketches, from left:

1   'Renaissance box'
2   'Box cut into two parts'
3   'Box cut into four parts'
4   'Two boxes put together'
5   'Two boxes with element between'
6   'Two boxes with element between absorbing smaller courts'
7   'Two boxes with element between, reappearance of smaller courts, unequal'
8   'Boxes put on plinth'
9   'Boxes put on plinth separated; plinth for each box separated from the other'

10 'Boxes on plinth; plinth pushed underneath boxes; arcades around periphery'
11 'Boxes on plinth; plinth pushed underneath boxes; arcades around periphery; third box added for executive & diplomat meeting'
12 'Possible allocations of functions. Executive–VIP/Ministers–Foreign Officers–Diplomats | Secretariat–Public. With roof garden, 3-2-1'
13 'Roof Garden – Offices – Entrance Floor – Basement Parking'

Ministry of External Affairs

Rajpath (Lutyen's Delhi), New Delhi, 2000

(invited competition, finalist)

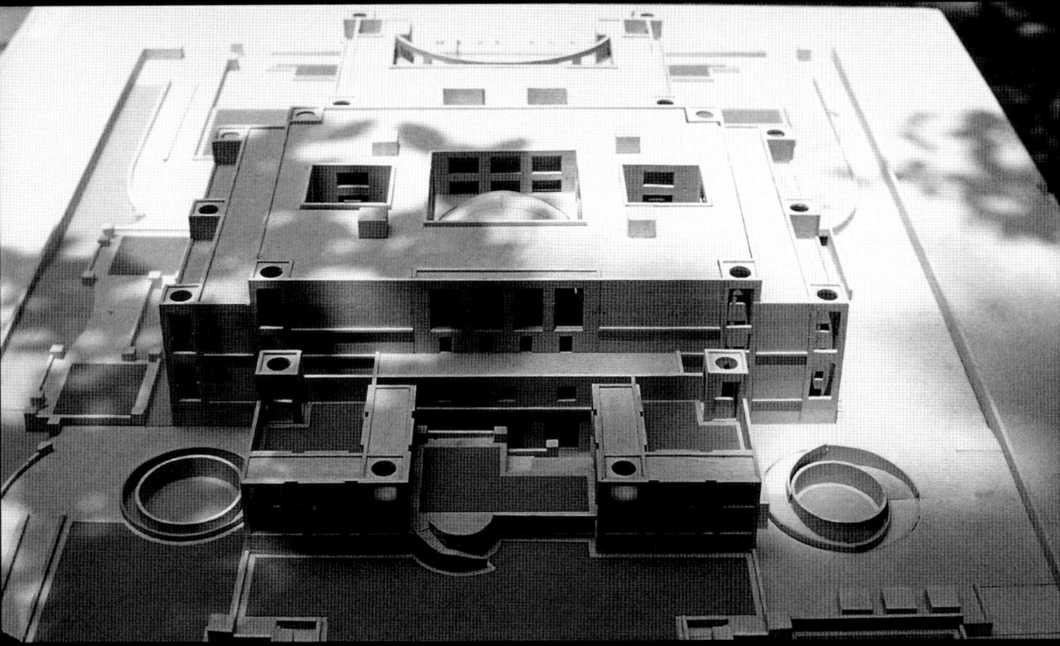

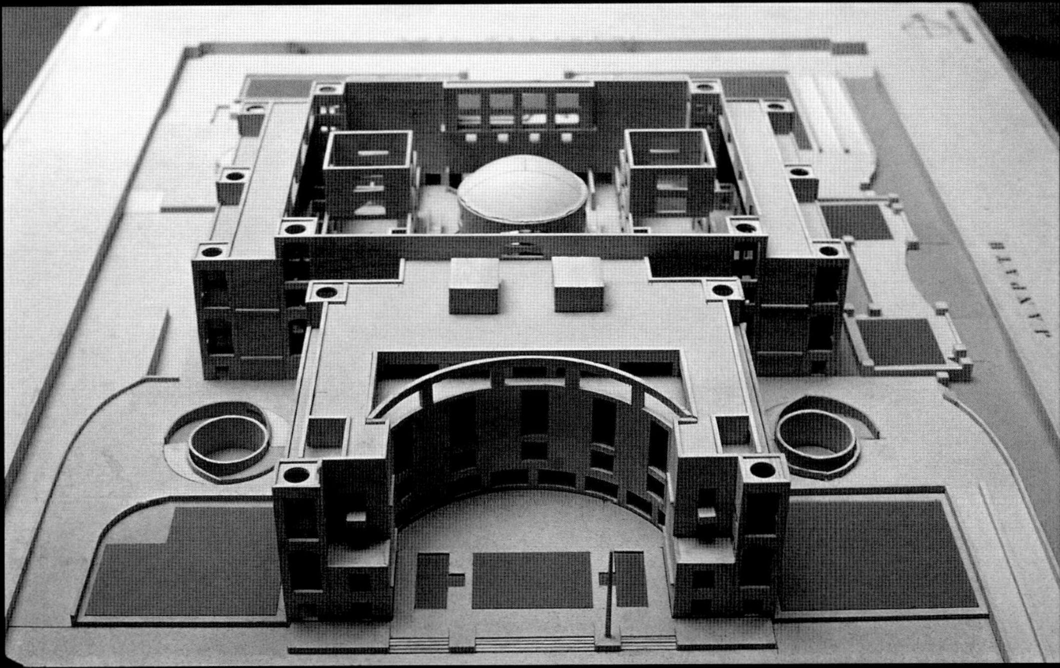

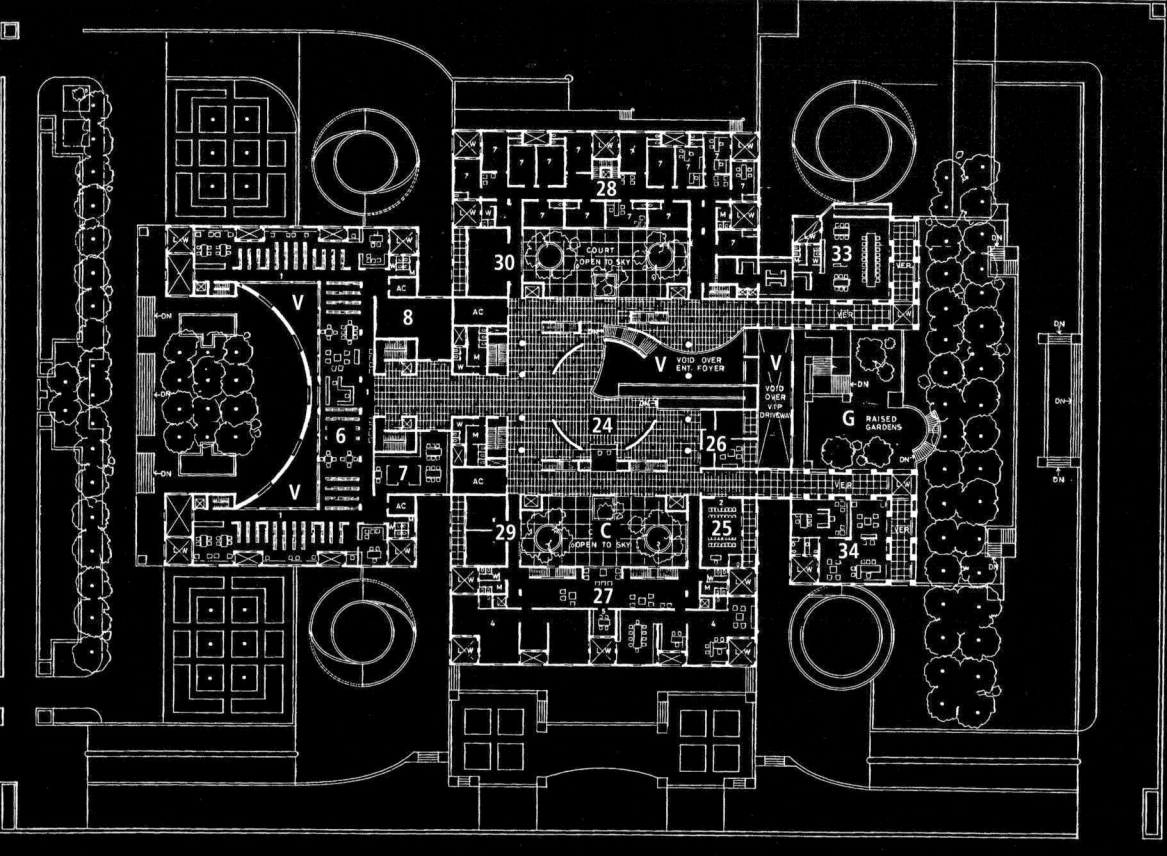

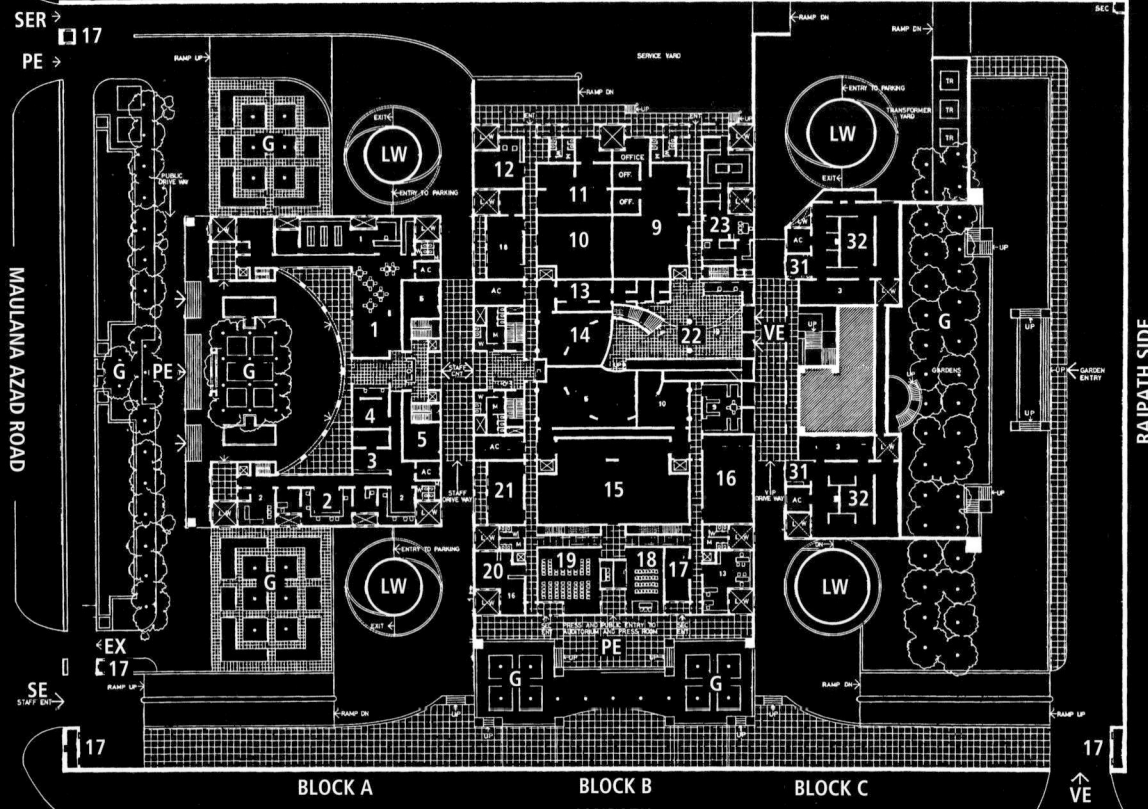

> Section.

> Definitive model in wood. Garden entry vie

< First floor plan.

< Ground floor plan.

BLOCK A
1 Cafeteria
2 CPV counter / Attestation cell
3 Haj cell
4 Protocol counter
5 Rooms for PAS / 'Daftaries'
6 Library
7 Map room
8 Rooms for PAS associates
BLOCK B
9 Maintenance wing
10 Central registry
11 Diplomatic bag section
12 Shredding room
13 Telephone exchange
14 Copy room
15 Media
16 Toshakhana
17 Security
18 Auxiliary auditorium (40 seats)
19 Press conference room (200 seats)
20 Staff counsel
21 Rooms for assistants / 'Daftaries'
22 VIP entrance foyer
23 Kitchen (for executive dining)
24 Reception – Hall of Nations
25 Conference room
26 VIP lounge / waiting
27 Ministers of State suite
28 Joint Secretaries' offices
29 Rooms for visiting Indian Ambassadors
30 Rooms for PAS assistants
BLOCK C
31 Transport cell
32 Service / store / equipment
33 Executive dining
34 Minister of External Affairs suite
GENERAL / SITE
PE Public entry
SE Staff entry
VE VIP entry
SRV Service entry
EX Exit
G Gardens
C Court
V Void to space below
LW Light well

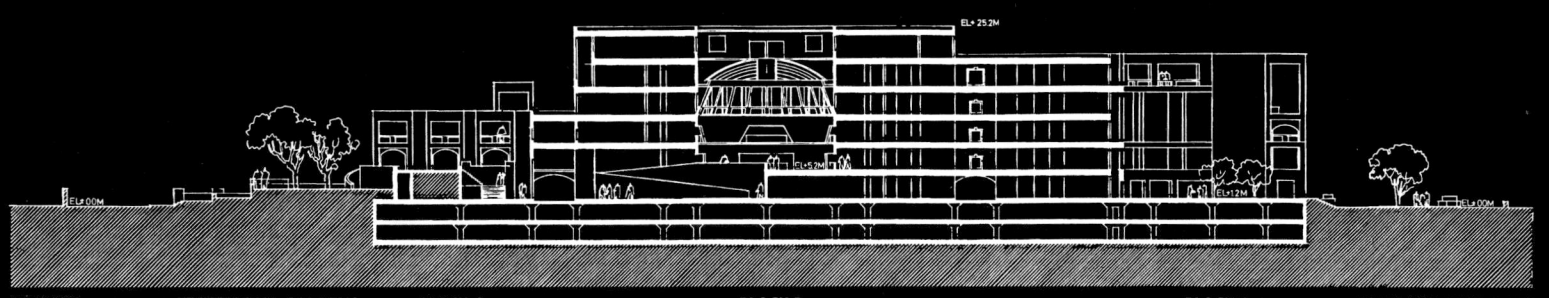

RAJPATH   CEREMONIAL GARDENS   BLOCK C   BLOCK B   BLOCK A   MAULANA AZAD ROAD

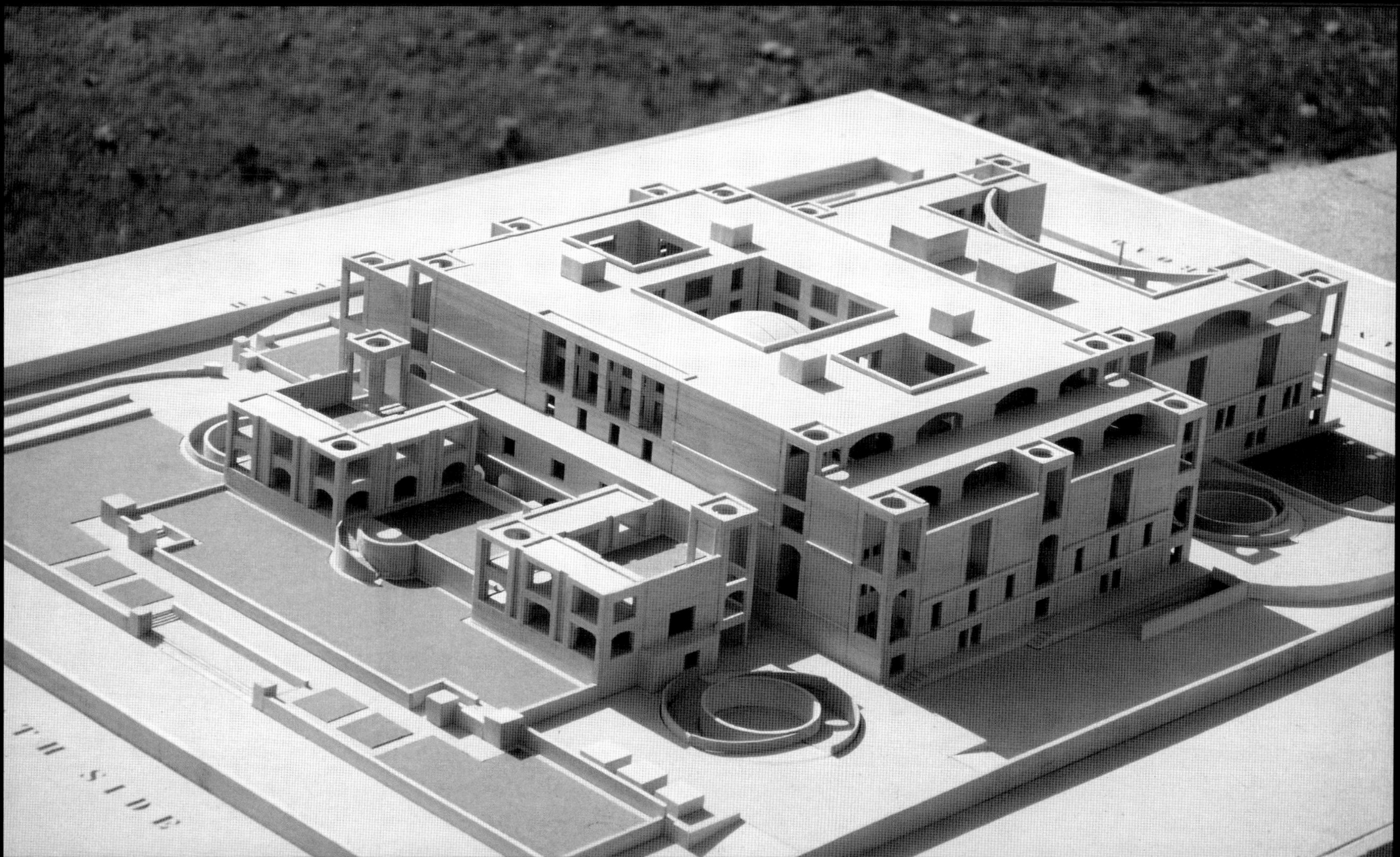

Writings

Editors' note:
Raje's ideas and thoughts presented in this chapter are collected from various lectures,
interviews, conversations, studio seminars and diary notes. They are grouped under the
broad themes of general thoughts on architecture, architecture in India, the association with
Kahn, his practice and elements of the practice that were of particular significance.

Architecture

Too often, the magnificent buildings are forgotten. The spirit of the buildings and the places they made are covered under the dust of time only to be inhabited by those who do not understand their very purpose. Such is the irony of the genius of them: the architecture, its era, its splendour is allowed to dissipate into the dark ages of the present. The idea is not to get out in the distant past, but to see if the present is inspired enough.

The country, over a great period of time, has witnessed civilizations come and go. The relics, the ruins and the buildings which have withstood the test of time are expressions in the ambience of eternity. Time stood still in the silence of the hills, the horizon and the expanse of skies, all manifest in single isolated columns to arcades, walls, openings and avenues without roofs. The lessons are locked into these, inviting anyone with enough curiosity, ready to explore and understand a deeper meaning which may offer clues to their origins. Every architectural composition in the past has been a model of a greater world, finite but unbounded. Its manifestation embodies a tight framework of parts, each having its own identity.

The above statement comes with the realization that building is an intervention. The changes it brings about are both physical and psychological in nature. Any attempt to make a physical change in such a context of the climate and culture of a place would be a direct attempt to change the inner relationships within the culture itself. However, it would take a great effort and understanding to appropriate the scale of physical form, as the physical form itself is a direct intervention. The celebrative character and the sequence of spaces that evoked a tremendous desire to communicate, through the language of ornament, an aura of myths and symbols. This architecture is then a model of the underlying principles that govern the universe and the forces that give it order. At the root of it is something deeply conceptual; design has not entered into it. An abstract concept that finds its expression in plan. Its geometry – making the intangible into a tangible way, knowledge into experience – a way of knowing.

The architecture in India is one for 'fair weather', transparent, accessible, contiguous, one that makes connections and encloses a hierarchy of public spaces which themselves become important nodes of activities. The post-colonial work has no conceptual structure and it remains compositional with such contradictions as mass has no weight, enclosures don't enclose, and light is considered for exterior modulations only. The structure dissipates in mid-air before it hits the ground and enclosures have no relationship with the volumes they enclose. The symbolism is without substance and presents meaningless monoliths.

New technology must realize forms that are compatible with the old patterns which are relevant both to the culture and climate of a given place. Such forms can generate new living traditions without snipping the lifeline between the old and the new.

Shastras need reinterpretation into contemporary language to show the connection between the forces that shape human behaviour and its mystical cover. The ideas of *vastu-shastra* must find their contemporary component, coming out of the need to discard outdated technologies and the need to recognize emerging changes in the social and economic order. The reason for Architecture to be is the reason for recognizing a spirit beyond basic needs. The reason for *shastras* is to put an order to wild speculations and make runaway thoughts into a comprehensive whole, and elevate the intellect to spiritual levels.

Building

I begin to formulate design elements which respond to both the inner needs and outer levels of measurable activities arising out of contextual circumstance. I sort out the spaces in plan that can respond to changes in time and are capable of adjusting themselves to the overall order that constitutes its framework. The spaces that are created outside the program of requirements are, architecturally, the most important spaces. They set up a rhythm and establish identities to the spaces that follow. The identity is stronger when the light characterizes the space along with the material that makes the enclosures. The order in plan must reflect the nature of space and the material with which the nature is defined. I believe that a close and compact plan not only ensures economy in space utilization, economy in structural design, economy in overall building expenditure, but a meaningful solution to a building in a hot and dry climate.

I use singular and complex horizons that offer changing vistas along with movement through spaces, bringing a number of spatial overlaps that are so vital to time–space concepts. There is a structural symmetry in nature at its cellular level and not 'form symmetries' in its external compositions. Conscious symmetry is different. It has idealized 'form compositions', transcending to the spiritual realm. A wheel must be symmetrical around its axis which is perpendicular to the direction of its movement. Symmetries have lead us to discover their inner source.

Breaking the programme down to identify spaces and formulate an order for the material chosen that is capable of meeting various scale of architectural elements ensures a certain continuity in projecting structural and spatial components, wilful but restricted within the framework of the general ordering principle. The details, however small or big, must respond to a scale. These are demonstrated beautifully in temple complexes, medieval cathedrals, mosques and *madrasas*, as well as in cities like Mandu and Jaisalmer. Here one observes that the parts of the buildings are responding to one another, building up the whole.

I see the scales and proportions of architectural elements as those that are directly related to the nature of material. Both concrete and brick as materials of construction have different strengths. Concrete is generous, but brick is not; space enclosed by concrete is not the same as enclosed by brick. The scales of buildings are directly related to the methods of fabrication. Most outdoor spaces, consciously or unconsciously designed, came through climatic considerations and social demand. The structures that enclose these spaces had an order. That order came out of the choice of material.

Practice

My colleagues are those who work with me on the project from the start. There is always a continuity and development of those concepts and ideas on which previously a substantial amount of work is done. The structural and mechanical engineering material inputs constantly test the architectural concepts and begin to become the mainstay in their own order. It is a happy moment when what to do meets the means of doing it.

The main critique comes from the structural engineer, to test the composition of plan in relation to the possibility of systems envisioned and in response to the basic material to be used either by choice or dictated by the demands made by the space which it serves. His discipline has to meet with the ordering principle on which the determinant elements of plan are established. The sense of light and the sense of space are to be strictly adhered to.

Making models at various stages of design development is a method that leads to a better understanding of the spaces in plans and sections, surface delineations and their geometry, volumes and their proportions, and above all, those members of the structure so crucial to bring natural light into spaces.

The construction site and the architect's office are two inseparable parts of the work activity that direct the process of design. Within this process lies the ability to correct and modify circumstantial responses arising out of measurable situations and abstraction of thought and ideas developed in the office and tested on site.

There are two categories of projects. Those that are realized in all their forms of completion, and those that have remained unrealized even though they are ready to be built. The ones that are unrealized have as much impact on the history of architecture as the ones that got an opportunity to be built.

Model Making

Indian Statistical Institute, Delhi, 1974. Wood blocks, chipboard. Volume study, open space relationships.

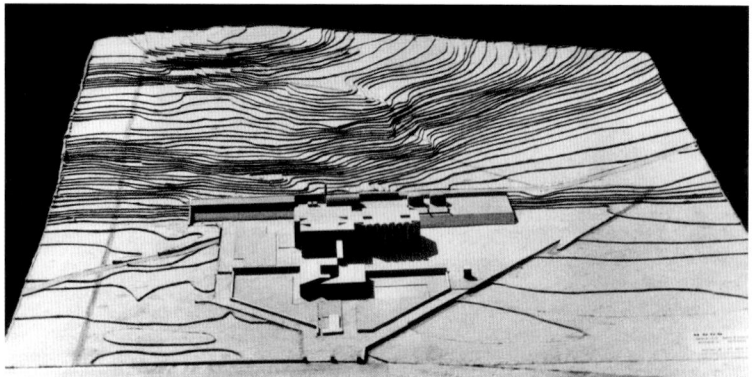

Mother Dairy, Bombay, 1980. Site model in wood blocks with land contours in chipboard.

Mother Dairy, Bombay, 1980. Definitive model in wood veneer.

The idea of model making or the intention behind a model is to consider the model as a tool to express or test one's thoughts and ideas – not necessarily to communicate with others, but primarily to oneself as author. It also serves to give shape in three dimensions – volume – to what cannot be expressed only in the form of a sketch or a drawing. The model establishes a connection between the thoughts, ideas, sketches; simultaneously identifying anchor points around which the whole project could make a beginning for development. I would consider this as an important stage in the design process.

Further moving on the track, it is vital to make the choice of material for the model at a given stage in design, one which would navigate the process to firm up a stage of commitment from 'tentative' to 'definitive'. The most definitive aspect of this stage is to understand the scale and proportions as demanded by the nature of the project. The characteristics of site which may be completely man controlled like in the urban areas or 'Nature' controlled where the elements of nature set up a visual relationship between the man-made and nature. Once this fundamental relationship is understood, the model can be made ready to examine the spaces and their consequences from within.

This becomes an important stage of the model because, in most cases, there is a marked difference in the spatial quality that the drawings represent and that expressed in the model. Hence, the model becomes a tool to clarify this disparity and represent clearly one's visualization of the 'interior' of the building; not in terms of 'interior design' but with reference to the space quality. This allows for one to look for the potential in exploiting aspects like the 'Structure' and the value of 'Natural Light'. Consequently, such models help in making an enormous commitment that is being undertaken in construction of the actual building or a complex of building in relation to what is around it.

Making models at various stages of design development is a method that leads to a better understanding of the spaces in plans and sections, surface delineations and their geometry and above all, those members of the structure so crucial to bring natural light into spaces.

Models are essential assistants when we are communicating with our engineers and other consultants. These models may be called engineering models, which could be models in parts or those of specific details, which help in establishing a dialogue with the consultants in furthering their feedback on the validity of an idea or the ways in which such ideas could be materialized.

Models have a definitive place along with the drawings – they may be plans, elevations, sections, isometrics or axonometrics. The material to be used for a specific purpose, which invariably depends on the expressive quality of the architecture that may not be completely evident in drawings.

The most difficult material to work with is wood. Solid block wood or the veneers of wood , where the planes of veneers represent and define the enclosures. But the important question may remain to be asked is; at what point in the design development process should wood find its entry? Wood is not a material which works along with certain changes in the thought process like say, clay or Plasticine, which can be instantly flattened or erased without leaving behind the footprints of its plan or layout. If one had a choice of a chisel and some clay, like a charcoal drawing, clay can be chiselled and moulded in seconds. The material doesn't resist change, since it runs concurrently with the pace of thoughts and ideas and at the end of its completion, an architect can see the whole model made of one material, as a monolith. Every monolith has weight, and weight is an important element in architecture.

Models made in chipboard, a gray coloured compressed cardboard, are more flexible in their making than wood. Chipboard with its gray colour does not radiate light. Its only impression also creates an impact in the sense of monolithic weight. All details become secondary to the colour of this material. The dark voids and the pattern of shadows animate all surfaces seen from various viewpoints.

The most impressive and complete model in its entirety, like a sectional axonometric drawing, where plans, elevations and sections are seen simultaneously, is the model made in transparent Plexiglas or acrylic sheet.

The transparency through various enclosing planes,

JCP House, Ahmedabad 1978. Study model in chipboard for surface and volume relationship.

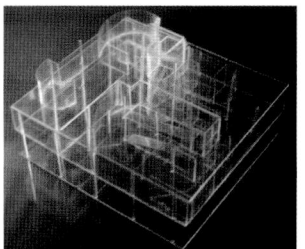

Gas Tragedy Memorial, Bhopal, Madhya Pradesh, 1982. Site model in wood blocks with wood veneer land contours.

Plexiglass model of Villa Savoye. Student model, 2nd year studio.

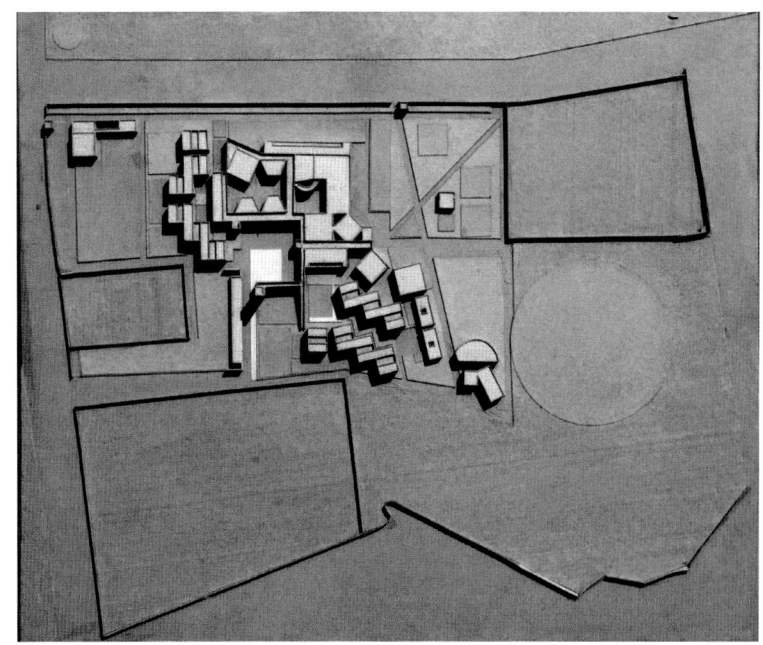

Indian Institute of Management, Ahmedabad, Phase 2, 1999. Site model in chipboard.

Kahn, Islamabad, 1965. Plasticine model.

Kahn, Levy Playground, 1967. layout and sculptural form study in Roma plasticine. A monolith.

inside and outside, lend the value of superimposition of planes and spaces all becoming self-luminous. The form, the structure, the space and the light present themselves as a single entity. Models made in acrylic or Plexiglas offer their transparency to orthographic projections simultaneously. Acrylic is a material which may provoke taking wrong decisions as the experience is that of the exploded view of elements of space and space itself.

I like to believe that temple builders made the models; so did the Persians and the Greeks. Islamic architects made models. The Renaissance architects like Michaelangelo, Boromini made models, since architecture was considered as a work of sculpture, the scaled-down models were the result of what the real thing would be like. A means of passing on instruction to the craftsmen, where the margins of error were minimized in the reality of construction. When the scale of projects were enormous, no good architect would risk the danger of getting into the unknown. The stakes are high also for his reputation. A sculpture can be judged but space is difficult because the real meaning of space comes out of experience of participation through structure and light, mass and volume, surfaces and textures.

Louis Kahn made models, or rather got them made under his supervision, in clay, in wood veneer, wood blocks or gray chipboard. Also some of his models were painted in monochromatic tones to highlight some specific features. The test of the model was to see if the 'form' remained as it was thought to be and that all 'details' were subservient to the form. His models were a 'work of art', never a commercial advertisement to seduce the promoters in funding the project. Frank Llyod Wright's models dealt with a much larger schema where in a specific building was a result of the overall order which included the topology of land, the anchor features of the site, the movement patterns and the public and private spaces. The models at the scale of a large neighbourhood or a precinct changed as thoughts and information on specific areas of design development changed. This was a kind of model which responded to the nature of change continuously over a period of time. The time and space truly changed and shaped the model to live in the present. The models therefore were records of their time, the philosophy and a way of life as interpreted and expressed by the architect.

Le Corbusier's models are to be seen in a broader schema at the scale of the city, to be understood in its volumetric disposition in space. The details of the specific projects were sorted out later. However, the actual proportions were studied and the designs developed accordingly. There was a concern for the building material at its real scale and value, but only at the stages when the buildings went into their production. Corbusier gave importance to flexibility and change and modified decisions on details as the building went up in construction. His models were not the end of everything, whereas for Kahn it was the final act before it became the building.

Supposing one wants to move beyond the Euclidian geometry, then one would have to define these spaces in mathematical terms; not only in terms of its aesthetics, but also in terms to express those values which are beyond the equations and the ratios. If one could attempt such a definition then the idea of building such a space is possible. Is it a warped space, a deformed space, distorted space – a space that does not carry any definition, but is still tangible? Then how does one, or what means are there to build such a model? Such forms are being generated by the computer, regardless of their purpose, as endless exercises. Do they address the questions raised above? Can the frontiers of space be touched by the glossary of these forms? In spirit of exploration these questions may come closer to answers that may be loaded with still more questions.

September 2002
Ahmedabad

1 Wild horses in stone. Ink, March 1980.
2 Beasts. Graphite, undated.
3 Speculations on Meditation Centre in Florida. Warm and humid. Ink, September 2003
4 Musings in sketchbook. Ink and graphite, November 1996 – January 1997.
5 Rewa Kund, Mandu. Ink and charcoal, November 1983.

Sketching

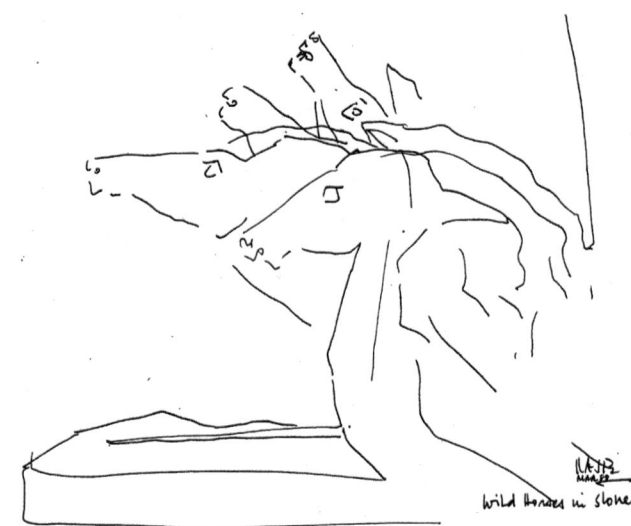

1

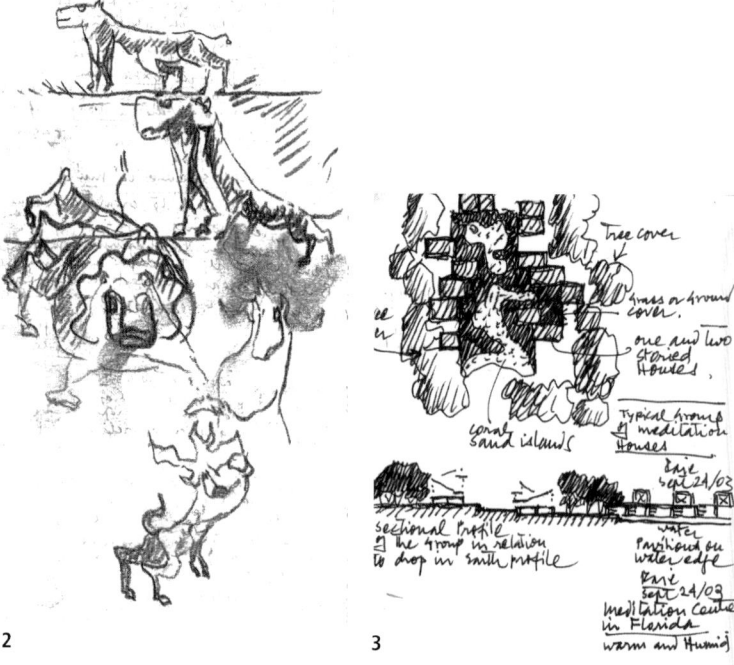

2   3

Sketching is an exploration in searching for form and spaces without any accuracy of dimensions and material choice. The thin or the thick lines with smudges suggest the density of mass with minute pores for desired intensity of light. The whole idea of sketching should remain extremely nebulous. Without an idea or feel for what one is looking for, the computer may turn out what seems to be acceptable in the very first attempts. The diagrams maybe so perfect that a trap could be laid and the rejection may take a long time in the absence of direct involvement of a certain feeling which is necessary to probe into the dark areas of ideas.

Sketching without formulation for a statement of problem, however diffuse it may seem, may lead to irrecoverable situations. The progressive development of a sketch without control over the overall scale of the project would become difficult to assess the nature of spaces and their desired relationships to overall character. There is a certain freedom from the mundane aspects of the programme of requirements. Those spaces which were not thought of earlier suddenly surface indicating the new beginning to reorganize or compose parts of building plans with interior and exterior spaces. The hard-line drawings which then follow gives up something which was not thought of before.

Unless the eye is disciplined and trained for minute observations in the visual context of a given place or position in space, it would be difficult for the hand to first record the impressions of what is being observed in the mind's eye and to coordinate the same impression the hand on paper. The impressions could be of such urgency that instant choice of medium to record is of the foremost necessity for the architect. In the absence of this the essence of what is being recorded would be lost, making room for what is described as meaningless record, pages after pages, incredible in quantum but devoid of character. Proportions in sketches are not necessarily essential. To change proportions is one's own prerogative to heighten the impact of communications.

To lend correct proportions in sketches may be generated from being self critical, until the hand draws what the eye sees.

The light has to be sensed. Its intensity lies in the first dense mass drawn with charcoal, or graphite or any other medium. It is trapped. It needs to be released.

It is difficult to sketch without some sort of an idea about the material. The material has a direct relationship with light. The material and its form, the character of which can only be enhanced in the presence of light. [Mostly parts of buildings with or without shadows]. The stronger the shadow, the stronger the [building] forms. The joints of the branches of trees, or small plants, rock formations, hoofs of animals. ...

Drawing with charcoal came from observing Kahn draw, and the subsequent development at various stages until the sketch became communicable through its substance and its graphic qualities. Both the Piranesi and Sant'Elias drawings were inspiring in their densities and tonal values. Their drawings directed towards spatial compositions. This was most important to learn. These architects were artists. Artists have to have a medium through which abstract ideas can become communicable. The sketch leaves an imprint of message to the artist. This is an inspiring moment without which the later development becomes characterless..

Satyajit Ray, Sergi Eisenstein and others sketched for the composition which could later be locked on the frame of the film when the cameras would roll. This is in anticipation of the movements that would follow. It is for a movie. Each frame following the other, realizing pictures in motion. In architecture the buildings don't move or fly. People move in them through spaces. The sensations and the experiences that the spaces offer need to be interpreted by the participants themselves. The overlaps of various images as perceived by participants is close to the editing which the movie maker makes. The architect's sketches, therefore, are inert, rooted in one place. The drama of these sketches is the drama of the graphic quality the sketches offer.

Sketching is helpful. But when one [student] takes sketches as a solution to a problem, the sketches stop serving their purpose. A sketch must make an effort to lay down a statement. The design will follow.

Undated, Ahmedabad

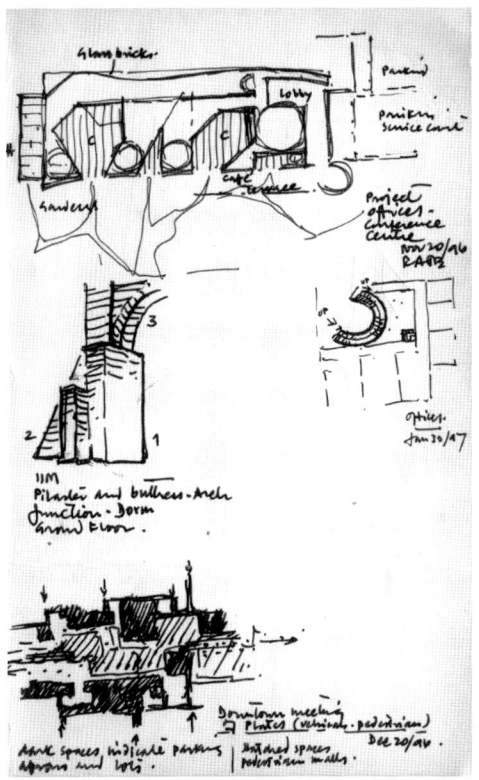

4

5

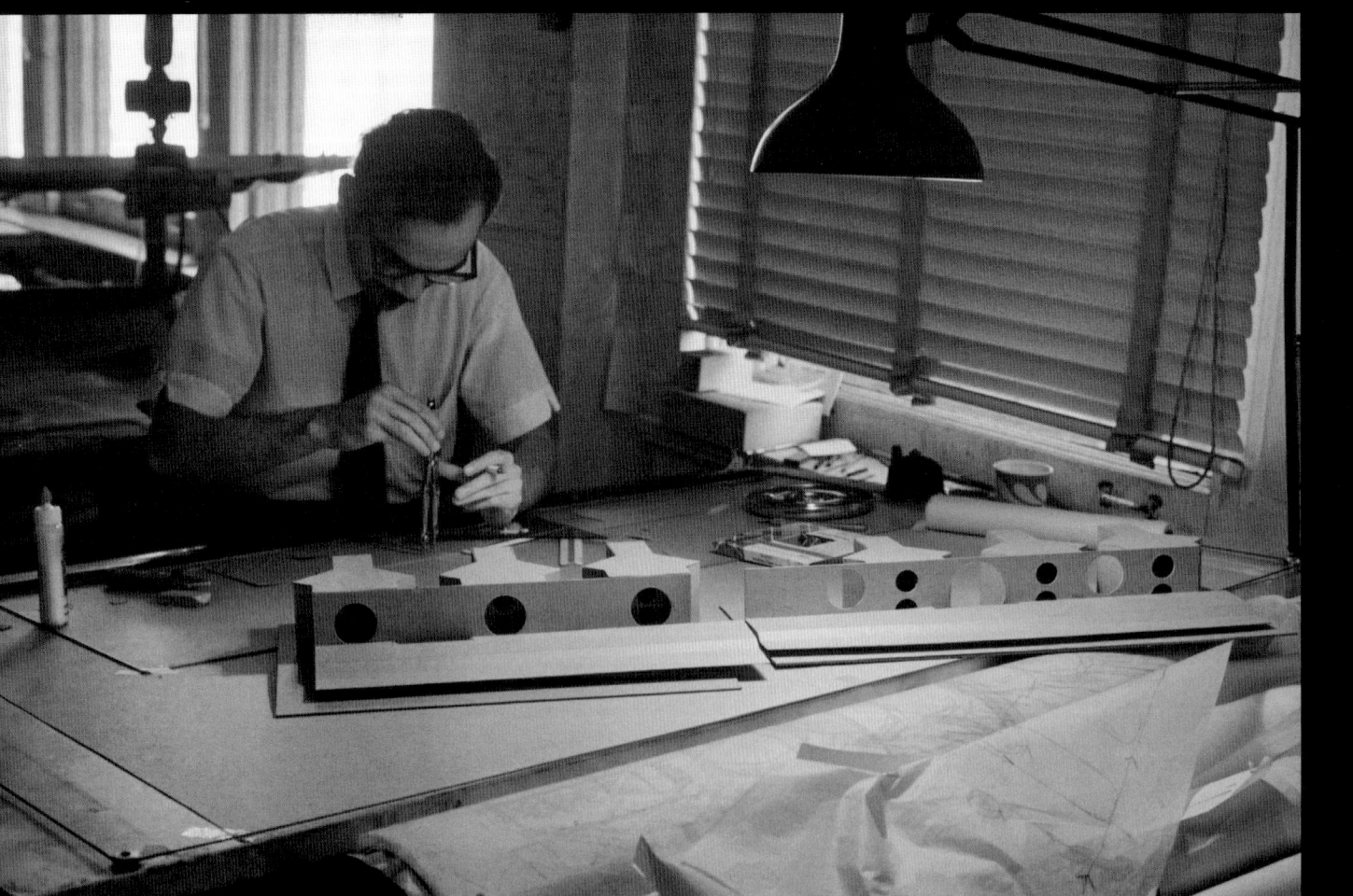

What I Learnt from Kahn

Louis Kahn was teaching all the time … in school, in the office, at the building site and in conversations. There was hardly a time when he was not talking about his values, attitudes, realizations, and architectural philosophy, conveyed in simple terms. Never a formal student of Kahn's, my learning occurred in the course of work and friendship during the years from 1964 to 1974.

At the time he was working on the Dacca Assembly building, Kahn loved to talk about Islamic architecture, particularly the Cairo Mosque or the built elements in Shiraz and Isphahan, in Persia (now Iran). He was delighted in showing us plans and diagrams, indicating how they were built. He also admired the architecture of the Ottoman Turks, particularly that of Sinan who built mosques in Turkey, during the 15th century. Kahn would talk endlessly about such buildings as a singularity of thought and its image, how they transcend material and bring one face to face with the experience of room-making. Hagia-Sophia was a fantastic room for him. The centre of the worship space in Ottoman architecture was another room. Invariably, the discussion would drift to the magnificent rooms of Gothic architecture.

In the course of these room-making discourses, Kahn would often talk about light, how light defines and characterizes space. Light itself would say 'this is the domed room and not a flat roofed room', or an arch, or a vault. Light could enhance the character of a particular space or structure that enclosed this space. These preoccupations of Louis Kahn were the lessons learned. Their manifestations in my work may not be obvious because I like to work with walls and vaults more than the more complex forms of Kahn. The lessons learned lead to a certain amount of restraint because at the heart of any endeavour is an awareness and expression of Order.

Choosing to work for and with Kahn, instead of studying with him provides a clue to a personal orientation towards a pragmatic orientation towards architecture. I am not a theoretician

in the sense of Kahn, but think in terms of putting certain ideas to test. The ideas may be hypothetical to start with, but if I find any way possible to push these ideas towards the truth, I begin to work on the development of these ideas in order to discover how far they might lead. With me, it is mainly the making-exercise rather than the abstract-exercise in terms of theoretical content even though I believe theory precedes design.

I first met Louis Kahn when he came to Ahmedabad to discuss the Indian Institute of Management. This project was to be designed at the National Institute of Design (NID) and Kahn had been invited to do it by NID. It was Kahn's desire, through NID, to meet with local architects regarding their experiences and understanding about the prospect of building in Ahmedabad. Kahn felt that local discussions would be helpful to him regarding the type of building, climatic conditions, the Indian way of life and similar topics. It was in this context that I first met Kahn.

After six months of becoming acquainted with Kahn he asked me whether or not I would be interested in going to Philadelphia to work with him. I thought this was a good opportunity even though I was doing my own work in Ahmedabad. After receiving a letter of invitation of sorts, I went to Philadelphia. Initially, I wanted to be there no more than a couple of years. However, I became deeply involved in the responsibilities given to me in Kahn's office and remained in Philadelphia for around five years from 1964 to 1969.

Curiously, in the light of my later role in the Indian Institute of Management, I had nothing to do with this project while in Philadelphia. This is because Kahn had asked me to work with him on designing the capital in Islamabad, Pakistan. This project absorbed the first year or so of my stay. Other major project commitments, also about a year each, were made on the Levi playground (a collaboration with Noguchi), the Media convent in a suburb of Philadelphia, and the Interama in Florida, conceived to serve as a place for cultural exchange with Central American countries. Near the end of my stay, I did a little work on the Kimbell Art Museum in Ft. Worth, Texas.

My role in the office was not unusual. I was given a project and became responsible for taking his instructions and preparing drawings and models for him, which is what he wanted. Through continuous dialogue, he made adjustments to drawings and the making of models at various stages of project development. The early stage drawings were not made to put ideas on trial; they were more accurately a type of conceptual, perhaps schematic, drawings up to the design development stage.

Consequently, a person in my role would not carry a project through to complete construction documentation, but would be reassigned to a new assignment. Sometimes, preliminary cost estimates were prepared at this early stage for Kahn, to develop an awareness of overall costs vis-à-vis the scope of the project. Occasionally, I would carry this work forward into the design development of plans and elevations. For the five years of my stay, most of what I did for Kahn had this preliminary sketchy but somewhat firm character.

To a certain extent, Kahn's office was international. It was staffed by individuals who came from countries around the world to work for him. Communication was not so much a problem in the office as Kahn's architectural language transcended cultural boundaries and values. It was not very easy, in a way, to understand Kahn because of the very special words that he used, words we could come to understand through constant exposure. Kahn was not particularly adept in communicating with ordinary lay people, and one might say that many architects had trouble discerning the meaning of his words. Basically, his language was the language of the art of architecture through which he tried to connect with the tradition, cultural heritage of those who would help him design, build and put his buildings to use. It was hardly conceived or useful for ordinary conversation.

Being around Louis Kahn was itself an intense, though casual, learning experience. At times, I was asked to attend his master's studio juries at the University of Pennsylvania. On other occasions, I was asked to accompany him while giving desk-to-desk crits to his students. In these ways, I benefited from instruction without having to pay the tab. Even so, the vibrant flow of projects and personal conversations was an additional, continuous source of insight and inspiration.

Le Corbusier was often a topic of conversation. In very intimate discussions, Kahn would talk about the works of Le Corbusier and how these inspired him from time to time. Although Kahn did not work in his Paris Atelier, he still considered Le Corbusier to be his teacher. There seemed to be two main sources of inspiration drawn from Corbusier.

The first deals with monumental nature of architectural work, the eternal spirit of Architecture. In this sense, Kahn came very close to the architectural realization of Le Corbusier even though their design languages were quite different.

The second inspiration appears to be the shared perception of new architecture which blends eclectic awareness with the modern experiences of space and structure. Even though he was much more committed to the making of a building as an expression of geometric structure and its components rather than the plastic architectural expression of Le Corbusier, the work of Kahn's teacher had a tremendous, oft-mentioned impact.

In many ways, Louis I. Kahn was a philosopher, but not in an academic sense. He could see and appreciate the kinship among Eastern and Western philosophies, without having the need to study them seriously. To an extent, Kahn was metaphysical in that he could transcend cultural values, different images and geographical barriers, an orientation more synchronic than systematic. He tended to focus on that which was in the forefront of his mind. Philosophically, what seemed most important to Kahn was the singularity of the artist, and he hardly missed an opening to emphasize that architecture is not something made by a committee.

Very often, he would punctuate this conviction with a discourse on how 'a camel is nothing more than a horse designed by a committee', or similar such contentions. Of final, far-reaching significance was acquiring an awareness of Silence in the making of architecture. This silence is not a silent silence, but one of an elevated inspirational nature. By Silence, Kahn does not mean peace or quiet or anything of the sort. Rather, it is a particular, extremely active state of mental awareness where ideas are beginning to gel, just before the firm definition needed to give root to form giving.

When beginning to work, Kahn individually pondered over many issues and concepts, a state where thoughts sort of criss-cross the mind, uncertain of true direction. Although active, this particular state is paradoxically a state of rest, where ideas and thoughts are without vectors, without any particular direction. This particular state was to Kahn really Silence, the very opposite of inactivity! It is within this Silence, a state of mind where things have not yet taken direction, that it is possible to realize the content and abstract form of an architectural problem. I think all great architects look for guidance from other great architects, and

I don't think Kahn was an exception to this. However, much of this guidance was more from the past than the present.

Kahn really loved Romanesque and Renaissance buildings tremendously. At the time he was working on the Assembly Building at Dacca, he thought his inspiration came straight from the Thermae of Carracalla in Rome. While working on other projects, he used to think of Carcassone and the walls of Albi Cathedral, and so forth. Islamic and Persian buildings, mentioned above were also extremely inspiring to Kahn. It is important to note that these were sources of inspiration, not discrete forms for direct use in architectural expression.

Of all modern architects, Le Corbusier stands out in terms of influence, examined previously in the text. One could say that Kahn actually avoided reaction to the work of contemporary colleagues and was reluctant to engage in professional-type criticism. Kahn was intensely involved in his own work, often spurred on by what he perceived as a late start on what he ought to have been doing earlier in his life. He was persistently absorbed in the problems immediately before him. When he found something interesting that held a lot of meaning for him, he simply avoided any mention of it. Frankly, he said he 'didn't want to burn his energies' on the work of others. He also said, 'Why should I analyse someone else's buildings? The architect who has made the plan, that particular architect, is the best person to interpret it in all its subtleties. Since I am an outsider, how can I interpret someone else's mind?'

Thus, in general, Kahn avoided reactiveness and criticism. But when he encountered awkwardness or shortcomings in buildings, he would respond with terse comments such as: 'Well, it seems certain that these architects have suddenly become aware of sculpture', or, more seriously, 'How could these architects forget the content of the real life behind the building?' It was Kahn's concern that a distinction should be drawn between that best left to circumstances and a greater awareness of people whose particular buildings are intended to serve, their patterns of behaviour and reactiveness. It was these kinds of issues that Kahn was most interested in and willing to discuss. Most interested in and willing to discuss.

There are several important lessons that I learnt from Kahn. The first has to do with the nature of an architectural plan. It takes a tremendous effort to make a plan because it is an abstract document within which a given architectural programme may be seen. It requires an ability to synthesize the programme in terms of plan elements so that there is a potential of place-making rather than merely space-making. It is this lesson and effort of place-making that is reflected in most of my work from time to time.

The architectural plan and building being made should have a proper sense of order appropriate to, and inherent within, the choice of materials and their structural expression. If there is a stronger order within a plan, it leads towards the exercise of making of openings, the thoughtful making of openings instead of just making openings that do not arise out of architectural or structural order.

This naturally leads to another major lesson learned, that of the light and handling of natural light in regard to the making of rooms; room-making in the broad sense of the term as buildings that have a sense of completion, was another basic tenet of Kahn's architectural philosophy.

Undated, from interview tapes

The building I really like is the Taj Mahal without so much as chewing on its meaning. The spiral and the Taj can be weighed in the same balance. Both have eternal presence. Both are timeless. Spiral is a diagram in motion, the Yin and Yang of the universe in perpetual motion. Centrifugal and Centripetal moving in and at the same time moving out without so much as touching one another. Perhaps one arm doesnot know that the other arm exists. Both are in perfect harmony. The Taj and the spiral. Expressing the laws of universe. Compression and Tension. Both energies co-exist. A Synergy in its symbol. Nothing can stop its eternal Throb. A rythm, a basic law of nature. A nature personified. Yin and Yang. The spirit of the spirit of Architecture.

Taj manifests in its expression an eternal Freeze. A distilled act, clear and transperent. A measurable space — An unmeasurable expanse. Its material and its form solidified in the act of its distillation. Nothing can be added to it. Nothing can be taken away. A touch of aggressive thought will disolve the entire creation into Nothingness. "Spiral" the two arms of the "Galaxy" ever moving and in its movement ever expanding! The umbilical chord with two "ends". What one end is attached to we "know". The other end is "unknown". This is where YOU take a chance, stick your neck out and "FIND OUT"

Raje
Dec 2002
June 2003
Ahmedabad

Appendix

1 House for Dr. J.C. Parikh, Sadra,1996.
2 Residential school for MSM Trust, Ahmedabad, 1995.
3 Gorwa Commercial Complex, Baroda, 1990.
4 Institute of Indology, Patan, 1981.
5 National Academy of Administration, Ghaziabad, 1986.
6 Jain ashram, Dharampur, 2000.
7 Testing Board Offices and Science Museum, Bhopal, 1995.
8 Residence for Rajan-Sajan Misra, Dehradun, 1998.

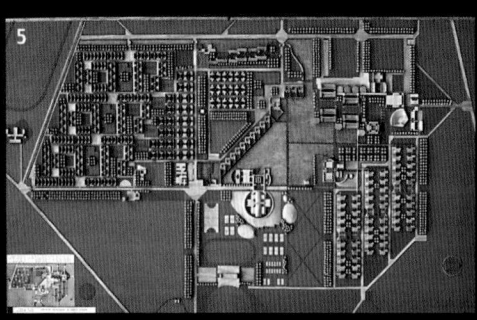
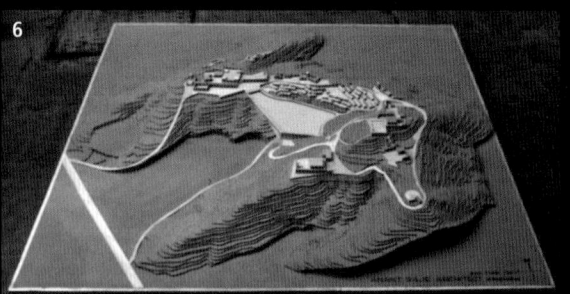

List of Works

1959   Toronto City Hall.
Competition entry.
In association with B.V. Doshi.

1970   Masterplan of Jawaharlal Nehru University, New Delhi.
Competition entry.
In association with B.V. Doshi.

1970   NBO Project, CEPT campus for Ahmedabad Education Society, Ahmedabad.
Unbuilt.

1971   Apartment for Kamala Chaudhary, New Delhi.
Unbuilt.

1973   'CONSERVE': INTACH offices, Ahmedabad.
Unbuilt.

1974   Residence for Mr. Choksi, Vallabh Vidyanagar.

1974   Housing project, Bhavnagar.

1974   Dormitories for National Institute of Design, Ahmedabad.
Unbuilt.

1975   Indian Statistical Institute for Planning Commission of India, New Delhi.
In collaboration with Kanvinde & Rai Architects.

1976   Agricultural Produce Wholesale Market Complex, New Bombay.
Partially completed.
Structural engineers: Sharad R. Shah.

1977   Mother Dairy (Vihar Dairy), Mumbai.
Structural engineers: Sharad R. Shah.

1978–81 Staff Housing, Indian Institute of Management, Ahmedabad.
Structural engineers: Sharad R. Shah.

1979   Dining halls and kitchens, Indian Institute of Management, Ahmedabad.
Structural engineers: Sharad R. Shah.
Mechanical engineers: Stein Doshi & Bhalla.

1980   Modern Bakery, Mumbai.
Unbuilt.
Structural engineers: Sharad R. Shah.

1981   Meat complex, Goa.
Structural engineers: Sharad R. Shah.

1981   Residence for Dr. Kulkarni, Ahmedabad.

1981   Institute of Indology, Patan.
Unbuilt.

1982   Residence for Dr. J.C. Parikh, Ahmedabad.
Structural engineers: C.B. Shah.

1982   Management Development Centre, Indian Institute of Management, Ahmedabad.
Structural engineers: Sharad R. Shah.
Mechanical engineers: Stein Doshi & Bhalla.

1982   Three dairies in Mumbai, Banaskantha and Mehsana for National Dairy Development Board.
Structural engineers: Sharad R. Shah.

1982   Central godowns for the Indian Dairy Corporation.
Structural engineers: Sharad R. Shah.

1982   Married students' quarters, Indian Institute of Management, Ahmedabad.
Structural engineers: Sharad R. Shah.

1983   Training institute for the Village Dairy Cooperative, Banaskantha (Gujarat).
Structural engineers: NDDB Anand.
Mechanical engineers: NDDB Anand.

Residence for Mr. Naushir Contractor, Ahmedabad.

Residence for Mr. Joshi, Ahmedabad.

Staff housing for Ahmedabad Textile Research Association
(ATIRA), Ahmedabad.
Structural engineers: Sharad R. Shah.
Mechanical engineers: SMPS Consultants.

District Collectorate Offices, Morena (Madhya Pradesh).
Under construction since 1985.
Structural engineers: Sharad R. Shah.
Coordinating agency: EPCO, Bhopal.

Office complex for Land Development Bank, Bhopal.
Unbuilt.
Structural engineers: Sharad R. Shah.
Coordinating agency: EPCO, Bhopal.

National Academy of Administration of Department of
Personnel and Training, Government of India, Ghaziabad
(Uttar Pradesh).
Invited competition: finalist.
Associate architects: R.J. Vasavada, Amita Raje.

Faculty and staff housing expansion, Indian Institute of
Management, Ahmedabad.
Structural engineers: Sharad R. Shah.

Gas Tragedy Victims Memorial for Government of Madhya
Pradesh, Bhopal.
Unbuilt.
Structural engineers: Sharad R. Shah.

Residence for Mr. Kanubhai Patel, Ahmedabad.
Structural engineers: Sharad R. Shah.

-90 Architect's residence (Schemes 1, 2, 3), Ahmedabad.
Unbuilt.

Indian Institute of Forest Management, Bhopal, Phase 1.
Associate architects: Gautam Bhatia, Amita Raje.
Structural engineers: Sharad R. Shah.
Mechanical engineers: Dr. P.C. Jain, Spectral.
Coordinating agency: BDA, Bhopal.

Residence for Mr. Sarkar, Orissa.
Unbuilt.

1988   Naval Academy, Government of India, Ezhimala (Kerala),
        Stage 1.
        Competition entry.
        Associate architects: R.J. Vasavada, Amita Raje.
        Structural engineers: Sharad R. Shah.

1988   Naval Academy, Government of India, Ezhimala (Kerala),
        Stage 2.
        Invited competition: finalist.
        Associate architects: R.J. Vasavada, Amita Raje.
        Structural engineers: Sharad R. Shah.

1989   Extensions to Management Development Centre, Indian
        Institute of Management, Ahmedabad.
        Structural engineers: Sharad R. Shah.
        Mechanical engineers: Dr P.C. Jain, Spectral.

1989   Residence for Mr. Harshvadan Mangaldas, Koba,
        Ahmedabad.
        Structural engineers: Sharad R. Shah.

1990   Headquarters for Bhopal Development Authority (BDA),
        Bhopal.
        Structural engineers: Sharad R. Shah.
        Mechanical engineers: Dr. P.C. Jain, Spectral.
        Coordinating agency: BDA, Bhopal.

1990   Housing at MOG Lines for HUDCO, Indore.
        Structural engineers: Sharad R. Shah.

1990   Wedding wall for Ms. Amrita Shodhan, Ahmedabad.

1990   Gorwa Commercial Complex, Baroda.
        Unbuilt.

1990   Residence for Mr. Indu Amin, Ahmedabad.
        Unbuilt.

1993   Mudra Institute for Communications, Ahmedabad, Phase 1.
        Associate architects: Amita Raje.
        Structural engineers: Sharad R. Shah.

1993   Commercial complex for HUDCO, Indore.
        Unbuilt.
        Structural engineers: Sharad R. Shah.

1994   Architect's apartment, Ahmedabad.
        Unbuilt.

1995   Testing Board Offices and Science Museum for Madhya Pradesh State Testing Board, Bhopal, Phase 1.
Associate architect: Amita Raje.
Structural engineers: Sharad R. Shah.
Coordinating agency: EPCO, Bhopal.

1995   Residential school for MSM Trust, Jetalpur, Ahmedabad, Phase 1.
Associate architect: Amita Raje.
Structural engineers: R. Lavingia.

1995   Studio for Linda, Koba, Ahmedabad.
Unbuilt.

1996   Factories, laboratories and offices for INTEC Polymers Ltd, Silvassa, Phase 1.
Structural engineers: Sharad R. Shah.

1996   Museum of Minerals and Mines, Nagpur.
In collaboration with National Institute of Design.
Unbuilt.
Structural engineers: Sharad R. Shah.

1996   Residence for Dr. J.C. Parikh, Sadra (Gujarat).
Unbuilt.

1996   Residence for Mr. Ranvir Khatau, Gandhinagar.
Unbuilt.

1997   Ravi Mathai Centre, Indian Institute of Management, Ahmedabad.
Structural engineers: Sharad R. Shah, Mahendra Raj.
Mechanical engineers: Dr. P.C. Jain, Spectral.
Acoustical engineers: Suri & Suri.

1998   Residence for Rajan and Sajan Misra, Dehradun.
Unbuilt.

1999   Campus annexe (Phase 2), Indian Institute of Management, Ahmedabad.
Unbuilt.

1999   International Buddhist Centre, Bodhgaya.
Invited competition.
Architectural team: Amita Raje, Saptak, Raiji, Sachin Bandookwala.

2000   Residence for Mr. Nandan Mehta, Ahmedabad.
Associate architect: Amita Raje.
Structural engineers: Vatsal Shah.

2000   Temple and religious centre for the Jain Trust, Dharampur, Gujarat.
Unbuilt.

2000   Indian Institute of Management Campus, Indore.
Competition entry.
Associate architect: Amita Raje.

2001   Offices for Ministry of External Affairs, Government of India, in the Lutyens zone, New Delhi.
Invited competition: finalist.
Associate architects: Gautam Bhatia, Amita Raje.

2008   Apartment for Mr. Kuntal Bhogilal, Mumbai.
Associate architect: Amita Raje.
Coordinating agency: S+PS Architects, Mumbai.

2008   Verandah renovation for Ms. Sheela Shodhan, Ahmedabad.

2009   Offices for Mr. Dahrmendra Vyas, Ahmedabad.
Associate architect: Amita Raje.
Structural engineers: Vatsal Shah.

2009   Pune generic house studies.
Unbuilt.

2009   Residence for Dr. Indira J. Parikh, Pune.
Unbuilt.
Coordinating agency: Girish Doshi Architects.

Journal of the Indian Institute of Architects, January–March 1976.

Architecture and Urban Design (A+U), Japan, August 1981.

DESIGN, New Delhi, July–September 1983.

Environmental Design, Journal of Islamic Environmental Design Research Centre, Rome, Italy, March 1984.

Journal of Space and Society, Rome, Italy, September 1986.

Architecture and Design (A+D), New Delhi, November–December 1987.

Catalogue of the Architecture of India, Festivals of India in Paris and Mumbai, 1985 and 1986

Commemorative issue, Indian Institute of Architects National Convention, Gujarat Chapter, 1987.

William J.R. Curtis, 'Modernism and the Search for Indian Identity', *Architectural Review*, London, August 1987.

William J.R. Curtis, *Modern Architecture since 1900*, second edition, Phaidon Press, London, 1987, Addendum: 'Recent World Architecture', p. 400 (Indian Institute of Forest Management, Bhopal, model illustrated).

Journal of the Indian Institute of Architects, December 1988.

Indian Architect and Builder, Mumbai, December 1988.

Design Journal, Seoul, Korea, February 1989.

William J. R. Curtis, 'Modernism and the Substructures of Indian Tradition', *Architecture 1900*, Montreal, UIA XVII, Summaries of Papers, pp. 424 ff.

Journal of the Indian Institute of Architects, February 1994: covering the presentation of the Institute's Baburao Mhatre Gold Medal, and publishing selected works.

Bhatt, Vikram and Peter Scriver, *After the Masters: Contemporary Indian Architecture*, University of Washington Press, 1991.

Bhaga, Sarabjit, Surinder Bhaga and Yashinder Bhaga, *Modern Architecture in India: Post Independence Perspective*, Galgotia Publishing Company, New Delhi, 1993.

Bhatia, Gautam, *Silent Spaces and Other Stories of Architecture*, Penguin Books India, New Delhi, 1994, pp. 70–77.

Architecture and Design (A+D), New Delhi, January–February 1995.

William J. R. Curtis, *Modern Architecture since 1900*, third edition, Phaidon Press, London, 1996, Chapter 34, 'The Universal and the Unique: Landscape, Climate and Culture', pp. 651–522 (Indian Institute of Forest Management, Bhopal, building illustrated).

Biography

1929	Born in Mumbai.
1954	Graduated in Architecture from Sir J.J. School of Fine Arts, Mumbai.
1955	Member, Indian Institute of Architects.
1956	Associate Member, Royal Institute of British Architects.
1956–59	Architect at Piloo Mody Architects, Mumbai.
1960–63	Architect at the offices of B.V. Doshi, Ahmedabad.
1964–69	Project Architect at the office of Louis Kahn, Philadelphia.
1969	Worked in association with Ar. George Mourious, Paris.
1969	Anant Raje Architects established in Ahmedabad, India.
1970	Doshi–Raje Architects established in Ahmedabad, India, for the Indian Institute of Management projects.
2009	Died in Ahmedabad, India.

Awards

Exhibitions

1987	Distinguished Professor's Award by the Centre for Environmental Planning and Technology (CEPT), Ahmedabad.
1987	Award for Outstanding Professional Achievement for Contribution to Design by the National Institute of Design (NID), Ahmedabad.
1991	'Architect of the Year' Award by J.K. Industries, India.
1992	Project Awards by the Journal of Indian Institute of Architects (JIIA) for the Indian Institute of Forest Management, Bhopal and Headquarters for the Bhopal Development Authority, Bhopal.
1994	Baburao Mhatre Gold Medal for Architecture by the Indian Institute of Architects (IIA) for 1993.
2000	Master Award for Lifetime Contribution in Architecture by J.K. Industries, India.
2001	Boromini Award, Rome: Nominated.

1979	Department of Islamic Art, Fogg Museum, Harvard University, USA: Recent Works.
1982	Venice Biennial, Italy: Works, Projects and Completed Buildings.
1985	Festival of India, Paris: Completed Projects.
1986	Festival of India Exhibition, Mumbai: Completed Projects.
1991	Hutheesingh Visual Arts Centre, CEPT, Ahmedabad: Retrospective Exhibition.

Lectures–Seminars

1959 Invited participant, seminar on 'Rural Housing in India', Roorkee University, conducted by Prof. Rene Eyeheraldi, Columbia, Prof. Ralph Borsodi, USA and Dr. Ensminger, Ford Foundation Representative in India.

1972 Invited participant, workshop–seminar on 'Housing for the Economically Weaker Sections of the Society', conducted by the Gujarat State Housing Board and Ministry of Housing, Baroda (Gujarat).

1973 Lecture on 'From Wright to Kahn', with visual material from the speaker's collection, at the Architecture Students' Association and the Indian Institute of Architects (IIA), Mumbai.

1980 Lecture at the School of Architecture, University of St. Luc, Bruxelles, Belgium.

1981–84, 87–89, 92–97 Seminars and lectures at the School of Architecture, University of New Mexico, Albuquerque NM, USA.

1984 Lecture at the Pratt Institute Overseas Programme, Rome, Italy.

1986 Lecture and seminars at the Architectural Association (Chetna Group), Bangladesh.

1993 Lecture and presentation of works at the Indian Institute of Architects, Kerala Chapter, Calicut.

1994 Lecture and presentation of works at the Academy of Architecture, Mumbai.

1994 Lecture and presentation of works at the Indian Institute of Architects, Nagpur.

1994 Lecture and presentation of works at the Indian Institute of Architects and Interior Designers, Pune.

1994 Lecture at the Australian Academy of Science, Canberra.

1995 Invited participant, Architecture conference at the School of Architecture, University of St. Luc, Bruxelles, Belgium.

1997 Lecture at the University of Alicante, Spain.

1999 Invited panelist at 'Chandigarh Perspectives', international conference to celebrate 50 years of the founding of Chandigarh designed by Le Corbusier; invitation by the Union Territory of Chandigarh.

1999 Lecture and presentation of work at the Urban Design Research Institute, Max Muller Bhavan, Mumbai.

2001 Lecture and workshops at the School of Architecture, University of Coimbra, Portugal.

2001 Lecture at the Ecole de Beaux Arts, Unit 8, Paris, France.

2001 Lecture at the School of Architecture, Mendrisio, Switzerland.

2001 Lecture and seminar at the offices of Shepley Bullfinch Richardson and Abbott, Boston, USA.

2003 Lecture and dialogue at the Forum for Exchange and Excellence in Design (FEED), Pune.

2006 Lecture at the School of Architecture, Colombo, Sri Lanka.

Teaching

1969–
2009
Professor at the School of Architecture, Centre for Environmental Planning and Technology (CEPT), Ahmedabad.

1970–75 Visiting faculty, School of Architecture, Punjab University, Chandigarh.

1970–75 Visiting faculty, School of Planning and Architecture (SPA), New Delhi.

1973–80 Evaluation Jury for Final Year Thesis Projects in Product Design, National Institute of Design (NID), Ahmedabad.

1974–75 Visiting faculty (November–January), Graduate School of Design (GSD), Harvard University, USA.

1975 Visiting faculty (February–March), School of Architecture, University of Texas, Austin, USA.

1981–
2001
Visiting faculty, Graduate Studios, School of Architecture and Planning, University of New Mexico, Albuquerque, USA.

1984 Design Workshop at the School of Architecture, Graduate School of Fine Arts, University of Pennsylvania, Philadelphia, USA.

1986 Visiting faculty, Graduate Studio, Department of Architecture, Rome University, Italy.

1994 Visiting Critic, School of Environmental Design and Architecture, University of Canberra, Australia.

2003 Invited Critic, Thesis juries at B.N. College of Architecture, Pune.

2006 Invited critic, Thesis juries at the School of Architecture, Colombo, Sri Lanka.

Consultations

1968–
2009
Advisor to the Environmental Planning and Coordination Organization (EPCO), Government of Madhya Pradesh, Bhopal.

Consultant to the Bhopal Development Authority, Madhya Pradesh.

Consultant to the Indore Development Authority, Madhya Pradesh.

1985 Member of the Advisory Board constituted by the Government of India for the memorial for the late Prime Minister of India, Smt. Indira Gandhi, New Delhi.

1986–94 Consulting member to discuss ways of improving architectural education in developing nations constituted by the Aga Khan Foundation for Islamic Architecture at MIT, USA.

1986–
2009
Member of the Advisory Board, Tata Energy Research Institute (TERI), New Delhi.

1992–94 Member of the Governing Council, National Institute of Design (NID), Ahmedabad.

Colleagues
1969–2009
(in alphabetical order)

Architectural associates
- Gautam Bhatia
- Gurusharan Patel
- Amita Raje
- M.S. Satsangi
- R.J. Vasavada

Structural
- R. Lavingia
- Mahendra Raj
- C.B. Shah
- Sharad Shah
- Vatsal Shah

Mechanical
- Dr. P.C. Jain I Spectral
- Rohit Shah I SMPS

Acoustical
- Suri & Suri

Costing and tenders
- Babubhai Jhethwa
- Vastupal Shah

Model making
- Babu Mistry
- Chandrakant Mistry

Photo labs
- Pranlal Patel and Anand Patel
- Parmanand Dalwadi

Studio assistants

Raje often said that his studio assistants were his 'extra hands' that enabled the speed at which drawings were made to keep up with the speed at which he thought. 'They must match,' he said, 'otherwise your thoughts leave you, and they get lost. If there are many hands, as soon as you think of something, it gets done and you begin to test whether there is any kind of relation between the two. In terms of all the abstractions you are talking about, when it comes to drawing them, are they inspired enough?' Students of architecture came to work for Raje in this spirit of apprenticeship. They were an integral part of his practice and defined the character of the studio.

p. 15   Anant Raje, 'Sources and Interpretations', first published in *DESIGN*, July/September 1983.

p. 22   Kitchen–dining complex at IIM Ahmedabad by Louis Kahn, 1972: Heinz Ronner and Sharad Jhaveri, *Louis Kahn: Complete Works, 1935–1974*, Princeton Architectural Press, 1987, p. 228.

p. 70   Site plan, J.C. Parikh residence: Ruparel, Mehul, 'Proportioning Systems as an Ordering Principle: An Inquiry into the Works of Architect Anant Raje', student thesis, School of Architecture, CEPT University, Ahmedabad, 2004.

p. 250   Wood model, MICA: photograph courtesy Darshan Soni.

p. 255   Floorplan of classroom building, MICA: Ruparel, Mehul, 'Proportioning Systems as an Ordering Principle: An Inquiry into the Works of Architect Anant Raje', student thesis, School of Architecture, CEPT University, Ahmedabad, 2004.

p. 259   Axonometric of classroom building, MICA: Ruparel, Mehul, 'Proportioning Systems as an Ordering Principle: An Inquiry into the Works of Architect Anant Raje', student thesis, School of Architecture, CEPT University, Ahmedabad, 2004.

p. 266   Floorplan of clubhouse, MICA: Ruparel, Mehul, 'Proportioning Systems as an Ordering Principle: An Inquiry into the Works of Architect Anant Raje', student thesis, School of Architecture, CEPT University, Ahmedabad, 2004.

p. 270   Wood model of dormitory cluster, MICA: photograph courtesy Darshan Soni.

p. 271   Wood model of dormitory cluster, MICA: photograph courtesy Darshan Soni.

p. 278   Axonometric, floorplans and sections of laboratory building, INTEC: Ruparel, Mehul, 'Proportioning Systems as an Ordering Principle: An Inquiry into the Works of Architect Anant Raje', student thesis, School of Architecture, CEPT University, Ahmedabad, 2004.

Acknowledgements

This book would not have been possible without the enthusiasm of the architectural community Raje was a part of: his colleagues in the profession and academia, associates, friends and, above all, students.

We would like to thank Gautam Bhatia and Rahul Mehrotra for their generosity, insights and interpretations in framing an introduction that speaks to the significance of Raje's work, which has eluded categorization and has had a silent life of its own. To Gautam and Rahul also go our sincere appreciation and gratitude for their support, encouragement and guidance during the entire process.

In addition, we are deeply grateful to:

The CEPT University at Ahmedabad, the University of New Mexico at Albuquerque, Forum for Exchange and Excellence in Design (FEED), Pune, and the B.N. College of Architecture, Pune, for providing us with video recordings of Raje's lectures. These provided invaluable insights into the architect's reflections on his projects and practice.

Manalee Nanavati, for her dedication to Raje and her belief in the book that led to countless hours of sorting through, cataloguing and organizing materials for the book.

Riyaz Tayyibji for help with the initial set-up.

Vivek Nanda, Parthiv Shah and Paulomi Shah, for their advice in navigating the world of words, books and publishing.

Indu Chandrasekhar, our publisher at Tulika Books, New Delhi, and Pankaj Mehta at Reproscan, Mumbai, for their expertise and engagement with the material, and for supporting it through the time it has taken us to put it together.

Raje's associates and friends for their insights, reflections and stories of a life and practice that, at the beginning of this project, was as overwhelming in its unbridled energy as it was intimate to illuminate: R.J. Vasavada, Sharad Shah, Haku Shah, Vijay Padaki, Miki and Madhavi Desai, M.S. Satsangi, Bernard Kohn, Georges Maurios, Ahmet Gulgonen, William J.R. Curtis, Attilio Petruccioli, Neelkanth Chhaya, Snehal Shah, Christopher Benninger, Charles Correa, B.V. Doshi. We have gained much from our conversations with them.

Our family and friends, for their quiet and steadfast support over the years.

And finally to Gauri Raje, who has been a constant presence during this project and who comes as close in spirit to her father as anyone possibly can: all our love, respect and admiration.

Contributors

GAUTAM BHATIA graduated in Fine Arts and went on to get a Master's degree in Architecture from the University of Pennsylvania in Philadelphia. A Delhi-based architect, he has received several awards for his drawings and buildings, and has also written extensively on architecture. Besides a biography on Laurie Baker, he is the author of *Punjabi Baroque*, *Silent Spaces* and *Malaria Dreams* – a trilogy that focuses on the cultural and social aspects of buildings. His most recent book, *Lie: A Traditional Tale of Modern India*, was published in 2010. Bhatia is currently working on *Below the Horizon – Ideas for the City*.

WILLIAM J.R. CURTIS is a historian, critic, painter and photographer. Born in 1948 in Birchington, Kent, England, he was educated at the Courtauld Institute, London and at Harvard University. He has taught at many universities around the world and in 2003–04 was Slade Professor of Fine Art in the University of Cambridge. Among his best known books are the classic *Modern Architecture since 1900* (Phaidon, third edition, 1996) and *Le Corbusier: Ideas and Forms* (Phaidon, 1986), both translated into many languages; *Balkrishna Doshi: an Architecture for India* (Mapin, Rizzoli, 1988); and *Denys Lasdun: Architecture, City, Landscape* (Phaidon, 1994). More recent works include: *Abstractions in Space* (Pulitzer Foundation, 2001), *The Structure of Shadows, Bell-Lloc* (Fundacion Bunka, 2009) and *Tuodoro Gonzalez de Leon: Complete Works* (Arquine, 2010). Curtis has written introductions to more than a dozen monographs on figures as diverse as Alvar Aalto and Raj Rewal, and contributes regularly to critical journals such as the *Architectural Review*, *Architectural Record*, *Il Giornale dell'Architettura*, *D'Architectures*, *Bauwelt*, *Architect's Journal* and *El Croquis* (with numbers on Alvaro Siza, Rafael Moneo, Tadao Ando, Miralles/Pinos, etc). He also exhibits and publishes his own paintings (*Mental Landscapes/Paisajes Mentales*, Circulo de Bellas Artes, Madrid, 2002) and his own photographs (*Structures of Light*, Alvar Aalto Museum, 2007). Among his numerous awards are: the Founder Award, Society of Architectural Historians, USA (1982); the Alice Davis Hitchcock Medal, SAH, Great Britain (1984); a National Honors Society Gold Medal in Architecture and Allied Arts, USA (1999); and a Medal of the Museum of Finnish Architecture (2006). Curtis lives in a remote rural spot in southwest France, and has long been interested in Indian architecture, ancient and modern.

RAHUL MEHROTRA is a practising architect and educator. He works in Mumbai and teaches at the Graduate School of Design at Harvard University, where he is Professor of Urban Design and Planning and Chair of the Department of Urban Planning and Design, as well as a member of the steering committee of Harvard's South Asia Initiative. His practice, RMA Architects (www.RMAarchitects.com), founded in 1990, has executed a range of projects across India. These diverse projects have engaged many issues, multiple constituencies and varying scales, from interior design and architecture to urban design, conservation and planning. As Trustee of the Urban Design Research Institute (UDRI) and Partners for Urban Knowledge Action and Research (PUKAR), both based in Mumbai, Mehrotra continues to be actively involved as an activist in the civic and urban affairs of the city. Mehrotra has written and lectured extensively on architecture, conservation and urban planning. He has written, co-authored and edited a vast repertoire of books on Mumbai, its urban history, its historic buildings, public spaces and planning processes. He is a member of the Steering Committee of the Aga Khan Awards for Architecture, and currently serves on the governing boards of the London School of Economics Cities Programme and the Indian Institute of Human Settlements.

AMITA RAJE was trained as an architect at CEPT University, although her interests include the fields of music, performing arts, textiles, social sciences and mathematics. She married Anant Raje in 1971, and was his associate in practice and teaching until his death in 2009. Amita currently heads the Anant Raje Foundation, established in 2010 with the aim to archive, restore and make available Raje's original works, notes, documents, sketches and various objects. She lives in Ahmedabad.

SHUBHRA RAJE is a practising architect and educator, dividing her time between the USA and India. A graduate of CEPT University and Cornell University, her practice (www.shubhraraje.com), founded in 2010, ascribes to an expanded definition of sustainability that moves beyond experimentation with new materials and technologies to include concepts like social and economic stewardship, with projects at varying scales from art installations to public institutions. She has taught at Cornell University, University of Colorado and CEPT University. Her encounters with Raje's work began as a toddler on his drafting table, and have continued through her student years and present research into his teaching methodologies.